Building English Skills

Purple Level

Building English Skills   Purple Level

Building English Skills   Yellow Level

Building English Skills   Blue Level

Building English Skills   Orange Level

Building English Skills   Green Level

Building English Skills   Red Level

Building English Skills

Purple Level

Prepared by the Staff of
The Writing Improvement Project

McDougal, Littell & Company
Evanston, Illinois

Staff of THE WRITING IMPROVEMENT PROJECT

Marilyn V. Kemp, Chairperson, English Department, New Trier Township High School East, Winnetka, Illinois

Eric Kraft, Writer and Editor, Stow, Massachusetts

Joy Littell, Editorial Director, McDougal, Littell & Company

Robert J. Lumsden, Evanston Township High School, Evanston, Illinois

William A. Seabright, Director of Design, McDougal, Littell & Company

Agnes Stein, English Department, Bloomfield College, Bloomfield, New Jersey

Marcia Baldwin Whipps, East High School, Salt Lake City, Utah

Project assistants: Pamela Kimball, Peggy J. Schleker, Patricia C. Stuhr

The Staff wishes to thank the more than 1500 students who contributed samples of their writing for analysis.

Acknowledgments: See page 287

ISBN: 0-88343-472-5

Chapters 1–5 and the Handbook contain, in revised form, some materials that appeared originally in *English Arts and Skills, Grade 12,* by Ronald J. Wilkins et al., copyright © 1965, 1961 by The Macmillan Company. Used by arrangement.

Contents

The page numbers for the Handbook (the second half of this book) appear in red.

Chapter 11 The Library and Its Reference Materials 255

Handbook

The page numbers for the Handbook (the second half of this book) appear in red.

13.0 The Semicolon, the Colon, the Dash, and Parentheses 232

14.0 The Apostrophe 241

15.0 Quotations 248

16.0 Spelling 254

17.0 The Plurals of Nouns 263

18.0 The Forms of Letters 268

19.0 Good Manuscript Form 276

The Composition Chapters (First half of text)

Vocabulary Development. Chapter 1 emphasizes *word distinctions, development of a critical vocabulary,* and *context clues.* An adequate vocabulary, and the ability to use synonyms precisely, are prerequisites to good writing.

Sentence Improvement. Chapters 2-5 provide an intensive program for sentence improvement based on a study of over 3000 student themes. This program is based on the belief that *the important problems of writing begin at the level of the sentence.* Some of these problems involve errors in grammar, but many of them are problems of meaning and sense. In each book, a chapter is devoted to those sentences which, though grammatically correct, are nonetheless unsatisfactory. In this book, for example, Chapter 2 deals with empty sentences, the circular sentences that say nothing (pages 30-32); it also deals with overloaded sentences, the sentences that contain too many ideas (pages 32-34).

The Paragraph. Chapters 6-8 provide an intensive study of the paragraph. All three chapters provide a wealth of first-rate models, along with helpful analysis.

The Composition. Chapter 9 provides a clear, workable blueprint for all expository writing longer than a paragraph.

The Research Paper. Chapter 10 provides a step-by-step method for writing a research paper. A sample research paper is included.

The Handbook (Second half of text)

The Handbook is arranged in 19 numbered sections, as follows:

Grammar. Sections 1-4 provide a thorough treatment of traditional grammar in a contemporary setting. Section 5 is an optional chapter on modern grammar.

Usage. Sections 6-10 deal with problems of usage.

Capitalization, Punctuation, Spelling, and Manuscript Form. Sections 11-19 deal with the mechanics of writing.

Special Features of the Handbook. The Handbook has some distinct advantages over other available handbooks:

1. The typographic arrangement is clear and attractive. Type and open space have been used to set off definitions and examples so as to make them easy to find and easy to read.

2. Since each topic is a short phrase (printed in red) rather than a rule, it is easy to locate.

3. Within each topic, there is a full explanation of each concept, followed by examples, and where appropriate, by the definition or generalization printed in boldface type.

Chapter 1

Vocabulary Development

Everything you read affects you in some way. What you read may cause pleasure or displeasure, even while it is meant to inform, persuade or amuse you. No matter what you read, you react. Part of your reaction is your criticism of the work. *Criticism* in this case means analysis and judgment.

What you feel about a work may be quite difficult to express. You may be able to say that you like or dislike a short story, for example, or that you think it is good or bad. However, if you must support and elaborate your opinion with specific reasoning, you may be at a loss for words.

Whether you continue your education or enter the business world, the situations that require precise criticism will increase. The purpose of this chapter is to help you equip yourself with a vocabulary to use in the evaluation of people and things and the analysis of literature and events.

Part 1
Studying Distinctions Among Words

Words that have like meanings are called **synonyms.** Most synonyms do not have exactly the same meaning. They are not interchangeable. Synonyms share the same general meaning, but have different shades of that meaning.

Why study synonyms? There are two good reasons. First, a knowledge of synonyms will make your reading more exact. A good writer chooses his words with care. If you know word distinctions, you will get more out of your reading. If you do not, you will be missing much of what a good writer has to say. Second, if you know word distinctions, you can state your own meaning more precisely. Your speech and writing will be more vivid and more persuasive. They will achieve your purposes more surely and more effectively.

Study the **synonymy** (comparison of synonyms) for *naive.** Note how all the words are related, and also how they differ in specific meanings.

> **naive** implies a being simple and innocent in a trusting way, but sometimes suggests an almost foolish lack of worldly wisdom [his *naive* belief that all advertising is honest].

> **ingenuous** suggests a childlike frankness or straightforwardness [his *ingenuous* delight in any kind of flattery].

> **artless** implies the appealing open and natural quality of one who is indifferent to the effect he has on others [a simple, *artless* style of folk singing].

> **unsophisticated** implies a lack of poise, worldliness, subtlety, etc. resulting from a limited experience of life [an *unsophisticated* farm boy].

*These distinctions are taken from *Webster's New World Dictionary*, Students Edition.

2

You can see that these four words are similar in meaning, yet distinct in the exact shade of meaning each conveys. If you are looking for a word with the general meaning that these four words share, you can search among the synonyms for the exact shade of that general meaning that best expresses your idea.

How can you learn the synonyms of words in common use? You can learn some of them by reading and attentive listening, but this is a slow process. A more effective method is to go to a dictionary. Among the standard dictionaries, you can find a full treatment of synonyms in *Webster's New World Dictionary*, Students Edition. *Webster's Dictionary of Synonyms* is also useful.

If you are interested in expanding your vocabulary, you will find the following procedure helpful:

1. Study a synonymy in a dictionary.

2. Write down the distinctions among the synonyms.

3. Compose sentences that illustrate these distinctions.

4. Try substituting one synonym for another in your sentences so that you will get a feeling for the distinctions among words.

Exercises
Distinctions Among Words

A. The word *suave* and its synonyms are an interesting example of the different implications carried by words of similar meaning.

> **suave** implies the smoothly gracious social manner of one who deals with people easily and tactfully, sometimes suggesting a surface politeness too smooth to be convincing [his *suave* manner with waiters]

> **urbane** suggests the social ease of a highly cultured person with much worldly experience [an *urbane* conversation on European theater].

diplomatic implies skill and tact in dealing with people and handling delicate situations, sometimes in such a way as to gain one's own ends [a *diplomatic* answer].

politic also expresses this idea, often emphasizing the immediate practical reasons for doing a thing [a *politic* move].

Use correctly in an original sentence each of the four synonyms above. Be sure that each sentence carries the precise meaning the word implies.

B. Look up the distinctions among the following groups of synonyms and use each synonym correctly in an original sentence.

1. likeness, similarity, resemblance
2. think, reason, cogitate, reflect, speculate, deliberate
3. aversion, antipathy, repugnance, abhorrence, loathing, revulsion
4. brave, courageous, bold, audacious, valiant, intrepid, plucky
5. bear, suffer, endure, tolerate, stand, brook

C. Consult your dictionary to answer the following questions.

1. You go to a play that someone has told you is *funny*. One scene makes you laugh until it hurts. Would you describe it as *amusing* or *comical?*
2. You can *criticize* a color-blind friend for the color combinations he wears, but can you *blame* him?
3. If your teacher asks you to read a *copy* of the Declaration of Independence, does she expect you to study a *duplicate* or a *facsimile?*
4. If you ran three miles you would undoubtedly be *tired*. Would you describe yourself more accurately as *weary* or *exhausted?*
5. When a candidate hears he has lost the election, he tries to face his supporters with *equanimity*. Would you describe his bearing as one of *composure* or of *nonchalance?*
6. Is an *intelligent* person necessarily *intellectual?* Explain.
7. There are *many* stars in the sky. Would you say the stars are *numerous* or *innumerable?*

8. What makes a *plot* a *conspiracy?*

9. Would you be more comfortable with someone who is *frank* or with someone who is *open?* How does an *outspoken* individual make you feel?

10. Are all *male* human beings *manly?* Explain. To whom is the word *mannish* applied?

D. Shakespeare was a master of the use of the exact word. Study the following passage:

> Good name in man, and woman, dear my lord,
> Is the immediate jewel of their souls:
> Who *steals* my purse *steals* trash: 'tis something, nothing;
> 'Twas mine, 'tis his, and has been slave to thousands;
> But he that *filches* from me my good name
> *Robs* me of that which not enriches him,
> And makes me poor indeed.

> —*Othello*

Look up the three verbs *steal, filch* and *rob* in the dictionary. Be prepared to explain why you think Shakespeare used each of these three words in its particular context.

E. Study the synonymy for the word *make* in *Webster's New World Dictionary,* Students Edition. Substitute a more precise synonym for *make* in the sentences below.

1. General Electric *makes* many kinds of appliances.

2. Mr. Jaspers was thinking about *making* a bird house for his backyard.

3. Marty *made* the bread dough into several long, thin loaves.

4. Meg *made* a trivet by gluing cork bottle stoppers together.

F. From your dictionary or a dictionary of synonyms, choose two synonymies that you find particularly interesting. Explain why you think it is important to know the distinctions among the synonyms given in each group, and make these distinctions clear by using each word in a sentence.

Part 2
Developing a Vocabulary of Criticism

By this time you are aware of two important facts about English words:

1. Most words in common use have more than one meaning.
2. You never get all of the meaning of a word in any one encounter with it.

For example, take the word *criticism*. You have long been familiar with its meaning of "finding fault." But the word is also used to name "the act of analyzing and of making judgments." This is the sense with which we are concerned at this point.

The act of making judgments is as common to your life as breathing. In fact, you cannot stay alive without making judgments. You have to analyze every situation in which you find yourself if for no other reason than to decide whether it is dangerous to you. In the classroom, the teacher asks a question. As a student, you must size up the question and determine whether you can make a reasonable answer. You must also reflect upon the importance to you of trying to make an answer. You may decide that you have not been carrying your weight in the classroom discussion and decide that it is time you did so. You may judge that you ought to make a try at an answer even though you are not sure of it.

This is one kind of analysis—the analysis of a situation. Every day you make countless other analyses and judgments. You judge the speech, actions and character of friends and others you meet. You judge clothes, food, books, news accounts and traffic conditions. For each of these judgments, there are exact and specific words that help you state your findings. More than that, these judgment words help you *think* about the things, people and events in the world around you. They help sharpen your perceptions and pinpoint your reactions.

You can make two kinds of judgments about things. You can react *subjectively*, which is to express your personal feelings about the thing you are criticizing. To react to something by saying it is great, okay or poor is to give only the thinnest of subjective judgments. These words say nothing about the thing you are dealing with. They only reflect your feelings about the thing, and not very precisely at that!

As an alternative, you can judge something by trying to name its qualities, or by being *objective*. To criticize something objectively is to use words that carry specific information to others about the thing you are dealing with. What can be said, for example, about another person? How can his personality, manner, intelligence or character be described? Here is a sample of possibilities:

Words Useful for Describing People

Personality	Manner	Intelligence	Character
cold	forthright	quick	strong
aloof	outspoken	keen	reliable
reserved	frank	sharp	selfless
retiring	candid	agile	dependable
restrained	straightforward	fine	trustworthy
cool	debonaire	incisive	spotless
warm	ingratiating	acute	determined
vibrant	patronizing	brilliant	certain
buoyant	charming	bright	sure
bubbly	devil-may-care	nimble	selfish
vivacious	carefree	alert	demanding
outgoing	footloose	astute	thoughtless
attractive	brusque	clever	driven
compelling	curt	ingenious	calculating
charming	rude	creative	egoistic

Words Useful for Describing People

Personality	Manner	Intelligence	Character
magnetic	bluff	slow	self-serving
appealing	blunt	dull	vain
fascinating	abrupt	dim	weak
beguiling	short	limited	sheepish
adorable	sullen	ignorant	helpless
bewitching	surly	foolish	limp
repulsive	glum	silly	spineless
repelling	sulky	senseless	insipid
revolting	grouchy	shallow	listless
hideous	sharp	irrational	irresolute
vile	cross	unreasonable	uncertain
unsavory	irritable	mad	wishy-washy
disagreeable	cantankerous		fickle
unpleasant	testy		
obnoxious	calculating		
odious			

Similarly, an objective judgment of a motion picture or TV program can go far beyond the vague, subjective judgments that underlie *great, dull,* or *poor.* The characters can be discussed in the terms listed above. But what about the acting, the pace, the story, or the sound effect? Another sample of possibilities as shown on the next page.

Words Useful for Criticism of Motion Pictures and TV Programs

Acting	Pace	Story	Sound Effects
inspired	brisk	contrived	complementary
natural	quick	artificial	supportive
realistic	lively	unbelievable	appropriate
relaxed	breakneck	calculated	jarring
truthful	hasty	maudlin	annoying
melodramatic	abrupt	clever	distracting
overblown	slow	bewildering	inappropriate
exaggerated	lethargic	baffling	intrusive
affected	leisurely	surprising	
unbelievable	relaxed	realistic	
unnatural	indolent		
wooden	halting		
uninspired	measured		
clumsy	irregular		
thoughtless	jerky		
careless			

Attempting to be objective in your judgments will have more than one benefit:

1. An objective criticism will carry more information and be more precise.

2. Making an objective criticism requires you to look at what you are criticizing with an open mind.

3. Searching for words to relay an objective criticism with precision and clarity will help you *think* more precisely and more clearly.

4. An objective criticism will earn the respect of your audience not only for the judgment you express but also for the critical effort that underlies it.

Exercises
Developing a Vocabulary of Criticism

A. What can be said about a dress? Make a list of judgment words that convey precise information. These will be nouns as well as adjectives. Avoid words like *lovely, divine, adorable*. Consult fashion pages of newspapers and magazines for suggestions.

B. What can be said about a sports car? Make a list of judgment words that carry concrete information. Consult a sports car magazine for suggestions.

C. What can be said about the weather? You can describe the weather, and you can also describe its effects: *depressing, enervating*, for example. Consult the first stanza of "The Eve of St. Agnes" by Keats for suggestions.

D. Think about a motion picture you have seen recently. What kinds of judgments can be made about it? What can you say more specifically than *great, dull* or *poor*? What about the acting, costumes, sound effects? You might think of the aspects of a motion picture for which Oscars are awarded.

E. Substitute a precise judgment word for each of the italicized words in the following sentences.

1. It was a *good* game.
2. Bobby is a *neat* dancer.
3. *Stories from the Twilight Zone* is a *great* book.
4. The music at the party was *poor*.
5. The movie was *funny*.
6. The Mercedes-Benz is a *terrific* car.

F. Below are ten subjective criticisms. Write a paragraph of objective criticism for two of the items. Example: a good audience

> The audience was familiar with the music and became involved with the soloist's interpretation of the sonata. When the program was over, the audience rose for a standing

ovation and demanded an encore, which the violinist obligingly gave.

1. an ideal vacation
2. bad news
3. a good friend
4. an elegant dinner
5. an ugly dog
6. nice hair
7. a comfortable house
8. soothing music
9. an appetizing meal
10. the perfect gift

Part 3
The Language of Literary Criticism

As you react with greater and greater maturity and sensitivity to the physical world around you, you will become more and more aware of the importance of having a vocabulary of criticism—a vocabulary that will help you describe and evaluate the people, places and things around you.

In your study of books, plays, motion pictures, and so on, you have perhaps already become aware of the need for such a vocabulary. You need special words to analyze the characters you meet—their words, actions and motives. You need special words to evaluate the style or form of a piece of writing.

For these purposes, you need more than just an understanding of the connotations of common words and a knowledge of common synonyms. You need a vocabulary characterized by depth and scope, a store of words from which you can take the *one word* that best conveys the *precise meaning* you have in mind.

If, for example, you are criticizing a scene from a novel in which a character describes a childhood of suffering and deprivation, a scene in which you feel the writer successfully moves the reader to a feeling of pity for the character, will you characterize the scene as *pathos* or as *bathos?*

If you are discussing a protagonist who is roguish and appealing and finds himself in a series of humorous or satiric adventures, will you classify the character as a *romantic idealist* or as a *picaresque hero?*

If a writer includes a passage that is intended to represent the thoughts of a character who is waiting to board an airplane, a passage that mixes memories, anxieties, and mundane concerns, will you say that the writer has used a *stream of consciousness technique* or *stark realism?*

If you are reading a review of a novel that is described as being in the tradition of the Gothic novel of Ann Radcliffe, will you expect it to be a novel about the ancient Goths, a novel set in a Gothic cathedral, or a novel that treats of horror for its own sake?

A good dictionary will answer these questions for you, but terms like those italicized above must become your stock in trade if you are to achieve that depth and breadth of language necessary to the understanding and enjoyment of literature.

Exercises
The Language of Literary Criticism

A. The following sentences contain words that will be useful to you in expressing judgments about books, motion pictures, plays, and so on. Examine carefully each underlined word and be able to tell the class exactly what each sentence means. If you are not sure, consult your dictionary.

1. The atmosphere of Poe's "The Fall of the House of Usher" is one of foreboding and mystery.

2. The mood of Barry's *Joyous Season* is not really joy at all but rather of a happiness that shows the leading character in tears at the final curtain.

3. Susan Glaspell builds up suspense in *Trifles* by skillfully introducing obstacles that the women must overcome to gain their ends.

4. Some people hold that the character of Holden Caulfield in *Catcher in the Rye* is not fully believable.

5. The imagery of Keats's poems is very rich.

6. The dialogue in Hemingway's short stories is racy and pungent.

7. Robert Frost relies less upon metaphor than upon tone to achieve his effects.

8. The most important aspect of poetry is sound, and therefore a poem must be read aloud to be fully appreciated.

9. "The Purloined Letter," by Edgar Allan Poe, was the first of a new genre, the detective story.

10. Bernard Shaw was regarded by his contemporaries as an iconoclast.

11. Tennessee Williams frequently uses the decadent South as his milieu.

12. Because of the sensational action of the new play, critics classified it as outright melodrama.

13. *Oedipus Rex* is an outstanding example of irony.

14. The climax of *The Bridge of San Luis Rey* comes at the beginning of the book with the collapse of the bridge, and justifies the telling of the tale.

15. In "Stopping by Woods on a Snowy Evening," the horse, without losing its identity as a horse, also becomes a symbol.

B. A comprehensive knowledge of words that describe people, places, and events is indispensable to good writing. Examine the words underscored below, define each exactly, and use each correctly in an original sentence. If you are not sure of any word, use your dictionary. Also, master the pronunciation of the word.

1. lethargic disposition
2. dour expression
3. vicarious enjoyment
4. mendacious personality
5. stentorian tones
6. scurrilous remarks
7. didactic literature
8. auspicious beginning
9. impeccably attired
10. indefensible conduct
11. sanguinary in nature
12. vacillating character

13. genteel manner
14. malodorous atmosphere
15. pertinacious individual
16. sophisticated manner

17. morbid obsession
18. abject poverty
19. ironic situation
20. poignant ending

C. Here is a test of your skill in evaluating people. Supply the name of an individual—fictional or historical—who you feel would fit each adjective given below.

Example: procrastinating: Hamlet

1. garrulous
2. ambitious
3. cunning
4. magnanimous
5. obsequious

6. quixotic
7. compassionate
8. treacherous
9. subservient
10. implacable

11. senile
12. naive
13. suave
14. egotistical
15. humble

D. *The Hairy Ape,* by Eugene O'Neill, carries the following paragraphs in its preface. Read them thoughtfully; then answer the questions that follow.

Eugene O'Neill is not only America's outstanding playwright: he is also chief of her dramatic rebels. But his rebellion is not against institutions or individuals; it is the more radical one aimed at spiritual slavery and effete convention. He is the dramatic apostle of a new vitality for man and art. His plays are a prologue to the great emancipation —the freeing of the human spirit. His leading characters are recruited from the ranks of those who, perhaps like himself, are the victims of a hypocritical civilization that represses and tortures the soul, while it romantically proclaims its liberty. Enmeshed in a confusion of restraints . . . they contend with tragic futility for self-expression. Even their goals of happiness are illusory. For most of them there is only defeat. But in the struggle each achieves a symbolic grandeur that is O'Neill's chief contribution to our theatre.

Man's good, he seems to say, is in courageous striving if

only he is true to his instinctive faith in his own spiritual value against the assaults of man-made conventions. In such strife he finds joy.

O'Neill came to this rebellion from a sousing in the romantic sentimentality of the theatre. As son of a great romantic actor he early acquired a loathing for the stuff of his father's dramas, in several of which, like *The Count of Monte Cristo*, he had to act for his bread. He was soon at work on a series of short plays, the stark realism of which shocked his father and seemed unsuited to the polite theatre of that day.

This passage calls for careful reading. Examine each word or phrase below with reference to the context in which it appears, and tell the class what you think it means. There may be differences of opinion. Listen to them. Then let the class, with the aid of your teacher, decide which interpretation is correct.

1. dramatic rebel
2. rebellion not against institutions or individuals
3. radical
4. spiritual slavery
5. effete convention
6. dramatic apostle
7. prologue
8. great emancipation—the freeing of the human spirit
9. hypocritical civilization
10. represses and tortures the soul
11. romantically proclaims its liberty
12. tragic futility
13. goals of happiness are illusory
14. symbolic grandeur
15. instinctive faith in his own spiritual value
16. man-made conventions
17. in such strife he finds joy
18. romantic sentimentality of the theatre
19. stark realism
20. polite theatre of that day

E. Select a short story or play that you have read recently. Describe as clearly and specifically as possible:

1. the character of the protagonist
2. the character of the antagonist
3. the nature of the conflict
4. the style of writing
5. the effect of the piece upon you

Part 4
Getting Meaning from Context

Whether you go on to college or to a job, you are going to meet an increasing number of new and unfamiliar words. They may be the vocabulary of psychology, law, chemistry, or whatever other college course you are taking. They may be political or economic terms in the news. They may be technical terms related to the industry in which you are working.

Wherever an unfamiliar word appears, you have the problem of figuring out its meaning—not necessarily all of its meanings, but enough meaning to make the passage intelligible. If you are to understand what you read—and you must read in order to participate in the life around you—you must have a method of dealing with unfamiliar words.

How do you get the meaning of an unfamiliar word which you come across in your reading? If you are reading a book or magazine in the back yard or on the bus, it is unlikely that you will have a dictionary close at hand. You will, therefore, need to use another method of getting the meaning of the word.

Sometimes you can get a clue to the meaning of a word from its root, prefix, or suffix. Sometimes you can get a clue from the **context,** the words with which the unfamiliar term is used. In using context clues, keep in mind that you are not trying to get the full meaning of the unfamiliar word. You are trying only to get enough meaning to go on with your reading, to make sense of the passage as a whole. It is well to state here once again a basic principle of language: you never get all the meaning of a word in any one encounter with it.

You may feel confident that you know the word *sensitive*, and yet you may not be aware of just how many ways it can be used. Each sentence below uses a different meaning of the word. In some sentences the word has a positive connotation, and in others a negative one. Compare the meanings of *sensitive* in each sentence.

Millie was very *sensitive* about being called the baby of the family. (irritable, touchy)

A *sensitive* seismograph picks up earth tremors not felt by inhabitants of the area. (able to measure small changes)

Joe's sunburn was painfully *sensitive*, and he howled as Amy brushed by him. (tender).

Carol was a warm and *sensitive* person who really listened to other people's problems. (sympathetic)

The eye is *sensitive* to foreign objects. This sensitivity triggers blinking and a flow of tears to expel the intruder. (quick to react)

In each sentence you only need to grasp one meaning of the word *sensitive*, but for you to get full use of the word, you need to know its multiple meanings.

Exercises
Getting Meaning from Context

A. From the context, work out the meaning of the following italicized words. Then consult a dictionary to find the other meanings for each word. In class, work out sentences illustrating these other meanings.

1. "Ninety feet down I found the pig iron standing on a ledge. It did not appear in the torch beam as an object from the world above, but as something *germane* to the place."

2. "On many occasions the smell of my pipe was my preservation and saved me from carrying in my clothes the *noxious* odors."

3. "It became clear as the party progressed through the snow that Marcel was only an *indifferent* climber."

4. "When we *cleared* the harbor entrance, I ordered full speed ahead."

5. "The birds that Holbrook snared were a welcome *supplement* to our scanty rations."

6. "At the station house an unemotional matron divested the famous *impersonator* of the last and best of her disguises."

7. "Now the tree under which he had done this carried a weight of snow on its boughs. No wind had blown for weeks, and each bough was fully *freighted*."

8. "And he did for me the unnecessary thing, the gracious thing, that we find done only by the great of heart. Things no training can teach, for they are done on the instant, with no *predicated* experience."

9. "Spring made a man feel good and sad, too, and wild sometimes, wanting to howl with the wolves or *strike* north with the ducks."

10. "The car careened on, charged the cliff face, rebounded, attacked the lower wall furiously with all its unwieldy weight like a great bumble bee, and tumbling over, crashed with a brief and distant *report* into the depths below."

B. The adjective *gross* has several meanings. Taking clues from the context, tell what it means in each sentence below.

1. The committee charged the Congressman with *gross* negligence in the execution of his duties.

2. If the *gross* weight of the package is given, remember that you must subtract the weight of the packaging to determine how much the contents weigh.

3. Trevor lost sight of the fleeing raccoon in the *gross* underbrush.

4. The *gross* form of the sculpture was now apparent, although the artist still had much of the detail to complete.

5. He was not invited to the party because not everyone could tolerate his *gross* language.

Part 5

Context Clues

Sometimes the context of an unfamiliar word will give you a definite clue to the meaning of the word. Professional writers, particularly textbook writers and newspaper reporters, take pains to explain unfamiliar words. An awareness of the devices writers use to provide an explanation will help you read smoothly through a passage without being interrupted by an unknown word. Six common types of context clues are explained and illustrated in this section.

How Context Reveals Meaning

1. **Definition.** The most obvious and straightforward method of revealing meaning is by outright definition. A form of the verb "to be" signals a definition.

> *Cinéma vérité* is a technique used to make a documentary film appear natural and spontaneous.

> The *sycophant* can be found wherever there is power; he is the individual who works his way into favor with flattery.

2. **Restatement.** Sometimes a writer will explain a term by restating it in other words. A restatement can take many forms. Certain words act as signals that a restatement will follow. Be alert to such signal words as these: *in other words, that is, to put it another way, or, this means.*

> One astronomer claims there is a total absence of *plasma*, or gaseous matter, in certain parts of the corona.

> Scientists are curious about the *optical properties* of the clouds covering Venus. In other words, they wonder whether sunlight filters through the clouds and reaches the surface of the planet.

The words *this, that, these* and *those* also signal a restatement.

> Irv was getting a degree in *topology*. This branch of mathematics deals with the properties of geometric figures that remain unchanged even when under distortion.

Commas, parentheses, or dashes may signal an appositive, which is another kind of restatement.

> A doctor will usually check the functioning of the *thyroid*, the gland which regulates body growth and metabolism, if the patient has a weight problem.

> Many of the more familiar metals are *malleable* (capable of being hammered into sheets) and *ductile* (capable of being drawn into wire).

With attentive reading of the context, you may find a restatement that helps you understand a word, even if no signals are present.

> Sara was *ambivalent* about Jack. She couldn't decide whether she admired him for leaving medical school to be a painter, or whether she considered him reckless and immature.

> In my home town there is a law against smoking in public, but the law has fallen into *desuetude*. Until recently, people have not felt it was their concern whether another person was smoking or not, and the law has not been used in forty years. Now people are beginning to ask that the law be enforced.

> Part of the effectiveness of her narrative is in her *understatement*. You know that being the only child living with these two crazy old people with their sleepwalking and fits of rage is a very strange growing up, but she treats it as just a little bit odd, no more.

3. **Example.** Sometimes a writer will give one or more examples to show the meaning of a word. Words that signal an

example are these: *such, such as, like, other, especially, particularly, for example, for instance.*

> Like Manhattan, each of the five *boroughs* is an administrative unit of New York City.

> There must be international agreement on punishments for hijacking and kidnapping. Such *guerilla tactics* cannot be tolerated by one nation without all nations being threatened.

4. Modifiers. A writer may clarify the meaning of a term in a modifying phrase or clause.

> It is hoped that both presidential nominees will be on their guard against the *chauvinistic* patriot who carries his devotion to obnoxious and pathological lengths and permits no criticism of any of our national institutions or methods.

5. Contrast. Occasionally a writer will make a contrast that enables you to grasp the meaning of an unfamiliar word.

> Both men were good writers, but each approached his work from a different standpoint. One was a *dilettante;* the other had to write for his daily bread.

> Unlike the other members of the band who resurfaced in other groups in later years, James was lost to the public after his *meteoric* fame as the lead singer.

6. Connecting words. A connecting word links two thoughts in a way that can shed some light on the meaning of an unfamiliar word. Study the examples to see how an unfamiliar word is illuminated both by the words to which it is connected and by the connecting word itself. Do the connecting words indicate the similarity or dissimilarity of the thoughts they connect?

> An ungraduated income tax takes money from the rich person at the same rate as from the poor person. A person who is paid enough to buy himself many luxuries may not

miss twenty percent of his salary; however, a person on a *subsistence* wage cannot be as offhand about giving up his twenty percent to the government.

There are disadvantages to color film for the professional photographer. No color film *renders* colors exactly as we see them. Moreover, the color results that any one film will produce will vary, depending on the age and storage conditions of the film.

One major objection to the proposed disarmament treaty was that there was no provision for inspection of *arsenals,* and therefore no assurance that weapons were not again being stockpiled.

Exercises
Using Context Clues

A. The following passages are taken from newspaper columns or from college textbooks. They are typical of passages you will meet in adult life. For each passage, do these two things: (1) figure out from the context the meaning of the italicized words, and (2) identify the method by which the context reveals the meaning.

1. *Plant pathology* treats abnormalities in the life of the plant.

2. The movement of soil by action of the natural agencies of water, wind, and ice is called *erosion.*

3. Louis Pasteur did one of his most famous investigations on *rabies,* the disease which makes dogs go "mad."

4. The points at which bones make contact or unite with one another are called *articulations.*

5. The fact that the lower vertebrates do not depend very much on the *cerebrum* can be demonstrated by removing this part of the brain and observing the general behavior of the animal.

6. To understand the principles involved in the treatment of cataract, it is first necessary to understand the *etiology,* or causes, of cataract.

7. The horizontal branches of the *banyan tree* and other species of figs often form numerous *prop roots* which grow downward until they enter the soil, where they branch and develop as ordinary roots.

8. The *marine* fishes respond only to notes of low frequency; fresh-water species are sensitive to frequencies of several thousand cycles per second.

9. Colbert was a defender of the economic theory known as *mercantilism.* According to this theory, a nation should make itself wealthy by taking in more *specie* (gold and silver) from selling and exporting its goods abroad than it spends abroad by buying and importing.

10. Theatre people in New York are always sighing for a *repertory theatre*—an institution with a permanent company of actors, a permanent staff of technicians, an intelligent and, no less important, intelligible policy.

11. All the organisms that cause red tides are *photosynthetic;* they use visible light to convert water and carbon dioxide into oxygen and food.

12. Milk contains a type of amino acid—*tryptophan*—which when given to volunteers produces a pronounced sedative effect.

13. The Indians carried provisions on their persons that could keep them for days, but the English were hampered by the necessity for frequent *replenishment* of supplies.

14. Although this Einstein model of the universe was an intriguing one and was based on a rather firm mathematical foundation, an important development occurred in 1929 which completely *invalidated* it.

15. If taxes sometimes seem *onerous,* what we get for them is probably the best bargain of our lives.

B. Choose a newspaper or magazine article in which the author's purpose is to inform readers about some subject. Be aware of how the author deals with terms that readers may not be familiar with. Write out sentences from the article in which the author uses context clues to clarify words and phrases. After each sentence, define the word or phrase as you understand it from the context.

Inferring Word Meanings

The six kinds of context clues you have just studied are visible and clear clues to word meaning. Many other contexts convey meaning in a more subtle way. In such contexts you must **infer** the meaning of an unfamiliar word.

Inference involves reasoning from known facts. When you encounter an unfamiliar word, search the context to see what can be known. Then try to determine what the connection is between the known facts and the unknown word. Rather than being steered by a specific device, you will have to derive the meaning of a word from the whole context.

Study the following examples. Do you see the reasoning that leads to a definition of each italicized word?

> He kept the *talisman* on a chain around his neck at all times. Once he had gone out to shovel the driveway without it and he had fallen and broken his arm. It didn't pay to take chances with a thing like that.

A talisman, which can be worn around the neck, is apparently an object that is supposed to bring good luck, since going out without it brought bad luck.

> In a series of settling tanks the solid waste *precipitates* out of the water, but the *effluent* is still too acidic to return to the river.

Since solid waste precipitates out of water in settling tanks, *precipitates* must mean something like *settles*. The *effluent* is water that is to be returned to the river, or water from the river that has been dirtied by some process.

Exercises
Inferring Word Meanings

A. In the following sentences you are to infer the meaning of the words in italics. Be ready to explain to the class what clues in the context led you to your definition. Compare a dictionary definition for each word with the definition you have constructed.

1. Eleanor, who has always suffered from *acrophobia*, could not be induced to go to the top of the Washington Monument for a view of the capital.

2. Each of these pianists is an erstwhile *prodigy*. Gould is supposed to have been able to read notes before he could read the printed word. He started playing the piano at the age of three, and gave his first recital at fourteen.

3. Americans have extended their high standard of living to more citizens since the Poverty Program of President Johnson, and yet is is still possible to find people living in *destitution* in the land of plenty.

4. An *indefatigable* worker, Thomas Edison often spent days and nights on his experiments, not even taking time to eat and sleep.

5. Moths and butterflies are the insects to which budding *entomologists* are first attracted.

6. Roots may extend far downward into the soil and spread *laterally*, much more widely than most people realize.

7. In 1921 the Russian government turned against modern art and Kandinsky thought it wise to leave his native land for good, settling again in Germany which, in turn, he left after the Nazis came to power. But since, according to him, the artist's first loyalty is to the satisfaction of an inner need, these displacements, despite their sadness, were *peripheral* to the creation of a lifework.

8. Of the American artists of the thirties and forties, some were traditionalists following *canons* of taste well formulated in the past; others were audacious innovators.

9. Man's response to the decline in fish harvest has been to try harder—an action more suicidal than *sapient*.

10. There has been speculation as to why the first national parks were established. In this period of relentless *disposition* of the *public domain*, it was reasonable to fear that even the most magnificent scenic sites might be plowed or grazed out of existence.

B. Examine the following passages, paying special attention to the italicized words. What is the special meaning of each word *in this context?*

1

Although it is difficult to generalize, too many of our universities have become huge circuses in which the sideshows overshadow the main attraction. "When a university president makes a speech calling for intellectual leadership," writes Dr. Hutchins, "he cannot be heard over the din his publicity man is making about the newest campus queen." Our colleges have involved themselves in activities which have only the most *tenuous relation* to the *academic function.* —MARTIN B. MARGOLIES

2

Certainly, some amount of criticism of the *bathos* and *sentimentality* that constitutes so great a part of our theatre fare today is justifiable. Serious students of literature should indeed maintain a *skeptical* attitude toward the commercially successful *floss;* they should be wary of gulping down uncritically the *mawkish sentiments* of the few who, by gently patting their audience on the head, comfort them with cheap and empty solutions. —LEONARD FLEISCHER

3

Burns brings an *element of complication* into what is otherwise the relatively simple *evolution* of English poetry. The influence of a half-foreign nationality, and the racy vigor of a son of the soil, quicken in him the germ of an unexpected originality. He is an *innovator,* but not after the manner of his English *contemporaries.* —LEGOUIS and CAZAMIAN

4

Languages die but words tend to be *immortal.* Catchwords, slang, and technical terms often disappear after a *brief run,* but many become established parts of the language, and once so established they persist. *Hosts* of Greek and Latin words are in use in dozens of the world's present-day languages. —JOHN CIARDI

5

The English language is an unpredictable medley, but no other can communicate such subtle shades of thought and feeling, such fine discriminations of meaning. The riches of its *mingled derivations* supply a multitude of synonyms, each with its own *distinction of implications.* —ELIZABETH DREW

6

Sincerity in the fullest sense must be more than a *temperamental disposition* to be frank. It is a simplicity of spirit which is preserved by the will to be true. It implies an obligation to *manifest* the truth and to defend it. —THOMAS MERTON

7

The *faculty* of creating is never given to us all by itself: It always goes hand in hand with the gift of observation. And the true creator may be recognized by his ability always to find about him, in the commonest and *humblest* thing, items worthy of note. —IGOR STRAVINSKY

Chapter 2

Effective Sentences

Many of the problems of writing are sentence problems. These problems are of two kinds:

1. Problems of grammar

2. Problems of meaning and sense

Sentence improvement is therefore treated at length in this book, both from the standpoint of grammar and from the standpoint of sense.

This chapter is devoted to those sentences which, though grammatically correct, are nonetheless unsatisfactory. These are the empty sentences, the circular sentences that say nothing. They are the overloaded sentences, the sentences that try to say too much. They are the illogical sentences, created by unrealized gaps in thought. These unsatisfactory sentences arise from clearly identifiable causes which can be isolated and presented to you without dependence on grammatical principles.

Part 1
Avoiding Empty Sentences

The function of a sentence is to convey facts, ideas, or feelings.

Writing cannot be done in haste. It cannot be done without thought. **Empty sentences** like the following result from haste and from failure to think before beginning to write.

> In cities and everywhere else there is too much traffic because there are too many cars and trucks and many of the cars and trucks take up too much room because they are so big.

This sentence starts out hopefully: *"In cities and everywhere else there is too much traffic because . . ."* The writer promises to explain why there is too much traffic. This is worth hearing about. What is the reason given? ". . . there are too many cars and trucks . . ." The writer clearly doesn't know any reason. He is simply saying, "There is too much traffic because there is too much traffic." As an afterthought, the writer added something about the size of cars.

This point about the size of many automobiles is a good one. It is related to traffic conditions in city streets. The writer's problem was to *think through* the relationship and to express it clearly. If he had *thought*, he would not have written "there is too much traffic because. . . ." He might have written:

> The existence of so many full-size luxury cars is increasing the tangle of traffic in our city streets.

Here is another example of an empty sentence:

> I think it is unfair to charge higher automobile insurance rates for men under 25 because it is not fair to charge men higher rates than women.

This sentence says only that higher automobile insurance rates are unfair because they are unfair. Why are they unfair? If the writer had reasons, he should have given them. If he did not have reasons, he should merely have expressed his opinion. By using "because," he led the reader to expect reasons and details. He might better have written:

> I think it is unfair to charge men higher rates for automobile insurance than women.

Exercise
Avoiding Empty Sentences

Rewrite the following empty sentences. Add any facts or ideas that you think will improve them.

1. I want to go to college because going to college will satisfy my long-felt desires.

2. Going to college is a necessity for entering the profession that I want to enter, for my profession requires a college education.

3. I thoroughly enjoyed the concert at the Auditorium because I liked the music.

4. The world is very beautiful in the early morning, for everything takes on added beauty when the sun is just coming up.

5. My teachers are not what I expected because I didn't know what to expect.

6. Having planned for a long time to buy a car, I was finally able to buy one as a result of my planning over a long time.

7. Athletics of all kinds should be provided in high school because all high schools need athletic teams to develop school spirit among the high school students.

8. If you're just starting, a $50.00 Gibson guitar would be just right for a beginner.

9. Everyone who drives should drive very carefully because reckless driving is dangerous.

10. Everyone needs a large vocabulary if he or she wishes to be successful in the future, for a large vocabulary is necessary for the person who wishes to go to the top in his or her career.

11. I believe in always trying my best in volleyball because I think that in that sport one must always give one's all and really try.

12. The excitement of the final quarter became so unbearable that I could hardly stand it any more.

13. That was the best novel I ever read because it wasn't boring at any time.

14. Being a paramedic would be a worthwhile and vital job because what they do is really important.

15. Once you have learned to swim and ride a bike, you can always swim or ride a bike because they are skills that stay with you and you can't forget them.

Part 2
Avoiding Overloaded Sentences

The guides to writing effective sentences are few and simple:

1. Say one thing at a time.

2. Say it clearly and directly.

Everyone has the experience of writing sentences that try to say too much. They become so crowded that the writer cannot remember what he started to say, and the reader becomes fatigued from trying to follow the thought. Such sentences are **overloaded sentences.**

When you find an overloaded sentence in your own writing, examine it carefully. Look for the main idea. Start over again with this subject-verb combination. Drop irrelevant details entirely. If the left-over details are important, start with a new subject-verb combination and pull the details together around it.

OVERLOADED Everyone should learn a second modern language today because the world is growing smaller and we need to know what is going on in other countries where there are many opportunities for young people to find interesting work.

IMPROVED Everyone should learn a second modern language today because in a shrinking world we need to know what is going on in other countries. A second language will open opportunities for young people to find interesting work abroad.

OVERLOADED I prefer a large university because there you can meet many kinds of people with different interests from many parts of the country where there are different ideas, and a wide experience with many kinds of people is an important part of education.

IMPROVED Experience with many kinds of people is an important part of education. In a large university you can meet people from many parts of the country and people with different interests. I prefer a large university because it provides this important part of education.

Exercise
Avoiding Overloaded Sentences

Rewrite the following overloaded sentences. There is no one right way to improve them. You may find it necessary to add words and details.

1. All colleges should be coeducational because men and women can work together with mutual respect for each other and interact socially as well as academically by being together on the campus.

2. Everyone wants to be a success, and this means making enough money to fulfill material needs and to pursue the goals that will make a person happy, which is the greatest thing in the world.

3. I like winter better than any other season of the year, for in winter I can skate and ski without getting too hot and too tired as I do in the summer, and I like to go to parties in the winter, and even school is exciting and interesting in the winter.

4. Hobbies can be a source of pleasure and relaxation from

business, and they can even lead to success in a vocation, and a student who enjoys designing, drawing, or even building aircraft models may become a pilot or an executive in an aircraft company.

5. Dogs are the best pets of all because they are friendly and intelligent, and they are easy to care for, and when a person gets home, his dog will always be glad to see him.

6. Participation in one or two extra-curricular activities in high school can be enjoyable and beneficial to the student if he or she doesn't join too many and neglect classwork, but maintaining good scholastic standing is necessary for a future vocational or college career.

7. A satisfying work is one of the ingredients of a happy life, so when you choose a career, be sure that it is something you will enjoy doing and that it will give you a feeling of fulfillment, self-worth and achievement.

8. Everyone should learn to cook because knowing how to cook makes one more appreciative of good food, and cooking a good dish brings a feeling of great satisfaction, and it is also useful to be able to prepare a meal in an emergency.

9. Trying to be an amateur painter, musician, or writer is better than simply studying art appreciation, music appreciation, or literature, though these have their rewards too, but trying to paint or write will make a person even more appreciative of the arts.

10. Juanita was chairperson of the committee and under her leadership more was accomplished than ever before, including an all-day educational forum and a fund-raising dance, both of which attracted many new members and brought the group much favorable publicity.

11. On the first day of our trip we drove as far as Chicago and just as we were about to stop for the night the car gurgled and stopped and we learned from the mechanic that it would take a day or two to repair the motor and that we'd have to stay over in Chicago.

12. A tunnel under the English Channel would be a good thing because it would make travel between England and the continent easier and more convenient and cheaper and many people cannot afford the passage now but would be able to drive from England to the continent and back.

Part 3
Avoiding Wordiness

A sentence that uses more words than necessary is boring. The extra words smother the meaning. The writer with a sharp eye can spot excess words and delete them during revision of his work.

One kind of wordiness arises from needless repetition of a word or from needless use of words with a similar meaning.

> We thought we had an *adequate* supply of *food* with *enough* for everyone *to eat.*
> Hard work *alone* is not the *only* thing you need.
> Jack is an *honest* person who *never tells a lie.*
> Carlene is the *kind* of individual of the *sort* you can trust.

Another kind of wordiness arises from the repetition of *that.*

> I thought *that* if I came *that* I might be able to help.
> We knew *that* Matt felt *that* he had been cheated.

In the last two sentences, the second *that* may be dropped.

In general, wordiness results simply from the use of too many words. The writer may use a clause or a phrase when a single word would suffice. Methods of avoiding or repairing wordiness are considered in Chapter 3 under the heading *Reduction.*

> WORDY   In the case of physics, you would probably agree that physics is too hard for most young people in the tenth grade.

> IMPROVED You would probably agree that physics is too hard for most tenth-grade students.

> WORDY   A year after we graduated we could look back and see that what we thought was an attitude on Ms. Stein's part of being very severe and demanding was really good training for later life.

REVISED When we looked back a year after graduation, we could see that Ms. Stein's severe and demanding attitude was good training for later life.

Awkward Repetition

Sentences lose their effectiveness if a word or phrase is repeated carelessly. Sometimes there is no substitute for a word, and it must be repeated. Awkward repetition is the use of a word or phrase a second or third time when it need not be repeated.

Awkward repetition can be corrected by using a synonym, by using pronouns in place of nouns, or by rewriting the sentence.

AWKWARD I have chosen a *topic* that is a frequent *topic* of conversation today. My *topic* is developing our own natural resources.

IMPROVED I have chosen a topic frequently heard in conversation today—developing our own natural resources.

AWKWARD My point is that too much *emphasis* is placed *on college education,* and this *emphasis on college education* makes many people go to college who don't need or want a *college education.*

IMPROVED My point is that too much emphasis on college education makes many people go to college for education they don't need or want.

AWKWARD Hamilton and Jefferson had entirely different ideas about government, but Hamilton and Jefferson both contributed much to our government.

IMPROVED   Hamilton and Jefferson had entirely different ideas about government, but they both contributed much to our country.

Exercise
Avoiding Wordiness

The following sentences are wordy or needlessly repetitive. Revise them to eliminate these faults.

1. The mirror was round in shape.

2. Maya Angelou wrote an autobiography of her own lfe.

3. The League of Women Voters is a non-partisan organization and is not in favor of any one political party or candidate.

4. A play which is very interesting and which is very different is the play *The Effect of Gamma Rays on Man-in-the-Moon Marigolds* by Paul Zindel.

5. Such factors as the right to own and sell property and the right to make a profit are characteristic of the free enterprise system in a capitalistic society.

6. It is my belief that the greatest invention since the wheel is, I think, the television.

7. Mary Ann was a great help to her team because of the fact that she had a willing spirit and wanted to help the team.

8. The committee held a lengthy discussion in respect to the matter of raising money for the prom.

9. Many nations in the world are anxious to improve their economic conditions, to rise from their present levels of poverty.

10. The graduating class heard much good advice and counsel from the commencement speakers on the occasion of their commencement exercises.

11. Since my parents spoke two languages, my mother speaking German and my father speaking French, I grew up learning both French and German from them and English in school.

12. The class discussed not only the problems of water conservation but also the problems of water pollution and the wastes that are poured into water from industrial plants.

Part 4
Avoiding Awkward Beginnings

The normal, easily readable pattern of English sentences is subject—verb—complement. A great many awkward sentences occur when this pattern is abandoned. Certain expressions used at the beginning of a sentence create awkwardness. They delay the thought, and they add nothing to it. Usually, they are not needed at all. The most common of these offending expressions are *The fact that, What I believe is, What I want is, Being that, The reason is.*

AWKWARD   *The fact that* Mary was sick should be taken into account.

BETTER   Mary's sickness should be taken into account.

AWKWARD   *What I believe* is that no one should be compelled to go to school.

BETTER   I believe that no one should be compelled to go to school.

AWKWARD   *What Terry needs* is a little encouragement.

BETTER   Terry needs a little encouragement.

AWKWARD   *Being that* there was no school yesterday, we have no homework assignments.

BETTER   Since there was no school yesterday, we have no homework assignments.

AWKWARD   *The reason* I chose this book *is* because of its title.

BETTER   I chose this book because of its title.

Exercise
Revising Sentences with Awkward Beginnings

Revise these sentences to remove their awkward beginnings.

1. Being that he was a new student in the high school, Bob felt lonely and apprehensive.

2. What I think is that everyone should work a ten-hour day and a four-day week in order to conserve our resources.

3. The fact that too many extra-curricular activities are often too time-consuming should be considered by the student before he joins too many clubs.

4. The reason I liked my summer work was because the work itself was pleasant.

5. What the stock market crash in 1929 did to many people was to make them bankrupt.

6. Being unhappy about losing my job, I lost my appetite too.

7. The reason there are so many accidents on the highways today is because people drive too fast.

8. What all Americans should do is learn to conserve energy.

9. The fact that many colleges have language requirements makes it necessary that one study one or two languages in high school.

10. The reason that Lori has been studying Russian and Spanish is because she wants to go into the diplomatic service.

11. What every diplomat needs is to be able to speak several languages.

12. The fact that the weather looked threatening made us postpone our picnic.

13. Being that the picnic was postponed, we decided to have a party indoors.

14. The reason that Jon is now working hard is that he nearly failed two of his midterm tests.

15. The old man being unable to keep up with the others, the group left him sitting by the roadside.

Chapter 3

Sentence Revision

Everyone is called upon at times to speak without preparation. In conversation and discussion, in class meetings, faculty meetings, or business conferences, a question will arise on which you must say something. In these situations there is little time to arrange your thoughts. You do your best, and the quality of your "best" depends upon previous experience and training.

In writing, the situation is different. There always comes a point at which you can go back over what you have written and put it in order. You can reorganize, you can rearrange your paragraphs, you can revise your sentences. This chapter deals with the kinds of revisions you will find it profitable to make in your sentences.

Part 1

Omitting Unrelated Details

The function of a sentence is to state an idea, to present facts, or to describe feelings. When unrelated details appear in a sentence, they interrupt the flow of thought.

In sentence revision, keep your mind on the main idea. Delete any detail that is not closely related to this idea.

> I would like to be an engineer like my brother, *who has a Mercedes* and works on big construction jobs all over the world.

Clearly, the Mercedes has nothing to do with being an engineer. It has a great deal to do with "my brother's" success as an engineer, but his success is another matter. It belongs in another sentence.

> It was so foggy over New York, *where we expected to spend two weeks,* that our plane could not land.

The expectation of spending two weeks in New York has nothing to do with the fog over the airport. If it is important at all, it belongs in another sentence.

Exercise
Omitting Unrelated Details

Rewrite these sentences, omitting details that are not related to the main idea.

1. We spent our vacation in Virginia, where George Washington lived, and we liked the state very much.

2. We usually go shopping on Saturday, which is the last day of the week, and buy our groceries for the next week.

3. The truck, which had burned on the highway and which was a Ford truck, was being dragged away by a crew of men who wore red shirts and caps.

4. Reading good books, which can fill our leisure time, is helpful in acquiring knowledge and an extensive vocabulary.

5. The new magazines, which came yesterday, are filled with articles on foreign policy and international affairs.

6. Important problems in American history are discussed by a panel of experts, one of whom is a friend of ours, on a weekly television program.

7. I had been absorbed in a television program, which was about the forthcoming election, and I had failed to notice that someone had entered the room.

8. The students at Roosevelt High School, located in the center of the city, can choose many courses from a varied curriculum.

9. The most beautiful scenes in Europe, which we visited last summer, are the lakes and mountains in the Alps.

10. TV weather forecasts, which are usually part of a news program, are based on scientific observation and knowledge.

11. Tourists love Florence, Italy, the home of the Medici, where Sue lost her purse when we were there last summer.

12. Ryan, who last year won the soccer award, went skiing in Aspen.

13. Much of the poetry of seventeenth century England, which suffered from great plagues, fires, and political revolutions, is called metaphysical.

14. They were afraid that the cold front, which was moving southward, would damage the orchards, located in Orlando where I was born.

15. San Francisco, where my sister lives, is one of the most colorful cities I have ever visited.

Part 2

Keeping Related Sentence Parts Together

In effective English sentences, the verb is closely tied to the subject; it is also closely tied to the complement. Similarly, the parts of a verb phrase are tied closely together. When these related sentence parts are widely separated by intervening words, the sentence is difficult to read. In general, keep closely related sentence parts together.

AWKWARD	The *fog,* after closely hugging the ground all day long, *lifted* at last.
	(Subject and verb separated)
REVISED	After closely hugging the ground all day long, the fog lifted at last.

AWKWARD	Jack *had* never in the four years of his high school career *received* such poor marks.
	(Parts of a verb phrase separated)
REVISED	Jack had never received such poor marks in the four years of his high school career.

| AWKWARD | You *have had,* whether you know it or not, your last chance. (Verb and object separated) |
| REVISED | Whether you know it or not, you have had your last chance. |

Exercise
Keeping Related Sentence Parts Together

Revise these sentences to bring related parts closer together.

1. The newest discoveries in science are to the average person awe-inspiring.

2. The refugees, after having been shunted around from one camp to another, were finally settled into homes of their own.

3. The TV announcer began, after a few opening remarks, his usual morning broadcast of the news.

4. The team had never, in all the games it had played, been so lucky as in this last game.

5. The family had, after a long vacation at the beach, returned to their home in the city.

6. The Student Council had, after much weighing of pro's and con's, gone to the convention.

7. The foreign ministers' conference will be, everyone hopes, of great significance.

8. The program committee has, even though several members believe it is not feasible, voted to give the choral concert.

9. The house across the street has, for the last four years, been unoccupied.

10. Computer programing is, according to an article I read, extremely complicated.

11. Because United States Presidents had fewer duties, they often vacationed for whole summers early in the nineteenth century.

12. Gary volunteered to give the oral presentation in history because he frequently enjoyed the attention.

13. He regretted only having two hands.

14. The Breitzmans were, having planned to go to Sweden after the Christmas season, disappointed that they were not granted their visas.

15. Because there was a fuel shortage, many big businesses were forced to close down this winter.

Part 3

Coordinating Related Ideas

There are times when ideas are so closely related that they should be joined in a single sentence. If the ideas seem of equal importance, they can be joined by a conjunction or by a semicolon in a compound sentence.

The coordinating conjunctions used to form compound sentences are *and, but, or, for, nor*. Each of these conjunctions has a specific meaning and therefore relates the parts of a compound sentence in a specific way: *and* and *nor* mean "in addition"; *or* means "an alternative"; *but* means "an exception"; *for* means "because."

> The seniors will take their tests on Monday, *and* the juniors will take theirs on Wednesday.
> Beth cannot solve the problem, *nor* can anyone else.
> Our team started last, *but* we gathered the most paper.
> Kate should apply now, *or* she may be too late.
> Bob decided to try, *for* he was sure there had been a misunderstanding.

Conjunctive adverbs and connecting phrases are also used to tie ideas together in compound sentences.

ADDITION	ALTERNATIVE	EXCEPTION OR CONTRAST
indeed	on the other hand	yet
in fact	at the same time	still
furthermore		however
moreover		nonetheless
also		
besides		

RESULT

consequently
as a consequence
therefore
hence
then

The choice of a conjunctive adverb depends upon the meaning the writer wants to convey. The point is that each conjunctive adverb specifies a particular meaning, just as the coordinating conjunctions do. The correlative conjunctions (*either–or; neither–nor; both–and; whether–or; not only–but also*) may be used to tie together the parts of a compound sentence.

Note: A comma is used before the coordinating conjunction in a compound sentence. A semicolon is placed before a conjunctive adverb, and a comma is usually placed after it. Here is an example of each:

> The ballet opens this weekend, and the tickets will go on sale tomorrow.
> The traffic was heavy; nevertheless, we arrived on time.

There are times when ideas do not need a conjunction between them. This is particularly true when the idea of "in addition to" is quite clear. The semicolon alone is better than *and* in these sentences.

It is raining here again; it was raining yesterday; it will rain tomorrow.

The outcome of the election was decisive; it was never in doubt.

Exercises
Coordinating Related Ideas

A. From the conjunctions given in parentheses, choose the one that best fits the meaning.

1. Usually the lake is still and placid, (and, but, or) today it is in constant motion.

2. Please buy me a straw pocketbook in Italy, (or, for, but) bring me some perfume from Paris.

3. Spices were once one of the world's most desired possessions, (but, or, and) they are now available to everyone at reasonable prices.

4. She cannot read her own handwriting, (nor, and, but) can anyone else read it.

5. Kathy looked after the children, (and, but, for) her mother was sick.

6. The wind roared in the treetops, (but, and, or) the windows of the old house rattled.

7. The Supreme Court gives a majority opinion, (or, and, but) it often gives a minority opinion as well.

8. We can go to Europe by ship, (and, or, for, but) we can go by jet.

9. Our weekend hike in the mountains was a great adventure (and, or, but) the sudden thunderstorms forced us to return home early.

10. Steve cannot go to the soccer match (but, nor, and) can he go to dinner with us.

B. Supply a suitable conjunctive adverb from the list on page 46. Copy the sentences, punctuating properly.

1. We had read all the news stories _____ we had even read all the advertisements.

2. The Senator's constituents wrote him about the legislation _____ he ignored the letters.

3. Lori had never learned to swim _____ she nearly drowned when the boat overturned.

4. Keith did not meet us at the appointed time _____ we waited.

5. We want to be in Salzburg for the Music Festival _____ we want to see the ruins of ancient Greece.

6. The seniors usually take their examinations early _____ they are free for a week before Commencement.

7. The audience waited expectantly _____ the speaker did not appear.

8. The books were piled on the table and on the floor _____ the bookshelves were filled to overflowing.

9. The sun shines most of the time _____ the state is called the Sunshine State.

10. Violets grow wild in this region _____ they even come up through cracks in the pavement.

Part 4

Avoiding Faulty Coordination

When ideas are closely related, they are read together with ease. One idea seems to complete the other; in fact, the second idea may help to explain the first. The main use of a compound sentence is to help the reader see a close relationship.

If unrelated ideas are joined in a compound sentence, the reader is confused, and the writer's point is lost. Sometimes the fault of joining unrelated ideas occurs because the writer has omitted something essential to the sense. His mind has raced ahead of his pen; consequently, a step has been left out.

CONFUSING   The airport was closed in by fog, and we missed the game.

IMPROVED   The airport was closed in by fog. *We were four hours late in arriving* and missed the game.

CONFUSING   I took the aptitude tests last spring, and I am not going into engineering.

IMPROVED   The aptitude tests I took last spring *showed that I am weak in mathematics.* I am not going into engineering because it requires mathematical skill.

Exercise
Avoiding Faulty Coordination

Revise the following sentences in order to avoid faulty coordination.

1. Six inches of snow fell during the night, and we were late to school.

2. The cost of living has risen sharply during the past few years, and personal incomes have risen too.

3. The admission requirements of the colleges have become more stringent, and the number of students entering college has increased.

4. The new Music Center cost one million dollars, and the city has increased the tax rate.

5. The sky is overcast, and we cannot go on our picnic.

6. The experts had predicted that Bartow would never get into office, and he ridiculed them in his acceptance speech.

7. Mother had completely forgotten to take the turkey out of the freezer, but fortunately the shrimp made a hit with the guests.

8. The camping trip was fun, and I needed an extra blanket.

9. Jack auditioned for the band yesterday, and he will choose a different activity.

10. Our team won the state tournament, and school was canceled the next day.

11. Jason won first place in the photography competition, and he is now our newspaper photographer.

12. Megan's car broke down, and we still arrived at the airport on time.

13. Illinois is called "The Land of Lincoln," and President Lincoln spent much of his life there.

14. The sky was dark and threatening, and the cross country meet was postponed.

15. Alex Haley spoke about his ancestry to a large crowd in Texas, and he is the author of the highly publicized *Roots*.

Part 5
Avoiding Stringy Sentences

Some sentences become overloaded because the writer strings a number of ideas together, placing an *and* between each idea. The result is that no one idea stands out; there seems to be no organization. You can revise stringy sentences in two ways:

1. Choose the conjunction that will show the real relationship between the ideas you are presenting.

2. Divide the sentence into two or more sentences.

STRINGY There is a water shortage in many parts of the country, and this shortage is causing concern, and the U.S. Department of the Interior is trying out methods of changing sea water to fresh water.

REVISED The water shortage in many parts of the country is causing concern; *consequently*, the U.S. Department of the Interior is trying out methods of changing sea water to fresh water.

STRINGY Scientists today are working in an invisible world, and they are dealing with genes, atoms, ions, and electrons, and no one has ever seen them, and some of them may not exist, but to understand modern science, we must understand the scientists' ideas of these invisible things.

REVISED Scientists today are working in an invisible world of genes, atoms, ions, and electrons. No one has ever seen them; *indeed*, some of them may not exist. But to understand modern science, we must understand the scientists' ideas of these invisible things.

Exercise
Revising Stringy Sentences

Revise these sentences. They have too many *and*'s. In each case, you will need to make two or more sentences.

1. Many scientists have dreamed of transmitting power through the air without the use of wires, and they have experimented for many years, trying to develop their ideas, and at last they seem to have come near the realization of their dream.

2. Recently the small colleges have been sorely pressed financially, and they need more money for salaries for their teachers, and they do not want to raise the costs of tuition to supply the needed funds.

3. Students nowadays may want to learn such languages as Arabic, Russian, and Hindustani, and these are not taught in many schools, and students may have to wait until they are graduate students to learn them.

4. They were to entertain their family and friends that night, and they decided to go on with it and try it and make the best of it.

5. She was a scholarly and accomplished book critic for a large newspaper and when she decided to write her own novel and had to quit the job, her co-workers wondered who could replace her.

Part 6
Subordination

The main clause is the basic structure in any sentence. It states the main idea of the sentence. Modifying clauses and phrases are used to add details or to explain the conditions that define or limit the meaning of the main clause.

The writer alone knows what his main idea is in each sentence he writes. If he writes only compound sentences, or only main clauses, he gives his reader no guidance; hence, the effectiveness of what he is saying is lost.

MAIN IDEA	LIMITING, EXPLAINING, OR DEFINING DETAILS
We can go to the concert (at any time?)	if the tickets aren't sold out. (under this condition)
Gary may need an assistant (why?)	to help with the correspondence. (explaining)
Raleigh went to his death (how?)	proclaiming his innocence. (defining details)

Materials of less importance can be subordinated (put in their proper place) by use of clauses. Adverb clauses are introduced by subordinating conjunctions, which express a great variety of relationships. (See Section 1.7 in your Handbook.) Nothing improves a sentence quite so much as substituting the right subordinating conjunction for a meaningless *and* that has been dropped thoughtlessly between two clauses.

WEAK   Jim took the heaviest pack, *and* he staggered slowly up the hill.

BETTER   *Taking* the heaviest pack, Jim staggered slowly up the hill. (participle)

WEAK   Mari was dressed in tennis dress, *and* she looked like a pro at the court club.

BETTER   *Dressed* in a tennis dress, Mari looked like a pro at the court club. (past participle)

WEAK   Pam worked hard for Sue's election, *and* she knew all along that Sue had no chance to win.

BETTER   Pam worked hard for Sue's election, *although* she knew all along that Sue had no chance to win. (adverb clause)

Subordination may also be used to join two related sentences smoothly and economically.

FAIR   Peg worked all night. She wanted the job completed on time.

BETTER	Peg worked all night to complete the job on time. (infinitive)
FAIR	Jack LeClerc is our guidance counselor. He did personnel work in the Navy.
BETTER	Jack LeClerc, *our guidance counselor,* did personnel work in the Navy. (appositive)
BETTER	Jack Le Clerc, *who did personnel work in the Navy,* is our guidance counselor. (adjective clause)

Upside-Down Subordination

This is the fault of placing an important idea in a subordinate clause or phrase.

FAULTY	The sailboat capsized, *nearly drowning the crew.* (The near drowning of the crew is more important.)
REVISED	The crew nearly drowned when the sailboat capsized.
FAULTY	Mrs. Brown was crossing at the corner *when a cyclist knocked her down.*
REVISED	Mrs. Brown was knocked down by a cyclist as she was crossing at the corner.
FAULTY	Jon lost control, *falling off the cycle.*
REVISED	Losing control, Jon fell off the cycle.

Exercises
Subordinating Ideas

A. Combine these sentences, converting one into either a phrase or a clause. Be careful to avoid upside-down subordination.

1. The match suddenly came to an end. The weary challenger fell against the ropes.

2. The scaffolding had been built beside the church. A workman had fallen off the scaffolding.

3. Last Sunday we were at home. Some guests came in for dinner.

4. We will vote next Tuesday for our favorite candidates. The candidates have made no promises of patronage to their supporters.

5. These plates are replicas of the marble squares in the floor of the cathedral. The cathedral is in Siena, Italy.

6. The chairperson of the committee left the meeting. The members of the committee stayed to finish the discussion.

7. The guests had been entertained well. They thanked their host and hostess profusely.

8. The team has played well throughout the season. It will probably win the championship game.

9. Cleopatra committed suicide in 30 B.C. Egypt became a province of Rome.

10. The haiku is a Japanese poem usually on some subject in nature, and consists of three lines totalling seventeen syllables.

B. Change the following compound sentences by subordinating one of the clauses. You may change it to either a subordinate clause or a phrase.

1. The new books are reviewed each Sunday in *The New York Times Book Review,* and the reviewers are important writers and critics.

2. The foreign ministers' conference was held in Geneva, and the ministers from many nations attended the conference.

3. Science education is encouraged by the federal government, and many grants are given to improve science instruction in the high schools.

4. Golfing requires skill and experience, and many people take up golfing as a means of getting exercise.

5. The actor forgot his lines, and he went into an impromptu performance.

6. The color of the water changed from a dull gray to a bright blue, and the sun came from behind a dark cloud and shone brightly on the lake.

7. The air feels cold, but the outside thermometer registers sixty-six degrees.

8. We picked the flowers yesterday and arranged them, but they are wilted today.

9. Cross-country skiing requires strength and stamina, and many individuals have found cross-country skiing a way to stay physically fit.

10. Newly-released movies are reviewed each week in *Time*, and the reviewers are often well known critics.

C. Correct the upside-down subordination in these sentences.

1. He was walking in the woods when he was struck by lightning.

2. The man who fell from the second-story window and fractured his leg was a window cleaner.

3. The book, which has caused a nation-wide sensation, is a novel about a small town.

4. The orchestra had begun the last number when someone shouted, "Fire!"

5. The politician, who was never elected to office, had tried five times.

6. Words, which can often be dangerous, are in reality only sounds in air or black marks on white paper.

7. The dancers, who seemed to be poetry in motion, presented a ballet.

8. The driver, who was killed when his car crashed into a tree, had fallen asleep at the wheel.

9. The outbreak of measles, which reached epidemic proportions, affected many children.

10. The special art exhibit was at the Chicago Art Institute which included only Van Gogh originals.

Part 7

Reduction

Reduction is the means by which bulky sentences are made compact and effective. Reduction can be achieved by changing a clause to a phrase or a phrase to a single modifier.

CLAUSE	We live in a house *which has high ceilings.*
PHRASE	We live in a house *with high ceilings.*
PHRASE	One of the players *on the Detroit team* was hurt.
WORD	One of the *Detroit* players was hurt.
CLAUSE	The men *who drive the buses* are on strike.
WORD	The *bus* drivers are on strike.
CLAUSE	The class elected José, *who is my closest friend.*
APPOSITIVE	The class elected José, *my closest friend.*

If the clauses of a compound sentence have the same subject, the compound sentence can be reduced by using a compound predicate. Similarly, two clauses with the same verb can be reduced by using a compound subject.

SAME SUBJECT	The men arrived at the camp late, *and they went right to bed.*
REDUCED	The men *arrived* at the camp late and *went* right to bed.
SAME SUBJECT	The tires are wearing thin, *and they will soon be useless.*
REDUCED	The tires *are wearing* thin and *will* soon *be* useless.
SAME VERB	The cups *were broken,* and the saucers *were broken.*
REDUCED	The cups and saucers *were broken.*

Exercise
Reducing Sentences To Make Them Effective

Rewrite these sentences, reducing the italicized words to a shorter construction.

1. Mr. Smith, *who is a banker and philanthropist,* gave a million dollars to Aurora College.

2. The boys and girls hiked up the mountain, *and when they were up there, they ate their supper there.*

3. The 1980 Olympics, *which will be held in Russia,* are to be televised.

4. Karen, *who is the valedictorian of her class,* has been accepted by several universities, *which are well known.*

5. The house had been burned, and *the garage had been burned too.*

6. The men and women in the choir sang a selection *which was very beautiful.*

7. The Student Government Association sent delegates to the annual convention, *which was meeting in Denver, Colorado.*

8. The pencils, *which are a special kind with soft lead,* are lying on the table, *which is in the living room.*

9. Canoeing on the Kankakee River, *which is in northern Illinois,* is an enjoyable summer activity.

10. Organizing a paper *which is long and difficult* requires an outline, *which may be a tentative one.*

11. Source material must be acknowledged, *and it can be acknowledged in a footnote or in the body of your paper.*

12. Questionnaires, *which were long and involved,* were sent to the high school seniors.

13. An analogy, *which is an extended simile or metaphor,* may be helpful in clarifying an issue.

14. The Sears Tower, *which is the world's tallest building,* is 1,454 feet high.

15. James Hoban, *who was an Irish-born architect,* designed the White House.

Part 8
Parallelism

The word *and* joins sentence parts of the same kind. It may join two nouns, two adjectives, two prepositional phrases, and so on. Similar sentence parts so joined are **parallel**. If the sentence parts joined by *and* are not of the same kind, **faulty parallelism** has occurred.

FAULTY	The child needs *sleep* and *to be fed at regular hours.* (noun joined to phrase)
REVISED	The child needs sleep and food at regular hours.
FAULTY	Nancy worried about the *test* and *if she would do well.* (noun joined to clause)
REVISED	Nancy worried about how she would do on the test. (When a parallel is impossible, change the sentence.)
FAULTY	The policeman told the driver to park his truck and *that he must go to the police station.* (phrase joined to clause)
REVISED	The policeman told the driver to park his truck and go to the police station.
FAULTY	We go into town *to dance, to buy food,* or *for a movie.*
REVISED	We go into town to dance, to buy food, or to see a movie.

And Which; And Who

A special kind of faulty parallelism occurs with *which* and *who.* The *and* should never appear before these words unless *which* or *who* appears earlier in the sentence.

STANDARD	Dr. Granjon was a person *who* loved people and *who* devoted her life to their care.
NONSTANDARD	There is a sign at the crossroads *and which* will direct you to our farm.
STANDARD	There is a sign at the crossroads *which* will direct you to our farm.
NONSTANDARD	We took our problem to the old repairman *and who* had never failed us before.

STANDARD   We took our problem to the old repairman,
who had never failed us before.

Exercise
Parallelism

Correct the faulty parallelism in these sentences.

1. She is ambitious, intelligent, and has persistence.
2. The ambitious executive wants success in business, an active social life for himself and his family, and he works for his community.
3. The teacher told the students to write the answers to the questions and that they must finish within the hour.
4. In the park I saw old men playing checkers, families picnicking, and students who were absorbed in reading textbooks.
5. Every town and city needs more parking space, more recreational facilities, and to have more money for these needs.
6. The class in reading learned to read faster and also reading with greater comprehension.
7. The explorers expected to find gold, to get rich, and an easy life.
8. The Puritans, a brave group and who suffered many hardships, influenced greatly the character of the American people.
9. All drivers using the turnpike and who cross the drawbridge must pay a toll.
10. The class read "Chicago," a poem by Carl Sandburg and who was an American poet.
11. The university attempts to teach students to think by requiring that they study logic, and they solve problems, and organizing in outline form their written work.
12. Preparing a manuscript for publication is an arduous task and that requires care and accuracy.
13. She asked for help with her geometry and that I explain the theorem again.
14. Mrs. Watkins asked for votes and to be elected.
15. This is an exciting novel and which you can get at the library.

Part 9
The Weak Passive

The subject of an active verb is the doer of the action. The subject of a passive verb is the receiver of the action. See Section 1.3 in your Handbook. There are many occasions when a passive verb form is useful and desirable. Sometimes the doer of an action is unknown or cannot be named.

> The old house had been torn down.
> The President was warned of the conspiracy.

Sometimes the passive verb is used to describe a common or ongoing experience.

> The Yankee games are played in the Stadium.
> The mail is delivered at one o'clock.

Sometimes the passive verb is used to avoid giving a direct order. Generally, in your Handbook, for example, rules and usages are stated with passive verbs:

> A participial phrase at the beginning of a sentence *is followed* by a comma.
> In standard usage, *bad is* always *used* after linking verbs.

The *weak passive* is the use of the passive when the active verb is more natural and direct.

> WEAK   A good time was had by everyone.
>
> BETTER   Everyone had a good time.
>
> WEAK   Much time is lost by students through poor planning.
>
> BETTER   Students lose much time through poor planning.
>
> WEAK   The ball was hit by Pete Rose right out of the park.
>
> BETTER   Pete Rose hit the ball right out of the park.

WEAK   My homework is not given enough attention by me.

BETTER   I do not give my homework enough attention.

Exercise
The Weak Passive

Revise these sentences to eliminate the weak passive verbs. Four
of the passive verbs are acceptable as they stand.

1. The book was discussed by the senior class.
2. Many gifts were bought by Mother when she went to town.
3. Dinner is served promptly at six o'clock.
4. The car was washed by us in the morning.
5. At the end of the program, a song was played by
the ensemble.
6. A letter was written by the class to the town's mayor.
7. Litter boxes have been placed at every corner.
8. The old house was bought and remodeled by us.
9. The store window was crashed into by a runaway car.
10. Arrangements had been made by me for the club to meet
at our house.
11. My tennis game is not given enough attention by me.
12. The dinner was enjoyed by all of the guests.
13. The article was printed in five languages.
14. The trailer court was destroyed during the storm.
15. A petition was written by the townspeople to the governor.

Chapter 4

Sentence Clarity

The purpose of the writer is to state his thoughts and feelings as exactly as possible. The more carefully they are stated, the greater effect they will have. If necessary words are left out, the meaning is incomplete. If modifiers are misplaced or left dangling, the writer's meaning is distorted. If there is a sudden shift in point of view, the reader is thrown off the track of the argument.

All of these errors can be caught in the process of revision. This chapter will help you to become alert to such errors and, by avoiding them, to write with ever-increasing clarity.

Part 1

Avoiding Omissions of Necessary Words

Omission of *That*

In some sentences the *that* introducing a noun clause must be stated to avoid confusion. When it is omitted the sentence can be read in two different ways.

CONFUSING	We heard all transportation, even Amtrak, was halted by the snowstorm.
IMPROVED	We heard *that* all transportation, even Amtrak, was halted by the snowstorm.
CONFUSING	We heard the team, coming off the field, were complaining about the referee.
IMPROVED	We heard *that* the team, coming off the field, were complaining about the referee.
CONFUSING	Lee found all the employees were unhappy about working on Saturday.
IMPROVED	Lee found *that* all the employees were unhappy about working on Saturday.

Omission of Part of a Compound Verb

The parts of a compound verb are often made up of verb phrases. If these parts differ in number or tense, the complete phrases must be used for clarity.

CONFUSING	The gas tank was filled, and the tires checked. (tank *was*; tires *were*)
REVISED	The gas tank *was* filled, and the tires *were* checked.

CONFUSING	The drawing *was* made, and the winners announced. (drawing *was*; winners *were*)
REVISED	The drawing *was* made, and the winners *were* announced.

Omissions in Comparisons

A comparison becomes awkward and confusing if necessary words are omitted.

CONFUSING	Pat is one of the fastest, if not the fastest, student on the team. (Pat is not one of the fastest student.)
REVISED	Pat is one of the fastest *students* on the team, if not the fastest.
CONFUSING	The storm will be as bad or worse than last week's blizzard.
REVISED	The storm will be as bad *as* last week's blizzard or worse.

Omission of Words in Idioms

An idiom is a group of words with a meaning different from the literal meanings of the words taken one by one.

The fisherman *held up* his catch.
The pilot *held up* his departure.

Many idioms like *hold up* are composed of a verb followed by an adverb. Here are some examples of idioms:

Idioms with *up*	Idioms with *down*	Idioms with *for*
hold up	turn down	love for
tie up	put down	need for
break up	hold down	respect for

Idioms with *in*	Idioms with *on*	Idioms with *off*
trust in	turn on	put off
pride in	put on	hold off
interest in	take on	turn off

When two idioms are used together in a compound construction, there is a temptation to drop the adverb from one of them. This omission is awkward and confusing.

FAULTY We were putting and taking off our coats all day.

CORRECTED We were putting *on* and taking off our coats all day.

FAULTY Mr. Andrews had no desire or need of more money.

CORRECTED Mr. Andrews had no desire *for* or need of more money.

FAULTY Carrie had a pride and respect for her work.

CORRECTED Carrie had a pride *in* and respect for her work.

Exercise
Avoiding Omissions of Necessary Words

Revise these sentences to correct the omissions.

1. We understood the guests were coming in a few days.
2. The house was empty and the windows cracked and broken.
3. Have you heard the concert has been postponed?
4. The clothes were packed, and the house turned over to its new occupants.
5. The team is one of the best, if not the best, team in the state.
6. The food on the boat will be as good or better than the food in the hotel.
7. She has a liking and pride in her music.
8. The paralegal is enthusiastic and thrilled with her new position.
9. Mary Pickford was one of the most popular, if not the most popular, motion picture star of the silent films.

10. She heard her name had been mentioned for the Cabinet post.

11. My dog is one of the most intelligent, if not the most intelligent, dog on our block.

12. The pilots were briefed on the flight, and the order given to proceed.

13. This novel by Faulkner is one of the best, if not the best, novel I have ever read.

14. The principal of the school decided the players could go to the game in the school bus.

15. The cakes looked and were similar to baking powder biscuits.

Part 2
The Placement of Modifiers

Single adjectives are usually placed just before the word they modify. Adjective phrases and clauses follow immediately after the word they modify. The only exception is the sentence in which both a phrase and a clause modify the same word. In this situation, the phrase precedes the clause.

We talked to the man at the store whom we met yesterday.

Many adverb modifiers can be moved from one place in a sentence to another without a change of meaning. Occasionally, however, moving an adverb produces unexpected effects. In general, be careful to place adverb modifiers so that they will express your meaning exactly.

CONFUSING   Linda was learning to dive *slowly*.

REVISED   Linda was *slowly* learning to dive.

CONFUSING   *Happily*, the play ended. (just in time!)

REVISED   The play ended *happily*. (happy ending)

CONFUSING   All the students can*not* get into the room.

REVISED   *Not* all the students can get into the room.

CONFUSING   Amy was praised for heroism *by the mayor.*

REVISED   Amy was praised *by the mayor* for heroism.

Exercise
The Placement of Modifiers

Revise these sentences to correct the misplaced modifiers.

1. The children sat looking at the parade in the window.
2. The class only has five dollars to spend for decorations.
3. The party never hopes to lose another election.
4. The dentist looked at the individual who sat in the chair stealthily.
5. Did you see the article about the new school in the paper?
6. All of the spectators cannot get into the stadium.
7. Pulitzer prizes are given annually for outstanding work in journalism and established by Joseph Pulitzer.
8. Her gift for her sister was a book of drawings on her birthday.
9. There is a package from Grandpa in your mailbox.
10. The thieves were arrested soon after the bank had been robbed by the police.
11. The ushers brought in extra chairs for the guests with cushioned seats.
12. Terry was praised for pitching a no-hitter by the coach.
13. Everyone should see a doctor to stay healthy at least once a year.
14. Wally Chambers talked about his football experiences during dinner.
15. I saw some geese eating my lunch at the lagoon.

Part 3

Avoiding Dangling Modifiers

When a phrase or clause is placed next to a word that it cannot modify sensibly, it is called a **dangling modifier.** Dangling modifiers often appear at the beginnings of sentences.

PARTICIPLE	Opening the door, chaos met our eyes. (This says that *chaos* opened the door.)
INFINITIVE	To be perfectly safe, good tires are necessary. (This says that *tires* are *perfectly safe.*)
ELLIPTICAL CLAUSE	While swinging a bat, his wrist broke. (This says the *wrist* swung a bat.)

To correct a dangling participle, supply a word for it to modify sensibly, or change the participle to a main verb and give it a subject. The phrase is thus turned into a clause.

FAULTY	Walking in the dark, my foot struck something soft.
CORRECTED	As I was walking in the dark, my foot struck something soft.
FAULTY	Standing on tiptoe, the inside of the room could be seen.
CORRECTED	Standing on tiptoe, *we* could see the inside of the room.
FAULTY	Hoping for prompt aid, this letter is addressed to you.
CORRECTED	I address this letter to you, hoping for prompt aid.

To correct a dangling infinitive, supply a word for the phrase to modify sensibly.

| FAULTY | To see the show this season, tickets must be ordered now. |
| CORRECTED | To see the show this season, *you* must order tickets now. |

To correct dangling elliptical clauses, supply the words that have been omitted to make the clause elliptical.

| FAULTY | When frozen, place the cream in a tray. |
| CORRECTED | When the cream is frozen, place it in a tray. |

Exercise
Avoiding Dangling Modifiers

Revise these sentences to correct the dangling modifiers.

1. Eleanor said, "I smelled oysters going downstairs for supper."
2. Entering the English classroom, four windows can be seen.
3. Looking at television, the electricity went off suddenly.
4. Looking up, the brilliant stars can be seen in the dark sky.
5. While walking in the park, the lake can be seen in the distance.
6. At the age of five, my parents sent me to camp.
7. Being rushed to the hospital, the siren of the ambulance made a weird noise.
8. After seeing Rome, other cities seem lacking in grandeur.
9. To hear well, the auditorium must be built properly.
10. When thoroughly cooked, serve the food in a casserole dish.
11. Paul found a wallet walking home from school.
12. Hoping to see the President, the streets were packed with people.
13. I knocked over the plants walking in the dark.
14. Driving toward the west, the sun was in our eyes.
15. We saw the Goodyear blimp driving down the expressway.

Part 4
Avoiding Needless Shifts

If you were looking at a movie and suddenly found that the pictures were showing upside-down, you would have at least a momentary feeling of confusion. Something like this occurs when a writer begins a sentence in one tense and suddenly shifts without warning to another tense. Shifts in number or person, and shifts from active to passive verb forms produce the same confusion.

There are times when it is necessary to shift from one tense to another or from active to passive. The need on these occasions will be readily apparent to the reader. It is the needless shift that causes confusion.

Shifts from Active to Passive

A sentence that starts out in one voice should usually continue in that voice. Remember that the subject of an active verb is the doer of the action; the subject of the passive verb is the receiver of the action. To change from active to passive is therefore a considerable change in point of view.

SHIFT IN VOICE   The district attorney *questioned* the bank president, and his files *were examined.*

IMPROVED   The district attorney questioned the bank president and examined his files.

SHIFT IN VOICE   We *telephoned* all our friends, and even strangers *were called.*

IMPROVED   We telephoned all our frends and even called strangers.

Shifts in Tense

If a sentence begins in the present tense, it should usually continue in that tense. If it begins in the past tense, it should not shift to the present.

FAULTY   We *are standing* in the street when the door *began* to open.

REVISED   We *are standing* in the street when the door *begins* to open.

ALSO ACCEPTABLE   We *were standing* in the street when the door *began* to open.

FAULTY   The class *was studying* quietly, and suddenly Jeff *lets* out a yell.

REVISED   The class *was studying* quietly, and suddenly Jeff *let* out a yell.

FAULTY	There *were* two seconds left when Laura *makes* the basket.
REVISED	There *were* two seconds left when Laura *made* the basket.

Shifts in Person and Number

The indefinite pronoun *one* is in the third person. It is referred to by the personal pronouns *he, his* and *him*. If you start a sentence with *one*, do not refer to it with the pronouns *you* or *your*.

SHIFT	If *one* hears a baseless rumor, *you* can either ignore it or try to find out how it started.
CORRECTED	If *one* hears a baseless rumor, *he* can either ignore it or try to find out how it started.

Many collective nouns like *group, class, club, crowd, team,* and so on, may be regarded as either singular or plural. The writer may decide whether the word is to be singular or plural, but once having decided, he must abide by his decision.

SHIFT	The club *has* (singular) decided that *they* (plural) will not elect new members this fall.
CORRECTED	The club *has* (singular) decided that *it* (singular) will not elect new members this fall.
SHIFT	The crowd roared *its* (singular) approval, and then *they* (plural) broke up the meeting.
CORRECTED	The crowd roared *their* (plural) approval, and then *they* (plural) broke up the meeting.

Exercise
Avoiding Needless Shifts

Revise these sentences to correct the needless shifts in number, person, tense, or voice.

1. Paula prepares the food for the party, and the house was filled with flowers.

2. The boys were on their way to Riverfront Stadium and are happy to be going to see a World Series game.

3. I think that if one goes to college, you should do your best to succeed.

4. The team was playing brilliantly when suddenly they begin to collapse.

5. The members of the class sold tickets for the homecoming dance, and the money was collected.

6. I was sitting alone in the house when suddenly someone begins to pound on the door.

7. Ed wrote his weekly theme by hand, but it was typed before it was given to the teacher.

8. The family plans a trip each year, and usually they go to some interesting place.

9. I heard a step on the porch, and then the dogs, hearing it also, begin to bark.

10. The mayor campaigned hard, but the election was won by the party in favor of the Charter-Council form of government.

11. When one reads a newspaper, you should read the important news and editorials as well as the sports page.

12. Sally and Jean were lying on the beach, and suddenly the tide begins to come in around them.

13. The army offers many courses of study for the enlisted personnel and they are offered also vocational training.

14. The class is studying frogs now, but they will study insects next week.

15. It has been my experience that if one wants to learn to write, you must write a composition of some kind each week.

Chapter 5

Sentence Variety

This section is for students who have mastered the basic elements of good sentences. It is for students who understand the subject-verb-complement order of English sentences and use this order to write clear sentences. It is for students who know where modifiers usually appear in a sentence and for those who regularly avoid ambiguities created by faulty omissions, faulty pronoun reference, and the like. In short, this section is for students who have achieved clarity in their writing and now wish to achieve effective and interesting sentences.

In natural English speech, we use three devices to secure interesting expression: the rise and fall of the voice, stress or accent, and rhythm. The voice falls between clauses, at the close of an introductory phrase or clause, and at the end of a sentence. We accent certain syllables in order to pronounce words correctly, and we also stress words to which we want to give special emphasis. Rhythm is achieved by a combination of voice falls and accents.

Speech is natural expression; writing is not. Some of the cleverest conversationalists we encounter have had little formal schooling. They speak easily with varying rhythms, but they may be totally incapable of recording these rhythms in written sentences. It follows that the smoothest writing, when read aloud, sounds like normal speech, for the successful writer gives the reader the feeling of speaking directly to him.

In writing, as in speech, a variety of rhythm is pleasing. Varied rhythm is achieved by using a combination of sentence patterns—by changing the kind and position of modifiers, by varying the length and kind of sentences.

Sentence variety is usually to be desired. However, *deliberate* repetition of the same pattern is a good device for securing emphasis and clarity. Note the repeated pattern in the first paragraph of this section.

The methods of securing variety suggested here are best used in revision. They are a means of curing monotonous passages. The writer who sets out in his first draft to begin each sentence in a different way is likely to find that his sentence structure interferes with his natural speech rhythms, producing self-conscious and awkward passages.

Part 1

Variety of Sentence Beginnings

Usually when every sentence in a passage begins in the same way, the effect is monotonous. A succession of sentences beginning with the same word or with the same kind of phrase or clause lulls the reader to inattention. As you read the two following passages, note the points at which your voice drops.

Sentences beginning with the same kind of phrase

Leaving the road, we plunged into the brush. *Coming to a creek,* we waded across. *Fighting our way through a tangle of vines,* we at last reached a path. *Turning left,* we climbed steadily uphill for an hour.

He was puzzled by the reaction of the crowd. *He* had tried to say something that would win their approval. *He* could not understand why they seemed hostile. *He* decided finally that it would not have mattered what he said.

Sentence variety can be achieved by beginning a succession of sentences in different ways—with adverb modifiers; infinitive, prepositional, or participial phrases; or with adverb clauses.

Jill worked conscientiously at the job until evening. (subject-verb)

Conscientiously, Jill worked at the job until evening. (adverb modifier)

To finish the job, Jill worked at the job until evening. (infinitive phrase)

Until evening, Jill worked conscientiously at the job. (prepositional phrase)

Working conscientiously, Jill stayed at the job until evening. (participial phrase)

Until evening came, Jill worked conscientiously at the job. (adverb clause)

Exercises
Varying Sentence Beginnings

A. Rewrite the following sentences, beginning each in accordance with the suggestion in parentheses.

1. Walter walked over to the bank in the morning to cash the check. (Prepositional phrase)
2. Someone had evidently notified the Coast Guard about us. (Single-word modifier)
3. Harry climbed into the back seat and held the precious package in his arms. (Participial phrase beginning with *holding*)
4. Drivers' licenses are issued in Alabama and Georgia to sixteen-year-olds. (Prepositional phrase)

5. Dad drives twenty miles to work every day.
(Adverb modifier)

6. Linda earned a thousand dollars during the summer by working at two jobs. (Participial phrase beginning with *working*)

7. Beth scored high on the test and won a valuable scholarship to the state university (Participial phrase beginning with *having scored*)

8. We will be glad to hire you, if there is a job open. (Adverb clause)

9. The Yankee pitching staff was in a state of collapse by midsummer. (Prepositional phrase)

10. The rain came down suddenly in torrents. (Adverb modifier)

B. Follow the directions for Exercise A.

1. We had been afraid of fire from the beginning. (Prepositional phrase)

2. Mike left the pool early and hurried home. (Participial phrase beginning with *leaving*)

3. The old motor was clearly not equal to the task. (Adverb modifier)

4. The little movie house closed because of poor attendance. (Prepositional phrase)

5. Only one of all our neighbors has a new car this year. (Prepositional phrase)

6. Virginia Woolf was among the first authors to make use of the stream-of-consciousness technique in writing. (Prepositional phrase beginning with *among*)

7. William Wordsworth celebrated nature in his poetry; he felt that nature was a source of "joy and purest passion" for man. (Participial phrase beginning with *celebrating*)

8. Hitler's forces were conquering Russia until winter set in. (Adverb clause)

9. The President issued the warning sternly. (Single-word modifier)

10. They do not give courses in home economics in the first semester. (Prepositional phrase)

Part 2

Variety of Sentence Structure

In student writing, a monotonous style arises chiefly from overuse of compound sentences. The compound sentence is a good and useful tool, but overuse dulls its edge. A succession of compound sentences is boring because the rise and fall of intonation is so regular. As you read the following passage, note the points at which your voice drops.

> The storm arose without warning, and waves started to bounce our boat around. Herb pulled in the anchor, and I reeled in our lines. It was impossible to get back to our dock, so Herb steered for the point. The wind was behind us, or we would never have made it. We got fairly close, and then we jumped into water up to our hips and pulled the boat ashore.

A succession of compound sentences can be avoided by changing one of the clauses. The clause may be made into a subordinate clause or a participial phrase. Some compound sentences can be changed into simple sentences with a compound predicate.

COMPOUND SENTENCE	We were delayed by a flat tire, and we missed the first touchdown.
PARTICIPIAL PHRASE	Delayed by a flat tire, we missed the first touchdown.
SUBORDINATE CLAUSE	Because we were delayed by a flat tire, we missed the first touchdown.
COMPOUND PREDICATE	We were delayed by a flat tire and missed the first touchdown.

Exercises
Varying Sentence Structure

A. Rewrite the following compound sentences, changing one of the clauses in each in accordance with the suggestion in parentheses.

1. The writer outlined recent discoveries about cancer, and he said that cancer could turn out to be several diseases. (Compound predicate)

2. Many people do not want to go to college more than two years, and junior colleges are growing rapidly. (Subordinate clause)

3. Sue has been an exchange student in France and she speaks French fluently. (Participial phrase)

4. I knew that the plane was late, and I took my time in getting to the airport. (Subordinate clause)

5. We flew at an altitude of 20,000 feet, and we passed over a bad electrical storm. (Participial phrase)

6. The Indian visitor was delighted by the students' knowledge of life in his land, and he stayed for three days. (Participial phrase)

7. Paul Norwood read the morning newspaper, and he discovered that he had not been elected after all. (Subordinate clause)

8. There is plenty of rainfall in this country, but it is not evenly distributed. (Subordinate clause beginning with *although*)

9. Everyone was late to work this morning, and there was a fire on the subway. (Subordinate clause beginning with *because*)

10. The disassembled Statue of Liberty was brought here in 210 wooden cases, and it arrived at Bedloe's Island in June, 1885. (Participial phrase beginning with *brought*)

B. Follow the directions for Exercise A.

1. Pam heard about the job early, and she was first to apply. (Participial phrase)

2. The American clipper ships appeared, and they swept other ships from the seas. (Subordinate clause beginning with *when*)

3. The book is long, and it requires careful reading. (Compound predicate)

4. News of the gold strike reached San Francisco, and there was a mad dash out of the city. (Subordinate clause)

5. The band uniforms have been delivered. They are packed for the trip. (Compound predicate)

6. The severe winter weather caused food and fuel shortages, and many people suffered greatly. (Subordinate clause beginning with *because*)

7. The mayor spoke to the district attorney and he urged him to proceed with the investigation. (Compound predicate)

8. The crowd left, and the hall was searched thoroughly. (Subordinate clause beginning with *after*)

9. Influenza vaccine is available to everyone, but we are still having epidemics. (Subordinate clause beginning with *although*)

10. Pittsburgh was still a small city, and Willa Cather came there is 1910. (Subordinate clause beginning with *when*)

Part 3
Variety of Sentence Length

A passage in which all the sentences are of about the same length, whether long or short, is monotonous. The insertion of a sentence of different length varies the rhythm and revives the interest of the reader. In the following passage from Hemingway's "Big Two-Hearted River," note how the short sentences are relieved by long sentences.

> He walked along the road feeling the ache from the pull of the heavy pack. The road climbed steadily. It was hard work walking up-hill. His muscles ached and the day was hot, but Nick felt happy. He felt he had left everything behind, the need for thinking, the need to write, other needs. It was all back of him.

Avoiding a Series of Short Sentences

Monotony is created especially by a succession of short sentences. There are times when a conscious series of short sentences is very effective, as in narrative, when it has the effect of building up suspense. The unconscious use of a succession of short sentences, however, creates an awkward effect. The effect can be overcome by combining the sentences. As you read the two passages below, note the points where your voice drops.

ORIGINAL Quietly we walked into the hall. It was very dark. Bob found a lamp. He turned it on. We sat down to wait for Mr. Manning. We waited for an hour. He didn't come.

REWRITTEN Quietly we walked into the dark hall. After Bob had found a lamp and turned it on, we sat down to wait for Mr. Manning. We waited for an hour, but he didn't come.

Short sentences may be combined in a number of ways:

1. By using a compound sentence.

TWO SENTENCES The plane stopped in Okinawa for repairs. We landed in Tokyo three hours late.

COMBINED The plane stopped in Okinawa for repairs, and we landed in Tokyo three hours late.

2. By using a simple sentence with a compound predicate.

TWO SENTENCES I stained the cabinet. Then I coated it with shellac.

COMBINED I stained the cabinet and then coated it with shellac.

3. By using a subordinate clause.

TWO SENTENCES Jeff sprained his ankle. He was practicing the javelin throw.

COMBINED Jeff sprained his ankle when he was practicing the javelin throw.

4. By using a participial phrase.

TWO SENTENCES   We were worried by some strange noises. They were coming from the engine.

COMBINED   We were worried by some strange noises coming from the engine.

5. By using a prepositional phrase.

TWO SENTENCES   The concert will take place at County Center. The date is February 10.

COMBINED   The concert will take place at County Center on February 10.

6. By using an appositive.

TWO SENTENCES   Susan Stein won first prize in the state instrumental competition. She is a soloist in our orchestra.

COMBINED   Susan Stein, a soloist in our orchestra, won first prize in the state tournament competition.

7. By using a single-word modifier.

TWO SENTENCES   Quietly we walked into the hall. It was very dark.

COMBINED   Quietly we walked into the dark hall.

Exercises
Varying Sentence Length

A. Combine the following short sentences in accordance with the suggestions in parentheses.

1. Ellen turned through the book. It was old. (Single-word modifier)
2. The judge came in. (Subordinate clause beginning with *when*) The spectators stood up.

3. We left Jean at home. She was watching television. (Participial phrase)

4. I read about your illness in the paper. (Subordinate clause beginning with *when*) I was reminded that I had not written you.

5. The engineers landed in helicopters on Ellesmere Island. It was the dead of winter. (Prepositional phrase beginning with *in*)

6. The doctor decided on an operation. She realized that it might not succeed. (Participial phrase)

7. I am going to Triton College in River Grove, Illinois. It is a junior college. (Appositive) It specializes in technical subjects. (Participial phrase)

8. We were delayed by an accident on the expressway. (Subordinate clause beginning with *because*) We missed the first act of the play.

9. The magnificent Bayeux Tapestry is a strip of embroidered linen that depicts the incidents preceding the Battle of Hastings. The Tapestry was commissioned in 1077. (Participial phrase)

10. We attended a lecture on consumer fraud. It was informative. (One word)

11. We have been building millions of houses a year. (Subordinate clause beginning with *although*) There are still not enough. Every year a greater number of new families is started. (Subordinate clause beginning with *because*)

12. Grover Cleveland was elected to a second term. (Subordinate clause) The country was on the verge of financial panic. People were jittery. (Main clause)

13. Sir Georg Solti is one of the finest conductors in the world. He directs the Chicago Symphony. (Appositive)

14. The play will open at the Shubert Theatre. The date is July 1. (Prepositional phrase)

15. Doctors discovered that Cleveland had cancer of the jaw. They decided on an operation. (Compound predicate) They put him on a battleship. They performed the operation secretly in New York Harbor. (Compound predicate)

B. Rewrite the following paragraph, making changes in sentence structure to create fluent, readable prose.

Many of today's novelists write as if by rote. Their works all appear to be taken from the same pattern. Readers must be more critical in their choice of books. The shelves of bookstores are teeming with mediocre if not inferior tales. The books are praised by their publishers as being "the greatest romance of the time" or "the year's most suspenseful novel." Even the writing is poor. Many writers are interested only in making money and not in producing good, solid literature. Few writers today are interested in contributing to the growth of the novel as a literary genre. At no other time have there been so many literary works available to the public.

Chapter 6

The Paragraph: Its Structure

Herbert Hoover established the image of himself as an Iowa farm boy steeped in the traditions of rural America. He spoke of the swimming hole under the willows, of trapping rabbits in cracker boxes in the woods down by the Burlington track, and of belly-whopping down Cook's Hill on winter nights. He recalled being taught by a neighboring Indian boy how to bring down pigeons and prairie chickens with a bow and arrow. Fishing, wrote Hoover, was "good for the soul of man," for all men were equal before fishes. He sang the praises of "the willow pole with a butcher'd-string line, fixed with hooks ten for a dime, whose compelling lure is one segment of an angleworm and whose incantation is spitting on bait." When he wrote his letter accepting the Republican nomination in 1928, Hoover referred to himself as "a boy from a country village, without inheritance or influential friends." —WILLIAM E. LEUCHTENBURG

You have just read a paragraph, a unit of writing complete in itself. A single paragraph is like a brick. Just as a brick is solid and substantial, so is a paragraph. Just as a brick is usually combined with other bricks to form a building, so is a paragraph usually combined with other paragraphs to form a composition. In this chapter we will discuss the basic structure of the paragraph.

Part 1
Defining the Paragraph

A paragraph is a group of related sentences with a single, unified idea that has been adequately developed. Usually one of the sentences is a topic sentence that states the main idea. The topic sentence usually comes first in the paragraph and is followed by the body of the paragraph. The body of the paragraph develops or explains what is said in the topic sentence. The paragraph sometimes ends with a clincher sentence that restates what the topic sentence has said.

The opening paragraph of this chapter is a good example of a well constructed paragraph. The first sentence tells the reader that Hoover represented himself as a simple farm boy. Having said that, the writer must explain or enlarge upon his idea. He does so in sentences two, three, four, and five. In the final sentence he clinches, or ties up the idea by restating Hoover's simple country background, the subject he introduced in his first sentence.

Like most definitions, the preceding definition of an ideal paragraph has some exceptions. You will be introduced to some of those exceptions later in the chapter, but for the present, we will work with the preceding definition.

Here are two more paragraphs for your examination. Determine how closely they meet the definition of an ideal paragraph.

Analysis 1

In the distance, when viewed from the Staten Island ferry or the piers of Hoboken, the 1,350-foot-high towers of New York's World Trade Center remind me uneasily of a double image of the mysterious, tombstonelike monolith that is discovered on the moon by space explorers in Stanley Kubrick's *2001: A Space Odyssey*. And I'm put off by the place when I'm in it, too. There is something decidedly spooky about the fact that the towers are identical twins, clones of one another. I leave the lobby of one building, stroll for a couple of hundred feet along an enclosed concourse, and then enter what appears in every way to be the building I just left. It's weird—Twilight Zone-y. All in all, the World Trade Center is not entirely of this planet or time continuum.

This paragraph is another good example of an ideal paragraph. The topic sentence engages the reader's interest by comparing the World Trade Center with the stone monolith in Kubrick's film. The body of the paragraph develops the main idea by describing the unusual aspects of the World Trade Center and sustaining the sense of strangeness. Every sentence supports the main idea. The paragraph ends with a clincher sentence that restates the idea in the topic sentence.

Analysis 2

Quite recently the peasants of Transylvania, a mountainous Rumanian province, discovered that they harbor a considerable tourist attraction. For the past few years visitors from the West have been coming round to inquire the whereabouts of Castle Dracula, home of the celebrated literary and cinematic vampire. The resulting confrontation between peasant and tourist is curiously ironic, a sort of mismeeting between a surviving folk culture and a thriving mass culture.

This paragraph has a serious flaw. While it has a strong topic sentence and a good clincher sentence, the body has not been sufficiently developed to justify the restatement of the clincher sentence. The writer has not discussed the "resulting confrontation," nor has he described the "surviving folk culture" or the "thriving mass culture." The body, consisting of only one sentence, is not an adequate development of the main idea.

The Elements of the Paragraph

You can well see that a good paragraph is not always easy to write. The writer of a paragraph must concern himself with all of these elements:

the topic sentence	unity	tone
the body	coherence	mood
the clincher sentence	adequate detail	

The topic sentence, the body, and the clincher sentence are the structural elements of a paragraph and they will be discussed in this chapter. The five remaining elements will be discussed in the following chapter.

Exercise
Analyzing the Paragraph

Examine the following paragraphs. Decide which are well developed, unified paragraphs and which are not. Be prepared to give reasons for your decisions.

1

In 1914 the United States was not so far from the early years of the Republic. There were men still living whose fathers had known Jefferson and John Adams and had been acquainted with Longfellow. In prairie towns women remembered the day Ralph Waldo Emerson had alighted from the train to talk to the local Chautauqua. There were thousands of men still alive who had fought under Stonewall Jackson at Chancellorsville or had stood with George Thomas at Chickamauga, even a few veterans who had marched with Winfield Scott on the Halls of Montezuma. A small company of loyal Democrats who voted for Woodrow Wilson in 1912 had cast their first votes for Martin Van Buren or James K. Polk. Negroes walked the streets of Savannah and Charleston who had been born in slavery.

2

Widen the scope of your horizon so that your vision extends beyond the walls of the room and you will still see the work of artists everywhere about you. The roaring airplane with its sleek fuselage is the result of the cooperative effort of engineer and industrial designer. The subway that thunders below has been made better looking and more efficient through planned design. The stream of people who enter the church on Easter Sunday reflects the current styles in fashion, and others who are seen at shops, theaters and fairs are decked out in the fashion designer's latest creations.

3

Skiing demands strong legs. As all professional athletes know, it is the legs that go first as the body ages. A skier can't count on many years in the sport and must start very young if he is to put in much time at the sport. Women have entered skiing in ever-increasing numbers. There is no reason that they cannot be as good at the sport as men. Boxers need strong legs, also. When you see a fighter's legs turn "rubbery," you know that he no longer has full control over his body.

4

At the risk of stating the obvious, it is worth remarking that success of communication depends upon the charm

(I use the word in its most serious sense) of the narrative. "Writings are useless," declared Theodore Roosevelt, speaking as president of the American Historical Association in 1912, "unless they are read, and they cannot be read unless they are readable."

5

If you relish paradoxes, consider the career of Horatio Alger, Jr. He made his fame writing books in which boys rose "from rags to riches"—yet he himself did not begin life in rags and did not die rich. The boys in his books got ahead by outwitting thieves and sharpers—yet he himself, a mild and generous little man who gave freely of his earnings to newsboys and bootblacks on the New York streets (the sort of boys who were his favorite heroes), was an easy mark for impostors. His books were, and are, generally regarded by the critical as trash—yet their sales mounted into the millions. He was one of the most popular of all American authors, if not of all authors of all time; and there can be little doubt that he had a far-reaching influence upon the economic and social thought of America—an influence all the greater, perhaps, because it was innocently and naïvely and undogmatically exerted.

6

While "instant" cameras of various types offer you "no muss, no fuss" convenience, they all have limitations. Cartridge-loading cameras are simple to handle, but they raise your film costs. Cameras that process a picture seconds after you've shot it have a very high film cost, don't give you the best possible prints, and cause problems when you want duplicates or enlargements. Cameras with automatic exposure prevent mistakes, but they can also prevent you from experimenting and improving your skill. In short, if you want the most for your money, don't buy convenience alone. In photography the "inconvenience" can be half the fun—and educational as well.

Part 2

The Topic Sentence

The topic sentence tells the reader what idea the paragraph is going to develop. For example, look at this sentence:

The children were excited.

You expect this paragraph to be about the excitement of the children, not about hunting big game in Africa or shooting the rapids of the White River. Once the writer has said "The children were excited," he has only one way to go: he must write about the children's excitement. That topic sentence, like every topic sentence, has a subject: it is about something. A topic sentence must also have a point of view: it must express an attitude toward the subject. In the sentence "The children were excited," the subject is *children,* and the point of view is *excited.* The writer can describe the children's excitement or he can explain why they were excited, and he will have written a paragraph.

Let's look at a topic sentence that has no point of view:

Christmas arrives on December 25.

While this sentence has a subject, *Christmas,* it has no point of view to develop. Once you have made that statement, you have nothing more to say. Suppose you revise the sentence as follows:

Christmas is the most exciting day of the year.

You now have a point of view that can be developed in some detail. You can write about the excitement: the colorful window displays, the happy smiles of little children, the jam-packed streets, or the thrill of getting and giving.

Here is another example of a topic sentence that would work:

Christmas can be an unhappy experience.

The writer could describe the loneliness of elderly people with no families, or the children whose families are too poor to buy presents for them.

On the other hand, the sentence "Christmas arrives on December 25" could be included in a paragraph. It could even be the first sentence, but it could not be the topic sentence. For example, we might begin a paragraph with "Christmas arrives on December 25." Our next sentence might be "It is a truly festive day." Now we could develop the idea that Christmas is a festive day. However, the topic sentence would not be our first sentence. The topic sentence would be the second sentence, "It is a truly festive day."

This last example alerts you to the fact that the topic sentence can be placed anywhere in the paragraph. While it usually is the first sentence in the paragraph, it can be placed somewhere in the middle of a paragraph or even at the end. You give your writing variety and interest by sometimes altering the usual pattern of putting the topic sentence first. Try putting it in the middle or at the end of the paragraph.

Exercises
Placement of the Topic Sentence

A. Find the topic sentence in each of these paragraphs, and note whether it is at the beginning of the paragraph, in the middle, or at the end. Give reasons for your decision.

1

Of two men who walk side by side along a country lane only one may know the names and natures of the plants and trees they see; yet we will not on that account call the other man immature. We will not call him immature unless his attitude toward such knowledge brands him so. If his lifework is such that he should, for effectiveness, know the names and natures of those plants and trees, but if he has chosen to bluff instead of to learn, then we can call him immature. We can call him so if he pretends to knowledge he does not possess. We can call him so, if, lacking a certain type of knowledge, he self-defensively holds that it is not worth possessing. We can call him so if this specific ignorance is but one expression of a kind of total obtuseness—a general indifference to the world he inhabits.—H. A. OVERSTREET

2

If our physical environment is worth saving, our emotional environment is even more deserving of protection, since the one provides us with means to sustain life while the other is our humanity; the one offers the necessities of survival, the other a life worth living. There is no government agency to protect our emotional environment and speak for its primacy in our lives. Yet the equivalent of air and water is the source of the ability to feel, to love, to endure. The most endangered of our vital resources is people.—DONALD E. CARR

3

Charles Bedou, at the age of forty, stands four and a half feet tall. When the towheaded Bedou was born, he weighed nearly nine pounds and was the size of any normal baby. Five years later, however, he was less than two feet tall; at ten, he was three feet; when he celebrated his eighteenth birthday, he was four-foot-six; and in the ensuing twenty-two years, he did not grow another inch. His body is all out of whack. His head and torso are the size of a much taller person's; his arms and legs are much too small. He is what is known as a dwarf.—SONNY KLEINFIELD

4

To combat popular opposition to the war, Wilson set up a Committee on Public Information, under George Creel. To arouse support for the war, the Creel Committee whipped up hatred of Germany and all things German, and in many communities the response of vigilante leaders went far beyond what Creel or Wilson had intended. The war, as Ludwig Lewison observed, was fought with a "peculiarly unmotivated ferocity." Aroused to fury at an enemy 3,000 miles distant whom they could not strike directly, civilians sought enemies within. Flying squads invaded farmhouses to force farmers to buy a quota of bonds, and if a farmer refused to buy at least the amount fixed by a private committee, they nailed a yellow placard to his house or splashed his home with yellow paint. Men suspected of disloyalty were forced to kiss the flag. Supposedly responsible Red Cross leaders warned that German-Americans had infiltrated the Red Cross to put ground glass in bandages; while in humorless patriotic zeal, sauerkraut was renamed "liberty cabbage," and Fritz Kreisler was driven from the concert stage.—WILLIAM E. LEUCHTENBURG

5

The classic example of the photographer who aims to make the uncommon common is the news photographer. His goal is not to record the ordinary and the everyday, but the extraordinary and the unusual. Wherever there is disaster, the newsman is there. If he cannot find disaster, he searches for the odd and the peculiar, the exotic, and the unfamiliar. His photographs, seen by millions, make momentary events and strange occurrences all over the world our common property. What more striking evidence could be offered of this power of photography than the atom bomb? The mushroom cloud, the very symbol of nuclear fission, has become known through photographs.—BEAUMONT NEWHALL

6

It was a bucket of bolts and barnacles. The staterooms were little more than cramped closets with iron bunks. The debris and litter of countless voyages were scattered about its deck. The *Vulcania* was a tired old ship. Her engines broke down in mid-voyage. Her third-class travelers had only one rusty shower room, its plumbing obsolete and its floors covered with fungus.

B. Here are ten sentences that would make good topic sentences for paragraphs. Put one line under the topic and two lines under the point of view, like this: <u>Minnesota</u> is a <u>winter wonderland</u>.

1. Dancing is superb conditioning for your body.
2. I enjoy the patter of rain on the roof.
3. Do you believe everything you read in the papers?
4. My mother cooks tantalizing roasts.
5. Despite your cynicism, you will like this play.
6. You will find bargains if you shop downtown.
7. The referee was unfair.
8. I must tell you that I really hate bowling.
9. Dave seems to be an unusually responsible member of the group.
10. Many adults are interested in comic books.

C. Develop one of the above sentences, or an original one of your own, into a paragraph of about six to eight sentences. Your topic sentence may be at the beginning of the paragraph or somewhere in the middle or at the end. Wherever your topic sentence is, underline its topic once and its point of view twice.

D. Write ten topic sentences of your own on any subject. Be sure that each has a topic and a point of view toward that topic. Keep your sentences for a later assignment.

E. Select three of the topic sentences you have written and develop paragraphs from them. In your first paragraph put the topic sentence at the beginning. In your second paragraph put the topic sentence in the middle. In your third paragraph put the topic sentence at the end. Keep your remaining sentences for a later assignment.

Part 3

The Body

The body of a paragraph is a group of related sentences that develop the idea in the topic sentence. The body proves or illustrates or explains the topic sentence.

Analyze the body of the following paragraph to determine what it tells you.

My work on the Plains brought me many friends, among them some of the truest and staunchest that any man ever had. You who live your lives in cities or among peaceful ways cannot always tell whether your friends are the kind who would go through fire for you, but on the Plains one's friends have an opportunity to prove their mettle. I found out that most of mine would as cheerfully risk their lives for me as they would give me a light for my pipe when I asked for it.—BUFFALO BILL

You undoubtedly discovered that the topic sentence is the first one. Its topic is *friends,* and the point of view is *truest* and *staunchest.* The body, which is made up of sentences two and three, explains the point of view.

Exercise
Determining How the Body of a Paragraph Works

In each of the following paragraphs determine what the topic sentence is. Then determine if the body does its job of developing the topic sentence. Be prepared to tell why it does or does not.

1

The truth seems to be that Horatio Alger never fully grew up to adult life, that he shunned its passions and battles and hard realities. Always, deep down in his heart, he wanted a boy's life—not a boy dominated by a stern father and dressed up in neat and proper clothes, but rather a boy free from parental supervision, free to soil and rumple his clothes, free to make a living for himself and test his budding self-reliance. Alger wanted also to be a man of letters, but could not achieve this ambition because his mind, while clear and logical, was childishly naïve, unimaginative, and bewildered by the complexities of mature life. After his books had become widely known, and people began to turn to him as an authority on slum conditions in New York, he was asked to serve on charitable and civic committees; but though he was happy to be treated as a person of importance he usually sat silent at board meetings; either he was too self-distrustful to speak or the problems discussed there took him beyond his depth.—FREDERICK LEWIS ALLEN

2

In the whole galaxy of youth presented in the novels of Charles Dickens, those juveniles who play important roles in the stories are but a few stars. Many more youngsters contribute to the story lines of the various books without playing principal roles, and there are incidental children everywhere underfoot, sometimes put into the books to make crusading or philosophical points, more often merely for fun. Dickens *liked* to write about children. Whereas other authors of the era studiously ignored children even as incidentals in their books, perhaps seeing nothing of interest in them, Dickens sprinkled them everywhere.—FRANK DONOVAN

3

Each year the stories of the yeti, or Abominable Snowman, a monster man-ape roaming the snows, come rolling down out of the Himalayas like an avalanche. "We stared in amazement and disbelief at those huge, apelike impressions in the snow," a Polish mountaineer announced last spring. "Lhakpa said she got a good look at the beast as it ripped out the throat of her only cow and slaughtered her yaks by smashing their heads with its huge fists," was another recent statement. A "hardened" police officer told reporters, "I'm convinced the girl saw a yeti. No other beast I know of could have mutilated her animals that way. One yak had been ripped apart and savagely knawed by a ferocious beast with phenomenal strength." A Frankenstein ogre incarnate? A vivid nightmare? But what about the yaks? And the police officer?—EDWARD W. CRONIN, JR.

4

As David Reisman and his collaborators pointed out two years ago in their brilliant analysis called *The Lonely Crowd*, the ideal now persistently held before the American citizen from the moment he enters kindergarten to the time when he is buried under auspices of a recognized funeral parlor is a kind of conformity more or less disguised under the term "adjustment." "Normality" has almost completely replaced "Excellence" as an ideal. It has also rendered all but obsolescent such terms as "Righteousness," "Integrity," and "Truth." The question is no longer how a boy ought to behave but how most boys do behave; not how honest a man ought to be but how honest men usually are. Even the Robber Baron, who represented an evil manifestation of the determination to excel, gives way to the moneymaker who wants only to be rich according to the accepted standards of his group. Or, as Mr. Reisman sums it up, the American who used to be conspicuously "inner-directed" is now conspicuously "outer-directed."—JOSEPH WOOD KRUTCH

5

Reasons why well-functioning mature adults do not use specific abilities are complex. Studies conducted at the University of Utah as a part of the Human Potentialities Research Project revealed that unconscious blocks are often present. In a number of instances a person with definite evidence that he has a specific talent (let's say he won a state-wide contest in sculpture while in high school) may not wish to realize this talent at a later time because he fears this would introduce a change in life-style. Sometimes fear of the passion of creation is another roadblock in self-actualization. On the basis of work at Utah it became clear that persons who live close to their capacity, who continue to activate their potential, have a pronounced sense of well-being and considerable energy and see themselves as leading purposeful and creative lives.—HERBERT A. OTTO

American he certainly was. Sam Clemens had the advantage, or disadvantage, of being brought up solely in his own country, remote from its coasts, with no contact with the outside world, in the days when America was still America. He lived, and died, before the motion picture had flickered the whole world with similarity, and before rapid transport had enabled every country to live on the tourists of all the others. His childhood was spent in an isolation from the outside world now beyond all conception. Nor was the isolation much relieved by mental contact. Like Shakespeare and Dickens, young Sam Clemens had little school and no college. He thus acquired that peculiar sharpness of mind which comes from not going to school, and that power of independent thought obtained by not entering college. It was this youthful setting which enabled him to become what he was.—STEPHEN LEACOCK

Part 4

The Clincher Sentence

A clincher sentence comes at the end of a paragraph and sums up what the paragraph has said. While the topic sentence has already said what the paragraph will be about, and the body has enlarged on the subject, the clincher sentence restates the point of the paragraph. It brings into sharp focus for the reader what the body of the paragraph has been about. In the following paragraph, note how the clincher sentence refers to the topic sentence and answers the question it poses in terms of the development of the paragraph.

Can we kill other human beings if we do not hate them? I suppose the answer must come from those in our fighting forces. Some young people will tell you that unless you hate the people of Germany and Japan, you cannot possibly win. On the other hand, many a young soldier going into the war will assure you that he cannot hate the individuals of any race. He can only hate the system which has made those individuals his enemies. If he must kill them in order to do away with the system, he will do so, but not because he hates them as individuals. If those who say that to win the war we must hate, are really expressing the beliefs of the majority of our people, I am afraid we have already lost the peace, because our main objective is to make a world in which all the people of the world may live with respect and good will for each other in peace.—ELEANOR ROOSEVELT

Exercises
Working with the Clincher Sentence

A. Identify the clincher sentence and the topic sentence in the following paragraphs. Be ready to tell how the clincher sentence restates the idea that is expressed in the topic sentence and ties up the development of the idea.

1

In the famous controversy about two cultures, one important point seems to have been overlooked: that if there truly is a gulf between the literary and the scientific culture, it cannot be bridged by science, but only by language. Language is the only means of communication between specialties as far apart as every individual's unique experience of his own life. Scientific specialization itself is human experience, and if it is to become part of the general culture it can only be so by communication through language. When there is a question of discussing and explaining our experiences of the other arts, music, or painting, we use words. If architecture aspires to the condition of music, all human experience aspires to words.—STEPHEN SPENDER

2

The human being is born ignorant. His body, to be sure, has certain kinds of "knowledge" that belong to it by nature.

Even the newborn infant "knows," for example, how to make the sucking motions that enable it to take in food for survival. But in all super-instinctual matters the ignorance of that newborn infant is total. His world has, so far, told him virtually nothing about itself. He is ignorant not only of such specific cultural skills as reading, writing, and arithmetic—through which there may later be opened up to him well-nigh incredible vistas—but of even his own survival needs. He can register discomfort, but he cannot be said to know that he is uncomfortable because his blanket has slipped aside and left him cold. He is at the total-ignorance level of a life in which the knowledge potential is enormous.
—H. A. OVERSTREET

3

One of the stoutly held myths of our day is that the television camera reveals true character. Like everyone else, I am a captive of this foolish notion: one can't help it, for the eye trusts what it *sees*, though it suspiciously screens what it *reads*, just as the ear filters, edits, and questions what it hears. This is why television is at once so powerful and so unpredictable a medium; the observing eye is mindless and restless, and, if it has nothing else more interesting to look at on the screen, will begin noticing a man's lapel width, or his nose, or the awkwardness of his hands. In the circumstances, viewers all think of themselves as excellent students of character who can spot the slightest trace of insincerity. But that is nonsense.—THOMAS GRIFFITH

B. Here are ten sentences. Some of them would make good clincher sentences, assuming that there were a proper body before them. Identify the ones that would *not* make good clincher sentences and be ready to tell why.

1. Thus it is clear that life can never again be the same as it was before World War II.

2. To answer your question, I must say that you are wrong on three counts.

3. Now, perhaps, you won't be taken in again by a confidence man.

4. Human beings have the potential to do noble things.

5. Before you sue, I think you should recognize certain truths.

6. Therefore, it seems that war seeks us out whether we welcome it or not.

7. I need to build a whole new system of priorities.

8. In this way we are duped even by ourselves on occasion.

9. Here is our chance to plan for the future.

10. Harder work, then, may be the solution to our economic ills.

C. You are now ready to write a paragraph that has a topic sentence, a body, and a clincher sentence. Go back to Exercise D on page 97. You have already developed three of those topic sentences. Take any three of the remaining seven topic sentences you wrote. Construct three paragraphs, each based on one of those topic sentences.

Part 5
Some Exceptions to Paragraph Form

Dialogue

When characters in a book talk to each other, they are engaging in dialogue. When writing dialogue, you must start a new paragraph each time a different character speaks, no matter how short or how long his speech is. The "he said" and "she said" are included in the same paragraph as the words spoken by him or her. These signals as to who is speaking are called *tags*. The following passage is an example of how dialogue and the tags should be paragraphed:

"He's gone," said the freckled man.

"Meaning Livius the Roman?" asked Average Jones.

"Exactly. Lucius Livius, son of Marcus Praenestinus."

"Are you the representative of this rather peculiar person, may I ask?"

"It would be a dull world, except for peculiar persons," observed the man on the settee philosophically. "I've seen very many peculiar persons lately by the simple process of coming here day after day. No, I'm not Mr. Livius's representative. I'm only a town-bound and interested observer of his."

"There you've got the better of me," said Average Jones. "I was rather anxious to see him myself."

The other looked speculatively at the trim, keen-faced young man. "Yet you do not look like a Latin scholar," he observed; "if you'll pardon the comment."

"Nor do you," retorted Jones; "if the apology is returnable."

"I suppose not," owned the other with a sigh. "I've often thought that my classical capacity would gain more recognition if I didn't have a skin like Bob Fitzsimmons and hands like Ty Cobb."—SAMUEL HOPKINS ADAMS

Exercise
Paragraphing Dialogue

Each of the following passages is dialogue, but it has been run together, without paragraphing. Determine where each new paragraph should be started.

1

He greeted the visitor. "Hello, Mike! What's that Abe tells me? Redcliff got lost?" "Seems that way," said Mike listlessly. "By gringo," Bill went on, "I shouldn't wonder. In that storm. I'd have waited in town! Wouldn't catch me going out in that kind of weather!" "Didn't start till late in the afternoon," Mike Sobotski said in his shivering way. "No. And didn't last long, either," Bill agreed while he shouldered into his overalls. "But while she lasted—."

2

"Now then, Podgers, I want to ask you about this clerk. What time does he arrive in the evening?" "At prompt six, sir." "Does he ring, or let himself in with a latchkey?" "With a latchkey, sir." "How does he carry the money?" "In a little locked leather satchel, sir, flung over his shoulder." "Does he go direct to the dining room?" "Yes, sir." "Have you seen him unlock the safe, and put in the money?" "Yes, sir." "Does the safe unlock with a word or a key?" "With the key, sir. It's one of the old-fashioned kind." "Then the clerk unlocks his leather money bag?" "Yes, sir."

3

Mrs. Pritchard studied the woods. "All I got is four abscess teeth," she remarked. "Well, be thankful you don't have five," Mrs. Cope snapped and threw back a clump of grass. "We might all be destroyed by a hurricane. I can always find something to be thankful for." Mrs. Pritchard took up a hoe resting against the side of the house and struck lightly at a weed that had come up between two bricks in the chimney. "Yeah?" she said, her voice a little more nasal than usual with contempt. "Why, think of all those poor Europeans," Mrs. Cope went on, "that they put in box cars like cattle and rode them to Siberia. Lord," she said, "we ought to spend half our time on our knees." "I know if I was in an iron lung there would be some things I wouldn't do," Mrs. Pritchard said, scratching her bare ankle with the end of the hoe. "Even that poor woman had plenty to be thankful for," Mrs. Cope said. "She could be thankful she wasn't dead."

4

Diessy raised his right shoulder toward his ear and held out one hand palm upward. "What have you on a ship? Swab deck, carry tray, wash dishes, push crates. Sometimes drink brandy with mate when he want a friend talking to him." He smiled at Father. "Luck is up and down. Once in

Martinique I own Hispano." "Diessy is Senegalese, Father Witherby," said Madolyn. Since when had she started this "Father Witherby"? That was the last straw. Father stirred his demi-tasse. With a bored sigh he said to Diessy, "You received your education in France?" "In school all over world. Mostly school of life. But I been in a school sometimes. In Germany, France, Russia. I learn all three languages." He looked at Father for a minute and then winked. "But enough of any—you think?" He shrugged. "My father say I must be learned man. That is why I not go home—to Senegal. I rather my father think I am learned man, not dishwasher. Father like to be proud of son, *n'est-ce pas?* You have son you are proud of?" "Yes," said Margaret suddenly. "He has John Junior. John Junior is not exactly a learned man but—."

5

"Come on, Hacker," said Allen. "Strike while the iron is hot." "You have nothing to lose but your chains, Hacker," said Whittier. "Mince pie tonight, Hacker," said Hugh. "Um ym." "Then you'd better get back there and start eating right away," said Mrs. Hacker, "before I call the police." "You're just the type who *would* rely on police," said Whittier. "But I'm not afraid of you or your police." "On the other hand, Whittier," said Hugh, "it might look very bad if Mrs. Hacker called the police." "We're going now, Hacker," said Allen. "This is your last chance." "Make up your mind, Hacker, before it's too late," said Hugh. "Nothing is to be gained by spending here." "You mean nothing is to be *lost* by spending here," Allen corrected. "I know what I mean," said Hugh. "That isn't it."

Implied Topic Sentence

Often a paragraph has no actual topic sentence. Instead, it may have an **implied topic sentence.** Here is an example of such a paragraph.

My work has taken me through some thirty states the past fifty years, particularly in the South and our great Southwest country. We are entirely responsible for dust storms and floods. We destroyed the buffalo grass, thus changing a grazing country into a wheat area. Buffalo grass was nutritious and furnished food for countless millions of buffaloes and antelopes—later for great herds of cattle. During the past twenty years our agriculturists have, through most of our states, industriously drained their acres; thus the surface water rushes off during winter and spring. There are protracted droughts throughout the summer. One of our most famous foresters told me a few years ago that we were cutting timber three times as fast as it grew.—WARREN KING MOOREHEAD

This paragraph is about the destruction of the land at the hands of man. It takes up the destruction of grazing land, the runoff of water, and the overcutting of the forests. The implied topic sentence might be "Man is destroying his Earth."

The following paragraph also has an implied topic sentence. Try to determine what it is.

As Pavlova's little bird body revealed itself on the scene, her instep stretched ahead in an incredible arch, the tiny bones of her hands in ceaseless vibration, her face radiant, diamonds glittering under her dark hair, her little waist encased in silk, the great tutu balancing, quickening, and flashing over her beating, flashing, quivering legs, every man and woman sat forward, every pulse quickened. She never appeared to rest motionless: some part of her trembled, vibrated, beat like a heart. Before our dazzled eyes she flashed with the sudden sweetness of a hummingbird in action too quick for understanding.—AGNES DE MILLE

This paragraph is a detailed observation of the dancing of the famous Russian ballet dancer, Anna Pavlova. The implied topic sentence might read "I once saw the great Pavlova dance in her superlative way."

Good writing is a relentless attention to words, sentences and paragraphs. Effective paragraphs are particularly important because they develop ideas that are impossible to convey in a single sentence. Good paragraphs working together to create compositions are the result of a mind working hard to engage another mind.

Chapter 7

The Paragraph: Its Other Elements

Now that you have worked with the topic sentence, the body, and the clincher sentence—the basic structural elements of a paragraph—you are ready to handle the other elements of a paragraph. They consist of the following:

unity   tone
coherence   mood
adequate detail

These five elements will be discussed in this chapter.

Part 1

Paragraph Unity

Writers sometimes make the mistake of violating the unity of a paragraph. In the heat of writing a paragraph, a writer sometimes includes ideas that really belong in a separate paragraph. On the other hand, he sometimes leaves out ideas that are really necessary to the paragraph he is writing. Another way in which he might violate unity is to shift the tone of his paragraph. For example, he might be writing a sternly serious paragraph and mix in a note of humor. He might even start with a topic sentence concerning one thing and end with a clincher sentence concerning something quite different. To achieve unity a writer must not omit ideas that belong in a paragraph or include others that don't belong. Every sentence in a paragraph must be necessary to the single end that the paragraph is trying to attain.

Examine the following paragraph to see if every sentence is needed and works together with the other sentences to one single purpose.

> A second spur that has driven me on has been, and still is, conscience. My grandfather on my father's side came off a farm within sight of the tower of St. Botolph's Church in Boston, England. The puritan conscience was perhaps part of my father's family's social heritage. In my attitude toward work I am American-minded, not Australian-minded. To be always working, and still at full stretch, has been laid upon me by my conscience as a duty. This enslavement to work for work's sake is, I suppose, irrational; but thinking so would not liberate me. If I slacked, or even just slackened, I should be conscience-stricken and therefore uneasy and unhappy, so this spur seems likely to continue to drive me on so long as I have any working power left in me.—ARNOLD TOYNBEE

You probably determined right away that the first sentence is the topic sentence. The topic is *conscience* and the point of view is *driven me on*. Now, if the remainder of the paragraph sticks to the matter of conscience goading the author, the paragraph will have unity. A quick re-reading of the paragraph shows that the paragraph does have unity because every sentence works to the purpose of substantiating the topic sentence. There is even a strong, clear rewording of the topic sentence in the last sentence, the clincher sentence.

Here is a paragraph that has some unneeded sentences. Look for them as you read.

In 1850, Pinkerton founded the country's first private detective agency, whose insomnolent logo (an open eye) and motto ("We Never Sleep") gave birth to the phrase "private eye." Of course, other people used Pinkerton's idea to start agencies of their own. They made lots of money in those days because policemen were very limited in number. A few agencies failed and went bankrupt, however. The Pinkertons pursued Jesse James, spied for Lincoln (himself a detective-fiction fan), and smashed the heads of striking steel workers for Andrew Carnegie before settling down to become a reputable multimillion-dollar corporation which now has some 37,000 employees. Only about five percent of Pinkerton's work today is investigative, but that still requires close to 1000 detectives nationwide, including part-time help.

What went wrong here? The writer made a very common mistake. Although he started out to deal with one subject, the Pinkerton Agency, he introduced the idea that other people set up agencies of their own. With that idea firmly rooted in his mind, he went on to speak of the money these companies made and the bankruptcy of some of them. He simply went along with the new idea he had introduced. Sentences two, three, and four do not belong in this paragraph, and thus there is a violation of unity.

Exercises
Paragraph Unity

A. Here are three paragraphs. Identify the one that has unity. Then, using your own words and ideas, supply missing words or sentences to the paragraph that needs them to achieve unity. Finally, delete the excess words or sentences from the paragraph that has these faults.

1

Of all the Indians I encountered in my years on the Plains the most resourceful and intelligent, as well as the most dangerous, were the Sioux. They had the courage of daredevils combined with real strategy. They mastered the white man's tactics as soon as they had an opportunity to observe them. Incidentally, they supplied all thinking and observing white commanders with a great deal that was well worth learning in the art of warfare. The Sioux fought to win, and in a desperate encounter were absolutely reckless of life.— BUFFALO BILL

2

Winter memories are the best memories of all. To sit before a roaring fireplace when the snow is on the ground and to remember the laughter of summer is to remember joyously. The wind howls but doesn't penetrate your warmth or security. Yes, winter memories are the best of all.

3

Poverty can often be a strong incentive for people. We all know, or have read stories about, a person who was born in a slum area and who, because of the grinding poverty he experienced, made up his mind to work and study so he could live a more gracious life. My uncle had a friend who grew up in a ghetto and who now is chief engineer at a radio studio. My uncle seems to know all kinds of people. He is very open and outgoing and makes friends easily. He lives a successful life as head mechanic at a large garage, and he makes more money than you might guess. Poverty can often be an asset rather than a liability.

B. All three of these paragraphs lack unity, either because some sentences introduce new ideas or because some sentences fail to support the idea in the topic sentence. If sentences do not belong in a paragraph, delete them. If sentences are needed to support the idea in the topic sentence of a paragraph, supply them.

1

I used to think I was a person, but I'm really just a bunch of numbers. In English class I sit in row 4 seat 2. If I'm not in that chair I am marked absent—even though I may be somewhere else in the room. The teacher doesn't know me; he merely knows if the chair is occupied. I'm a number on a driver's license. I'm an ID number, and I'm a locker number. I had a combination lock that was numbered. However, I changed to a lock that opens with a key. That kind of lock is much safer than a combination lock. Mine cost only a dollar, but it is a good, strong lock. You can see that I am just a bunch of numbers.

2

I enjoy being a joiner. My days and evenings are filled, and I avoid boredom. I belong to a stamp club, I play in the school orchestra, I am a member of the chef's club, and I belong to the city's drum and bugle corps. I get a lot of companionship and pleasure being in these organizations, and I have made a lot of friends. Friendship is a valuable thing. Everyone needs friends. You need someone in whom to confide, and you need friends when you are depressed. You can well believe that I love being a member of active groups.

3

We made an exciting trip to the West last summer. It was thrilling to observe what I had always been told—that America is as scenic as Europe. We saw the Rocky Mountains, which are huge masses on the landscape. They were surprisingly green. I had expected them to be solid rock. We saw lakes that we had never seen before except in travelogues. A highlight of our trip was seeing the Pacific Ocean, which I had never seen before. I will never forget the fun we had on that trip.

Part 2
Coherence

A paragraph must be coherent, so that the reader can easily follow the writer's train of thought. The ideas must be arranged in a logical order and clearly related to each other.

The Order of Ideas in a Paragraph

The order of ideas in a paragraph is determined by the nature of the content. The three most frequently used ways of ordering the ideas in a paragraph are as follows:

> chronological order
> spatial order
> order of importance

Chronological Order

Chronus was the ancient god of time. From his name we get the word *chronological*, which means "in the order of occurrence." For example, if you wanted to explain a process, such as the steps you go through in assembling an engine, you would list these steps in sequence. It wouldn't make any sense at all to list the steps in the wrong order. If you wished to explain how an accident happened, you would tell about the skid your car went into before you would tell of your car's hitting another car broadside. That is the order in which these actions occurred.

Here is a paragraph in which the ideas are arranged chronologically. What kind of time is evident here?

> Easily the most conspicuous feature of the planet is the white caps that cover its polar regions. They display a fascinating rhythm of advance and retreat. At the end of winter in each hemisphere the polar cap covers some four million

square miles. As spring comes, it begins to diminish—rather slowly at first, then at an increasing rate. Near the middle of spring dark rifts appear. They grow steadily and soon split the cap into several sections. Disintegration of the fragments then proceeds rapidly. But the cap never disappears completely: even in midsummer a tiny dazzling spot remains near the pole.—GERARD DE VAUCOULEURS

You saw the passage of time in this paragraph as it traces the melting of the ice cap in seasonal time, from early spring until midsummer.

Spatial Order

Spatial order is the order of things as they are arranged in space. For example, a writer wishing to describe a country church has to decide whether to describe it first from the outside or the inside. If inside, he must decide whether to describe the church from the altar to the front door or from the high ceiling to the parquet floor or from side to side. In short, he can't describe things at random; if he did, the reader of his paragraph would have no logical sense of the arrangement and structure of the church in his mind. Spatial order is most often used with descriptive writing. In the following paragraph, note how carefully the writer selects what she wants to describe so that the reader can "see" the room and feel its atmosphere.

At that time we were living in a second-floor apartment on West 10th Street. The lobby was an asset to the tenants: large, faintly grand, a polished place that smelled strongly of Liquid Veneer and dimly of cats. It was illuminated by paired bracket-lamps, each with one eye blinded by economy, and the melting hues of their Tiffany glass shades reminded me of half-sucked candy. Two staircases—one for the tenants on the east side of the building and one for the tenants on the west—opened out and upward with expansive, old-fashioned gestures; and in each French window stood a twirled iron tripod holding a pot of those plants which somehow cling to life through all: spitting radiators, north light, neglect of janitors. For me the lobby had a soothing elegance; it brought to mind the baronial halls in illustrations by Reginald Birch.—ELIZABETH ENRIGHT

This paragraph of spatial order moves methodically through the lobby, noting its prominent features and describing in sufficient detail what it looked like.

Order of Importance

The order of importance is usually used in writing a paragraph of explanation or argument. Most often a writer moves from the least important idea to the most important idea. He moves, for example, from the least important reason, to more important reasons, to the climax of his argument. Thus, he ends on a strong note. He can also use the reverse of that order. By starting with the most important idea, he can catch the reader's immediate attention and he can then dwindle off to less important material.

The following tongue-in-cheek passage from *Candide* builds to its conclusion, and though the conclusion is as faulty as the examples leading to it, the form is that of a logical argument.

Pangloss taught metaphysico-theologo-cosmolonigology. He proved admirably that there is no effect without a cause and that in this best of all possible worlds, My Lord the Baron's castle was the best of castles and his wife the best of all possible Baronesses. " 'Tis demonstrated," said he, "that things cannot be otherwise; for, since everything is made for an end, everything is necessarily for the best end. Observe that noses were made to wear spectacles; and so we have spectacles. Legs were visibly instituted to be breeched, and we have breeches. Stones were formed to be quarried and to build castles; and My Lord has a very noble castle; the greatest Baron in the province should have the best house; and as pigs were made to be eaten, we eat pork all the year round; consequently, those who have asserted that all is well talk nonsense; they ought to have said that all is for the best."—VOLTAIRE

Not every paragraph needs a specific order of ideas. For example, if you wish to write about the fun you had at a party, it wouldn't matter if you wrote about the food first and the band second, or the opposite way around. If you were describing a raging storm, it wouldn't matter if you first described the downpour of water or the devastating power of the wind. Depending on his subject, a writer sometimes combines orders for an effective paragraph.

Exercises
Order of Ideas in a Paragraph

A. Each of the following paragraphs is developed in a different way: chronological order, spatial order, or order of importance. Determine the order of ideas in each paragraph and be ready to explain your choice.

1

South of New Orleans, down along the stretch that is called the Lower Coast, the land trails off to a narrow strip between river and marsh. Solid ground here is maybe only a couple of hundred feet across, and there is a dirt road that runs along the foot of the green, carefully sodded levee. It once had state highway markers, but people used the white-painted signs for shotgun targets until they were so riddled they crumbled away. The highway commission has never got around to replacing them. Maybe it doesn't even know the signs are gone; highway inspectors hardly ever come down this way. To the east is the expanse of shifting swamp grass, and beyond that is the little, sheltered Bay Cadoux, and farther still, beyond the string of protecting, is the Gulf. To the west is the Mississippi, broad and slow and yellow.
—SHIRLEY ANN GRAU

2

You have heard it repeated, I dare say, that men of science work by means of induction and deduction and that,

by the help of these operations, they wring from nature certain other things (which are called natural laws and causes), and that out of these, by some cunning skill of their own, they build up hypotheses and theories. And it is imagined by many that the operations of the common mind can be by no means compared with these processes. To hear all these large words, you would think that the mind of a man of science must be constituted differently from that of his fellow men. But if you will not be frightened by terms, you will discover that you are quite wrong, and that all these terrible apparatus are being used by yourself every day of your life.
—THOMAS HENRY HUXLEY

3

There was a long part of her diary which was given over to an account of her life with me. At some point she mentioned the way we'd married in haste in 1943 when I was being drafted into the Army and how that hectic time had been brightened by the promise of the life we'd begun when I got back. Then there was the leave spent together in San Francisco. She'd just heard of her brother's death, but we'd been able then to keep a good heart because the war's end was at least visible. Then came the year in the trailer while I was finishing college, the year I'd written my play and we'd talked of how great it would be to get out with jobs of our own and our own apartment. Then how I'd got involved with Larris in promoting his cartoon books and how we'd traveled all over the country on that scheme. How we'd saved money on different occasions to buy a house, had spent the money and started saving all over again.—R. V. CASSILL

4

She dressed her tiny self carefully, donning a clean white camisole and her black Sunday frock. After she had drunk her tea and eaten a slice of thinly margarined toast, she washed her cup and saucer in some water she had drawn from the bathroom the evening before and put them away on her "kitchen" shelf in the clothes closet. Then she tiptoed down the steep stairs to the bathroom and washed her face and hands—"a lick and a spit" as she called it.—HUGH GARNER

B. The sentences in the following paragraphs are not in logical order. Study the paragraphs to determine what the proper order should be and write down the numbers of the sentences in the correct order of ideas. Note the order you now have. Is it chronological, spatial, order of importance, or a combination of orders?

1

1. During 1902 we made upward of fourteen hundred flights, sometimes going up a hundred times or more in a single day. 2. I recall sitting in it, ready to cast off, one still day when the breeze seemed approaching. 3. Our runway was short, and it required a wind with a velocity of at least twelve miles an hour to lift the machine. 4. We had to go ahead and discover everything for ourselves. 5. That's just a sample of what we had to learn about air currents; nobody had ever heard of "holes" in the air at that time. 6. It came presently, rippling the daisies in the field, and just as it reached me I started the glider on the runway. 7. But the innocent-appearing breeze was a whirlwind. 8. I tilted my rudder to descend. 9. It jerked the front of the machine sharply upward. 10. Then the breeze spun downward, driving the glider to the ground with a tremendous shock and spinning me out headfirst.

2

1. Many evenings as I prepared the material for this chapter, I found myself drifting from my subject, the brain, to wander deep into the fascinating lives of electronic computers. 2. Exploring the living brain, however, proves to be a different kind of venture and makes enormous demands of our own brain. 3. No matter how remarkable and intricate the computer may be, man made the computer, and so he knows what he put into it and how it functions. 4. The intricate details of computer structure and function by no

means provide easy reading, but I soon realized that compared to the infinite mysteries of the living brain, computers are a logical and relaxing subject. 5. Fortunately the brain is the most flexible and adaptable organ in the body, and an examination of itself is inevitably the challenge the human brain must accept.

3

1. When I first started going to motor races, they were conducted mostly on small dirt tracks up to a mile in length, their curves modestly banked. 2. The colossal rear tires kicked up magnificent rooster tails of dust. 3. The straightaways were short, forcing cars to bunch up fiercely on the corners. 4. There was a lot of hammin' and frammin' as the cars circled the track. 5. At the peak of the maneuver, their front wheels were sideways to the direction in which the cars were traveling. 6. The herd hurtled into the turns in a fantastic blur of dust, heat, noise, speed. 7. As the cars churned around the turns, they drifted into long, graceful slides. 8. It was one of the most spectacular sights in sport.

4

1. The equation between human ingenuity and human wisdom has become dangerously unbalanced. 2. If he waged war, the enemy was relatively close at hand, while elsewhere in other corners of the wilderness, downstream or across the earth, other human beings carried on the more civilized affairs of mankind until it was their turn to play the spear game. 3. The more power man wields the more he has need of unthinking self-control, and the unselfishness to behave in such a way today that the human species may survive and future generations may have reason to speak of us with kindness and respect. 4. If long ago man invented a spear and then used it unwisely, the most damage he could do was to kill, one at a time, a number of his fellow men. 5. Modern weapons reflect the evil face of man's technological genius, for with one strike they can kill thousands of individuals. 6. With the gift of power goes the burden of responsibility.

7. Even a brief thermonuclear tournament might destroy or devastate all life on this planet, including innocent plant and animal bystanders.

The Use of Linking Words and Expressions

Coherence is achieved in two ways. While arranging your ideas in a logical order is one element in achieving coherence, using linking words and expressions is another element in achieving coherence.

Linking words help the reader follow the line of thought from one idea to another. Pronouns such as the following are useful words for this purpose because they refer to words and ideas in preceding sentences.

he, him, his	they, them, their
she, her, hers	this, that
it, its	these, those

In the following paragraph, note how the words in red refer to a previously mentioned person, thing, or idea.

Animals talk to each other, of course, there can be no question about that; but I suppose there are very few people who can understand them. I never knew but one man who could. I knew he could, however, because he told me so himself. He was a middle-aged, simple-hearted miner who had lived in a lonely corner of California among the woods and mountains a good many years, and had studied the ways of his only neighbors, the beasts and the birds, until he believed he could accurately translate any remark which they made. This was Jim Baker. According to Jim Baker, some animals have only a limited education and use only very simple words and scarcely ever a comparison or a flowery figure; whereas certain other animals have a large vocabulary, a fine command of language, and a ready and fluent delivery; consequently, these latter talk a great deal, they like it, they are conscious of their talent, and they enjoy "showing off."—MARK TWAIN

Linking expressions, or connectives, also help to move the idea of the paragraph smoothly from sentence to sentence. Here are some of the most commonly used linking expressions:

TO ADD IDEAS

also	in addition	and then
too	likewise	further
besides	again	furthermore
in the second place	nor	as a result
equally important	moreover	in the same fashion

TO LIMIT OR CONTRADICT

but	however	at the same time
yet	although	on the other hand
and yet	nevertheless	on the contrary
still	otherwise	nonetheless

TO ARRANGE IN TIME OR PLACE

first	finally	soon	here
second	at this point	sooner or later	nearly
next	meanwhile	afterward	opposite to
presently	eventually	at length	adjacent to

TO EXEMPLIFY

for example   for instance   in fact   in other words

TO SUM UP

in short	on the whole	for the most part	in any case
in brief	to sum up	in any event	as I have said

In the following paragraph, note how the linking expressions, shown in red, help to move the idea of the paragraph smoothly from sentence to sentence.

I don't live in the past very much. In fact, I hardly live there at all. My memory is just awful for things that happened last week, let alone what happened fifteen, twenty, or twenty-five years ago. I've never kept a diary or journal or even a scrapbook. I don't know why exactly; there just never seemed to be time. Every now and then, though, I'll run across an old newspaper clipping my parents saved, or maybe a school yearbook, and that'll trigger the memory of some experience or feeling I had many years ago. I rarely remember details—what I was wearing or what somebody said to me or whether the sun was shining—and I'm sure that the few things I do remember vividly are colored by the way I feel about them now, today. Still, certain incidents stand out, and they're important to me, at least right at this moment. How important they were to me when they actually happened, I don't really know.—BILLIE JEAN KING

Exercise
Using Linking Words and Expressions

Read the following paragraph carefully. Determine what pronouns and what linking expressions help to make the paragraph coherent. Copy them in order, numbering each with the number of the sentence in which it appears. You may have more than one pronoun or linking expression in some sentences.

1. In 1959 Dr. L. S. B. Leakey found at Olduvai the massive-jawed, small-brained creature who has come to be known as *Zinjanthropus*. 2. Although detailed anatomical data are not available, the creature would appear to be not too distant in its anatomy from some of the known, and possibly much later, man-apes. 3. It, however, is remarkable for two reasons. 4. First, it was found in association with clearly shaped stone tools, long known but never found in direct contact with human remains. 5. Thus this creature was not merely a user of chance things which he picked up; he was a thinker who shaped. 6. Second, late last July Doctors J. F. Evenden and Garniss Curtis of the University of California announced that *Zinjanthropus* was nearly *two* million years old. 7. They had dated the creature by a new "clock" involving the use of potassium-argon radioactive delay. 8. If this dating method is correct, the history of tool-using man will thus have been carried back almost a million years before the Ice Age.—LOREN EISELEY

Part 3
Adequate Detail

Some writers do not supply enough details to help the reader understand what they are trying to explain or describe. The necessary details may be in the writer's mind, but the reader can respond only to what is on the page before him, not what is left out. The reader needs adequate details in order to respond fully and intelligently to what a writer is saying. Note the plentiful details that make the following paragraph full and interesting.

> Edinburgh is a city of pure drama. It sits on a natural terrain of ridges, hills, ravines, and stupendous rocks as sharp-edged as a piece of crumpled steel. An amalgam of light and shadow, brightness and gray mist, it joins two separate parts: an Old Town, whose craggy skyline is one of the most dramatic in the world, and a New Town, an eighteenth-century concept of fine residences that is Europe's largest stretch of Georgian houses. A subtle, somber, yet exciting city, it can thrill or chill a visitor, for its striking townscapes—its Castle, its sky-piercing churches, its superb crescents—are marvelously thrilling to the eye, but its inner life is pulled back out of sight. At night the city becomes a tomb, the yellow streetlamps flickering in the mist.—FRANCES KOLTUN

This paragraph is rich in descriptive detail. For that reason you can respond to it. Not only are the details plentiful and varied, but they also give the reader a strong impression of the character of the city.

Here is the same paragraph as it might have been written by someone who didn't give sufficient details. Do you think it would capture a reader's interest?

> Edinburgh is a dramatic city. It is made up of an Old Town and a New Town. It has many unusual characteristics to thrill the visitor. At night the city is dark and mysterious.

Exercises
Supplying Adequate Details

A. Here are some ideas for paragraphs. Choose two of the ideas and amplify them. Stick to the subject, but enrich the ideas with enough details to develop them into effective paragraphs.

1. I dislike winter in Wisconsin. Snow and cold only complicate my life.
2. I read more books in grade school than I read now. Somehow, there doesn't seem to be time enough to read.
3. Saturday is the busiest day of my week. I have all kinds of things to do.
4. I don't hate myself, but I am not proud of myself either. I have certain weaknesses.
5. We had a picnic on the Fourth of July. I was completely exhausted when I went home that night.

B. Here are more ideas for paragraphs. Select three and enrich them with enough detail to develop them into effective paragraphs.

1. The program was wonderful. Everyone talked about it for weeks.
2. The garbage at the camp site was scattered all over the area. It was not an inviting place to set up our tent.
3. I received an unusual birthday present. I really liked it.
4. The car was fully loaded. We were prepared to start our vacation.
5. The man looked cold and hungry. He stopped briefly at the door of the restaurant.
6. The accident was the worst I have ever seen. The ambulance arrived within minutes.
7. I could tell that a serious storm was about to break. The sky to the west of us was an ominous black.
8. I have chosen a career. Hard as it may be to prepare for it, I am sure I will succeed.
9. The zoo was an exciting place. It was hard to decide what to see first.
10. Homeowners can save money by doing their own basic repair jobs. Certain tools are necessary for these repairs.

Part 4

Tone

The **tone** of a piece of writing reveals the writer's attitude toward his subject. For example, his tone may be angry, amused, bitter, satirical, flippant, naive, bored, or sarcastic. His subject matter usually determines the tone a writer wants to achieve, and he uses any of a great number of techniques to achieve that tone. These techniques are the coloration the writer gives his paragraph. He might use specifically chosen words. He might use figurative language. He might omit details that detract from the tone he wants to achieve. He might skillfully employ rhythm. He might construct sentences to work to his purpose.

Writing, however, can't use some of the devices that the voice can use. For example, a speaker can put sarcasm into the way he voices a biting word. He can shout or whisper to achieve a certain tone. He can modulate the pitch of his voice. He can use gestures and change his facial expressions as he speaks. Think for a moment how vocal emphasis can alter the tone of a simple statement. The simple statement "He is a good citizen" can take on a number of different tones. The speaker might say, "*He* is a good citizen?" Or he might say, "He is a *good* citizen!" A speaker can create a number of tones merely from the inflection he gives his words.

In writing, you don't have those inflections available to you. You must depend largely on the words you use, on the way you place those words, on the way you construct your sentences, or on the way you arrange the ideas in your paragraph. If you want to achieve a certain tone in your writing, you have to work very carefully to achieve it. It doesn't appear accidentally.

Notice how tone is achieved in the following paragraph.

> The strange things you want in this life! When I was nine or ten years old I wanted a middy blouse more than anything on earth. I wanted it so badly that I dreamed about it;

whined through my nose for it. But my mother shook all her blonde curls in a sort of vivacious horror: "No, honey! Never! Heavens, shades of Radcliffe girls with chafing dishes and bulging calves all leaping at a basketball together and having a corking time. Corking! That's the sort of word that goes with middy blouses. No, Baby. Over my dead body." And since my mother was the one sun in my sky (my father had been killed in Belleau Wood) I resigned myself to the quaint little smocked dresses that she chose for me.—
ELIZABETH ENRIGHT

The writer presents her mother as a somewhat frivolous, empty-headed woman as she vivaciously shakes "all her blonde curls." We are even reminded of the mistakenly stereotyped "dumb blonde." The writer's use of the word *quaint* signifies that her mother apparently chooses styles from the past for her daughter, childish clothes that help the mother appear younger. The mock horror the mother exhibits about Radcliffe girls, with their muscular calves and their interest in athletics, reveals the mother as flighty, lacking in wisdom and unsympathetic to her daughter's feelings. The writer's tone is one of acceptance. She wryly accepts things as they are. She is not angry—only disappointed.

Exercises
Analyzing Tone

A. Determine the tone of each of the following paragraphs and be able to explain how the tone is created.

1

My first suitor came from Holland. He was called Wilhelm and his teeth were too regular; he was much older than I; he had a long, sad face; at least, thus it was that others made me see him when they had taught me to consider his defects. As for me, at first I found his face thoughtful rather than long and peaked. I did not yet know that his teeth—so straight and even—were false. I thought I loved Wilhelm. Here was the first man who, through me, could be made happy or unhappy; here was a very serious matter.—GABRIELLE ROY

2

It is some time before dawn, in the late spring, as I write this. The seagulls have more than an hour before it will be their moment to fly in from the river, screeing and crying, and then fly back. After them, the pigeons will murmur, and it will be day, perhaps a hot and sticky day. Right now the air is deliciously cool, but I find myself shivering. I find myself imagining the cold, the bitter cold, of that morning when Death came in full panoply, like one dressed for dinner. That morning so very long ago.—AVRAM DAVIDSON

3

"Crime, Watney," remarked my friend, Mr. Schlock Homes, laying aside the financial section of the journal and reaching for his Yellowbole and shag, "is the contrived and exhibited manifestation of the subconscious negation of theosophistic impregnation and authoritative influence. It has the added disadvantage, of course, of being illegal, which so often forces its perpetrators into opposition to the law."
—ROBERT L. FISH

4

Mrs. Brennan took snuff. She got it out of her grandson's store, going in and helping herself from the big tin on the second shelf. It was a habit her family deplored. Mrs. Brennan did not like snuff much. It was one of the things she had got over. It made her cough. But the fact that her family deplored her taking it prevented her from giving it up completely. She drank a little, too. Not much; just enough to get "tiddly." That was what she called it, "I'm a little tiddly today," she'd say, and the family didn't like that either. Nor did she, save for the fun of shocking them and the interest outwitting them gave her.—STUART CLOETE

5

The lights were going on in the St. Anselm Hotel for the first time. The last mason had left a week ago. The last painter and carpenter had left two days ago. The last decorators were still busy, in some of the rooms on some of the floors, working overtime, working like mad, unrolling carpets, tacking up drapes, unpacking mirrors. Everyone was new at his job, from the manager down to the merest bellboy; everyone was confused, highly excited, uncertain just what was expected of him. Everyone was asking the personnel member just over him what to do and how to do it, and then getting it wrong because he'd been told wrong. The bellboys were asking the bell captain, the bell captain was asking the desk clerk, the desk clerk was asking the manager. It stopped there; the manager had no one higher than himself to ask. So he passed the blame in reverse direction, and it started down the line again: to desk clerk, to bell captain, to bellboy. Then, when it got there it had to stop once more and start up-rank again. But everyone was making allowances, so there was no great harm done, except to nervous energy. Everyone knew no one could be expected to be letter-perfect. Everyone knew they'd do better in a day or so, or a week. Everyone knew things would calm down and straighten out.

—CORNELL WOOLRICH

6

It's a story they tell in the border country, where Massachusetts joins Vermont and New Hampshire. Yes, Dan'l Webster's dead—or, at least they buried him. But every time there's a thunderstorm around Marshfield, they say you can hear his rolling voice in the hollows of the sky. And they say that if you go to his grave and speak loud and clear, "Dan'l Webster—Dan'l Webster!" the ground'll begin to shiver and the trees begin to shake. And after a while you'll hear a deep voice saying, "Neighbor, how stands the Union?" Then you better answer the Union stands as she stood, rock-bottomed and copper-sheathed, one and indivisible, or he's liable to roar right out of the ground. At least, that's what I was told when I was a youngster.—STEPHEN VINCENT BENÉT

B. Write an original paragraph in which you establish a specific tone. State what the tone is and explain how you achieved it. This is as important to the exercise as the paragraph itself. Choose one of the following tones or choose one of your own: disgust, anger, patience, formality, foolishness, stupidity.

Part 5
Mood

It is easy to confuse tone with mood. Simply remember that tone is the writer's attitude toward his subject, while **mood**, on the other hand, is the attitude that is evoked in the reader. Look at this paragraph to see the difference.

> Michael Lowes hummed as he shaved, amused by the face he saw—the pallid, assymetrical face, with the right eye so much higher than the left, and its eyebrow so peculiarly arched, like a "v" turned upside down. Perhaps this day wouldn't be as bad as the last. In fact, he knew it wouldn't be, and that was why he hummed. This was the bi-weekly day of escape, when he would stay out for the evening, and play bridge with Hurwitz, Bryant, and Smith. Should he tell Dora at the breakfast table? No, better not. Particularly in view of last night's row about unpaid bills. And there would be more of them, probably, beside his plate. The rent. The coal. The doctor who had attended to the children. Jeez, what a life. Maybe it was time to do a new jump. And Dora was beginning to get restless again.—CONRAD AIKEN

This is a picture of a self-satisfied man. He is "amused" by his face, but he is not ashamed of it, as is revealed by his humming as he looks at it. The reader, however, sees something sinister in the "pallid" face with its rakishly formed eyebrow. The man is somewhat upset about unpaid bills, but it is little more than a passing annoyance. The reader finds him less than candid with his wife when he plans to play cards but not to tell her. Apparently he is a loser at cards. The thought rolls through his mind that he should duck out on his wife and his unpaid bills. In short, the reader doesn't have much reason to like Michael Lowes. The way the writer feels about Mr. Lowes is *tone*; the way the reader feels about him is *mood*.

Here is another paragraph. What mood is created here?

> On leaving his house one morning at his usual early hour for going to the Law Courts, Chief Inspector Ganimard noticed the curious behavior of an individual who was walking along the Rue Pergolese in front of him. Shabbily dressed and wearing a straw hat, though the day was the first of December, the man stooped at every thirty or forty yards to fasten his bootlace, or pick up his stick or for some other reason. And, each time, he took a little piece of orange peel from his pocket and laid it stealthily on the curb of the pavement. It was probably a mere display of eccentricity, a childish amusement to which no one else would have paid attention: but Ganimard was one of those shrewd observers who are indifferent to nothing that strikes their eyes and who are never satisfied until they know the secret cause of things. He therefore began to follow the man.—MAURICE LEBLANC

In this paragraph the description of the man's behavior attracts the attention of the Chief Inspector. It also attracts the reader's attention. The mood created is one of mystery—at least curiosity. The reader knows something will develop from the circumstances described.

Exercises
Tone and Mood

A. Determine the tone and the mood of each of the following paragraphs and explain how they are created.

1

Aristide Valentin, Chief of the Paris Police, was late for his dinner, and some of his guests began to arrive before him. These were, however, reassured by his confidential servant, Ivan, the old man with a scar, and a face almost as gray as his moustaches, who always sat at a table in the entance hall—a hall hung with weapons—Valentin's house was perhaps as peculiar and celebrated as its master. It was an old house, with high walls and tall poplars almost overhanging the Seine; but the oddity—and perhaps the police value—of its architecture was this; that there was no ultimate exit at all except through this front door, which was guarded by Ivan and the armory. The garden was large and elaborate, and there were many exits from the house into the garden. But there was no exit from the garden into the world outside; all round it ran a tall, smooth, unscalable wall with special spikes at the top; no bad garden, perhaps, for a man to reflect in whom some hundred criminals had sworn to kill.—GILBERT K. CHESTERTON

2

Orlo Vay, the Chippewa Avenue Optician Smart-Art Harlequin Tinted-Tortus Frames Our Speciality, was a public figure, as public as a cemetery. He was resentful that his profession, like that of an undertaker, a professor of art, or a Mormon missionary, was not appreciated for its patience and technical skill, as are the callings of wholesale grocer or mistress or radio-sports-commentator, and he tried to make up for the professional injustice by developing his personal glamor.—SINCLAIR LEWIS

3

A man testifying before a judge:

Had he ever been a spy himself? No, he scorned the base insinuation. What did he live upon? His property. Where was his property? He didn't precisely remember where it was. What was it? No business of anybody's. Had he inherited it?

Yes, he had. From whom? Distant relation. Very distant? Rather. Ever been in prison? Certainly not. Never in a debtors' prison?—Come, once again. Never? Yes. How many times? Two or three times. Not five or six? Perhaps. Of what profession? Gentleman. Ever been kicked? Might have been. Frequently? Ever been kicked downstairs? Decidedly not; once received a kick on the top of a staircase, and fell downstairs of his own accord. Kicked on that occasion for cheating at dice? Something to that effect was said by the intoxicated liar who committed the assault, but it was not true. Swear it was not true? Positively. Ever live by cheating at play? Never. Ever live by play? Not more than other gentlemen do. Ever borrow money of the prisoner? Yes. Ever pay him? No. Was not this intimacy with the prisoner, in reality a very slight one, forced upon the prisoner in coaches, inns, and packets? No. Sure he saw the prisoner with these lists? Certain. Knew no more about the lists? Certain. Knew no more about the lists? No. Had not procured them himself, for instance? No. Expect to get anything by this evidence? No, not in regular government pay and employment, to lay traps? Oh dear no. Or to do anything? Oh dear no. Swear that? Over and over again. No motives but motives of sheer patriotism? None whatever.—CHARLES DICKENS

B. Write three paragraphs of your own, each having a different tone and mood. State the tone and mood of each.

Chapter 8

Types of Paragraphs

There are many types of paragraphs for writers to use. Professional writers have an idea and a purpose in mind when they write, both of which determine the type of paragraph they use. The following types of paragraphs are the most familiar and will be discussed in this chapter.

the paragraph of details	the paragraph of definition
the paragraph of description	the paragraph of reasoning
the paragraph of comparison and contrast	the paragraph of argument and persuasion
the paragraph of narration	the paragraph of analogy
the paragraph of explanation	

While content and purpose govern the type of paragraph a professional writer uses, he doesn't sit down and say to himself, "I think I'll write a paragraph of argument and persuasion today." Rather, he might decide to write about the energy shortage and try to convince people to be more sparing of natural resources. If he is at all logical, he will develop his paragraph by the method of argument and persuasion. He will do that, perhaps without even thinking of a method of development. You, too, might be as logical and suit the proper form to the ideas you wish to convey. Because you are probably a relatively inexperienced writer, however, you will be able to control your paragraphs more successfully if you are consciously aware of the type you are using.

Part 1
The Paragraph of Details

Developing a paragraph by the use of details is the most frequently used method of developing an idea. You present your idea in the topic sentence, and then develop the idea by giving details that support or illustrate what you have said in the topic sentence. In the following paragraph, pick out the topic sentence; then determine what details are used to develop the main idea. Is there a clincher sentence?

The Feudal Ages from the ninth to the fifteenth century was a period of force, of violence, and of disorder. It was literally an age in which the strongest took what he could, and the weaker nobles and the common people protected themselves as best they might. A leader who did not excel as a fighter usually gave way to one whose arm was stronger, whose sword thrust was keener and whose battle ax cut deeper. It was an age in which assassination was used frequently to rid a noble or prince of his enemies. It was an age in which treachery abounded and faith was not kept except with the strong. Even the Church was disorganized in the earlier period. Few of its members were able to read and some higher churchmen were only a little less unscrupulous than other great nobles. The rights of peasants and women were not deeply respected, although in the later Feudal Age (1100–1450 A.D.) a more chivalrous spirit was shown to noble ladies.—ROSCOE LOUIS ASHLEY

The topic sentence is the first one. Although it presents three ideas, they overlap and support each other to form a single idea: that one time span in the Feudal Ages was marked by the use of force, of violence, and of disorder. The paragraph is generous in its use of supporting evidence and reinforces the topic sentence thoroughly and vigorously. Did you notice, however, that there is no summarizing clincher sentence? In fact, the writer ends, not by restating the topic sentence, but by telling us that things were better for noble ladies in a later period of time.

While this information is closely related to that of the topic sentence, it does not sum up what the topic sentence says. Clearly the last part of the last sentence in the paragraph is leading into the paragraph that will follow. If the writer were writing a one-paragraph article, and this were it, he would probably have substituted a different sentence for the last one. However, writers seldom write one-paragraph articles. Instead, they usually write multi-paragraph articles in which it is necessary to tie the paragraphs together so that no one of the paragraphs is an entity in itself. For that reason, often a paragraph doesn't meet all the rules governing a single paragraph.

Imagine, if you will, that a paragraph is a brick. It is the basic unit of which a building is made. When you start to build, however, you put mortar on it to join it with other bricks. The brick is no longer a separate unit. Now it is tied to other bricks and loses some of its individuality. So it is with paragraphs in a multi-paragraph theme. They must have verbal mortar, which we call transitions, joining them to each other, and thus they can't always meet the definition of an ideal paragraph.

Exercises
The Paragraph of Details

A. Here is a paragraph that uses details. Find the topic sentence and explain how the details develop or support the idea in the topic sentence.

Writers are not highly regarded in America. I know this sounds odd, but it is true. Everyone uses a pen, and everyone believes he or she could write a book if there were only time. Recently I heard the expression, "I could write a book about that place." Another person, after reading a book about his own profession, said he could write a better book. The point is, each assumed as a matter of course that he could write a book, but he would never claim to be able to carve a statue or compose music or paint a picture or design a building. Even if writers do not offer to write a book they have a plot for a novel, which they present to a writer, free.

—WILLIAM MCFEE

B. Here are some subjects for a paragraph developed by the use of details. Choose one of the subjects, or one of your own, and write a paragraph. You may use any one of the sentences as your topic sentence, or you may alter it to make it more interesting. However, be careful that it is a subject that can be developed by the use of details. Give your body sufficient length to develop your idea, maintain unity and coherence, and conclude with a clincher sentence.

1. I enjoy bird watching.
2. Mobile homes can be very comfortable.
3. Autumn is a season of regrets.
4. Is there a more unpleasant place than a dentist's office?
5. Hunting is a cruel and unnecessary sport.
6. Some people have annoying habits.
7. You can learn a lot by watching TV.
8. Our basement looks like a wall-to-wall dump.
9. I can't seem to get going in the morning.
10. I think I am a pretty independent person.

Part 2

The Paragraph of Description

Persons, places, and things are the subjects for description. While describing the outer surface of any one of these subjects is relatively simple, an external description is seldom enough.

Usually, you want to capture the essence, the inner qualities of the person, place, or thing you are describing. It may be sufficient to stick to externals in a police description of a wanted criminal, but you don't have occasion to write many police descriptions. To say, for example, that a person is five feet six inches tall, that she is a female Caucasian, that she has blue eyes and black hair, is to say nothing of what kind of person she is. To reveal her inner qualities, you might note that she has a shy smile, that her hands and eyes are in constant motion, that she always looks away from the person who talks to her.

If you were to describe the Statue of Liberty, you might wish to convey the idea that immigrants who sailed in to New York, passing the Statue of Liberty, must certainly have felt the symbolic strength of her welcoming smile, and have been thrilled by her quiet dignity and the lighted torch she holds. There is more to be said about her than a mere inventory of her size and weight and color.

Describing a Person

Read the following description of a person:

> Before the prisoner left for Texas, the police took the traditional mug shots of him. In these photographs, Abel looks something like an unfrocked monk who had been caught blaspheming. A scowl clouds his ascetic face, and the sparse fringe of brownish-gray hair around his ears and the back of his head is disarranged. He is looking down an aquiline nose with tired eyes, and his receding chin is darkened by a one-day growth of beard. The collar of his white shirt is unbuttoned, and his striped tie is askew. Looking at this face, one might think immediately of a clerk who has worked too long in the same department. The photograph brings to mind an observer's remark: "He has a genius for the inconspicuous," and the surprise of the foreman of the Abel jury, John T. Dublynn, who exclaimed when he first saw the defendant: "He could be walking down the street and he could be anybody."—SANCHE DE GRAMONT

You probably feel some distaste for the person described here because the writer has been selective in what he tells you about the man. That is, he tells mostly unpleasant things about Abel and fails to tell any good things. Abel might, for instance, have had a pleasant smile. He might have been witty. He might have had attractive eyes. The writer chooses, however, to note that his subject "looks like an unfrocked monk"! The writer also tells us that he wears a scowl, that he looks down his nose, that he has a receding chin, that his hair is mousey, and that he is unshaven. You form a dislike for the man.

Exercise
Describing a Person

Write a paragraph describing someone you know. Don't merely describe his or her physical appearance; try to select facts that reveal his or her inner qualities. Even though you like this person, you probably are aware of some faults. Describe him or her with these faults in mind.

Describing a Place

You have five senses—touch, taste, smell, hearing, and sight —and ideally a piece of descriptive writing will appeal to at least one of the five. In other words, a piece of descriptive writing will enable you to "feel" whatever the writer is describing or enable you to "hear" it or "smell" it. The sense most often appealed to is the sense of sight. At some time, you have undoubtedly heard a person say, "The writer described the setting so well that I could almost see it."

In describing a place, try to capture the quality or the feeling of it by choosing words that convey an atmosphere. What kind of feeling does the following description of a place convey?

It was a lovely morning. The last stars withdrew while we were waiting, the sky was clear and serene but the world in which we walked was sombre still, and profoundly silent. The grass was wet; down by the trees where the ground sloped it gleamed with the dew like dim silver. The air of the morning was cold; it had that twinge in it which in Northern countries means that the frost is not far away. However often you make the experience—I thought—it is still impossible to believe, in this coolness and shade, that the heat of the sun and the glare of the sky, in a few hours' time, will be hard to bear. The grey mist lay upon the hills, strangely taking shape from them; it would be bitterly cold on the Buffalo if they were about there now, grazing on the hillside, as in a cloud.—ISAK DINESEN

Notice how this description appeals to the senses: the feel of wet grass and cold air, the colors of dim silver and grey mist. The words *serene, sombre, profoundly silent* capture the feeling of this place in the hours before the heat and glare of the day.

Exercises
Describing a Place

A. Write a paragraph telling what you see about you at this moment. Then write a second paragraph in which you keep what you see, but add appeals to one of the other five senses. For example, if you describe what you see in a room, mix in a description of how the room smells, or what you hear in the room.

B. Write two paragraphs, each a description of a place. Make one a description of a place you like and the other a description of a place you dislike. Appeal to as many senses as you can without overwriting your descriptions. Don't tell the reader which paragraph is about a place you like and which is about a place you dislike. Help the reader determine your attitude by the words and phrases you use. As an example of a place you like, you might describe the kitchen while the Thanksgiving banquet is cooking. In describing the kitchen you could appeal to the sense of sight and the sense of smell. You might also want to appeal to the sense of hearing. As an example of a place you dislike, you might describe a crowded street, with the smell of exhaust fumes and the sound and sight of the congestion going on there.

Describing a Thing

Describing a thing is much the same as describing a place. Again, you employ as many of the senses as you can comfortably use. You might make a point of using a simile or a metaphor because it is often easier to describe a thing by comparing it with some other thing.

The following paragraph is a description of a thing. Read carefully to see what senses the writer appeals to and what comparisons he uses, if any.

But the object that most drew my attention, in the mysterious package, was a certain affair of fine red cloth, much worn and faded. There were traces about it of gold embroidery, which, however, was greatly frayed and defaced; so that none, or very little, of the glitter was left. It had been wrought, as was easy to perceive, with wonderful skill of needlework; and the stitch (as I am assured by ladies conversant with such mysteries) gives evidence of a now forgotten art, not to be recovered even by the process of picking out the threads. This rag of scarlet cloth—for time and wear and a sacrilegious moth had reduced it to little other than a rag—on careful examination, assumed the shape of a letter. It was the capital letter A. By an accurate measurement, each limb proved to be precisely three inches and a quarter in length. It had been intended, there could be no doubt, as an ornamental article of dress; but how it was to be worn, or what rank, honor, and dignity, in by-past times, were signified by it, was a riddle which (so evanescent are the fashions of the world in these particulars) I saw little hope of solving. And yet it strangely interested me. My eyes fastened themselves upon the old scarlet letter, and would not be turned aside. Certainly, there was some deep meaning in it, most worthy of interpretation, and which, as it were, streamed forth from the mystic symbol, subtly communicating itself to my sensibilities, but evading the analysis of my mind.—NATHANIEL HAWTHORNE

Perhaps you recognize this "thing" as the famous "A" that the heroine of *The Scarlet Letter* had to wear on her breast. Notice how the writer invests it with mystery. There is something strange and compelling about the letter that makes him unable to take his eyes off it. It is a "mystic symbol."

Exercise
Describing a Thing

Write a paragraph describing a thing that has some unusual qualities about it, preferably a thing that requires comparisons in describing it. For example, if you were describing a stone, you could say that it looked like a plump little pillow embroidered in tiny black stitches.

Mixing Descriptions

A writer often mixes two or more descriptions together. In describing a dance, for example, he might write about a thing (the music) and the people (the dancers). In describing a picnic, the writer might talk about a place (the park) and the thing (the food).

Exercises
The Paragraph of Description

A. Write a paragraph in which you mix two descriptions.

B. Here are some subjects for paragraphs of description. Choose one of these subjects, or one of your own. Write a paragraph of description of a person, place, or thing—or some combination of them. Employ as many senses as you reasonably can.

1. A well baked pizza is a work of art.
2. At 4:00 the traffic on the expressway started bunching up, and we were slowed to 15 miles per hour.
3. The garden showed all shades of the rainbow in its lavish display of flowers.

4. There is one comedian I like better than all others.

5. Fall is a lovely season.

6. The smell and sound of the ocean surf lulls one into sleep.

7. The beginners' ski slope is a wild confusion of people, noise, and color.

8. There is nothing else like the shine and smell of a new car.

9. At the touchdown, the stands exploded with frenzied cheers.

10. Puppies are cuddly creatures.

Part 3

The Paragraph of Comparison or Contrast

Using Comparison

In making a **comparison,** a writer shows the similarities between two or more people, places, or things. Read the following comparison carefully.

Naturally, it would be as wrong to deny film its visual glories as it would be to deny opera its music. The novel quality of film is the visual experience, just as one of the important aspects of opera is the music. But a film is also theater drama, including sound and music; and opera has been known to be excellent theatrical drama apart from its music. As a matter of historical record there have been intermediate states. Legitimate plays have been filmed, with the camera expanding audience awareness. Television programs are often examples of well-made plays which are simply filmed. At least two operas, Purcell's *Dido and Aeneas* (baroque) and Berg's *Wozzeck* (modern), have been said to use music and action cinematically. It is not a question of reducing any one form to another, which is where much of the jealousy and confusion between, for example, films and novels originates. It is a matter of recognizing that all dramatic art does not spring out of a vacuum. Originalities of expression and content do advance beyond the media of the past—or, much more accurately, new qualities appear. But it is not a mystery where film borrows and where it is new. Therefore, it becomes nonsense to deny science fiction film the capacity to embody sophisticated science fiction ideas on the screen as well as in the written form, just as it would be foolish to argue against the Greek dramatists, or Ibsen, Shaw, and others, that ideas cannot be made to work on the stage.—GEORGE ZEBROWSKI

You can detect in the first sentence that some kind of relationship between film and opera is going to be established. The second sentence makes clear that the relationship will be one of comparison. If there were any doubt in your mind, it is resolved in the third sentence, where the likeness between film and opera as theater drama is noted. The paragraph continues to note similarities, and is thus a paragraph of comparison.

Here is another paragraph in which comparison is used. What is the comparison?

Many experts believe that the chimpanzee is next to man in intelligence. The Yerkes, however, reasonably expect that the gorilla would be, in view of the more pronounced resemblance in structure of the nervous systems in the gorilla and man. It may be that the former judgment is colored by human performances. The gorilla is sullen, untamable and ferocious, shy, wary, and slow-moving. The chimpanzee, on the other hand, is more lively, tractable, gregarious, and "humanizable"—besides being of smaller size, and less dangerous to man than the gorilla. The fact is that psychologists know a great deal about the intelligence of the chimpanzee, whereas the gorilla's is relatively unknown. Meanwhile, it should be stated that gregariousness and amiability are not quite identical with intelligence. And if gorillas do not go out of their way to show affection for their human hunters and captors, this can scarcely be adduced as evidence against a respectable I.Q.—WESTON LA BARRE

Using Contrast

In using **contrast,** the writer shows how two things differ. What two things are contrasted in the following paragraph?

> *Culture* puts the focus on the customs of a people. *Society* puts it upon the human beings who practice those customs. You can see and count the individuals who make up a society. You do not see a culture so directly. A picture of a way of life emerges from long-continued investigation. The anthropologist watches which individuals from a society do what, in what sequence, and for how long. He tries to be alert for what they might do but, in fact, seldom or never do. He listens to what they say and notes what they fail to say. He observes the objects they make and how they make them. From his enquiries he can derive the regularities in behavior that are the culture.—JACK ALLEN *et al.*

The contrast here, of course, is between culture and society.

Here is another paragraph of contrast. Can you identify what is being contrasted?

> The history of India provides both an inspiration and a challenge to the historian. It inspires by its vast range and scope, its color, its variety, its rich cluster of personalities; it challenges with its complexities, its long periods of obscurity, its unfamiliar movements, and its stark contrasts between luxury and poverty, between gentleness and cruelty, creation and destruction. For the few with gorgeous processions and rainbow pageantry there were the many with mud huts and a handful of rice or millet a day, with the burning heaven for a canopy and the stifling dust for perfume.—PERCIVAL SPEAR

Combining Comparison and Contrast

Sometimes it suits the needs of a writer to combine comparison and contrast in the same paragraph, just as you use similarities and differences to clarify your own thinking. When you buy a car, you determine how much it is like some other car and how it differs from that car. You are often inclined to compare and contrast one friend with another. Which of the points in the following paragraph show comparison, and which show contrast?

> It is to be assumed that if man were to live this life like a poem, he would be able to look upon the sunset of his life as his happiest period, and instead of trying to postpone the much feared old age, be able actually to look forward to it, and gradually build up to it as the best and happiest period of his existence. In my efforts to compare and contrast Eastern and Western life, I have found no differences that are absolute except in this matter of the attitude toward age, which is sharp and clearcut and permits of no intermediate positions. The differences in our attitude toward sex, toward women, and toward work, play and achievement are all relative. The relationship between husband and wife in China is not essentially different from that in the West, nor even the relationship between parent and child. Not even the ideas of individual liberty and democracy and the relationship between the people and their ruler are, after all, so different. But in the matter of our attitude toward age, the difference is absolute, and the East and the West take exactly opposite points of view.—LIN YUTANG

The writer speaks of the similarities in attitudes and relationships in Eastern and Western life. However, there is a striking contrast between the East and the West in their attitude toward age. The writer points out that this difference is "absolute," and he relates enough facts to make his point clear.

Exercises
The Paragraph of Comparison or Contrast

A. Write a paragraph in which you compare or contrast two places you know well. Be sure your topic sentence makes clear whether you are presenting a comparison or a contrast.

B. Select one of the following subjects, or one of your own, and develop it into a paragraph. Your topic sentence will make clear whether you are presenting similarities, differences, or a combination of the two.

1. Novels are much like short stories, only longer.
2. There are some similarities between riding a skateboard and riding a surfboard.
3. The riding experience in a small car is different from the riding experience in a large car.
4. Animals in zoos live different lives from animals in their natural habitat.
5. Although stage plays and movies are somewhat alike, they have their differences.
6. Life in a small town is quite different from life in a large city.
7. Men and women have essentially the same goals in life.
8. All performers have some qualities in common.
9. A hit-and-run driver who kills is no different from a murderer.
10. For several reasons I would rather take a train than a bus.

Part 4

The Paragraph of Narration

You are often involved in narration. When you tell a friend what happened to you on Friday night, you are narrating, telling a little story or anecdote. Such a story doesn't need a plot and characters and setting, as a real short story must have. Your only concern in telling your story is to convey to the listener or the reader a short account of whatever it was that happened to you. Here is a paragraph of narration. Note how simply and directly it is written.

> During the night we had already prepared our rescue net, and when with a rising sea Skipper Mees brought the *Insulinde* alongside the wreck, four persons were able to jump into the net. At the second attempt three succeeded in jumping across. In the meantime the day had fully dawned.

Again we tried. Everything cracked and creaked as we touched the wreck, but we got nobody across. We tried anew for the fourth time. The *Insulinde* thumped against the doomed ship, seeming to tear everything on board from its moorings, but no one jumped. The fifth attempt—again in vain. The sixth: no man saved. Six attempts in the furious surf in a raging storm—and five men still aboard the lost ship! Six times hurled against the wreck, again seeking space, again up and through the breakers to the waiting men, again alongside the ship. Six times under almost impossible circumstances, through ground swells and a treacherous surf, each time the *Insulinde* scraping the hard sand of the reef. I can assure you that it wasn't much fun.—KLAAS TOXOPEUS

This paragraph tells a brief but exciting story. It is actually an adventure tale in miniature.

Here is another paragraph of narration. See if you can re-tell the story line.

Statistics, it is sometimes said, can be made to prove anything. If you play around with the right figures in the right way you will always get the right answer. A good example of this once arose in a firm which made vitamin pills. Its sales department found that there was a definite relationship between the number of pills sold and the death rate. As the former increased the latter decreased in strict proportion. So on this basis the firm had only to step up production and sales enough to bring the death rate down to zero and then below zero, by which time it would have brought about the resurrection of the dead. On their own the statistics were sound enough, but the conclusions they led to were obviously absurd.—HENRY C. KING

Exercises
The Paragraph of Narration

A. Not all subjects, of course, can be treated in a narrative paragraph. Below is a list of subjects. Which of them could be subjects for narration? Think through each of the subjects carefully, because some of the subjects can be developed as narrative paragraphs and others as paragraphs using details. For example, think about a subject like this:

I'm lucky to have such a loving family.

You could develop this idea in a paragraph of details, giving examples of the love that members of your family express to each other. You could also develop the idea in a paragraph of narration by recounting an actual experience that revealed your family's love. Be ready to tell what it would be possible to say if you were to write paragraphs on the subjects.

1. A course in auto mechanics should be a must for everyone who drives a car.

2. A careless remark can hurt a sensitive person.

3. Two people can communicate even though they speak different languages.

4. Why are lakes such popular resort areas?

5. My mother's love of moving furniture around distresses my father.

6. I have one, only one, true friend.

7. She worked hard for her promotion.

8. Everyone likes some kind of music.

9. When I saw how beautiful the world looks at five o'clock in the morning, I decided I would get up early more often.

10. Courses in speech are helpful to many students.

11. If I told you about my trip to New York, you wouldn't believe me.

12. Attending a live concert certainly beats seeing it on TV.

13. I'll never forget the day I started ninth grade.

14. A magnet attracts metal filings.

15. I find it hard to believe what an expert can do with a skateboard.

16. Things were somehow more relaxed when I was in grade school.

17. I was late for band practice today.

18. Not everyone has a family like mine.

19. The best movie I have ever seen was _____.

20. Despite its blatant commercialism, Christmas is still an exciting time of the year.

B. Select a subject and develop it into a paragraph of narration. You may select one of the subjects in the preceding exercise, or a subject of your own.

Part 5
The Paragraph of Explanation

One of the purposes of a paragraph of explanation is to give reasons for something that happened. For example, you might want to explain why your football team lost, why you were late for an appointment, why you forgot to return a phone call, or why you failed a test. Explanations of this kind are not difficult to write because they are reconstructed from your own experience.

Explaining How Something Works

To explain how something works requires a logical presentation of ideas and enough information to enable the reader to follow your thinking and understand what you are saying. The following paragraph is an explanation of how something works.

Echo-sounding apparatus consists essentially of two pieces of equipment. One transmits sound signals through the water, and the other receives these signals after they have been reflected back from the sea floor. Sound waves travel through water at a more-or-less constant speed—about one mile per second. Thus the depth of water can be calculated from the time between transmission and reception of a given signal. On most early models, automatic echo-sounding was possible only to depths of about five hundred fathoms (or three thousand feet). Individual measurements of greater depths had to be made by using an ordinary clock to estimate the time gap between transmission and reception of sound waves. Consequently, even as late as 1939, comparatively few soundings had been made in the deeper parts of the oceans.—KEITH CLAYTON

After the writer tells you that echo-sounding apparatus consists of two pieces of equipment, he explains how each piece works. He also explains how earlier equipment worked and why it limited scientific investigation.

Explaining an Idea

Explaining an idea or a concept is probably the most difficult kind of explanation because it is more complex. The following paragraph explains three Hindu concepts.

A unique idea that pervades all Hindu thinking and forms, as it were, the mental atmosphere which the traditional Hindu breathed, is the concept of *karma*. *Karma* is literally "action" and the concept may be described as the law of consequences. Every action, good or bad, has its consequence or fruit. The consequence comes back to the individual, the fruit must be plucked or the crop reaped, by a law from which there is no escape. This idea is closely linked with that of transmigration of the soul, or reincarnation, since the fruits of one's actions clearly cannot all be experienced in a single physical existence. These two ideas are intimately interwoven into the texture of the Hindu mind, from the prince to the peasant, from the philosopher to the worldly-wise merchant. They serve as a justification of the whole system of caste, justifying both the claims of the privileged and the disabilities of the lowly.—PERCIVAL SPEAR

After reading this paragraph, you can understand why explaining ideas can be so complex. Considering that the concept is philosophical in nature and foreign to our culture, the writer has achieved a truly fine explanation. It is clear, intelligent, and interesting.

The Paragraph of Explanation

A. The following subjects are starting points for paragraphs of explanation that involve reasons. Choose one of these, or one of your own, and write a paragraph of explanation.

1. He was unable to keep up with the rest of the class.
2. The Paris world of fashion no longer dictates women's clothing styles.
3. Victims of criminals are now being told their rights.
4. When it is winter in the United States, it is summer in Australia.
5. Diet pills can have harmful side effects.
6. Pilots often try to get into the jet stream.
7. Automobile insurance is costly.
8. Color photography is more popular than black and white.

B. Write a paragraph that explains a process—how something works. Explain how a helicopter can stay in the air, how a hurricane develops, how to grow tomatoes, how to bowl. Choose a subject of your own, but be certain that it describes a process.

C. Write a paragraph explaining an idea. For example, you could write about brotherhood or sisterhood, charity, respect, prejudice, selfishness, self-denial, or any other idea you would like to explain. Because most ideas are too large to handle in a single paragraph, limit your subject accordingly.

Part 6

The Paragraph of Definition

If a writer used the word *sesquipedalian* in a book you were reading, you would expect him to define the word, for the term isn't widely used. If someone described you as *analphabetic*, you would certainly want to know what he meant. You might be confronted with words like *abecedarian*, *syzygy*, and *hemi-*

demisemiquaver, which you might not understand. Even shorter and more common words may need definition, especially if the author uses them in an unusual way.

The following paragraph is one of definition. Notice that the author tries to explain the meaning of a word in a conversational, informal way. He doesn't settle merely for a dictionary definition.

> The equality of all men is one of the most fundamental aspects of the democratic doctrine, but it is frequently misunderstood. Those who believe in democracy do not hold that all men are *identical*, but only that in some *basic* respects they are all *equal*. In the Jewish-Christian religious tradition, all men are equal before God. His challenge to every human being is the same, although man's response to that challenge varies enormously. In the classical humanist tradition, from the Greeks onward, all men share—ever and above differences of race, religion, nationality, and class—one common trait: the ability to reason. In this view, men are more than members of a particular social, economic, or national group. Their basic equality comes from what they have in common rather than from what separates them.—
> WILLIAM EBENSTEIN

Exercises
The Paragraph of Definition

A. Here is a good beginning for a paragraph of definition. Examine it closely and then complete the paragraph by explaining both the positive and the negative sides of liberty as you would define them.

> In the dictionary, liberty is defined as freedom from external restraints or compulsion. The definition is not incorrect but is too narrow, because liberty means freedom *from* having to do something, as well as freedom *to* do something. In this sense, liberty may be said to possess two sides—a positive and a negative.

B. Defining something well and interestingly can be difficult. Try to define some simple object that you see every day. For example, you might think it easy to define a chair: "A chair is something one sits on." However, you sit on desks, on the floor, on the corner of a bed. So you try again: "A chair is something with four legs," or "A chair is made of wood." You can see that these definitions, too, are inadequate because they do not define a chair as distinct from other things. Choose one of the following things to define, or something of your own choice. Be sure to choose something commonplace and try to define it absolutely.

A yard
A chicken
A cold in the head
A pair of eye glasses
A ballpoint pen

Part 7

The Paragraph of Reasoning

To reason with someone, you must take him carefully through the steps you took to arrive at a conclusion. You can't browbeat him or outshout him. You must be logical and persuasive. Here is a paragraph of reasoning. What is the topic sentence? What are the steps in reasoning that the writer goes through?

The German decision of 1917 gives a perspective to Wilson's neutrality policies that was not available at the time. It seems likely that Germany would have unleashed its submarines the moment it had enough built to make such a tactic feasible. It would have done so irrespective of American policy. Once Germany declared unrestricted warfare on all vessels, the United States would have been forced, as the price of peace, either to suffer without retaliation heavy loss of life at sea or to end its trade with Europe. An embargo on American commerce would have been even less practicable in 1914 than it had been during the Napoleonic wars. Once the Germans had enough U-boats, they could not have been stopped from declaring unrestricted warfare by anything less than a strong show of American force—and American force was not great enough in these years to be effective—or by total American collaboration. World War I was a revolutionary effort to change the distribution of power in Europe. Since Germany believed, probably correctly, that it could not overthrow Allied supremacy without destroying American commerce, it is not clear that there was any policy open to the United States which would not ultimately have led to American intervention.—WILLIAM E. LEUCHTENBURG

Exercise
The Paragraph of Reasoning

Write down a non-debatable fact and construct a list of reasons why it is a fact. Then develop your reasons into a paragraph with a good, topic sentence and a clincher sentence. Here is an example of what you are to do.

FACT:

Football is America's favorite spectator sport.

REASONS:

1. The rules are easy to learn, so it is a game most Americans can understand as they watch.

2. People like violence. Football, with the possible exception of hockey, is the most violent game we have.

3. Sitting in the stands on a beautiful fall afternoon is pleasant.

4. People enjoy the excitement and sociability of the crowd of spectators.

You may develop one of the following subjects, or one of your own.

1. Some people fear flying.
2. A circus appeals to young and old alike.

3. Athletes are much admired.
4. Many people take their dogs to obedience school.
5. It is possible to be over-educated for a job.
6. A typewriter is a surprisingly complicated machine.
7. The handicapped often do more and better work than people who are not handicapped.
8. The water heater uses more energy than any other appliance you have.
9. We live in fear of the lawless.
10. There are good reasons why we should have a 30-hour work week.

Part 8

The Paragraph of Argument or Persuasion

Argument and persuasion work hand in hand. Though they are sometimes treated as separate processes, it is almost impossible to separate the one from the other. Therefore, accept these definitions somewhat warily. Argument is the presentation of a point of view. Assume, for example, that a person has attacked you for being a conservationist. You reply to the person by *arguing* in favor of conservation, giving as many convincing reasons as you can in its favor. You are not, you understand, trying to *persuade* the person to pick up every discarded soft-drink can he sees, or to ride everywhere in a car pool. You are simply presenting an argument without necessarily trying to persuade the person to act upon the information you give him.

As you can see, people seldom argue without also trying to persuade. You are not likely to write an editorial in the student newspaper arguing the case for shorter school days or less homework unless you are trying to persuade somebody to do something about the length of the school day or the amount of homework that is given. See if you can find both argument and persuasion in the paragraphs that follow.

In our day the Constitution has been used to shield racketeers, gangsters, and those suspected of radicalism from the necessity of testifying about their activities before courts and legislative investigating committees. It has prevented the censorship of books, magazines, and movies offensive to many groups; upset the convictions of criminals found guilty by juries; blocked religious instruction in the public schools. Constitutional restraints (Fourth Amendment) on police make warrants necessary for searches of homes and offices for evidence of crime and forbid the police to use the third degree or drugs to get confessions from persons accused of crime. When these things occur, some citizens are likely to object that the courts are soft on criminals and that constitutional rights which protect enemies of society and members of despised political minorities should be abolished or, at least, cut down. The ordinary lawabiding citizen has no need of such protection, they argue. With crime rising in our major cities, with juvenile delinquency spreading among youth, with the spread of illegal gambling, drug addiction, sex offenses, with the competition between the United States and the Soviet Union and China for world leadership, should we not strengthen the hand of government and law-enforcement officers?

Did you notice how many factual occurrences the writer uses to introduce his point of view? These undeniable occurrences gain the attention and respect of the reader and arouse his curiosity as to the purpose of the argument. The writer then presents some likely objections to the occurrences and ends with a question that is designed to persuade you to his point of view. Both argument and persuasion in this paragraph are handled with intelligence and skill.

Here is another paragraph by the same writer. Is his handling of argument and persuasion any different from his preceding paragraph?

We reject the implication that a responsible citizen must participate in the political process. Those who vote simply because they have been told that they should—and feel guilty if they do not—may be among those who vote for mules, favor the first names on the ballot, and elect dead men to offices that have been abolished. We believe that a person who is mature and responsible will vote because he senses the relationship between the quality of the society in which he lives and his own well-being. He will want, therefore, to cooperate with others in order to ensure that the conditions of progress for himself and the society are maintained. By eliminating the burden of guilt about political participation, we may be able to arrive at an understanding whereby free, willing individuals spontaneously take part in the political process in order to extend the area of creativity for themselves, in order to express more adequately the obligation they feel toward the society, and to discharge more handsomely the debt they believe they owe society.

In this paragraph, the writer reverses his previous order of argument and persuasion. He begins with a direct, uncompromising statement of what he believes and then gives the reasons to support that statement. While he uses reasons instead of facts as arguments, his reasons appeal to society's highest moral and ethical standards. It is difficult to resist this kind of persuasion.

Exercise
The Paragraph of Argument or Persuasion

Combining both argument and persuasion, write a paragraph on a subject you know well and have strong feelings about. For example, you might wish to write about the women's movement, student power, cheating, testing, class bullies, or any other subject you feel strongly about.

Part 9

The Paragraph of Analogy

An analogy is a comparison in which you usually compare something difficult to understand with something very much like it but easier to understand. For example, a computer might be compared with the brain. There are circuits in each, each has a memory, and each gives answers and solutions. While nothing is ever exactly like something else, it is relatively easy to understand a computer by showing in what ways it is similar to the brain.

In the following paragraph of analogy, what is being compared?

> It is a curious phenomenon of nature that only two species practice the art of war—men and ants, both of which, ironically, maintain complex social organizations. This does not mean that only men and ants engage in the murder of their own kind. Many animals of the same species kill each other, but only men and ants have practiced the science of organized destruction, employing their massed numbers in violent combat and relying on strategy and tactics to meet developing situations or to capitalize on the weaknesses in the strategy and tactics of the other side. The longest continuous war ever fought between men lasted thirty years. The longest ant war ever recorded lasted six-and-a-half weeks, or whatever the corresponding units would be in ant reckoning.—NORMAN COUSINS

It is not too difficult to see that the art of war as practiced by men and by ants is being compared.

Here is another paragraph of analogy. What is being compared?

> Machines and tools have always been created in the image of man. The hammer grew from the balled fist, the rake from the hand with fingers outstretched for scratching; the shovel from the hand hollowed to scoop. As machines became more than simple tools, outstripping their creators in performance, demanding and obtaining increasing amounts of power, and acquiring superhuman speeds and accuracies, their outward resemblance to the natural model disappeared; only the names of the machine's parts show vestiges of their human origin. The highly complex machinery of the modern industrial age has arms that swing,

fingers that fold, legs that support, teeth that grind, and male and female parts that mate. Machines feed on material, run when things go well, and spit and cough when they don't.—JOHN H. TROLL

You are probably aware that machines and tools are considered to be extensions of parts of the human body. This paragraph reveals the specific comparisons between them.

Exercise
The Paragraph of Analogy

Select one of the following comparisons, or one of your own, and develop it into a paragraph of analogy. Be sure to make specific, believable comparisons.

1. Civilization is like a beehive.
2. Supervising a kitchen is like running a factory.
3. Reading is like sailing away in a tall ship.
4. Vacation is like have a battery charged.
5. Friendship is sometimes like a boxing match.

Review Exercise
Types of Paragraphs

Study the following paragraphs and determine how each was developed. Be ready to support your answer.

1

She was a big awkward woman, with big bones and hard rubbery flesh. Her short arms ended in ham hands, and her neck was a squat roll of fat that protruded behind her head as a big bump. Her skin was rough and puffy, with plump molelike freckles down her cheeks. Her eyes glowered from under the mountain of her brow and were circled with expensive mauve shadow. They were nervous and quick when she was flustered and darted about at nothing in particular while she was dressing hair or talking to people.—
ALICE WALKER

2

Earthquakes are caused by stresses that develop within the upper layers of the earth, usually within the crust. As the stresses build up, the rocks are increasingly distorted until they can no longer withstand the pressure. Suddenly they fracture, or break, and spring back toward their original positions. The sudden fracture of the rocks causes the development of the shock waves that we call an earthquake. The shocks of a severe quake may last for several minutes, its waves spreading out in every direction from the original break. Often the first violent break is followed by aftershocks as other stresses fracture other rocks in the area. Sometimes these aftershocks are very severe and very frequent and they may take weeks or months to die away.—KEITH CLAYTON

3

By the summer of A.D. 79, life in Pompeii and Herculaneum must have been very pleasant. Set in a fertile countryside with a warm climate, both towns could offer visitors delicious fruits in abundance and a variety of delicate wines from the vineyards that flourished on the slopes of Vesuvius. Pompeii, with its shops, offices, and busy market, its amphitheatre, public baths, and taverns, had all the bustle of a typical Roman country town. Herculaneum was smaller, quieter, and more secluded. There were no chariots rattling through its cobbled streets as they did through the streets of Pompeii, and its inhabitants—mainly wealthy people—were content to live away from the hurly-burly of trade and commerce. Life was carried on in quiet dignity.—HENRY GARNETT

4

One of the most striking things about volcanoes is their great variety of both appearance and behavior. Most people's mental image of a volcano is typified by the symmetrical cone of Fujiyama, the sacred Japanese mountain near Tokyo. By contrast, Mauna Loa, in Hawaii, consists of a much more gently sloping cone. It is built up from an enormous heap of basalt, about seventy miles in diameter at its base. Some volcanoes erupt periodically; others destroy themselves in one great cataclysm; still others erupt continuously but quietly, like a pan of stew bubbling over a low flame.—KEITH CLAYTON

5

On reaching Hispaniola, Captain Lowther sighted and approached a French vessel which had a cargo of wine and brandy. Pretending that he was a merchant who desired to purchase certain wines and brandies of the Frenchman's ample stock, he went on board to view the liquors. The pirate then carried his deception further by offering a price for the greater part of the cargo, which the Frenchman refused. This annoyed the buccaneer, so he stepped closer to the French captain and whispered in his ear that they were going to take all the cargo anyway without paying anything. Terror-stricken, the Frenchman collapsed, and Lowther ordered the immediate removal of thirty casks of brandy, five hogsheads of wine, and other valuable goods in the cargo. As the Frenchman had given in so easily, Lowther presented him with five pounds for his trouble.—EDWARD ROWE SNOW

6

The river was dark and swift, and there were jagged panes of ice along the banks, encrusted with snow. The valley was gray and cold; the mountains were dark and dim on the sky, and a great, gray motionless cloud of snow and mist lay out in the depth of the canyon. The fields were bare and colorless, and the gray tangle of branches rose up out of the orchards like antlers and bones. The town lay huddled in the late winter noon, the upper walls and vigas were stained with water, and thin black columns of smoke rose above the roofs, swelled, and hung out against the low ceiling of the sky. The streets were empty, and here and there were drifts of hard and brittle snow about the fence posts and the stones, pocked with soil and cinders. There was no telling of the sun, save for the one cold, dim, and even light that lay on every corner of the land and made no shadow, and the silence was close by and all around and the bell made no impression upon it. There was no motion to be seen but the single brief burst and billow of the smoke. And out of the town on the old road southward the snow lay unbroken, sloping up on either side of the rocks and the junipers and the dunes. A huge old jack rabbit bounded across the hillside in a blur of great sudden angles and settled away in the snow, still and invisible.—N. SCOTT MOMADAY

7

What I mean by education is learning the rules of this mighty game. In other words, education is the instruction of the intellect in the laws of Nature, under which name I include not merely things and their forces, but men and their ways; and the fashioning of the affections and of the will into an earnest and loving desire to move in harmony with those laws. For me, education means neither more nor less than this. Anything which professes to call itself education must be tried by this standard, and if it fails to stand the test, I will not call it education, whatever may be the force of authority or of numbers upon the other side.— THOMAS HENRY HUXLEY

8

If we take a golf ball to pieces we find that it is made of a series of concentric layers. On the surface is a white, hard material that makes up the thin outer crust. The rest of the ball is made of quite different materials. Immediately beneath this outer covering is a layer built up of thin rubber strands. Within this layer is a small, hollow rubber ball that contains a thick, sticky liquid. Most people, on seeing a golf ball for the first time, would find it impossible to describe its interior without first taking the ball to pieces. But in fact we can discover quite a lot simply by observing the behavior of the ball and by examining the crust. We could start by shaving off a sliver of the crust and weighing it. If we then compared its density (that is, its weight per unit volume) with the whole ball, we should find that the figures are different. The fact that the ball bounces well suggests that it contains some highly elastic material. From our knowledge of its density and its elasticity, we might well deduce that the interior was made of rubber.—KEITH CLAYTON

9

Proceeding from worship to daily life, we find further differences between the Hindu and the Muslim. The Hindu, for example, is in the main a vegetarian, and some are so strict as to abstain from eggs and even from red-colored vegetables like the beet. In particular he regards beef, that mainstay of so many millions in the West, with repulsion bordering on horror. The Muslim has no such feelings about meat in general and beef in particular, but for him pork is unclean and wine is forbidden. The Hindu observes frequent short fasts; their vogue was utilized by Mahatma Gandhi in his long fasts for political or moral purposes. The Muslim has his month of fasting, whose observance is a point of honor. While these are curious customs indeed, they are things that need not affect basic processes of thought or standards of value.—PERCIVAL SPEAR

10

She tried to be sexy and stylish, and was, in her fashion, with a predominant taste for pastel taffetas and orange shoes. In the summertime she paid twenty dollars for big umbrella hats with bows and flowers on them and when she wore black and white together she would liven it up with elbow-length gloves of red satin. She was genuinely undecided when she woke up in the morning whether she really outstripped the other girls in town for beauty, but could convince herself that she was equally good-looking by the time she had breakfast on the table. She was always talking with a lot of extra movement to her thick coarse mouth, with its hair tufts at the corners, and when she drank coffee she held the cup over the saucer with her little finger sticking out, while she crossed her short hairy legs at the knees. —ALICE WALKER

Chapter 9

The Composition

A composition is a piece of writing that develops an idea or expands a topic in a coherent and unified manner. The paragraphs in a composition must adequately develop a topic or an idea, must be logically connected, and must form a complete whole.

In this chapter you will study the following basic steps involved in writing a composition.

1. Choosing and limiting your subject
2. Writing down your ideas
3. Organizing your ideas
4. Outlining
5. Writing your first draft
6. Revising
7. Writing your final draft

Following this step-by-step procedure will enable you to write an effective composition, one that proceeds in an orderly manner toward the goal you wish to achieve.

Part 1
Choosing Your Subject

The first step in writing any composition is to decide on a subject. What is worth writing about? It is anything worth thinking about. What is a worthwhile subject for your composition? It is anything that interests you. Remember, however, that you must develop your subject in a coherent and unified manner. Therefore you must ask yourself whether you know enough about your subject to discuss it in some depth. If you do not, are you willing to research the subject enough to allow you to develop it more fully? Will you be able to do the required research? Is the information available? Do you know where to find it? The range of subjects available to you is limited only by your own interests and the available information.

If you are interested in social problems, you might want to write about efforts to revitalize the residential areas of large cities or the difficulties retired people encounter when living on a fixed income or the prospects for programs of preventive medical care.

If you watch television, you might want to write about the portrayal of American family life on situation comedy series or the quality of network news programs.

Your composition will benefit from your genuine interest in the subject you choose to write about. On the other hand, your composition will suffer if your interest in it is slight.

Limiting Your Subject

The composition you will write will consist of five paragraphs and will total approximately 500 words. Because you will not be able to develop any broad or general subject within those limits, you will have to limit or narrow the scope of your subject. Consider the subject of communication. It is a boundless subject, and an adequate treatment of it would fill many volumes. If you were to limit it, you might follow a process similar to the following, continually dividing each large subject into two smaller ones. In each pair, the subject in boldface type is the one chosen for further subdivision.

UNLIMITED:	Communication
SLIGHT LIMITATION:	History of Communication **Modern Communication**
2000-WORD LIMITATION:	Postal Service Today **Television Today**
1000-WORD LIMITATION:	Television Entertainment Today **Informative Television Today**
500-WORD LIMITATION:	Consumer Information *via* Television **The Limitations of Network News**

Exercise
Limiting the Subject

The following list of subjects is too large for adequate treatment in a 500-word composition. Within each subject, find three narrow subjects suitable for a composition of that length. Keep your list of subjects for a later exercise.

1.	Energy	6.	Sports
2.	Government	7.	Art
3.	Superstition	8.	Rivers
4.	Cities	9.	Stars
5.	Transportation	10.	Literature

Determining the Controlling Purpose of Your Composition

It is important to write down a clear statement of your controlling purpose and keep it in front of you through all stages of your composition. If the nature of your subject forces you to revise your original controlling purpose, make the necessary change, but be sure that all parts of your composition reflect that change. Your composition and your controlling purpose must work hand in hand: your composition should achieve what your controlling purpose sets out to do. Keep referring to your controlling purpose and employ it as a guide as your work progresses.

In a statement of controlling purpose, the most common verbs are *to explain, to show, to demonstrate.* For example, if you chose to write on the subject of network news, your controlling purpose might be stated like this:

> The controlling purpose of this composition is to show that network news programs do not adequately inform the public.

This statement will not appear in your composition, at least not in the form of a statement of purpose, nor will it be your title. It is intended for your own use as a way of controlling your thinking and writing, helping you to stick to the point and to stay on course.

Exercises
Determining the Controlling Purpose of a Composition

A. In the exercise on page 171 you limited each of ten broad subjects to three possible subjects for compositions of 500 words. Choose three of these limited subjects and write for each a statement of the controlling purpose that you would follow in developing the composition. Save your statements for use in a later exercise.

B. Choose a subject for your own composition and limit it sufficiently for a 500-word paper. Then write a one-sentence controlling purpose for your composition.

Part 2
Writing Down Your Ideas

You have chosen a subject and limited it. You have also established a controlling purpose for your composition. Your next step is to write down your ideas on the subject you have chosen.

The purpose of this step is to get as many ideas as possible down on paper. You will organize and polish those ideas later, so don't concern yourself with order, relative importance, or phrasing. At the top of your paper, write your title if you already have one. If not, leave the space blank, to be filled in later. Write your controlling purpose below your title space so that you can use it to guide your thinking. Then begin to jot down whatever ideas come to mind.

As you begin to write down ideas, you may find that you haven't as many ideas on your subject as you thought you had. You may have to do more extensive reading or research in the subject you have chosen. You may find that you are not certain of the accuracy of some points. If so, you will have to check these points in reference books or other source material. (See Chapter 11 on The Library and Its Reference Materials.) When you have completed any additional research, you can add to your list of ideas.

Your first list of ideas might look something like this (ignore the asterisks):

TENTATIVE TITLE

CONTROLLING PURPOSE The controlling purpose of this composition is to show that network news programs do not adequately inform the public.

a half hour of news is too short
television too dependent on
visual stories

* everybody sees television
* television polls have an undue
    influence
  oversimplification in TV news
  shallowness
  depth possible in newspapers
  television dependent on brief
    stories
  paternal newscasters
  newspapers more idea-oriented
  television more personality-
    oriented
  Jefferson's notion of an informed
    populace
  uninformed or misinformed public
    will act foolishly
  intrusive commercials
* rise in newspaper cost
  decline in newspaper readership
  public dependence on TV news
* economics of television
* emergency programing
* famous newscasters
* famous reporters
* portable cameras
* history of TV news
* ratings of news shows

A review of the list of ideas will show you that some are not closely related to the controlling purpose of the composition. These unrelated ideas, marked with asterisks, should be eliminated so that the focus of the composition remains clear and well-defined:

  everybody sees television
  television polls have an undue
    influence
  rise in newspaper cost

emergency programing
famous newscasters
famous reporters
portable cameras
ratings of news shows

Two ideas are too broad to be treated within the limit of 500 words. These unmanageable ideas should also be eliminated:

economics of television
history of TV news

When reviewing your list of ideas, ask yourself the following questions:

1. Is this idea directly related to the controlling purpose?
2. Can this idea be developed adequately, along with the others, in 500 words?

If the answer to either question is no, the idea should be eliminated.

After you have reviewed your list of ideas and eliminated all those that are unrelated or unmanageable, study those that remain in search of ideas for your tentative title. Try to write two or three possible titles at this time. They will also help to focus your work as you write, and you can eliminate two later. Possible titles for this subject include the following:

What's the Use of Network News?
Sorry, Mr. Jefferson
Network News Is Not Enough

As you develop your composition further, you may find that some of the remaining ideas are not so appropriate to your purpose as they had seemed earlier, or that some ideas cannot be adequately developed within the limits of your composition. If so, do not hesitate to eliminate those ideas. Your composition will be further improved by the elimination of every inappropriate or unmanageable idea.

Exercises
Writing Down the Ideas

A. In Exercise A on page 172, you wrote a controlling purpose for each of three limited subjects. Select two of these controlling purposes and list under them all the ideas that come to your mind for developing that subject. After studying your lists, (1) eliminate every idea that is irrelevant to the controlling purpose, and (2) eliminate every idea that cannot adequately be developed in a 500-word composition. Save these lists for use in a later exercise.

B. Do the same as above for the subject you have chosen for your composition.

Part 3
Organizing Your Ideas

After eliminating those ideas that are unmanageable within the 500-word limit of your composition and those that are not directly relevant to your controlling purpose, you are left with only those that are manageable and relevant, and it remains now to order them into a coherent pattern for development.

First examine your remaining list of ideas in search of major points. Look for three major points, corresponding to the three paragraphs that will make up the body of your composition.

In the ideas on the subject of network news programs, notice that "oversimplification in TV news" is a major point in support of the controlling purpose. The following ideas are related to this point:

a half hour of news is too short
television too dependent on visual stories
shallowness
television dependent on brief stories
paternal newscasters
intrusive commercials

A second major point is "depth possible in newspapers," and the following ideas are directly related:

> newspapers more idea-oriented
> television more personality-oriented
> decline in newspaper readership
> public dependence on TV news

The third major point seems to be "Jefferson's notion of an informed populace," with related idea that "uninformed or misinformed public will act foolishly."

There are now three major ideas to be developed:

> oversimplification in TV news
> depth possible in newspapers
> Jefferson's notion of an informed populace

The first job of organization has been accomplished: grouping into three major categories. The second job is to determine in what order each of the major points should be developed in order to present the reader with an orderly and logical piece of reasoning. To determine a logical order of development, ask yourself which of the major points, if any, cannot be understood without the others. Clearly these must follow the others.

The controlling purpose of the composition on the subject of television news is as follows:

> The controlling purpose of this composition is to show that network news programs do not adequately inform the public.

Since the composition will be building to the conclusion that network news programs do not adequately inform the public, it seems logical that the major idea of oversimplification in television news should come last. Jefferson's notion of an informed populace would logically come first, since it establishes a reason for concern over the inadequacy of television news. And the comparison of the depth possible in newspapers can fall between the two, partly as a link between the past—the informed populace that Jefferson had in mind—and the present —the ill-informed public of the television age. Thus the final order of ideas in developing the composition will be as follows:

Jefferson's notion of an informed populace
depth possible in newspapers
oversimplification in TV news

The groups of subordinate ideas can now be organized into a logical order of development under their respective major points. New ideas are almost certain to come to you at this time, and the act of organizing the ideas is likely to make some seem less potent than they had seemed at first. Do not hesitate to add or eliminate at this stage.

At this point in the organization it was necessary to do some additional reading on Jefferson's notion of an informed populace because it lacked sufficient supporting ideas. The grouped ideas for the composition on the subject of television news programs might now resemble the following:

Jefferson's notion of an informed populace
    vital to democracy
    political decisions based on reason
    uninformed public would focus on personality
    fear of demagogues

depth possible in newspapers
    long, careful analyses of issues
    declining newspaper readership
    increasing dependence on television

oversimplification of TV news
    television too dependent on visual stories
    intrusive commercials
    dependence on brief stories
    shallowness
    paternal newscasters

Exercises
Organizing the Ideas

A. Refer to the lists of ideas you developed for two subjects in Exercise A on page 176. Organize each set of ideas into three major points and related subordinate ideas. Then order the ideas in the sequence in which you would expect to develop them in a 500-word composition. Save this work for use in a later exercise.

B. Do the same as above with the ideas you have listed for your own composition.

Part 4
Outlining

Your preliminary organization of your ideas will now serve as the basis for an outline. The outline will show all the ideas in this sequential and logical relationship to one another. An outline is, in effect, a schematic diagram of the relationships among ideas.

Two outline forms are in wide use. One is the **sentence outline,** in which all ideas are expressed in complete sentences; the other, briefer form is the **topic outline,** in which the ideas are expressed in words or phrases. You will make a topic outline for your composition.

Outlining Procedure

1. Leave space at the top of the page for a final title.

2. Write the statement of your controlling purpose two spaces below the line allotted for the title.

3. Use standard outline form. The following example is a sample arrangement of numerals and letters that will constitute the form of your outline.

```
I.
   A.
   B.
      1.
      2.
         a.
         b.
            (1)
            (2)
               (a)
               (b)
II. (etc.)
```

4. Number your main headings with Roman numerals. Use capital letters for subtopics under each main heading. Divide your subtopics in descending order of importance: first Arabic numerals, then small letters, then Arabic numerals in parentheses, then small letters in parentheses.

5. Indent subtopics, placing the letters or numerals directly below the first letter of the first word in your preceding topic or subtopic.

6. Do not use the words *Introduction, Body,* and *Conclusion* in your outline. These are merely organizational terms used in planning a composition.

7. Use only one idea for each topic or subtopic.

8. Do not use a single subtopic. Use either two or more or none at all. A topic cannot be divided into fewer than two parts.

9. Begin the first word of each topic and subtopic with a capital letter. Do not use periods after topics or subtopics.

10. Make all main topics parallel in form. Make each group of subtopics parallel in form. For example, if the first main topic is a noun, all the other main topics must be nouns. If the first subtopic under the main topic is an

adjective, the remainder of that group of subtopics must also be adjectives.

Example of an Outline

Following is a completed outline, sharpened and refined, for the body of the composition on the subject of television news programs. Notice that parts I and V have not yet been completed; these will be, respectively, the introduction and the conclusion. Notice also that the title has not yet been decided.

The controlling purpose of this composition is to show that network news programs do not adequately inform the public.

I.

II. The function of news in a democracy

    A. Jefferson's notion of an informed populace

        1. Capable of evaluating political issues

        2. Capable of basing decisions on reason

    B. Jefferson's fears for an uninformed populace

        1. Inability to make intelligent decisions

        2. Inclination to focus on personalities

        3. Tendency to follow demagogues

III. Newspapers and television as sources of news

    A. Traditional dependence on newspapers

    B. Advantages of newspapers

    C. Decline in newspaper readership

    D. Increasing dependence on television

IV. Limitations of television news reporting

    A. Brevity

    B. Dependence on visual stories

    C. Interruption by commercial breaks

    D. Focus on personalities

V.

Exercises
Making an Outline

A. In the following list you will find all the ideas necessary for a topic outline on the subject of oil.

Arrange the ideas in outline form, using every item and numbering and lettering each item properly as a main topic or a subtopic. Which item could serve as a title?

Supports modern technology
In everyday life
Effect of oil on our economy
Creates jobs
Chemical composition
In international trade
Possible substitutes for oil
Oil-rich areas
History of oil
The uses of oil
Varieties
In transportation
Important facts about oil
Energy value
In Industry
Viscosity
Creates pollution problems
Oil and Society

B. Briefly review the following outline and then correct it, keeping in mind the following points: (1) Every topic and subtopic must relate to the controlling purpose. (2) Main topics should be parallel in form; each group of subtopics should be parallel in form. (3) Subtopics should never be fewer than two. (4) Organizational terms should never be used. (5) In a topic outline, complete sentences should not be used.

LIFE IN AN INSTANT CITY

I. Introduction: The instant city a relatively new phenomenon

II. Profile of typical instant city
   A. Residential area
      1. Single-family dwellings
      2. Contrasting with suburban homes
   B. May also include industrial area
   C. Commercial areas included by design

III. Describe the population
   A. Economic mix
   B. Backgrounds—includes blue-collar workers and professionals

IV. These cities are luring people away from suburbs and more established urban areas
   A. Convenience
      1. Self-contained transportation network
   B. Leisure activities
      1. Boating
      2. Social organizations
      3. Many provide entertainment complexes
   C. They provide some of the advantages of a city with the feeling of a small town
   D. Education
      1. Centralized schools, for economy
      2. Recruiting teachers

C. In Exercise A on page 176, you organized the ideas for two subjects into the major points and their related ideas in the order you would develop each of them in a fve-paragraph composition. Now put the ordered ideas for these two subjects into proper topic outline form according to the instructions in this section.

D. Do the same as above with the order of ideas for your own composition.

Part 5
Writing Your First Draft

You now have a statement of controlling purpose and an outline of the body of your composition to work from. You are now ready to begin the actual writing of a first draft, which will include all the information in your outline and also an introduction and a conclusion.

While the work you have already done will serve as a base for the writing itself, you may find that you have a difficult time beginning. If you find it so, begin with the second paragraph, which is the first paragraph that appears on your outline. The information for this paragraph is already at hand, and the introduction can be written later, even as the last writing you do for the composition.

Keep in mind that you are writing a first draft. Concentrate on getting your ideas expressed in a logical manner, and don't worry too much about sentence structure, word choice, or punctuation. These matters can be adjusted when you revise the first draft.

Remember that the composition will have three basic parts —a beginning, a middle, and an end. These basic parts are usually called the introduction, the body, and the conclusion. The composition as a whole will be only as strong as the weakest of these parts. The following sections will consider the writing of each part in turn.

The Introduction

The introduction to a composition serves two purposes: it *introduces* the reader to the subject, and it *interests* the reader in the subject. In a five-paragraph composition, the introduction should be limited to a single paragraph. Many techniques can be used to construct an effective introduction, including the use of a quotation, startling statistics, or an interesting anecdote.

The composition on the subject of television news programs might begin with any of the following introductions.

QUOTATION: Mails from the North—the East—the West —the South—whence, according to some curious etymologists, comes the magical word NEWS.—THOMAS DE QUINCEY

STATISTIC: According to a recent survey conducted by The Center for the Study of Public Information, a full sixty percent of American voters get all their information about political issues from nightly television news programs.

ANECDOTE: In conversation over lunch one day last week, I asked a friend of mine whether she thought the water control bill should pass. "I don't know anything about it," she said. "Was it on TV?"

Each of these introductions goes beyond merely getting the reader's attention; each tells the reader what the subject of the composition will be: specifically, the news. But two of the three, the final two, are stronger than the first because they raise the key issue of the composition: the question of the adequacy of television news programs as the public's primary source of political information. The first might be strengthened by the addition of a statement like the following.

It is certainly true that the news comes from all directions, but if we get our news solely from television, it might be said that we are getting more magic than fact.

Regardless of the device used to open a composition, the introduction should never be merely a lifeless restatement of the controlling purpose such as the following:

This composition will discuss the shortcomings of television news programs.

Remember that the controlling purpose is a device that the writer of a composition uses to keep the composition focused on a single purpose; it will never serve the two functions of an adequate introduction—to introduce the subject and to interest the reader.

Exercises
Writing an Effective Introduction

A. Choose three of the following introductions to rewrite and expand in order to make them both informative and interesting. Use a quotation, a statistic, or an anecdote.

1. It seems to me that the invention of the camera changed our understanding of cultures around the world.
2. Everyone should know something about the history of his or her local community.
3. We really know very little about this small and fragile planet we live on.
4. Many people underestimate the skill required to train animals to perform in films.
5. The Nobel Prizes have an interesting history.

B. Keeping in mind the purposes and possibilities for effective introductions, write a first paragraph for your composition. Remember that it should both introduce the subject and interest your reader. Review your introduction to decide whether it completely covers the controlling purpose of your composition. The first sample introduction by Thomas de Quincey, for example, would have been misleading without the additional statement. The reader would have expected the composition to treat news in general rather than television news specifically.

The Body

The body of the composition is the longest section. Here the points are made, the issues raised and discussed. In a five-paragraph composition the body consists of the three paragraphs in the middle, and the writer must accomplish his or her purpose within that body. The following concerns should serve as a guide in the writing of the body.

1. **Use your outline as a guide.** The outline was written as an aid to establishing a clear and appropriate pattern of development for the ideas that the composition is meant to express. If you do not follow the outline, you will lose the logical structure that the outline was designed to provide.

2. **Keep your purpose in mind.** Make the body of your composition accomplish what your controlling purpose promises you will accomplish. If you set out to demonstrate the truth of an assertion, be certain that you demonstrate it forcefully, clearly, and fully.

3. **Divide your writing into paragraphs.** Develop each main topic in your outline into a single paragraph in your composition. Begin each paragraph with a topic sentence, and support each topic sentence with the information you have included in your subtopics. Develop each topic and subtopic fully.

4. **Provide clear transitions.** Transitional devices at the beginning of paragraphs indicate how each idea is logically related to the ideas in preceding paragraphs. It is crucial that your reader be able to follow the development of your thoughts if he or she is to be able to understand them.

Using Transitional Devices

Transitional Words and Phrases. Just as the linking expressions or connectives in Chapter 7 are used to achieve coherence within a paragraph and to help the reader move smoothly from one idea to another, certain words and phrases are used to help the reader move smoothly from one paragraph to another. The following transitional words and phrases are the ones most often used in the first sentence of a new paragraph.

TO INDICATE TIME RELATIONSHIPS

before	earlier	once	sooner or later
during	later	then	at this point
after	soon	in time	at the same time
afterward	first	eventually	until
at last	next	finally	recently

TO INDICATE LOGICAL RELATIONSHIPS

since	besides	furthermore
therefore	consequently	and then
because	inevitably	as a result

TO INDICATE SIMILARITY

as	also	similarly	in the same way
like	again	another	equally important
and	likewise	moreover	
too	equally	in addition	

TO INDICATE CONTRAST

but	however	otherwise
yet	although	in contrast
nor	nevertheless	on the contrary
still	nonetheless	on the other hand

Each of the following sentences is the first sentence of a paragraph. Notice how the transitional devices serve, in each case, to link the new topic to that of the preceding paragraph. You can even guess what the preceding paragraph was about without having read it.

Still, solar power will never totally eliminate the need for other sources of energy.

Later, the Romans established an outpost of the Empire near what is now the border of England and Scotland.

His attitude toward freedom of speech was *equally* contemptuous.

Pronouns. The use of a pronoun to refer to an idea in the preceding paragraph can also create a link in the mind of the reader. The words *this, that, these,* and *those* are frequently used as transitional devices, sometimes as pronouns and sometimes as adjectives.

Great care must be taken in the use of these words as adjectives. They must be followed by a noun that makes the reference clear to the reader. Consider the sentence "This cannot continue indefinitely." The reader would be justified in wondering, "This *what* cannot be continued indefinitely?" Such a sentence must make it clear what is being referred to; for example, "This waste," or "This conduct."

Other pronouns can also function as transitional devices. The following sentences, which could serve as opening sentences of paragraphs, demonstrate how the technique works.

> *That* attitude soon changed, however.

> Never before have *these* issues seemed so critical or *their* resolution so important.

> *This* procedure has been effective in the past, but stronger measures are required today.

Repetition. The flow of meaning from one paragraph to the next can be smoothed by the repetition of a key word in the opening sentence. Notice how repetition of a word is used as a transitional device in the following examples.

> **1**
>
> Mass production has made it possible for a great number of people to own reproductions of significant works of art. It is now only a matter of taste that determines whether a person hangs an inexpensive reproduction of a lithograph by Picasso or a cat calendar on that blank spot on the living room wall.
>
> But taste is not the only consideration for collectors of high-priced original prints.

The people who spend their time wondering about such things predict that the next boom in home entertainment will not be swimming pools or television tennis games but computers.

The typical home computer setup will be no larger than a component stereo system and will serve equally well as an accountant, a family nutritionist, a heating engineer, or a chess opponent.

Repetition need not be limited to a single word; sometimes a writer will use a single word or phrase in the second of two paragraphs to refer to the whole idea developed in the first. In such cases the repetition serves much the same purpose as the use of a pronoun. Notice how this device works in the following examples.

3

To the manufacturers, the recall rate for American cars is startling testimony to the overall ability of the industry to turn out a product that does what it is supposed to do in a dependable and predictable manner. To the owner of a car recalled for a defective seat-belt harness, however, the recall rate is a shocking indictment.

Reliability, it would seem, is in the eye of the beholder.

4

On an increasingly large number of golf courses in the winter months one can see lines of weekend skiers gliding along without fear of broken legs or the price of the next lift ticket.

But safety and economy are not the only reasons for the rise in popularity of ski touring.

Exercises
The Body of the Composition

A. Find a magazine article on a subject that interests you and examine it for transitional devices. Write down the opening sentences of ten paragraphs from the article that make use of the transitional devices discussed in this section. Explain how the devices work in each paragraph.

B. The body of your composition will consist of three paragraphs. Write the body now, keeping the following points in mind:

1. Test your ideas against your controlling purpose as you write.
2. Use your outline as your guide.
3. Develop the ideas in each paragraph completely.
4. Provide clear transitions between paragraphs.

The Conclusion

As its name implies, the conclusion of the composition should bring matters to a close. The reader should be left with a sense that what should have been said has been said. It is always a good technique to return in the conclusion to the ideas you used in your introduction. This reiteration serves to remind the reader of the key ideas and leaves him or her with a feeling of completeness.

If the paragraphs in your composition have adequately developed your topics and are logically connected, your concluding paragraph will form the complete whole, making the structure complete and stable.

Our model composition might have a conclusion like the following.

The situation is deplorable, but what are we to do? People can't be forced to read newspapers. They can't be forced to study political and economic issues in detail. The power of the television image will remain, no matter what we do, but television news programs might be improved to the point where they provided more of the substance of information. Network news programs could be expanded to an hour. The focus of the programs could be directed to larger issues, not just to the events of the day. Instead of one or two paternal newscasters, the public could be offered a variety of men and women, reporting from a variety of political perspectives. These changes are small, but they would go a long way toward making television news contribute to a truly informed populace.

Notice that the conclusion begins with the use of the word *situation* as a repetitive device, providing the transition from the preceding paragraph. The writer offers suggestions for improvement of the situation and returns to a key idea of the introduction and the composition as a whole: that an informed public is essential to a democratic society. The reader has, in the course of reading the composition, learned why an informed public is necessary, why dependence on television news has made for an inadequately informed public, and now learns in the conclusion what might be done about it.

With the draft of the entire composition complete, the writer is at last in a position to select a final title for the work. The title, like the introduction, should both inform and interest the reader. It should not be clever without substance, but neither should it be accurate without life.

Exercises
Writing an Effective Conclusion

A. Write the concluding paragraph of your composition, including in it an echo of the ideas and techniques you used in your introduction. Refer again to your controlling purpose and try to include all its essential ideas in your conclusion.

B. Choose a title for your completed composition.

Part 6

Revising

The best compositions are largely the products of work done in this final stage. It is in revision that your ideas will achieve their best and most succinct expression. Following the steps listed below will enable you to make visible improvements in your first draft.

1. **Read your composition aloud.** The importance of this step cannot be overemphasized. Nothing else will show you so clearly where your ideas were not fully developed or where your thinking was fuzzy or where your sentences were awkward. If possible, read your work to someone who will be critical of it. Use the criticism in your revision.

2. **Revise for content.** Is your purpose clear from the outset? Have you said enough? Is your information accurate? Are your ideas laid out clearly?

3. **Revise for form.** Have you organized your composition clearly and logically? Have you given each main idea its own paragraph and introduced it with a topic sentence? Are your paragraphs coherent? Are all your ideas clearly related to each other? Have you made connections between ideas by using transitional devices?

4. **Revise for wording.** Have you used the most precise words to express your ideas? Review the information on synonyms and antonyms in Chapter 1. Use a dictionary or thesaurus to check the meanings of key words in your composition and to locate synonyms for them. If you find synonymous words with meanings closer to what you had intended, revise the wording.

5. **Check for capitalization, punctuation, and spelling.** Obviously, faults of these kinds will distract your reader from the content of your work. If necessary, consult Sections 11–17 in the Handbook.

A Model Composition

Following is a revised, completed composition based on the outline that appears on page 181.

NETWORK NEWS IS NOT ENOUGH

According to a recent survey conducted by the Center for the Study of Public Information, a full sixty per cent of American voters get all their information about political issues from nightly television programs. A democracy that gets most of its news from such shows is a democracy in great jeopardy, for half-hour news programs provide the public with the illusion of information, not the substance. This insubstantiality is the result not of a conspiracy to misinform or under-inform; it is an inherent shortcoming of television as an information medium, at least as currently organized.

The introduction offers a statistic and asserts the purpose of the composition: to show that television news programs, as currently organized, are not a sufficient means of informing the citizens of a democracy.

The importance of solid information to a democracy did not escape Thomas Jefferson, who felt most strongly that a democracy could survive only when the public was well-informed about current affairs. In his view, an informed public would have the ability to evaluate political issues and make political decisions on the basis of reason, not on preconception or whim. But he feared a public that received false or inadequate information. They would be unable to make intelligent decisions; instead they would focus on personalities, not issues, and would be likely to follow demagogues. Jefferson could not have foreseen television, but he clearly anticipated its impact.

The first paragraph of the body of the composition corresponds to topic II and its subtopics in the outline. The first sentence is the topic sentence; the rest of the paragraph develops the statement it makes. Repetition of the key word information serves as a transition from the introduction.

Until recently the dominant source of information in America has been the newspaper. By its very nature—the fact that it is in print and can be read at the reader's own pace—a newspaper can provide long and careful analyses of issues and events. But recent polls show a precipitous decline in newspaper readership. Each year, more and more Americans get most of their information not from a newspaper, but from television.

Again the key word *information* is repeated, linking this paragraph to the preceding one and to the introduction. The words *until recently* locate the paragraph in time. The paragraph corresponds to topic III in the outline.

But television, unlike a newspaper, is by its very nature an inadequate medium for communicating information. Because it is a visual medium, relying on stories that can be filmed, it cannot probe the complexity and interrelatedness of the issues that confront the citizens of a complex world. Television news programs are prisoners of time, dominated by periodic commercial breaks and dependent on brief stories that can never provide the depth that is possible in newspapers. The visual image encourages a focus on personalities rather than issues, a focus that is demonstrated by the attitude of the newscasters themselves, who adopt a wise and paternal manner. This focus on personalities is exactly what Jefferson feared from an ill-informed public.

Two words, *but* and *unlike,* provide a transition from the preceding paragraph and indicate a contrast between its topic and the topic discussed here. The paragraph corresponds to topic IV in the outline.

The situation is deplorable, but what are we to do? People can't be forced to read newspapers. They can't be forced to study political and economic issues in detail. The power of the television image will remain, no matter what we do, but television news programs might be improved to the point where they pro-

The final paragraph constitutes the conclusion of the composition. The writer returns to the problems posed in the introduction, echoes a phrase from the introduction in the words *the substance of information,* and returns to

vided more of the substance of information. Network news programs could be expanded to an hour. The focus of the programs could be directed to larger issues, not just to the events of the day. Instead of one or two paternal newscasters, the public could be offered a variety of men and women, reporting from a variety of political perspectives. These changes are small, but they would go a long way toward making television news contribute to a truly informed populace.

Jefferson's concerns in the closing words. As a whole, the conclusion is prescriptive, offering the reader a possible solution.

Exercise
Revising a Composition

Revise your composition, following the suggestions in this section. Prepare a clean, final version.

Chapter 10

The Research Paper

A research paper is a formal composition of some length based on information gathered from reliable sources, and organized and shaped by the writer's own thinking and judgment. The search for suitable source materials related to your subject, together with the planning and writing procedures you studied in connection with Chapter 9 (Writing a Composition), requires an extended period of time. In order to use your time wisely, each step of the planning, research, and writing must be carefully controlled along the way.

Because a thorough research paper takes weeks to complete, choosing a subject for which reference books and articles are not readily available can be a costly error in terms of time. Careful attention to planning and organizing your paper is also important because mistakes become increasingly difficult to correct once you are involved in the actual writing. You must allow enough time to read your source materials and to judge the usefulness of that reading for your subject. You must allow enough time to write and revise your paper; and, finally, you must prepare accurate footnotes and a final bibliography.

While a research paper is a more ambitious undertaking than a composition, footnotes and a bibliography are the only aspects that are entirely new. When your teacher makes the research paper assignment, work out a time schedule, with your teacher's guidance, that will help you work through each stage in a thorough and unhurried way.

This chapter will discuss the procedures in writing a research paper. The basic steps are these:

EIGHT STEPS IN WRITING A RESEARCH PAPER

1. Choosing and limiting your subject
2. Preparing a working bibliography
3. Preparing a preliminary outline
4. Reading and taking notes
5. Organizing notes and writing the final outline
6. Writing the first draft
7. Writing the final draft with footnotes
8. Writing the final bibliography

Part 1

Choosing Your Subject

Choosing the right subject is extremely important to the success of your paper. To start your thinking, you may wish to make a list of ten subjects that come to your mind as possibilities for a research paper. Then check your list against the following guidelines.

1. **Choose a subject that interests you.** Choose a subject that you want to learn more about. If your subject does not really interest you, your paper will probably not be interesting to the reader either.

2. **Choose a subject for which a wide range of source materials is readily available.** Subjects that are too recent in development, or too technical in nature, will have few, if any, source ma-

terials If you have doubts about source materials for any of the subjects on your list, consult your school librarian to find out how much information the library has.

3. **Choose a subject of some significance.** A subject of lasting interest will be challenging and gratifying to pursue. After all, you will be spending much time and effort on this assignment, and what you learn should be a significant addition to your store of knowledge as well as that of the reader.

4. **Choose a subject that can be presented objectively.** Your purpose is to sift through and reshape an accumulated body of information, not to indulge in arguments and persuasion. Argument and persuasion are right for debates, but not for a research paper. Your paper should be an objective presentation of your subject, not an emotional one.

5. **Avoid straight biography.** Biography requires long, intensive research, involving letters, interviews, and unpublished material not available to the average person. If the person is well known, biographies already exist and using them as resource material, even if they are in unusual quantity, results merely in a rehashing of already published information. Bringing your own thinking and direction to bear on a biography is virtually impossible.

Limiting Your Subject

As you learned in Chapter 9, limiting your subject is of vital importance in writing a good paper. A research paper will be approximately 2,000 words in length, and your subject must be limited so that your research can be handled within the time allotted yet the coverage of your subject can be thorough.

Example 1

Suppose you were interested in art and wanted to do a paper on some aspect of it. Limiting your paper might proceed in the following steps:

1. Art
2. Painting
3. History of painting

At this point, stop to consider whether your subject can be handled in a 2,000-word paper. Obviously, the history of painting is far too large to be covered in that length, so we will have to narrow it further.

4. Turn-of-the- century realism in American painting
5. The Ash Can School
6. The paintings of John Sloan

If you examine the last two subjects, you will probably realize that your source material may be too limited to cover either of the subjects adequately. Whatever information you could find would tend to be repetitious and therefore frustrating. Subject number 4 might be exactly right. It has enough breadth for you to move around in, yet it is specific enough to concentrate on.

Example 2

Here is an example of a subject for a literary paper. Suppose you were interested in the works of Stephen Crane. Limiting your subject might proceed like this:

1. Stephen Crane
2. The works of Stephen Crane
3. The realism of Stephen Crane
4. *The Red Badge of Courage*

You have worked your way down to what seems to be a manageable subject: one book. However, the subject is still too general because there are countless ways in which to discuss a book. You need to focus on a particular aspect of the book that you feel will lend itself to a wide variety of source materials. You decide on the following subject for your paper:

The realism of Henry Fleming in Stephen Crane's *The Red Badge of Courage*

Limiting Your Subject

Bring to class three subjects that interest you as possible choices for a research paper. Limit each one properly and be sure that each one can be adequately researched. You will probably have to work in the library to complete this assignment. It is a vital first step in your research paper.

Part 2

Preparing a Working Bibliography

When you have decided on your subject, in consultation with your teacher, your next step is to search for and collect your source material. While the *Readers' Guide* and specialized reference books will be your best sources, you should first consult a good encyclopedia for a general overview of your subject.

If you have limited your subject properly, you won't find an article on your specific subject. Look for a general article on the larger subject of which yours is a part. This overview of the whole subject may suggest related ideas that you will want to consider as your subject takes shape. It may also suggest a modification in your original subject. While a shift in idea is not serious at this point, consult your teacher for approval.

Recommended Sources

At this point, you may wish to review Chapter 11 (The Library and Its Reference Materials) so that you can use your library time wisely. The following sources are the most important for a research paper.

1. **The card catalog.** Suppose you are doing a paper on William Faulkner. You would first look at all the subject cards with his name. In addition to all the books Faulkner has writ-

ten, you will find major biographies and works of criticism mainly concerned with him. However, many books that may have informative chapters on Faulkner may not be entered. Look at "American Literature," "Twentieth Century Literature," "Literature of the South," "The Novel," "Literary Criticism," and any other general subjects that may seem related. The description of the book on the card will tell you whether the book is worth investigating.

2. **The Readers' Guide.** This source will list current magazine articles on your subject. For most subjects, past articles are as useful as present ones, and the library has cumulative bound volumes of past years.

3. **Specialized Reference Books.** Turn to Part 3 in Chapter 11 and review the list of reference books. If any of them relate to your subject, consult them in your library. They often suggest titles of additional books that may be useful.

In preparing a working bibliography, your objective is to accumulate as many books and articles as you think might be helpful to you in some way. Because you cannot always tell whether the information on a catalog card or in the *Readers' Guide* or in a bibliography will be helpful to you, it is wise to include sources you may be doubtful about at the moment. If some sources turn out to be of little help, you can later drop them from your bibliography.

Guidelines for Selecting Source Materials

The following guidelines will help you in selecting source materials.

1. **Is the book or article included in any of the bibliographies you have consulted?** In addition to the bibliographies in reference books, many of the books from the card catalog will contain their own bibliographies. When you find such a bibliography, check your own working bibliography and add promising new sources. If the same books or authors appear in various bibliographies, they are probably worth investigating.

2. **Is the author an authority on the subject?** While you may not know this at the beginning, an author who has written several books or whose name is included in various bibliographies may be an authority on the subject. As you read, be on the alert for writers whose opinions are mentioned or quoted.

3. **What is the value of a promising book?** A book on the space age published in 1958 may not be as authentic as one published in 1977. A book on a famous scientist, written by a friend or relative, may not be as accurate as one written by an authority on scientific thinking. A third edition of a book would be more valuable than the first or second edition.

4. **If a magazine article looks promising, what kind of magazine did it appear in?** In general, popular interest magazines such as those on the newsstand are not suitable sources for a research paper.

5. **If a book looks promising, for what audience is it intended?** Many interesting books are intended for younger readers and are not suitable for research papers. Books of a highly technical nature are usually not suitable either.

Bibliography Cards

For each bibliography source, use a 3 x 5 card or slip of paper. Because you will be referring to each card time and again for specific information, be sure you fill out each card carefully and completely.

Bibliography cards have three purposes:

1. To record all the information needed to find the reference in the library when you are ready to take notes from it.

2. To record the information needed to prepare the footnotes for your paper.

3. To record the information needed to prepare the final bibliography for your paper.

Here are the correct forms of bibliography cards, from three different kinds of sources: a book, a magazine article, and an encyclopedia article.

Book

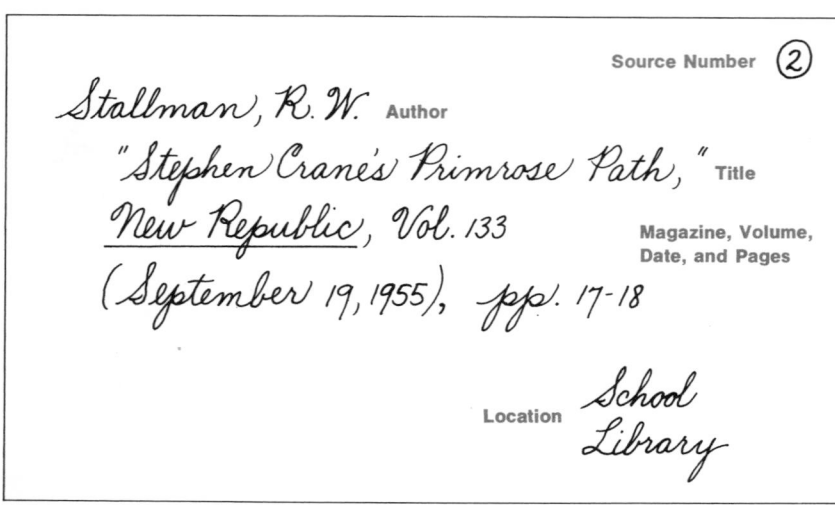

Source Number ①

Ellison, Ralph Author

Shadow and Act Title

New York : Random House, 1964
Publishing Information

809.8
EL 5 Call number

Location *Public Library*

Magazine Article

Source Number ②

Stallman, R. W. Author

"Stephen Crane's Primrose Path," Title

New Republic, Vol. 133 Magazine, Volume, Date, and Pages

(September 19, 1955), pp. 17-18

Location *School Library*

Encyclopedia Article

"The American Civil War" Title

Encyclopedia Americana Reference

Vol. 6 (1975), pp. 782-819 Volume, Date, and Pages

Ref.
031 Location *School*
En1 Call Number *Library*

On these sample bibliography cards, note that the titles of books are underlined and the titles of articles are enclosed in quotation marks. Note also the correct abbreviations and punctuation.

Here is some additional information that will be helpful in preparing bibliography cards:

1. If a book has an editor rather than an author, use *ed.* (editor) or *eds.* (editors) after the name: *Todd, William, ed.*

2. If no publication date is given, use the copyright date: *c. 1970.*

3. If neither publication nor copyright date is given, use the abbreviation *n.d.* (no date).

4. Information such as the above is usually found on the title page of a book, encyclopedia, or pamphlet. Sometimes pamphlets have the information on front or back covers or on the last page. Magazines may have the information on the front covers or on one of the first few pages.

5. If you use a newspaper article, give the writer's name (if

there is one); the title of the article in quotation marks; the name of the newspaper, underlined; and the date and the page number.

6. The source number in the upper right-hand corner of your card is important because it will save you a great deal of time as you are writing the first draft of your paper. Instead of having to write out all the information on the bibliography card every time you credit the use of an idea or a quotation, you can merely jot down the number of the card to identify the source.

As you continue the work on your paper, you will understand the importance of including the complete bibliographical data for each source.

Exercise
Preparing a Working Bibliography

Using all available facilities, prepare a working bibliography for your chosen subject.

Determining the Controlling Purpose of Your Paper

Now that you have chosen your subject, prepared your working bibliography, and done some background reading, you are ready to bring your subject into sharper focus by deciding exactly what aspect of your subject you are going to write about. You need to formulate a controlling purpose for your paper— a formal, exact statement of what your paper is going to be about. Once you have refined your controlling purpose to the extent that it presents your purpose as clearly as you want it to, you can use it to direct your note-taking, and to help you write a good outline and a good paper.

It is possible that as you read you will want to revise your controlling purpose, but stating it as clearly as possible now will help you select the right material for your note-taking.

Material that does not relate directly to your controlling purpose does not belong in your paper or your notes.

You will recall that on page 202, the student interested in Stephen Crane decided to write a paper on the realism of Henry Fleming in Stephen Crane's *The Red Badge of Courage*. While this statement may be suitable as a title, it is not sufficiently focused for a statement of controlling purpose. The statement must be recast into one that requires proof, such as the following:

> *Controlling Purpose:* to demonstrate that Henry Fleming, the protagonist of Stephen Crane's *The Red Badge of Courage*, is an accurate portrayal of a Civil War soldier by comparing him with actual soldiers through their letters and diaries.

Exercise
Stating the Controlling Purpose

Write out the controlling purpose for your paper, stating it as exactly as you can at this point in your procedure.

Part 3
Preparing a Preliminary Outline

The clear statement of your controlling purpose and the nature of the resources in your stack of working bibliography cards will help you prepare a preliminary outline for your paper. At this stage your outline will be only tentative and rough in form, but the major divisions and some subdivisions will suggest themselves. The first major topic will be devoted to your introduction and the last major topic to your conclusion, so at the present you need be concerned only with the topics in between.

This preliminary outline will function merely as a general guideline to your reading. As your reading progresses and you gain more information, you can revise and extend your outline accordingly. If you find that your source material does not contain enough information to develop a major topic sufficiently, you may have to delete that topic entirely and substitute one that is better covered. Your reading may also suggest an entirely new topic that you may want to develop. Make notes or revisions on your outline as you pursue your reading, so you have all the information in one place when you are ready to prepare your final outline.

Keep the statement of your controlling purpose before you at all times so that you can judge the relevance of your material when preparing your preliminary outline and also when taking notes on your reading. If, as a result of your reading, you find that major topics need revising, you may need to revise your controlling purpose accordingly.

Here is an example of how a rough preliminary outline of the paper on Stephen Crane might look:

The Realism of Henry Fleming in Stephen Crane's *The Red Badge of Courage*

CONTROLLING PURPOSE: to demonstrate that Henry Fleming, the protagonist of Stephen Crane's *The Red Badge of Courage,* is an accurate portrayal of a Civil War soldier by comparing him with actual soldiers through their letters and diaries.

I. (Introduction)

II. Soldiers in battle

    A. Risks
    B. Fears

III. Change in attitude

    A. Urgency
    B. Rage
    C. New Purpose

IV.   Desertion

    A.   Mental problems

    B.   Physical problems

    C.   Excuses

V.   Expectations versus realities of battle

VI.   Soldiers mature

VII.   (Conclusion)

Exercise
Preparing a Preliminary Outline

Prepare a preliminary outline for your paper in the following form:

1. Put the title of your paper at the top.
2. Below the title, write your controlling purpose.
3. Follow standard outline form. (See pages 179–181.)
4. Keep the details of your outline to a minimum so you can revise and expand more easily as your reading progresses.

Part 4

Reading and Taking Notes

Keep your controlling purpose and your preliminary outline before you as you read and take notes, so you can keep a strong control over the direction of your paper. Take notes on 4 x 6 cards so they don't get mixed up with your 3 x 5 bibliography cards. Be sure to use a separate card for each note or for each set of related facts about one topic from the same source. Remember that the grouping of your cards under separate topics will be necessary when you write your final outline. For example, if you have two different ideas on one card, you may need one idea for the beginning of your paper and the other for the end of your paper. Sorting out your cards would be almost impossible with both ideas on one card.

A Sample Note Card

Here is a sample note card containing both a paraphrased idea and a direct quotation and showing the position and spacing for each part of a note card.

Sample Note Card

Fears in Battle Guideline   Source Number ④

Note   Most soldiers feverish with impatience before battle. Nothing "brings ... such crucial trial as the throbbing emotions that immediately precede the clash of arms."

Page Reference *page* 339

Here is an explanation of the parts of a sample note card.

1. **The guideline** is a heading that identifies the note on the card. It corresponds to a topic or subtopic on your preliminary outline. Include on the card only ideas pertaining to the guideline and use a different card for each source. If your reading does not yield enough information for your guideline, you may need to delete the topic from your outline and discard the corresponding note cards. If your reading yields new or different information, revise your outline and your guideline accordingly.

2. **The source number** corresponds with the number of your working bibliography card and is the source from which the note was taken. By checking the card in the working bibliography, you can obtain all the information on the source whenever you need it.

3. **The page reference** must be exact for two reasons: (1) You may want to refer again to the source to verify the facts, and (2) you may need the page reference for footnotes.

4. **The note,** of course, is the most important part of the card because it is this part that you are going to use in writing your paper. Except for direct quotations, all notes should be paraphrased in your own words to avoid plagiarism.

Plagiarism

Because plagiarism is intellectually dishonest and therefore a form of stealing, it is an extremely serious offense and can result in severe penalties, even no credit for the course. The following forms of plagiarism are the most frequent:

1. Failure to document with quotation marks any material copied directly from other sources.

2. Failure to acknowledge paraphrased material (someone else's ideas)

3. Failure to provide a bibliography

4. Use of others' work as one's own, particularly in the creative arts

5. Use of others' ideas as one's own for themes, poems, musical compositions, or art work.

Improving Your Skill at Taking Notes

Here are some suggestions to improve your skill in taking notes:

1. Be accurate. Double-check statistics and facts to make sure you have them right. When you summarize or paraphrase

a writer's words, be sure you do not misinterpret or distort his meaning.

2. Distinguish between fact and opinion. Label opinions: "Dr. Graves thinks that . . ." or "According to Grace Jackson, . . ." Be careful to note differences in opinion and to point out such differences in your notes.

3. Take notes as quickly as possible. Omit all words or phrases not essential to meaning; use abbreviations. Be careful, however, not to take notes so brief that when you need to use them you cannot understand what you have written.

4. Copy a direct quotation exactly, including punctuation, spelling, and grammar. Be sure to use quotation marks both at the beginning and at the end of the quotation so that you can easily separate the quotation from paraphrased material.

5. Any words inserted by the writer in the text of a quotation must be enclosed in brackets. (See Section 13.13 in your Handbook.) Parentheses must not be used. Insert brackets in ink if your typewriter does not have them.

6. Indicate the omissions of nonessential parts of a quotation by ellipses. (See Section 13.14 in your Handbook.)

7. If you can't get all the information on one side of a card, write *over* in parentheses at the bottom of the card, flip the card over and continue on the back. If you have more than two lines, you probably have too much material for one card.

Exercise
Reading and Taking Notes

Complete your reading and your note cards. Adjust or revise your preliminary outline, and make any final revisions of your controlling purpose.

Part 5
Organizing Notes and Writing the Final Outline

A research paper is longer and more complex than a short composition and your outline will be correspondingly so. Remember, however, that much of your work has already been done. The guidelines on your note cards will provide the divisions and subdivisions of your outline and your next step is to divide your note cards into separate piles in order to write your final outline.

Put each note card with the same guideline into a separate pile. Each of these piles of cards should relate to one of the major or minor divisions of your preliminary outline. Study these piles of cards to see what information each contains and the extent to which the information conforms to the information on your preliminary outline. Refer to your controlling purpose often as you study your cards.

Gradually, some topics will emerge as major divisions of your subject, some as subdivisions and others as sub-subdivisions. If some cards reveal insufficient material on a subdivision and you feel that subdivision is important, you may have to do more reading. If the subdivision is not important, you can either combine it with another subdivision if it is closely related or delete the information and the card entirely.

This is the point at which you decide exactly what you are going to include in your paper and what you are going to leave out. Keep checking your controlling purpose to see that all your usable material is relevant to your subject. Don't be afraid to delete information that is not relevant. The decisions you make at this point will be reflected in your paper.

Finally, when you have chosen your main topics and sub-topics and tested each note card for relevance to your controlling purpose, begin to organize the topics for your final outline. Try to decide in what order your topics would move most logically toward the conclusion you have determined in your controlling purpose. Feel free to move an entire main topic from one place to another or to shift your note cards to different positions.

Write down your main topics in various orders and study them, thinking about how logically you can make transitions between topics. If a transition from one topic to another seems forced, something is probably wrong. Either you need to re-arrange your topics or you need to revise the emphasis or the direction of one of them.

When you are finally satisfied with the order of your material, test it once more against your controlling purpose in the following ways:

1. Does it begin at the beginning and move logically to the conclusion?

2. Are the main topics the most important ideas?

3. Do the subtopics relate specifically to the main topics?

4. Is there any unnecessary duplication of topics or subtopics?

5. Do all the main topics relate clearly to the controlling purpose?

6. Will the transition from one topic to the next be clear and logical?

7. Will the conclusion correspond to that of the controlling purpose?

8. Have you included too much information anywhere so that your paper will not be well balanced?

9. Have you included enough information to develop your ideas well?

When you are satisfied with the answers to these questions, you are ready to write your final outline. If you have any doubts about standard outline form, check pages 179–181. Remember that a good outline is not necessarily a long, elaborate one. Try to keep it within reasonable bounds.

Organizing Notes and Writing the Final Outline

Organize your note cards and write your final outline.

Part 6

Writing the First Draft

At this point you have the title of your paper, the statement of your controlling purpose, your final outline, and your note cards sorted to fit your outline. With all these in front of you, you are ready to write your first draft. This is the time to get all your information on paper as fully and freely as you can. Don't worry about style and form or the mechanics of punctuation. Your main purpose is to get all your ideas down in a form that you will be able to follow when you are ready to revise and polish your paper.

Follow your outline and keep your controlling purpose in mind. Begin a new paragraph for every topic and subtopic on your outline and make some attempt at paragraph transitions, although you can work these out more carefully later.

Write your entire paper in the third person. Never use *I*, *me*, or *my* because you will be in danger of injecting your own opinion, and personal opinion has no place in a research paper. Use the information on your note cards and be sure to include the source number in the upper right-hand corner of your note card when you use other people's ideas or direct quotations. You will need these sources for your footnotes. To save time, you can write the first few words of a direct quotation, and the source numbers will help you locate it very quickly when you need to copy it carefully and completely on your final draft.

As you write, keep in mind that the first paragraph of your paper will constitute your introduction, in which you set forth your controlling purpose. Your final, or concluding, paragraph should round up all your ideas in a restatement of your controlling purpose.

Writing the First Draft

With your controlling purpose and your outline before you, and using your note cards, write the first draft of your paper.

Part 7

Writing the Final Draft with Footnotes

Before writing your final draft, you may wish to review the suggestions for revising a composition on page 193 and the recommendations for manuscript form in Section 19 of your Handbook. Because you have spent so much time and effort thus far, you will want to do your best job on revising and polishing your paper.

Long Quotations

If direct quotations are more than three typed lines long, indent them five spaces from both the left and the right margins. Single space each line and do not use quotation marks. If the quotation is the beginning of a paragraph in the source, indent the first word an additional two spaces.

Footnotes

Uses

1. To indicate source of material that is directly quoted

2. To give credit for other people's ideas even though you write them in your own words
3. To give the source of diagrams, figures, or statistics

Numbering

There are two common ways of numbering footnotes, both using Arabic numerals:

1. Consecutively throughout the paper, beginning with number 1 on the first page and ending with number 20 on the last page, if that is the total number of footnotes.

2. Numbering beginning over on each successive page: numbers 1 and 2 on the first page, numbers 1, 2, and 3 on the second and successive pages. Check with your teacher to see which way he or she prefers.

Place the Arabic numerals slightly above the material to be footnoted, usually after the last word of a sentence or a direct quotation. For example:

This same feeling was expressed by many Federals and Confederates. Bruce Catton, the Civil War Historian, wrote that "the instinctive loyalty of all these men went...to the army."[1]

Position

Footnotes may appear in a paper in one of two ways: at the bottom of each page or on a separate page at the end. The actual form of each is the same.

If footnotes are to appear on each page, you must be careful to allow enough room at the bottom of each page for all the footnotes on that page. This will also include a one-inch margin of blank space at the bottom of each page.

When you have typed the last line of text on a page, skip a line. Then type a line that extends across the page, from the left margin to the right. Skip another space, and then type your first footnote. The bottom of your page will look like this:

This same feeling was expressed by many Federals and Confederates. Bruce Catton, the Civil War historian, wrote that "the instinctive loyalty of all of these men went...to the army.[1]

---

[1]Bruce Catton, This Hallowed Ground, p. 360.

Form

1. Number each footnote with an Arabic numeral to correspond to the material in the text (See above).

2. Indent each footnote five spaces, just as you do for paragraphs. Observe the text margin at the right. If the footnote runs to a second or third line, bring those lines back to the left margin.

[14]"Hypnotism Spots Epileptic Whose Fits Are Neurotic," Science News Letter, Vol. XX (May 13, 1970), p. 296.

3. Single space each footnote but double space between footnotes.

4. Place a period at the end of each footnote.

5. The first time a work is mentioned, the footnote should contain the author's first and last names, the title (magazines and book titles underlined to represent italics; articles and parts of works in quotation marks), the volume number (Capitalize Vol. and put the number in capital Roman numerals.), the date if the reference is a magazine, and the page or pages (in Arabic numerals).

[1]G. D. H. Cole, A Short History of the British Working Class Movement, Vol. III, p. 125.

[2]Robert A. Dahl, "Workers' Control of Industry and the British Labour Party," American Political Science Review, Vol. XLI (October, 1967), pp. 890–93.

6. To refer to sources already cited in previous footnotes in full form, use a shortened form for footnotes.

(a) To refer to a reference mentioned in the immediately preceding footnote, use *Ibid.*, the abbreviation for the Latin *ibidem*, meaning "in the same place." *Ibid* should be underlined because it is a foreign word. It can never be used as a first footnote on a page unless footnotes are numbered consecutively throughout a paper and an *Ibid.* just happens to refer to the preceding footnote which is on the preceding page. If the page number differs from that given above, place a comma after *Ibid.* and write the page number:

[15]Lawrence Battistini, Japan and America, p. 145.

[16]Ibid.

[17]Ibid., pp. 170–173.

(b) To refer to a work cited earlier in full form but not in the immediately preceding footnote, you should write the author's last name only and the page or pages.

[18]W. Pratt, "Japan and the Pacific Problem," Newsweek, Vol. XXXI (June 7, 1948), p. 22.

[19]Norton Ginsberg, et al., "What Future for the Japanese Economy?" The Round Table, Vol. DCCXVI (Dec. 16, 1971), p. 12.

[20]Pratt, p. 33.

Of course, if references by other authors with the same last name are used, you will also have to include the author's first name or initials.

If more than one work by the same author has been referred to, then you should write the author's last name and the title— in shortened form, if you desire.

[21]Thomas Hardy, _The Mayor of Casterbridge_, p. 56.

[22]Hardy, _Jude the Obscure_, p. 68.

[23]Hardy, _The Mayor_, p. 59.

If you refer to a reference with an extremely long title, you may use ellipses.

It is not necessary for identification purposes to give the complete title:

[24]Eva E. Dye, "Women's Part in the Drama of the Northwest," _Transactions of the Twenty-second Annual Reunion of the Oregon Pioneer Association for 1894..._, p. 42.

7. The last line of the last footnote in the paper should be one inch (6 spaces) from the bottom of the last page even though the text is not a full page.

Basic Forms for Footnotes

Books

1. One author:

   ¹Robert Johnson, <u>Battles and Leaders of the Civil War</u>, Vol. II, p. 45.

2. Two authors:

   ²Otto Eisenschiml and Ralph Newman, <u>The American Iliad</u>, pp. 488–89.

3. Three authors:

   ³Otto U. Faulkner, Tyler Kepner, and Hall Bartlett, <u>The American Way of Life—A History</u>, p. 67.

4. Four or more authors. If you have more than three authors, you need list only the name of the first author and then use the abbreviation *et al. (et alii),* which means "and others":

   ⁴Rewey Belle Inglis et al., <u>Adventures in English Literature</u>, p. 57.

5. No author given: If you have a book with no author given, you start with the title:

   ⁵<u>The Lottery</u>, pp. 28–32.

6. If you wish to refer to a book written by an author using a pseudonym, you may supply the real name in parentheses:

   ⁶Mark Twain (S. L. Clemens), <u>The Adventures of Huckleberry Finn</u>, p. 20.

7. If you have an editor of a book, write his name followed

Basic Forms for Footnotes

by (ed.). If you have two or more editors, write their names followed by (eds.):

⁷J. N. D. Anderson (ed.), The World's Religions, p. 143.

⁷J. E. Smith and E. W. Parks (eds.), The Great Critics, p. 143.

8. If you have a translator of an original work, put the name of the translator after the title of the book:

⁸Homer, The Odyssey, trans. E. V. Rieu, p. 129.

9. If you wish to note that you are using a particular edition of a book, put the information within parentheses:

⁹Sir Alan Gardiner, Egyptian Grammar (2d. ed. rev.), p. 27.

10. If you use a book or monograph that is part of a series, put the name of the series in quotes and, with other information, within parentheses:

¹⁰Virgil K. Whittaker, The Religious Basis of Spenser's Thought ("Stanford University Publications: Language and Literature," Vol. VII), p. 34.

11. If you wish to refer to only one volume with a special title that is part of a work of several volumes under one general title, list the author, title, and volume number, followed by the general title of the work:

¹¹T. C. Chamberlin and R. D. Sailsbury, Geology, Vol. 1: Geologic Processes and Their Results (2d. ed. rev.), p. 153.

Basic Forms for Footnotes

12. If you use a component part by one author of a larger work edited by other authors, list the particular author, the title of the part (in quotation marks), and then cite the title of the collection (underlined), followed by the names of the general editors:

[12]Roy P. Baler, "Psychological Pattern in 'The Love Song of J. Alfred Prufrock,'" <u>Twentieth Century English</u>, ed. William S. Knickerbocker, p. 384.

13. To refer to a volume of poems, write the name of the poet, the title of the poem in quotation marks, the title of the collection underlined, and the number of the page on which the poem appears:

[13]Edgar Lee Masters, "Ann Rutledge," <u>Spoon River Anthology</u>, p. 194.

14. Classical references. Books are indicated with small Roman numerals. If the classical work is not divided into books, all the divisions are indicated with Arabic numerals. There should be no punctuation between the author's name and the title of the work, and none after the title:

[14]Cicero <u>Tusculanae disputationes</u> ii. 2. 52–54.

[15]Aristotle <u>Poetics</u> 20. 35–37.

15. Scriptural references. The names of the books of the Bible, of the Apocrypha, and of the Apocalyptic, and the names of the versions of the Bible should be abbreviated when exact chapter and verse references are given. The names of the books should not be underlined:

[16]Acts 1: 1–3.

Basic Forms for Footnotes

16. If you wish to refer to a book with several authors and more than one volume, write the names of the authors, the title of the book (underlined), the volume number, and page or pages:

[17]Meriwether Lewis and William Clark, History of the Expedition of Captains Lewis and Clark, Vol. I, p. 291.

Magazines, Encyclopedias, Reports, Pamphlets, Newspapers

1. To refer to an article in a journal or periodical, give the author's name, the title of the article (in quotation marks), the name of the journal or magazine (underlined), the volume, if there is one, the date of issue, and the page or pages:

[1]B. F. Trueblood, "Hague Conference and the Future of Arbitration," Atlantic Monthly, Vol. XCVII (June, 1906), p. 723.

If an author's name is not given, put the title first:

[2]"To End a Scandal," Time, Vol. LXXVII (May 26, 1961), p. 63.

2. To refer to an article in an encyclopedia, give the author's name, the title of the article, the name of the encyclopedia (underlined), volume, and page:

[3]Milton H. Erickson, "Hypnotism," Collier's Encyclopedia, Vol. X, p. 316.

If an author's name is not given, put the title first:

Basic Forms for Footnotes

[3]"Hypnotism," Collier's Encyclopedia, Vol. X, p. 316.

It is not necessary to give the names of the many editors of encyclopedias, such as the *Encyclopaedia Britannica,* but for a special encyclopedia with one editor, you should give the name of the editor:

[4]E. E. Kellett, "Spinozo," Encyclopaedia of Religion and Ethics, ed. James Hastings, Vol. XI, p. 251.

3. If you wish to refer to a report or pamphlet, give the author's name, the title (underlined), the date and place of the report, and the pages:

[5]James W. Angell, Financial Foreign Policy of the U.S., A Report to the Second International Studies Conference on the State and Economic Life, London, May 29, 1933, pp. 8–10.

If the report is by an association rather than an author, start with the name of the association:

[6]American Medical Association, Medical Relations under Workmen's Compensation, A Report Prepared by the Bureau of Medical Economics, p. 3.

4. To refer to an unsigned newspaper article, write the headline (in quotation marks), the name of the newspaper (underlined), the date, and the page. Sometimes the section and the column may also be given:

[7]"The Reading of Adults," Chicago Daily News, Aug. 6, 1975, p. 4.

[8]"The Influence of TV on Reading," New York Times, Sept. 10, 1975, Sec. 4, p. 10.

Basic Forms for Footnotes

Other Sources

1. To refer to an interview rather than a printed source, write the name of the person interviewed, the identification of the person, and the date:

[9]Interview with Dr. Philip H. McDevitt, Superintendent of Evanston Township High School, Evanston, Illinois, May 15, 1977.

2. If you wish to refer to a letter that has not been published, write the name of the person who wrote the letter, the position he holds, and the date of the letter:

[10]Letter from Hon. Jimmy Carter, President of the United States, Washington, D.C., May 22, 1977.

3. If you wish to refer to information in private files, put the name of the material and the place where it can be located:

[11]Final Report on Plagiarism, by Clarence W. Hach and the Curriculum Committee of the English Department, Evanston Township High School, May 23, 1961 (in the files of the English Department).

4. If you wish to refer to a thesis or dissertation, put the name of the author, title of work (in quotation marks), and the university where the work was completed, the date, and the page:

[12]H. L. Reynolds, "The Number of Commas in Early Renaissance Poetry," (unpublished Ph.D. dissertation, Department of English, University of Chicago), p. 78.

5. When you wish to refer to a book review, include the

Basic Forms for Footnotes

name of the author of the work being reviewed, the title of the work, the name of the reviewer, the place where the review appeared, date, volume and page:

¹³Henry Aiken, "Review of The Moral Nature of Man," by A. Campbell Garnett, Ethics, Vol. LXIII (January, 1953), pp. 140–42.

6. When you wish to refer to a citation taken from a secondary source, write the name of the author and the title of the original source and the page and then the place where it was quoted:

¹⁴Donald A. Stauffer, The Nature of Poetry, p. 58, quoted in Paul Engle and Warren Carrier, Reading Modern Poetry, p. 99.

Reference Words and Abbreviations Used in Footnotes

Here are some of the more common reference words and abbreviations used in footnotes.

bk., bks.	book or books
ca. (or *c.*)	*circa,* "about" or "near." Used with approximate dates: *ca.* 1776; "*ca.*" is preferable to "*c.*," which can also mean "chapter" or "copyright."
cf.	*confer,* "compare." Used, for example, when you wish to have your reader compare footnotes 22 and 23, which follow: *cf.* footnotes 22 and 23 or *cf.*

Ernest Hemingway, *The Sun Also Rises*, p. 15.

c., ch., chs., (or chap., chaps.)	chapter(s)
col., cols.	column(s)
comp.	compiled or compiler
ed., eds.	editor(s), edition(s)
e.g.	*exempli gratia*, "for example"
esp.	especially (as in "pp. 208–232, esp. p. 220")
et al.	*et alii*, "and others"
et seq.	*et sequens* and *et sequentes*, "and the one following," "and those that follow." But cf. "f.," "ff."
ex., exs.	example and examples
f., ff.	and the following page(s) or line(s). These abbreviations are replacing *et seq.*.
fig., figs.	figure(s)
fn.	footnote (Cf. "n.")
ibid.	*ibidem*, "in the same place"; i.e., the single title cited in the note immediately preceding.
idem	(no period; sometimes *id.*) "the same." Used in place of *ibid.* when the footnote is to the same source on exactly the same page as that referred to in the note immediately preceding.
i.e.	*id est* "that is"
illus.	illustrated, illustrator, illustration(s)
l., ll.	line, lines
ms.	manuscript
mss.	manuscripts
n. or nn.	note or notes (as "p. 48, n. 2").
n.b., N.B.	nota bene, "note well"

n.d.	no date
no., nos.	number(s)
op. cit.	*opere citato,* "in the work cited." If several different items have come between the first mention of a book and a subsequent reference to it in a footnote, the last name of the author is repeated, followed by *op. cit.* and the correct page number.
p. or pp.	page(s)
par., pars.	paragraph(s)
passim	"throughout the work, here and there" (as pp. 79, 144, *et passim*)
pref.	preface
pseud.	pseudonym, a pen name: e.g., Mark Twain, pseud.
rev.	review, reviewed (by); revised (by), revision
sec. (or sect.), secs.	section(s)
ser.	series
sic	"thus, so" If the word "*sic*" in brackets [*sic*] is inserted in a quotation, it shows that you are recognizing and pointing out an error or a questionable statement. For example: There were nine [*sic*] men on the bench at the time of his election. Your own additions to quotations are shown by bracketing those words added: "He [Herman Wouk] was a member of the New York Writers' Club."
st.	stanza
trans. (or tr.)	translator, translation, translated ("by" understood in contex)
vol., vols.	volume(s)
vs.	*versus,* "against"; also verse

Writing the Final Draft with Footnotes

Write the final draft of your paper with the footnotes. Leave a three-inch margin at the top of your first page and number each page beginning with page 2. Reread your paper several times to check the following:

1. Does your introductory paragraph engage the reader? Is it well developed? Does it set forth the controlling purpose of your paper?

2. Does your paper follow your outline exactly? Is it well paragraphed? Do your ideas flow logically from sentence to sentence?

3. Are your paragraph transitions natural and logical?

4. Does your concluding paragraph sum up your ideas and restate your controlling purpose? Is it a logical result of what you set out to prove?

5. Have you numbered all the ideas and direct quotations in the text and footnoted them correctly?

6. Have you tested the force and accuracy of specific words? Do you have interesting sentence variety?

7. Have you checked spelling, punctuation, and usage?

Your final paper will be evidence of your intelligent understanding of your subject, your discrimination in research, your care in refining your paper, and your accuracy in footnote and bibliography form.

Part 8

Writing the Final Bibliography

Most research papers have at the end a bibliography, a list of references actually used in writing the paper. (Sources listed on your bibliography cards that were consulted but not referred to in the paper are not listed.) This bibliography serves two purposes: (1) it shows what research was done; (2) it provides a list of references for those who may be especially interested in your topic and wish to investigate it further.

In preparing your bibliography, arrange all of the items alphabetically by the last name of the author. If no author or editor is given, the first word of the title (ignoring *A, An,* or *The*) determines the order.

Use the following forms for the different types of entries:

1. For a book—one author:

> Wright, Richard. <u>Black Boy</u>. New York: Harper and Row, 1945.

2. For a book—more than one author:

> Strunk, William, and E. B. White. <u>The Elements of Style</u>. Toronto, Canada: Macmillan, 1959.

3. For a book—compiled by an editor:

> Gold, Robert S. (ed.). <u>Point of Departure</u>. New York: Dell, 1967.

4. For a book—only one chapter used:

> Wilson, J. Dover. "The Theatre," <u>Life in Shakespeare's England</u>. Middlesex, England: Penguin, 1968, pp. 197–237.

5. For a magazine article—author given:

> Wills, Garry. "The Impeachment Man," <u>Atlantic Monthly</u>, Vol. 233 (May, 1974), pp. 79–84.

6. For a magazine article—no author given—alphabetized by title:

> "Open Secret," <u>Newsweek</u>, Vol. XXI (Jan. 11, 1943), pp. 62–63.

Treat pamphlets or reports like magazine articles unless no author is given; then use the following form:

7. For a pamphlet or report—no author given:

> American Medical Association. Medical Relations Under Workmen's Compensation, a Report Prepared by the Bureau of Medical Economics. Chicago: American Medical Association, 1976.

8. For an encyclopedia article—author given:

> Baines, Anthony Cuthbert. "Bagpipes," Encyclopaedia Britannica, Vol. 2 (1968), pp. 1036–37.

9. For an encyclopedia article—no author given—alphabetized by title:

> "Sarah Lawrence College," Collier's Encyclopedia, Vol. 20 (1968), p. 427.

10. For a newspaper article—no byline—alphabetized by title:

> "Making the Most of Your Summer," Chicago Tribune, June 15, 1976, p. 56.

11. For a newspaper article—byline given:

> Smith, John Justin. "Seeking the Trail of Jesus," Chicago Daily News, April 13–14, 1974, Sec. 2, pp. 19–20.

12. For a bibliographic entry for a casebook:

> Marcus, Mordecai. "The Unity of The Red Badge of Courage," Stephen Crane's The Red Badge of Courage: Text and Criticism, eds. Richard Lettis, Robert F. McDonnell and William E. Morris. New York: Harcourt, Brace, 1960, pp. 189–95.

13. For non-print material:

> "Shakespeare's Stratford," 76 frames, color with teaching guide, Literary Backgrounds, n.d.

14. For a book containing an article that first appeared in another source which is to be acknowledged:

> Van Ghent, Dorothy. "On Pride and Pre-
> judice," Pride and Prejudice: An Au-
> thoritative Text, Backgrounds, Re-
> views and Essays in Criticism, ed.
> Donald J. Gray. New York: Norton,
> 1966, pp. 362–73. Reprinted from
> Dorothy Van Ghent, The English Novel,
> Form and Function, New York: Holt,
> Rinehart, 1953, pp. 105–23.

Here are a few miscellaneous rules to follow:

1. If there are any facts of translation, editions, series, volumes, and the like, they should come immediately after the title, each item separated by a comma.

2. If the publication date is not given on the title page of a book, the copyright date should be used.

3. Page numbers are given only for articles from encyclopedias and periodicals and for pages of books only if a single chapter is used.

4. Each entry should be single-spaced, and there should be a double space between entries.

5. The second and following lines of each entry should be indented five spaces so that the last name of the author stands out. This is exactly the opposite of footnote form.

6. Put a period at the end of each entry.

7. If you have two references by the same author, you need not repeat the author's name. A straight line will be sufficient:

> Randolph, Vance. Ozark Mountain Folks. New
> York: The Vanguard Press, Inc., 1972.
>
> ————. Ozark Superstitions. New York: The
> Columbia University Press, 1977.

8. A bibliography may be divided into different classes in order to point out the types of sources used: books, pamphlets, periodicals, encyclopedias, and miscellaneous, such as newspapers, speeches, and interviews. In this plan, center each heading and arrange the sources alphabetically with each group.

9. If no author is given, the entry should be alphabetized by the first important word of the title.

Here is a sample bibliography divided into different classes.

BIBLIOGRAPHY

Books

Anouilh, Jean. The Lark, tr. by Christopher Fry. London: Oxford University Press, 1956.

Fry, Christopher. A Phoenix Too Frequent. London: Oxford University Press, 1951.

Grierson, S. H. J. G. Metaphysical Lyrics and Poems of the Seventeenth Century. Oxford: Clarendon Press, 1961.

Rothe, Anna (ed.) Current Biography. New York: H. W. Wilson Co., 1977.

Stanford, Derik. Christopher Fry Album. London and New York: Peter Nevill Ltd., 1972.

————. Christopher Fry, An Appreciation. London and New York: Peter Nevill Ltd., 1977.

Thor, with Angels. London: Oxford University Press, 1971.

Thrall, William Flint and Addison Hibbard. A Handbook to Literature. New York: Odyssey Press, 1966.

Whiting, B. J., et al. (eds.) The College Survey of English Literature. New York: Harcourt, Brace and Co., 1952.

Periodicals

Brown, John Mason. "Seeing Things," Saturday Review of Literature, Vol. XXXIII (Dec. 2, 1950), pp. 44–46.

Clurman, Harold. "Theatre: From Paris to London," New Republic, Vol. LXXII (June 5, 1970), pp. 21–22.

————. "Theatre: Two Ladies," New Republic, Vol. LXXIII (Nov. 27, 1950), p. 22.

Downes, Mollie Panter. "Letters From London," New Yorker, Vol. XXIV (Feb. 11, 1970), p. 85.

"Enter Poet Laughing," Time, Vol. LVI (Nov. 20, 1970), p. 10.

Hobson, Harold. "Poetic Drama Ascendent," Christian Science Monitor, (March 25, 1970), Magazine Section, p. 10.

"Theatre," Newsweek, Vol. XXVI (Nov. 24, 1976), p. 27.

Tomlinson, Elizabeth. "The Metaphysical Tradition in Three Modern Poets," College English, Vol. I (December, 1974), pp. 208–22.

Willis, James R., Jr. "The Metaphysical Lyric," Interpretations of The Lark, ed. William O. Matterly. New York: Morgan Publishing Co., 1975, pp. 91–103. Reprinted from The American Intellect, Vol. X (Spring, 1971), pp. 16–30.

Unpublished Material

Lundgren, Ralph. "The Boy with a Cart," A production thesis, Washington University, August, 1974.

Shank, Jon Beck. "Saints in Question," A poetry play with preface. Unpublished Master's thesis, Department of English, Brigham Young University, June, 1973.

Other Sources

————. Personal interview with Christopher Fry, Playwright, London, England, May 22, 1970.

————. Letter from Christopher Fry, Playwright, London, England, June 10, 1971.

Exercise
Writing the Final Bibliography

Following the correct form for your entries, prepare your final bibliography. Assemble your research paper in the following order.

1. Title page in whatever correct form your teacher requires
2. Page containing title at top, statement of controlling purpose beneath it, followed by your final outline
3. The text of your paper
4. The final bibliography

THE REALISM

OF

HENRY FLEMING

IN

STEPHEN CRANE'S

THE RED BADGE OF COURAGE

by

Craig Pirrong

3 English H
Mrs. Ichkoff
March 8

The Realism of Henry Fleming

in Stephen Crane's <u>The Red Badge of Courage</u>

<u>Controlling Purpose</u>: to demonstrate that Henry Fleming, the protagonist of Stephen Crane's <u>The Red Badge of Courage,</u> is an accurate portrayal of a Civil War soldier by comparing him with actual soldiers through their letters and diaries.

    I. A comparison of war experience
        A. Memoirs of actual Civil War soldiers
        B. Experiences of soldiers in <u>The Red Badge of Courage</u>

   II. Soldiers' attitudes toward battle
        A. Risks of combat
        B. Fear of cowardice
        C. Nervousness before battle

  III. Soldiers' change in attitude during battle
        A. Sense of urgency
        B. Feeling of rage
        C. Emergence of unity of purpose
            1. Abandonment of self
            2. Loyalty to army

   IV. Problems of desertion
        A. Mental struggle
        B. Physical exhaustion
        C. Rationalizations

    V. Differences between expectations and actualities of battle
        A. Physical
        B. Mental

   VI. Growing maturity of soldiers
        A. Coping with stress
        B. Attitude toward death

  VII. The reality of war experience
        A. In the Civil War
        B. In <u>The Red Badge of Courage</u>

Stephen Crane's The Red Badge of Courage was the first novel to explore the real feelings of a soldier going into action for the first time. Before The Red Badge, American fiction concerning the Civil War concentrated on the heroic deeds of soldiers and was marked by over-glorification and inaccuracy. However, the letters and diaries of actual Civil War soldiers reveal that these soldiers were more concerned with their feelings than their deeds. By examining the memoirs of Civil War soldiers and comparing them with experiences in The Red Badge, one can see that Stephen Crane's novel is an accurate portrayal of the reality of a soldier's emotions and resulting actions during the war.

Henry Fleming, the protagonist in The Red Badge, like many actual Civil War soldiers, feared the consequences of an impending battle. Henry thought that "as far as war was concerned he knew nothing of himself."[1] He also thought that "the only way to prove himself was to go into the blaze, and then figuratively to watch his legs to discover their merits and faults."[2] Many Civil War soldiers had the same feelings as Henry. Bell Wiley, a historian who has done extensive research on the Common Private of the Civil War, wrote that soldiers were more concerned with the question of how they would stand up in battle than they were over the chance of being wounded or killed.[3] One private wrote, "'I have a marked dread of the battle field, for I...have never seen a person die...& I am afraid

---

[1]Stephen Crane, The Red Badge of Courage, in The Complete Novels of Stephen Crane, ed. Thomas A. Gullason, p. 206.

[2]Ibid., p. 209.

[3]Bell Irvin Wiley, The Life of Billy Yank, p. 68.

that the groans of the wounded & dying will make me shake
nevertheless I hope & trust that strength will be given me
to stand & do my duty.'"[4]

The methods that soldiers devised to avoid battle or
to alleviate their doubts about their courage were many.
Some would self-inflict wounds; others would leave the front
on the pretense of a broken musket, helping a wounded
comrade, being ordered to do some special task by an
officer, illness or a "call of nature." Many never
returned.[5] Like Henry, some soldiers tried to relieve their
fear of battle by calculating the odds of their being hit
or their chances of running. Officers, as well as common
soldiers, computed the risks of combat. Before the Battle
of Perryville, three brigade commanders discussed the
chances of their getting hit and of their troops' running.
The generals predicted that their troops would stay and
fight and that they themselves would not be hit, but all
three were killed and their brigades were routed.[6] Like
Henry's own calculations, the officers' calculations
were wrong.

Some soldiers tried to hide their fear and go into the
fight as bravely as possible. One of these real soldiers
was Elbridge Capp. Like Henry, who felt that he had to "go
into the blaze," Elbridge said to himself, "'I must face the
danger.'"[7] Others resolved to let death solve their

---

[4]Bell Irvin Wiley, The Common Soldier of the Civil War,
p. 56.

[5]Wiley, Billy Yank, p. 86.

[6]James M. Hillard, "'You Are Strangely Deluded':
General William Terrill," Civil War Times Illustrated,
Vol. XIII (February, 1975), p. 18.

[7]Elbridge Capp, Reminiscences of the War of the
Rebellion, p. 135.

problems. One of these soldiers said, "'I'm willin ter die ...but I don't want ter be no coward.'"[8] Another private, Sam Watkins, said, "I had made up my mind to die."[9] Henry had these same feelings, thinking "that it would be better to get killed directly and end his troubles."[10] He thought it better to "fall facing the enemy, than to play the coward."[11]

The descriptions of Henry's feelings immediately before and during battle were consistent with the accounts of both Federal and Confederate soldiers. Before facing fire for the first time, Henry was "in a fever of impatience."[12] Most soldiers experienced this same feeling. One wrote that nothing "brings...such crucial trial as the throbbing emotions that immediately precede the clash of arms."[13] Another private said that "the knowledge of an impending battle always sent that thrill of fear and horror."[14]

Once the firing started, however, Henry's feelings, as well as those of most soldiers, changed. Henry had been advised that a man changed in battle, and he found it was true.[15] Before he went into action, Henry's main concern was for himself. After the battle opened in earnest, however, his outlook changed: "He suddenly lost concern

---

[8] William Hinman, Si Klegg and His Pard, p. 400.

[9] Sam R. Watkins, Co. Aytch, p. 234.

[10] Crane, p. 220.

[11] Wiley, Billy Yank, p. 68.

[12] Crane, p. 219.

[13] Hinman, p. 339.

[14] Capp, p. 140.

[15] Crane, p. 219.

for himself, and forgot to look at a menacing fate."[16]
He became an automaton.

> He was at a task. He was like a carpenter who
> has made many boxes, making still another box,
> only there was furious haste in his movements. . .
> Following this came a red rage. He developed the
> acute exasperation of a pestered animal, a
> well—meaning cow worried by dogs. His impotency
> appeared to him, and made his rage into that of a
> driven beast.[17]

Civil war veterans' reminiscences echo Henry's change from
fear to indifference, rage and urgency. One private wrote,
"'Strange as it may seam to you, but the more men I saw
killed the more reckless I became.'"[18] Henry Morton Stanley,
the famous explorer, also described this feeling of urgency.
He wrote, "We plied our arms, loaded, and fired, with such
nervous haste as though it depended on each of us how soon
this fiendish uproar would be hushed."[19] Oliver Norton, a
Pennsylvania infantryman wrote, "I acted like a madman....
The feeling that was uppermost in my mind was a desire to
kill as many rebels as I could."[20] A third soldier, like
Henry, wished to grapple face to face with his enemies:
"'I was mad...;how I itched for a hand—to—hand struggle.'"[21]
    Gradually a feeling of unity—oneness—with the army,
the corps, the regiment manifested itself in both the

---

[16]Ibid., p. 225.

[17]Ibid., pp. 225—226.

[18]Wiley, Billy Yank, p. 71.

[19]Henry Morton Stanley, "Henry Stanley Fights with
the Dixie Grays at Shiloh," The Blue and the Gray,
Vol. I, ed. H.S. Commager, p. 354.

[20]Oliver Norton, Army Letters, p. 91.

[21]Wiley, Billy Yank, p. 72.

average Civil War private and in Henry Fleming. Throughout
The Red Badge Henry calls himself "part of a vast blue
demonstration."[22] When he first came under fire, Henry
thought that

> He became not a man but a member. He felt that
> something of which he was a part—a regiment, an army,
> a cause, or a country—was in a crisis. He was welded
> into a common personality which was dominated by a
> single desire. For some moments he could not flee,
> no more than a little finger can commit a revolution
> from a hand.
> There was a consciousness always of the presence of
> his comrades about him. He felt the subtle battle
> brotherhood more potent even than the cause for which
> they were fighting. It was a mysterious fraternity
> born of the smoke and danger of death.[23]

This same feeling was expressed by many Federals and
Confederates. Bruce Catton, the Civil War historian, wrote
that "the instinctive loyalty of all of these men went...
to the army."[24] Henry Morton Stanley wrote that, "there were
about four hundred companies like the Dixie Greys, who
shared our feelings."[25] Sergeant Thomas H. Evans, a member
of the regular army, said that an "abandonment of self"[26]
emerged in battle. At the surrender of the Army of Northern
Virginia, one private, "unwilling to outlive his army,"[27]

---

[22]Crane, p. 205.

[23]Ibid., p. 225

[24]Bruce Catton, This Hallowed Ground, p. 360.

[25]Stanley, p. 354.

[26]Thomas H. Evans, "'There is no use trying to dodge
shot,'" Civil War Times Illustrated, Vol. VI (August,
1967), p. 43.

[27]William C. Davis, "The Campaign to Appomattox,"
Civil War Times Illustrated, Vol. XIV (August, 1975), p. 40.

shouted, "'Blow, Gabriel, blow!'"[28] These loyalties became "more potent even than the cause for which they were fighting."[29]

On the other hand, flight from the field of battle was not uncommon to Civil War soldiers. In fact, "there was a considerable amount of malingering, skulking, and running in every major battle."[30] Henry's own reasons for running were similar to those of many who fled from an actual battle. When the Confederates charged for the second time, Henry ran. He saw "a revelation."[31] When he fled, "There was no shame on his face."[32] A soldier in the Twelfth Connecticut was much like Henry. William DeForest described the soldier in these terms: "He did not look wild with fright; he simply looked alarmed and resolved to get out of danger;... he was confounded by the peril of the moment and thought of nothing but getting away from it."[33]

Soldiers who fled from the field of battle were generally beset with a conflict between their bodies and their souls. When the Rebels charged for the second time, Henry was exhausted and dismayed. "He seemed to shut his eyes and wait to be gobbled."[34] William Hinman echoed Henry's feelings, saying that a soldier had to

---

[28]Ibid.

[29]Crane, p. 225.

[30]Wiley, Common Soldier, p. 26.

[31]Crane, p. 230.

[32]Ibid.

[33]John William DeForest, A Volunteer's Adventures, p. 63.

[34]Crane, p. 230.

...go through the struggle...between his mental and
physical natures. The instinct of the latter at such a
time—and what soldier does not know it?—was to seek
a place of safety, without a moment's delay. To fully
subdue this feeling by the power of will was not...
such an easy a matter as might be imagined....Some
there were who could never do it.35

Soldiers who ran usually tried to rationalize their actions.
Henry thought that he had been right in running because he

...was a little piece of the army. He considered the
time, he said, to be one in which it was the duty of
every little piece to rescue itself if possible. Later
the officers could fit the little pieces together
again, and make a battle front. If none of the little
pieces were wise enough to save themselves from the
flurry of death at such a time, why, then, where would
be the army? It was all plain that he had proceeded
according to very correct and commendable rules.36

Henry again tried to demonstrate to himself that he was
right by "throwing a pine cone at a jovial squirrel."37
When the youth saw that the squirrel fled rather than let
the missile strike him, Henry felt that, "Nature had
given him a sign."38

Actual combatants who ran from battle gave somewhat
less symbolic and complicated, yet similar, excuses. George
Townsend, a hospital steward, stumbled on a group of
skulkers at the Battle of Cedar Mountain and recorded:

Some of these miserable wretches...muttered that they
were not to be hood-winked and slaughtered.
"I was sick, anyway," said one fellow, "and felt
like droppin' on the road."

35Hinman, p. 398.

36Crane, p. 233.

37Crane, p. 234.

38Ibid., p. 235.

"I didn't trust my colonel," said another; "he ain't
no soldier."
"I'm tired of the war, anyhow," said a third, "and
my time's up soon; so I shan't have my head blown
off."[39]

One soldier who deserted his comrades at the Battle of
Corinth said on his return that he had not run, but had been
detailed to guard a water tank. His comrades never let him
live it down.[40] Another soldier, nicknamed "Spinney," said
he had run because he thought that the bullets were calling
his name.[41]

Henry found battle time to be very different from what
he had conceived it would be. At first, he "had the belief
that real war was a series of death struggles with small
time in between for sleep and meals."[42] He learned later,
however, that battle took up very little time in a soldier's
life.[43] He also thought that "Secular and religious
education had obliterated the throat-grappling instinct."[44]
However, when the Confederates were attacking for the first
time, and Henry "wished to rush forward and strangle with
his fingers,"[45] he realized that this thought was wrong,
too.

---

[39]George A. Townsend, "A Camp of Skulkers at Cedar
Mountain." The Blue and the Gray, Vol. I, ed. H.S.
Commager, p. 493.

[40]Wiley, Billy Yank, pp. 87-88.

[41]Warren Lee Goss, "Yorktown and Williamsburg,"
Battles and Leaders of the Civil War, Vol. II, eds. Robert
U. Johnson and Clarence C. Buel, p. 197.

[42]Crane, p. 205.

[43]Ibid.

[44]Ibid.

[45]Ibid., p. 225.

Many actual soldiers also experienced a difference between their expectations and the realities of battle. Henry Morton Stanley wrote, "It was the first Field of Glory I had seen in my May of life, and the first time that Glory sickened me with its repulsive aspect, and made me suspect it was all a glittering lie."[46] Sam Watkins wrote, "I had heard and read of battlefields...but I must confess that I never realized the 'pomp and circumstance' of the thing called glorious war until I saw this."[47] Some were so naive about the realities of war that they were surprised that the enemy was firing bullets.[48] This difference between the untrained soldiers' image of war and the realities of combat was well portrayed in The Red Badge of Courage.

Under the stress of combat, both Henry Fleming and many actual Civil War soldiers rapidly matured. Henry's attainment of maturity was both quick and dramatic. Early in The Red Badge, Henry felt the need to make excuses to escape the reality of his cowardice, but by the end of the book, Henry was able to look upon his feats, both bad and good, objectively. He thought that "He could look back upon the brass and bombast of his earlier gospels and see them truly."[49] Earlier, when Henry had been walking with a wounded soldier called the tattered man, Henry felt guilty and embarrassed because he himself had no wound, while everyone around him had a "red badge of courage."[50] To escape his guilt and embarrassment, Henry ran from the

---

[46]Stanley, p. 357.

[47]Watkins, p. 42.

[48]Ibid. and Stanley, p. 353.

[49]Crane, p. 298.

[50]Ibid., p. 240.

tattered man, feeling that he "could have strangled"[51] his
wounded companion. By the end of The Red Badge, however,
Henry realized that the tattered man had actually been
trying to help him, and he felt guilty for deserting this
man who had cared for him and aided him.[52] When Henry had
outgrown the selfishness of immaturity, he could finally
say of himself that "He was a man."[53]

Henry's attainment of maturity was common to many
adolescent soldiers. Bell Wiley wrote, "One of the most
interesting things about the boy soldiers was the speed
with which they matured under the stress and strain of army
life."[54] Sam Watkins, a Confederate private, wrote that
early in the war "we wanted to march off and whip twenty
Yankees. But we soon found that the glory of war was at home
with the ladies, not upon the field of blood and...death....
I might say the agony of mind were very different indeed
from the patriotic times at home."[55] One soldier wrote:

> With the new troops, they have not been called on to
> train or restrain their nerves. They are not only
> nervous, but they blanch at the thought of danger....
> What to them, on joining the service, was a terrible
> mental strain, is soon transformed into indifference.[56]

This view of the experience of war is also similar to
Henry's. Before Henry had attained his maturity, he was
nervous and afraid of how the strain of battle and the

---

[51]Ibid., p. 245.

[52]Ibid., p. 297.

[53]Ibid., p. 298.

[54]Wiley, Billy Yank, p. 301.

[55]Watkins, p. 21.

[56]Frank Holsinger, "How It Feels To Be Under Fire,"
The Blue and the Gray, Vol. I, ed. H.S. Commager, p. 308.

thought of death would affect him. After he had "become a man," however, Henry could say matter-of-factly that "He had been to touch the great death, and found that, after all, it was but the great death."[57]

Henry's final understanding of the meaning of life and death has emerged from his experiences during war. His diverse emotional experiences, his growth to maturity, and his eventual feeling of unity with his comrades all parallel the experiences that actual Civil war soldiers have recorded in their letters and diaries. These parallel experiences reveal that The Red Badge of Courage is an accurate representation of real life under the conditions of the Civil War.

---

[57]Crane, p. 298.

BIBLIOGRAPHY

Books

Capp, Elbridge. Reminiscences of the War of the Rebellion. Nashua, New Hampshire: The Telegraph Publishing Co., 1911.

Catton, Bruce. This Hallowed Ground. Garden City, New York: Doubleday and Co., Inc., 1956.

Crane, Stephen. The Red Badge of Courage, in The Complete Novels of Stephen Crane. Ed. Thomas A. Gullason. Garden City, New York: Doubleday and Co., Inc., 1967.

DeForest, John William. A Volunteer's Adventures. New Haven, Connecticut: Yale University Press, 1946.

Hinman, William. Si Klegg and His Pard. Cleveland: N. G. Hamilton and Co., 1892.

Holsinger, Frank. "How It Feels To Be Under Fire." The Blue and the Gray. Vol. I. Ed. H.S. Commager. Indianapolis: Bobbs-Merrill Co., Inc., 1950.

Johnson, Robert U. and Clarence C. Buel. (eds.) Battles and Leaders of the Civil War. Vol. II. New York: Thomas Yoseloff, Inc., 1956.

Norton, Oliver. Army Letters. Chicago: O.C. Deming Co., 1903.

Stanley, Henry Morton. "Henry Morton Stanley Fights with the Dixie Grays at Shiloh." The Blue and the Gray. Vol. I. Ed. H.S. Commager. Indianapolis: Bobbs-Merrill Co., Inc., 1950.

Townsend, George. "A Camp of Skulkers at Cedar Mountain." The Blue and The Gray. Vol. I. Ed. H.S. Commager. Indianapolis: Bobbs-Merrill Co., Inc., 1950.

Watkins, Sam R. Co. Aytch. New York: The Macmillan Co., 1962.

Wiley, Bell Irvin. The Common Soldier of the Civil War. Gettysburg: Historical Times Inc., 1973.

Wiley, Bell Irvin. The Life of Billy Yank. Indianapolis: The Bobbs-Merrill Co., Inc., 1951.

Periodicals

Davis, William C. "The Campaign to Appomattox," Civil War Times Illustrated, Vol. XIV (April 1975), p. 40.

Evans, Thomas H. "'There is no use trying to dodge shot,'" Civil War Times Illustrated, Vol. VI (August 1967), p. 43.

Hillard, James M. "'You Are Strangely Deluded': General William Terrill," Civil War Times Illustrated, Vol. XIII (February 1975), p. 18.

Chapter 11

The Library and Its Reference Materials

Knowing how to use library resources efficiently is an asset to every student. Whether you do research in literature, history, science, or other disciplines, the library is an indispensable tool.

To make effective use of the library, however, it is necessary for you to know (1) how books are classified and arranged, and (2) how to use the card catalog.

Reference books are also a valuable source of information. They include dictionaries, encyclopedias, almanacs, catalogs, atlases, biographical reference books, literary reference books, and magazines.

This chapter will give you the basic information you need to make the best use of the library.

Part 1
The Classification and Arrangement of Books

Finding any book you need requires a knowledge of how books are classified and how they are arranged on the shelves.

The Classification of Books

Fiction. Works of fiction (novels and anthologies of short stories) are usually arranged in alphabetical order by author. When there are two or more books written by the same author, you would find them shelved alphabetically by title. For example, Ray Bradbury's books would be found under *B*. His *Dandelion Wine* and *Fahrenheit 451* would be followed by *Martian Chronicles*.

Nonfiction. Most libraries—including high school libraries —use the Dewey Decimal System, named for its originator, the American librarian, Melvil Dewey. There are ten major classifications in the Dewey Decimal System; all books fit into one of these classifications.

THE TEN MAJOR CLASSIFICATIONS ARE THESE:

000–009 **General Works** (encyclopedias, handbooks, almanacs, etc.)
100–199 **Philosophy** (includes psychology, ethics, etc.)
200–299 **Religion** (the Bible, theology, mythology)
300–399 **Social Science** (sociology, economics, government, education, law, folklore)
400–499 **Language** (languages, grammars, dictionaries)
500–599 **Science** (mathematics, chemistry, physics, biology, etc.)
600–699 **Useful Arts** (farming, cooking, sewing, nursing, engineering, radio, television, gardening, inventions)

700–799	**Fine Arts** (music, painting, drawing, acting, photography, games, sports, amusements)
800–899	**Literature** (poetry, plays, essays)
900–999	**History** (biography, travel, geography)

As you can see from the major categories of the Dewey Decimal System, each discipline has a classification number. For example, all books on the fine arts are classified between 700 and 799, and all history books will be found between 900 and 999. The system becomes more detailed as each of these major groups is subdivided. The table below subdivides works in literature as follows:

800–899	**Literature**	810	**American literature**
810	American literature	811	Poetry
820	English literature	812	Drama
830	German literature	813	Fiction
840	French literature	814	Essays
850	Italian literature	815	Speeches
860	Spanish literature	816	Letters
870	Latin literature (classic)	817	Satire and Humor
880	Greek literature (classic)	818	Miscellany
890	Other literature	819	Canadian-English literature

The numbers in a particular classification combined with the letter of the author's last name make up the **call number.** The call number helps you locate the book on the shelf once you have found it in the card catalog.

Arrangement of Books on the Shelves

You can see that books are arranged numerically on the library's shelves in order of classification. Most libraries prominently mark their shelves with the numbers indicating the books to be found in each particular section. Like fiction books, nonfiction books are arranged alphabetically by authors' last names under their subject classification.

Biographies are one of the most popular kinds of books in libraries. The Dewey Decimal System division for them is 920. However, large libraries will often place biographies in a separate section because of the large number of these books. In this case, they will have a "B" on the spine of the book and on the catalog card. If you are looking for a particular biography and are unable to locate it, ask the librarian for assistance.

Reference Books are located in the library's reference room or area. They are categorized in the Dewey Decimal System and often with the letter "R" or "Ref" above the classification number. Usually, a reference book may not be checked out from the library.

Exercise
The Classification and Arrangement of Books

Using the Dewey Decimal Classification summary on pages 256 and 257, assign the correct classification number to each of the following books:

1. *The Book of Jazz*, by Leonard Feather
2. *Ancient Greece*, by Roger Green
3. *Economics and the Public Purpose*, by John Kenneth Galbraith
4. *The Concise Oxford Dictionary of Current English*, ed. J. B. Sykes
5. *The Treasury of House Plants*, by Rob Herwig
6. *Law and Everyday Life*, by Elinor Swiger
7. *Decisive Battles of the Civil War*, by Joseph Mitchell
8. *Fireside Book of Humorous Poetry*, ed. William Cole
9. *The Teenager and Psychology*, by Robert Gelinas
10. *Camping and Woodcraft*, by Horace Kephart
11. *Masters of the Drama*, by John Gassner
12. *Handbook of the World's Religions*, by A. M. Zehavi
13. *Explorations in Chemistry*, by Charles Gray
14. *Highlights of the Olympics*, by John Durant
15. *Tomorrow's Math*, by C. Stanley Ogilvy

Part 2

Using the Card Catalog

The **card catalog** will determine whether the library has the book you want and, if so, where you will find it. The card catalog is a cabinet of small drawers or file trays containing alphabetically arranged cards. Each card bears the title of the book and the classification or call number of the book. (Sample cards are found on pages 259 and 260.)

There are usually three cards for the same book in the card catalog. There are the *author card*, the *title card*, and the *subject card*. The convenience of having three different ways of finding a book is described here.

The Author Card. Perhaps you are writing a paper for an elective film class about the Moving Picture Industry. Narrowing your topic to famous Hollywood screenwriters, you choose to investigate a source on the subject by Thomas Dardis. You look up his name in the card catalog and find that the author card will appear like this:

810.90   **Dardis, Thomas**
D

       Some time in the sun / by Thomas Dardis. New York: Scribner, [1976]
      274 p. : ill

    Bibliography: p. 253–256

Author cards for all books by an author will be filed together alphabetically according to title. Books *by* an author are followed by books **about** an author.

The Title Card. If you know the title of a book but not the author's name, the title card will help you locate the book. Look in the card catalog for a card bearing the title at the top of the card.

The place of the title card in the catalog is determined by the first letter of the first word in the tile. (*A*, *An*, and *The* do not count as first words.)

810.90
D   **Some time in the sun**

       Dardis, Thomas
           Some time in the sun / by Thomas
       Dardis. New York: Scribner, [1976]
           274 p. : ill

       Bibliography: p. 253–256

                  ○

The Subject Card. In your investigation of the movie industry, you may not have a particular book in mind. However, you suspect there are many books on your particular subject. In the card catalog you will find a subject card similar to this:

810.90
D   **Moving Picture Industry—Hollywood**

       Dardis, Thomas
           Some time in the sun / by Thomas
       Dardis, New York: Scribner, [1976] 274 p. : ill

       Bibliography: p. 253–256

       The Hollywood years of Fitzgerald, Faulkner,
       Nathanael West, Aldous Huxley, and James
       Agee.   ○

Subject cards are most useful when you want information on a specific topic from a variety of sources. Cards for all books on a particular subject are cataloged together. The subject card may also indicate that a book has chapters on a single aspect of the topic you are interested in, and the publication date on the card will help you find the most up-to-date book on your subject.

The Information on Catalog Cards

The three types of catalog cards—author, title, subject—carry the same information. This information includes:

1. The call number.
2. The title, author, publisher, and date of publication.
3. The number of pages, and a notation on whether the book has illustrations, maps, table, or other features.

Cross Reference Cards

Occasionally, while researching a particular subject, you will find a card that reads *See* or *See also*. The "See" card refers you to another subject heading in the catalog which will give you the information you want.

```
Conservation of energy resources

     see

Energy conservation
```

The "See also" card refers you to other subjects closely related to the one you are interested in. This card may be helpful to you in making sure that your research on a particular topic is complete.

Compare the cross reference cards and see how they both will be beneficial to you in doing thorough research of a topic:

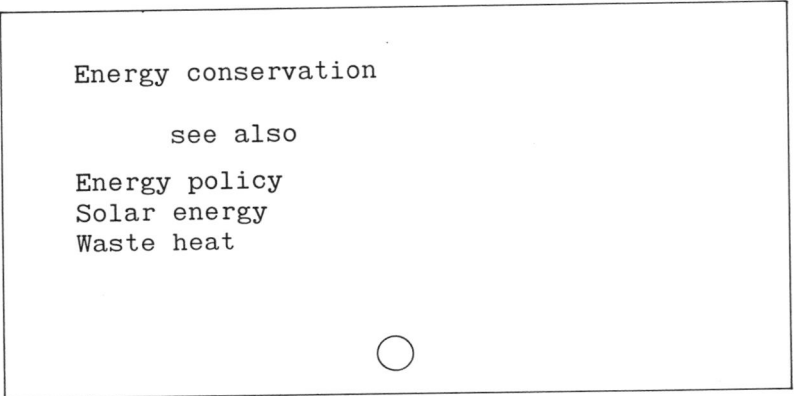

Guide Cards

Besides the catalog cards, you will find guide cards in the cabinet trays. The guide card bears a tab that projects above the other cards. It will aid you in finding other catalog cards quickly. For example, in researching the topic of television advertising, you will find catalog cards easily by means of alphabetically arranged guide cards like these:

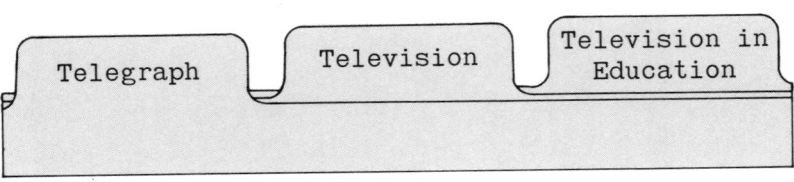

Exercise
Using the Card Catalog

Use the card catalog to find the author, title and call number of a book on the following subjects:

1. A history of Western music
2. A book about motorcycles
3. A novel on frontier and pioneer life
4. A collection of Greek myths
5. A book on Chinese cooking
6. A dictionary of usage and style
7. A book on playing chess
8. A book on the discovery of North America
9. A book showing how to draw maps
10. A biography of Henri Matisse
11. A source book of medieval history
12. A book of personal narratives of slaves
13. A history of firearms
14. A book on educational tests and measurements
15. A novel by William Faulkner

Part 3

Using Reference Materials

One of the best ways to obtain information on a particular topic is to consult a reference work. Libraries have either a reference section or a reference room. It is here that you will find just about everything you want, from a *Newsweek* article that reviews a recently published novel to a college catalog from a local junior college.

Reference works include the following: dictionaries; encyclopedias; pamphlets, handbooks, and catalogs; almanacs and yearbooks; atlases; biographical reference books; literary reference books; and magazines.

Reference works are tools, and like tools, should be used in definite ways. Most reference works have prefaces which describe how information is arranged, show sample entries, and explain the symbols and abbreviations used in the book. Before using any reference work for the first time, you would be wise to at least skim the preface.

The basic types of reference books are described in this section.

Dictionaries

The most widely used reference books in the library are the general dictionaries. General dictionaries fall into three major categories:

1. **Unabridged** dictionaries are dictionaries with over 250,000 entries.

2. **"College"** or **"desk"** **dictionaries** generally carry 130,000 to 150,000 entries.

3. **Concise** or **"pocket"** dictionaries are those with a smaller number of entries.

Unabridged Dictionaries. An unabridged dictionary may contain up to 500,000 words. It gives uncommon, as well as common meanings of many words, and explains in detail how they are used. The best known unabridged dictionaries are the following:

> *Webster's Third New International Dictionary*
> *The Random House Dictionary of the English Language,*
> *Unabridged Edition*

You will find at least one—if not both—of these in your school or community library.

College or Desk Dictionaries. A college or desk dictionary is a quick and convenient reference. It provides information you would normally need about definitions, spellings, pronunciations, and matters of usage. It usually contains a special section which gives biographical information about well known people, and articles on such topics as pronunciation, spelling, and dialects.

Your school or local library probably carries several different college dictionaries. The best known are these:

The American Heritage Dictionary of the English Language
The Macmillan Dictionary
*The Random House Dictionary of the English Language,
    College Edition*
Thorndike-Barnhart Dictionary
Webster's New Collegiate Dictionary
Webster's New World Dictionary of the American Language

Dictionaries about Language. Another group of dictionaries is available to you. Each of these deals with a specific aspect of our English language: synonyms and antonyms, rhymes, slang, Americanisms, etymology, and so forth.

As a young writer, you need to be concerned with precision in your writing. A help in finding the precise word you are looking for is a **thesaurus,** or dictionary of synonyms.

A thesaurus should be used only as a "memory-jogger," to help you find words that are already in your vocabulary. You are treading on dangerous ground if you select from a thesaurus a word you don't know in place of a word you do know. From your study of Chapter 1, you know that most synonyms are not interchangeable.

A list of reliable thesauruses follows:

Roget's International Thesaurus
Roget's Thesaurus in Dictionary Form
Roget's Thesaurus of English Words and Phrases
Webster's Collegiate Thesaurus
Webster's Dictionary of Synonyms

Additional dictionaries dealing with our language are the following:

*Abbreviations Dictionary: (Abbreviations, Acronyms,
    Contractions, Signs and Symbols Defined)*
Acronyms, Initialisms, and Abbreviations Dictionary
Brewer's Dictionary of Phrase and Fable
A Dictionary of American Idioms
Dictionary of American Slang

Dictionary of Literary Terms
A Dictionary of Slang and Unconventional English
A Dictionary of Word and Phrase Origins (3 Volumes)
Harper Dictionary of Contemporary Usage
Mathews Dictionary of Americanisms
The Oxford Dictionary of English Etymology
Wood's Unabridged Rhyming Dictionary

Special-Purpose Dictionaries. Finally, there are special-purpose dictionaries that deal exclusively with music, medicine, foreign language, and many other subjects. These include the following:

FOREIGN LANGUAGE:

Cassell's Dutch Dictionary
Cassell's French Dictionary
Cassell's German Dictionary
Cassell's Italian Dictionary
Cassell's New Latin Dictionary
Cassell's Spanish Dictionary

HISTORY:

Concise Dictionary of American History
Dictionary of American History
A New Dictionary of British History

LITERATURE:

Dictionary of Fictional Characters
Dictionary of Literary Terms
Dictionary of World Literary Terms
Webster's Dictionary of Proper Names

MATH AND SCIENCE:

Compton's Illustrated Science Dictionary
Dictionary of Biology
Dictionary of Science and Technology
The International Dictionary of Applied Mathematics

MUSIC AND ART:

Grove's Dictionary of Music and Musicians (10 volumes)

Harvard Dictionary of Music
Bryan's Dictionary of Painters and Engravers (5 volumes)
McGraw-Hill Dictionary of Art (5 volumes)

Encyclopedias

General Encyclopedias. An encyclopedia (from the Greek *enkyklios paideia*, which means "general education") is a collection of articles alphabetically arranged in volumes on nearly every conceivable subject. It is designed for quick reference, and provides you with general information on various fields or branches of learning.

Guide letters on the spine of each volume and guide words at the top of the pages assist you in finding information. It is best, however, to check the general index when looking for information. It may list several good sources. For up-to-date information on a topic, check the yearbook which many encyclopedias include.

Never use an encyclopedia as your only source. Use it only to obtain a general survey of your subject. The library is a storehouse of information; an encyclopedia should be used only as a door to that storehouse.

Most libraries include the following encyclopedias in their reference section:

GENERAL ENCYCLOPEDIAS

Collier's Encyclopedia (24 volumes)
    Publishes *Collier's Yearbook*; Volume 24 includes a
    bibliography and Index
Encyclopaedia Britannica (30 volumes)
    Publishes *Britannica Book of the Year*; includes separate
    Index and Atlas for the set (more details follow)
Encyclopedia Americana (30 volumes)
    Publishes *Americana Annual*
World Book Encyclopedia (22 volumes)
    Publishes annual supplement; Volume 22 includes
    Research Guide and Index

The *Encyclopaedia Britannica* is unique in its organization. In dealing with the great amounts of knowledge known to humankind, the *Britannica* has broken down its encyclopedia into three parts: the *Propaedia* (*pro* meaning "prior to"), the *Micropaedia* (*micro* meaning "small") and the *Macropaedia* (*macro* meaning "big").

The *Propaedia*, or Outline of Knowledge and Guide to the *Britannica*, presents more than 15,000 different topics, arranged according to fields or areas of knowledge. For each topic in the Outline, there are references to the *Macropaedia* of three kinds: (1) whole articles, (2) sections of articles, (3) other references. These references make possible systematic study or reading on any subject in the encyclopedia.

The *Micropaedia*, consisting of 10 volumes, is a ready reference and index to the entire encyclopedia. As a ready reference, it is a short-entry encyclopedia. Its more than 100,000 entries, arranged in alphabetical order, give the most important and interesting facts about their subject. Often this is all you will want to know. But when a subject is also treated in depth in the *Macropaedia*, the *Micropaedia* becomes an index.

The *Macropaedia*, which contains knowledge in depth, is the main body of the *Britannica*. The *Macropaedia's* 19 volumes contain 4,207 long articles by world-renowned contributors on major subjects.

Encyclopedias on Specific Subjects. Encyclopedias on a wide variety of specific subjects fill library shelves. To give you some idea of the diversity of encyclopedias, here is a partial list:

ENCYCLOPEDIAS ON SPECIFIC SUBJECTS

ART:

Encyclopedia of Modern Art
LaRousse Encyclopedia of Byzantine and Medieval Art
LaRousse Encyclopedia of Prehistoric and Ancient Art
LaRousse Encyclopedia of Renaissance and Baroque Art

HISTORY:

An Encyclopedia of World History
Encyclopedia of American History

HOBBIES AND INTERESTS:

Encyclopedia of Gardening
The Illustrated Encyclopedia of World Coins
The International Encyclopedia of Cooking

LITERATURE:

The Concise Encyclopedia of English and American Poets and Poetry
The Concise Encyclopedia of Modern Drama
LaRousse Encyclopedia of Mythology
McGraw-Hill Encyclopedia of World Biography (12 volumes)
McGraw-Hill Encyclopedia of World Drama (4 volumes)

RELIGION AND OCCULTISM:

Encyclopaedia of Occultism
Encyclopaedia of Religion

SCIENCE AND MATHEMATICS:

The Concise Encyclopedia of Archeology
Encyclopaedia of Animal Care
The Encyclopedia of Chemistry
Grzimek's Animal Life Encyclopedia (13 volumes)
The Illustrated Encyclopedia of Aviation and Space
International Encyclopedia of Social Sciences (17 volumes)
The Mammals of America
The Pictorial Encyclopedia of Birds
Universal Encyclopedia of Mathematics

SPORTS:

The Baseball Encyclopedia
Encyclopedia of Auto Racing Greats

Pamphlets, Handbooks, and Catalogs

The Vertical File. Pamphlets, handbooks, booklets, and clippings on a variety of subjects are available in most libraries. These subjects include information about vocations, travel, census data, and program schedules. It is here you may find college catalogs, too. All of this information is kept in a set of file cabinets called the **vertical file.**

One of the most important ideas behind the vertical file is that the information in it is current. This file can be an invaluable source to you when writing a report on a contemporary topic, seeking current statistics, or looking up information on careers.

Information about Vocations, Colleges and Universities. The reference section of the library can be a starting point in seeking information about careers and about colleges. Again, depending on the size of your library, the availability of materials does vary. Here is a list of some resources you might use:

> *Encyclopedia of Careers and Vocations*
> *Barron's Guide to the Two-Year Colleges*
> *Barron's Profiles of American Colleges*
> *Lovejoy's College Guide*

The 300 section of your reference area will provide related material. Many libraries also have on reserve many college catalogs.

Almanacs and Yearbooks

Published annually, almanacs and yearbooks are useful sources of facts and statistics on current events, as well as on matters of historical record in government, economics, population, sports, and other fields:

> *Guinness Book of World Records*
> *Information Please Almanac, Atlas and Yearbook*

Statesman's Yearbook
Statistical Abstract of the United States
Women's Rights Almanac
World Almanac and Book of Facts

Atlases

We usually think of an atlas mainly as a book of maps, but it also contains interesting data on a number of subjects. The excellent *National Geographic Atlas of the World*, for example, lists some of the following topics in its table of contents: "Great Moments in Geography," "Global Statistics," and sections on population, temperature, oceans, and place names. Below is a list of other widely used atlases:

Atlas of World History
Atlas of World Wildlife
The Britannica Atlas
Collier's World Atlas and Gazetteer
Goode's World Atlas
Grosset World Atlas
The International Atlas from Rand McNally
The Times Atlas of the World

Biographical References

There are brief biographical notations in dictionaries and longer biographical articles in encyclopedias. Often, however, a better source is one of the specialized works listed below:

Current Biography. Biographies of current newsworthy individuals are published here monthly. Each issue is indexed. All copies are bound in an annual volume with a cumulated index of people in that particular volume as well as previous annual volumes. Also found at the end of the annual volumes are the names of the people in *Current Biography* according to their profession. Biographies of internationally known persons are found here, but Americans are well represented throughout this reference.

Dictionary of American Biography. This is the most famous and most reliable of all American biographical dictionaries. Alphabetically arranged, this twenty-two-volume work carries articles on the lives and accomplishments of prominent deceased Americans. The work contains 14,870 biographies of Americans from the colonial days to 1940. It is kept up-to-date by supplements. The length of the articles varies from half-page sketches to chapter-length essays.

Dictionary of National Biography. This multi-volume dictionary is the most famous and the most reliable of British biographical dictionaries. Its accurate and concise information makes it a most valuable source. It includes only Englishmen who are no longer living.

The International Who's Who. Alphabetically listed, this source provides brief biographical sketches of prominent living people of all nations. This publication includes thousands of personalities and provides a valuable source for current biographies.

Webster's Biographical Dictionary. This is a source of biographical facts about past and present noteworthy people. More than 40,000 individuals are listed alphabetically and pronunciation keys are given for each name.

Who's Who. Principally concerned with British personalities, this source provides a very brief description of the life and accomplishments of each individual included. You would probably need to refer to another source if you needed information.

Who's Who in America. This volume provides biographical sketches, listed alphabetically, of prominent Americans who are known either for their positions or their accomplishments. Published every two years, this book can guide you to other sources in seeking detailed information about a particular person.

Who's Who in America also has regional editions: *Who's Who in the East (and Eastern Canada)*, *Who's Who in the Midwest*, *Who's Who in the South and Southwest*, and *Who's Who in the West.*

Who's Who in American Women. Unusual in its title, this book not only lists outstanding American women, but women of international acclaim.

Books about Authors. For biographical information about authors, and critical evaluations of their works, the following sources are especially useful:

> *American Authors: 1600–1900*
> *British Authors Before 1800*
> *British Authors of the Nineteenth Century*
> *Contemporary Authors*
> *Cyclopedia of World Authors*
> *Twentieth Century Authors*
> *Twentieth Century Authors: First Supplement*
> *World Authors: 1950–1970*

Literary Reference Books

The following are valuable reference books on the history of literature, on quotations and proverbs, for locating poems and stories, and for finding information about writers:

> *Bartlett's Familiar Quotations*
> *Book Review Digest*
> *Contemporary Poets*
> *Cyclopedia of Literary Characters*
> *Encyclopedia of World Drama*
> *Granger's Index to Poetry and Recitations*
> *Illustrated Encyclopedia of the Classical World*
> *A Literary History of England*

A *Literary History of the United States*
Mencken's *A New Dictionary of Quotations*
The Oxford Companion to American Literature
The Oxford Companion to Classical Literature
The Oxford Companion to English Literature
The Oxford Companion to the Theatre

From the above list, three widely used reference works are the following:

Bartlett's Familiar Quotations. This is one of the best known of the dictionaries of quotations. Its completeness and accuracy have made it notable for over a century.

Quotations are arranged chronologically by author in the main section of the book. A shorter section of passages from the Bible, Koran, and the Book of Common Prayer follow. To find the complete source of a quote, you should use the main index in the back of the book. Whether you know the entire quotation or simply have a general idea of its topic, you would be able to find it in the index.

For example, study this quotation from a poem by the American poet, Walt Whitman:

"I hear America singing, the varied carols I hear."

You may find a reference to this quotation in three places:

1. under Walt Whitman entries in the main index of the book.
2. in the index under the first line of the quote.
3. under the subject heading of America.

Whatever your recollection or your need for a quotation on a particular subject, *Bartlett's* is an excellent source.

Book Review Digest. Arranged alphabetically by authors of the book reviewed, this digest gives short quotations from selected reviews from many popular American and English periodicals. If a work of fiction has had four or more reviews or a work of nonfiction has had two or more reviews, and if the book is hard-bound and has been published in the United States, it will appear in this digest. It is published monthly and accumulated annually.

You will find this to be a good source in finding both unfavorable and favorable reviews of particular books.

Granger's Index to Poetry and Recitations. This source includes an index of first lines as well as an index of authors to assist you in finding a poem if its title is unknown to you. By using this reference book, you will also be able to locate not only a quotation but an entire short work. For example, let us say you need to find an anthology or book containing the poem "The Love Song of J. Alfred Prufrock" by T. S. Eliot. You would look up this title in the *Index* and under the poem's title you will find listed a number of books containing this poem. The titles, however, are coded, and you will find the code explained in the front of the book.

Granger's Index to Poetry and Recitations is a standard, worthwhile source for any student of literature.

Magazines

The *Readers' Guide to Periodical Literature* lists the titles of articles, stories, and poems published during the preceding month in more than 100 leading magazines. It is issued twice a month from September through June and once a month in July and August. An entire year's issues are bound in one hardcover volume at the end of the year. Articles are listed alphabetically under *subject* and *author* (and *titles* when necessary). You will find the *Readers' Guide* invaluable when looking for articles on a subject for a composition.

The following excerpt from the *Readers' Guide* illustrates how articles are listed:

CANADIAN general electric company-GSW ltd merger.
See Household appliances industry—Consolidations and mergers

CANAVERAL NATIONAL SEASHORE
Defending a barrier beach. Nat Parks & Con Mag 50:27 N '76

CANCER

Diagnosis

New way to screen for cancer. Sci N 110:310 N 13 '76 ———— title of article

Nutritional aspects

How dietary factors combat cancer. Sci N 110:310-11 N 13 '76

CANDIDATES, Political.
How will the good guys fare in '76? Republican candidates. il Nat R 28:1229-33 N 12 '76 ———— name of magazine
Scientist-candidates for Congress. F. C. Bennett. il Phys Today 29:63-4 O '76

CANDY
No-cook sugarplums. Good H 183:154 D '76 ———— volume number

CANNIBALISM (microorganisms)
Sex-specific cannibalism in the rotifer asplanchna sieboldi. J. J. Gilbert. il Science 194:730-2 N 12 '76 ———— page reference

CANS
Safe-opening can lid. S. Bronson. il Pop Sci 209:72 N '76 ———— date of magazine

Manufacture

See Container industry

CANTWELL, Robert, 1908- ———— author entry
Outdoors. Sports Illus 45:88+ N 22 '76

CAPITAL
Effects of capital shortage on business expansion; excerpts from address. W. D. Witter. por Intellect 105:131-2 N '76

CAPITAL, Venture
Venture capital. T. P. Murphy. See 2d issue of each month of Forbes, July 15, 1976-

CAPITAL investments
Capital outlays: a warmer glow. il Bus W p46-7 N 15 '76

CAPITAL punishment ———— subject entry
Dusting off old sparky. J. K. Footlick and L. Howard. il Newsweek 88:35-6 N 29 '76
In cold blood. G. F. Will. Newsweek 88:116 N 29 '76

CAPITALISM
Should we dump the present economic systems and start again from scratch; excerpts from address, June 1976. S. Amin. il UNESCO Courier 29:9-12 O '76

CAPITALISTS and financiers
See also
Millionaires ———— "see also" cross reference

CAPLAN, Frank
(ed) How to select the right toys for your child; excerpt from The parenting advisor. il Fam Health 8:48-50+ N '76

CAPLAN, Jerry L.
Raku reduction stenciling. il Ceram Mo 24:58-9 N '76 ———— illustrated article

CAPLAN, Lincoln
(ed) See Evans, W. Walker Evans on himself

CAPRARO, Albert
At home with top U.S. designers. C. Porcelli. il por House B 118:92-3 N '76*

CAPSICUM. See Peppers ———— "see" cross reference

Exercises
Using Reference Materials

A. **Dictionaries and Encyclopedias.** Using the dictionaries and encyclopedias listed on pages 264–269, indicate the best source for answers to these questions. Include the page reference.

1. Where did the phrase "ugly duckling" originate?
2. Find a short article on cryogenics.
3. In what epic is Hector an important character?
4. How did Currier and Ives become famous?
5. What are the basic steps in computer data processing?
6. What were the "Jim Crow" laws?
7. Compare the form of the Miltonic sonnet with the Shakespearean sonnet.
8. Describe "op art."
9. What are the four main blood groups?
10. What was the original meaning of the word *flivver*?
11. Who wrote the ballet "Slaughter on Tenth Avenue"?
12. Was Robin Hood a real or legendary character?
13. What is existentialism?
14. Find an illustration and description of a lute.
15. What is the story of Scylla and Charybdis?

B. **Almanacs, Yearbooks and Atlases.** Using the almanacs, yearbooks and atlases listed in this chapter, indicate the best source for answers to these questions. Include the page reference.

1. Find a list of the major North American turnpikes.
2. How is a patent issued?
3. What are the major land uses in the United States?
4. Who is the mayor of Los Angeles?
5. What are the warning signs of a heart attack?
6. What is the law on succession to the presidency?
7. Whose portrait is on the $20 bill?
8. Compare the number of American participants in World War II and the Vietnam War.
9. How many times has the United States won the Olympic Games since 1900?

10. Find a map showing climates of the world.
11. What is the National Guard?
12. Find a list of the state compulsory school attendance laws.
13. What play has had the longest Broadway run?
14. Which states have a sales tax?
15. What are some of the endangered species of birds in North America?

C. **Biographical References.** Using the biographical references listed in this chapter, give the best source for answers to these questions. Include the page reference where you found the information.

1. What series of novels did Upton Sinclair write?
2. Find a list of Isaac Bashevis Singer's works in English translation.
3. What is the setting of Joseph Heller's novel *Catch-22?*
4. What made Bill Mauldin, the cartoonist, famous?
5. What part did Charlotte Corday play in the French Revolution?
6. Which novel of Jessamyn West's became a popular movie?
7. How has Jacques Cousteau graphically shared his experiences as a marine explorer?
8. What were some of Clarence Darrow's most famous cases?
9. Where can you find a picture of Geoffrey Chaucer?
10. What is the background of most of J. P. Marquand's novels?
11. What was Henrik Ibsen's contribution to drama?
12. What story influenced William Golding in the development of his novel *Lord of the Flies?*
13. What honor was Gwendolyn Brooks given by the state of Illinois?
14. What was the ultimate success of Clarence Day's family sketches?
15. What physical handicaps made drawing difficult for James Thurber?

D. **Literary Reference Books.** Use the literary reference books listed in this chapter to answer the following questions. After each answer write the name of the reference book you used.

1. What was a morality play?

2. What influence did the McGuffey readers have on American education?

3. Find a poem on freedom.

4. On what occasion did John F. Kennedy say, "Let us never negotiate out of fear, but let us never fear to negotiate"?

5. In what century was the Tower of London built?

6. What was the "theater of the absurd"?

7. What are some of the treasures housed in the British Museum?

8. Who wrote the poem "Renascence"?

9. What was meant by Manifest Destiny?

10. What forced the magazine *Literary Digest* to cease publication?

11. Who are the main characters in the musical comedy *Of Thee I Sing*?

12. What were the Leather Stocking Tales?

13. How favorable were the reviews of John Steinbeck's *The Grapes of Wrath*?

14. Where was Tin Pan Alley?

15. What is the plot of Frank Norris' novel *The Pit*?

E. Readers' Guide to Periodical Literature. Use the excerpt from the *Readers' Guide* on page 276 to answer the following questions:

1. Under what subject will you find articles on the manufacture of cans?

2. Give the complete magazine title of the following abbreviations:

Fam Health	*Phys Today*
Bus W	*Ceram Mo*
House B	*Nat R*

3. On what page in *Good Housekeeping* can you find a recipe for candy sugar plums?

4. What magazine has an article on the Canaveral National Seashore?

5. Who has made a speech on the effects of capital shortage on business expansion?

F. Using Reference Materials for a Research Paper. The American novelist, Sinclair Lewis, is best known as a satirist of the American middle class. In a study of his major novels, *Main Street* and *Babbitt,* some background study of his life and writings would be valuable. From the reference sources listed in this chapter, find the specific books which will answer these questions. Include the page references.

1. Comprehensive biographical information.
2. Find reviews of *Babbitt* and *Main Street.*
3. What Minnesota town is the locale for *Main Street?*
4. What was Lewis' reason for declining the Pulitzer Prize in 1926?
5. Compare Sinclair Lewis with Willa Cather as an interpreter of small town life in America.
6. What is the entry under "babbitt" in the unabridged dictionaries?
7. On what occasion did he say, "Our American professors like their literature clear and cold and pure and very dead"?
8. What is the plot of *Arrowsmith?*
9. What was the title of his address in Stockholm on receiving the Nobel Prize for Literature?
10. Were the critics justified in accusing him of romanticism?

Handbook

A detailed Table of Contents of the Handbook appears in the front of this book.

How To Use the Handbook

This Handbook is your reference book. In it the concepts of grammar and usage are organized so that you can study them efficiently and refer to them quickly.

To use the Handbook well, you should first leaf through it to become familiar with its organization and contents. Note especially the following:

Organization of the Handbook

Grammar (Sections 1–5)   Sections 1–5 provide a comprehensive treatment of English grammar. They give the rules and explanations for grammatical questions you want answered.

Usage (Sections 6–10)   Sections 6–10 are a guide to English usage. When you are puzzled about which form of a word to use in your writing, turn to the appropriate part of these sections.

Forms and constructions marked STANDARD are accepted as standard usage—the kind of usage that is appropriate at all times and in all places. Forms and constructions marked NONSTANDARD are not accepted everywhere. While they may go unnoticed on the playing field or in the locker room, in many other situations they mark the user as careless or untrained in the English language.

Capitalization (Section 11)

Punctuation (Sections 12–15)

Spelling (Sections 16–17)

Good Form (Section 18–19)

Throughout the Handbook are many exercises that test your understanding of the concepts explained. These exercises are the first steps in putting what you learn here to practical use. The next steps are in your own writing and speaking.

1.0 The Classification of Words

The words in our language have been classified into eight large groups according to the jobs they perform in a sentence. These eight groups are called the eight **parts of speech.** Here are the parts of speech.

nouns	adjectives	conjunctions
pronouns	adverbs	interjections
verbs	prepositions	

In addition to the parts of speech, there are three kinds of words, formed from verbs, that do many different jobs. These words are called **verbals.** Verbals are all formed from verbs and have several of the characteristics of verbs. They are unlike verbs, however, in that no verbal can stand by itself as a complete verb. The verbals are the *infinitive,* the *participle,* and the *gerund.*

This section provides a comprehensive treatment of the parts of speech and the verbals.

1.1 The Noun

Certain words in the language are used as labels with which we identify people and things.

A noun is the name of a person, place, or thing.

Things named by nouns may be visible, such as *hats, buildings,* and *books.* Things may be items that we perceive with our other senses: *odors, sounds, tastes.* Other things are abstract and not observed through the five senses: *beliefs, ideas, wishes,* and so on.

PERSONS	PLACES	THINGS
Walter Mondale	Philadelphia	dictionary
principal	school	patience
artist	plantation	capitalism

A **common noun** is the name of a whole group of persons, places, or things. It is a name that is common to the whole group: *stone, glass, minister, building.*

A **proper noun** is the name of an individual person, place or thing.

A proper noun always begins with a capital letter.

COMMON NOUNS	PROPER NOUNS
sunshine	Beverly Sills
television	Statue of Liberty
modesty	India
mountain	Pennsylvania Avenue

As the above list shows, a noun may consist of more than one word. Each word in a proper noun is capitalized.

Any word that can be immediately preceded by *the* is a noun: *the* bridge, *the* George Washington Bridge, *the* language. Many proper nouns, but not all of them, can be preceded by *the: the Astrodome, the New York Hilton,* not *the* President Carter or *the* Canada.

Exercise A: Find all the nouns in the following sentences.

1. The savage cartoons precipitated a storm of criticism.
2. The old farmer made hay while his son shone on the gridiron.
3. Sequoias have a remarkable resistance to fire, fungi, and insects.

4. The anteater can eat 100,000 termites at a time.

5. Mt. Rushmore in South Dakota bears sculptures of famous American patriots.

6. The theory that life exists on Mars is being tested.

7. The game of soccer is becoming increasingly popular with many Americans.

8. I read that lions have headaches, tigers suffer from sinus trouble, and horses and chimpanzees have ulcers.

9. Paul Revere, silversmith, was among the fifty citizens who donned warpaint and feathers for the Boston Tea Party.

10. Some scientist claims to have discovered the cure for which there is no disease.

Exercise B: Decide which of the following are common nouns and which are proper nouns. Write the proper nouns, beginning each with a capital letter.

1. village, greenville, chicago, city
2. indian, warrior, girl, pocahontas
3. ruler, napoleon, prince, queen elizabeth
4. newspaper, *the new york times*, biographer, book
5. mountain, appalachian mountains, pike's peak, st. lawrence seaway
6. gulf of mexico, lake, canal, panama canal
7. scholarship, student, principal, national merit scholarship
8. algebra, spanish, biology, latin
9. state, north carolina, country, united arab republic
10. settler, puritan, citizen, lord baltimore

1.2 The Pronoun

Since it would be awkward and cumbersome to repeat the name of a person or thing every time we wish to refer to it, we use other words in place of names. These words are pronouns. They may be used in a sentence in any way that a noun is used.

A pronoun is a word used in place of a noun.

The noun for which the pronoun stands and to which it refers is its **antecedent.**

> *Beth* had forgotten *her* excuse. (*Beth* is antecedent of *her.*)

> The *students* were taking *their* exams. (*students* is antecedent of *their.*)

> Mr. Ryan is the *person* to *whom* you should report. (*person* is the antecedent of *whom.*)

Sometimes the antecedent of a pronoun appears in a preceding sentence.

> The labor *mediators* entered the dispute. *They* studied the issues carefully. *They* were confident *it* could be settled. (*They* in each sentence refers to the antecedent *mediators;* *it* refers to *dispute.*)

Indefinite pronouns do not often refer to any specific noun. The indefinite pronoun itself may be the antecedent of a personal pronoun.

> The *cones* were ripe. *Some* fell to the ground. (The antecedent of the indefinite pronoun *Some* is *cones.*)

> *Each* of the girls brought *her* father. (The antecedent of *her* is the indefinite pronoun *Each.*)

There are six kinds of pronouns:

personal pronouns	interrogative pronouns
compound personal pronouns	relative pronouns
demonstrative pronouns	indefinite pronouns

Personal Pronouns

Pronouns used in place of persons' names are called **personal pronouns.** They permit us to identify the person speaking, the person spoken to, and the person spoken about. Personal pronouns are also used to refer to things.

First Person (the person speaking)
I, me, my, mine, we, us, our, ours

Second Person (the person spoken to)
you, your, yours

Third Person (the person or thing spoken about)
he, she, it, they
his, hers, its, their, theirs
him, her, them

Personal pronouns change their form, or spelling, for different uses in sentences. This change of form is called the **case** of pronouns. There are three cases: *nominative, possessive,* and *objective.* Personal pronouns also change their form to show the difference between singular (one) and plural (more than one). This change of form is called the **number** of pronouns.

The following table shows the forms of the three *persons,* for the three *cases,* and for the *number* of all of the personal pronouns.

Personal Pronouns

Singular

	NOMINATIVE	POSSESSIVE	OBJECTIVE
First Person:	I	my, mine	me
Second Person:	you	your, yours	you
Third Person:	he, she, it	his, her, hers, its	him, her, it

Plural

	NOMINATIVE	POSSESSIVE	OBJECTIVE
First Person:	we	our, ours	us
Second Person:	you	your, yours	you
Third Person:	they	their, theirs	them

Third person pronouns that refer to male persons are in the **masculine gender.** Those that refer to female persons are in the **feminine gender.** Pronouns that refer to things are in the **neuter gender.**

Here are some important things to remember about pronouns:

> The pronoun *it* is called a personal pronoun even though it refers to things more often than to persons.

> Both *it* and *you* are the same in nominative and objective case forms.

> Countries, ships, and airplanes are sometimes referred to by the feminine pronouns, *she, her, hers.* Animals may be referred to by *it* and *its* or by *he, his, she, her, hers,* depending on the sex of the animal.

> The words *mine, yours, hers, ours,* and *theirs* are always used as pronouns. The words *my, your, its, our,* and *their* are always used as modifiers before nouns. They are **possessive pronouns.** *His* may be used either as a pronoun or as a modifier.

> This car is *mine.* (pronoun)
> Here is *my* key. (modifier)
> The beehive is *theirs.* (pronoun)
> I traded my trouble for *his.* (pronoun)
> Today is *his* birthday. (modifier)

Compound Personal Pronouns

A **compound personal pronoun** is formed by adding *-self* or *-selves* to certain of the personal pronouns, as follows:

FIRST PERSON:	myself, ourselves
SECOND PERSON:	yourself, yourselves
THIRD PERSON:	himself, herself, itself, oneself, themselves

There are no other acceptable compound personal pronouns. Never say *hisself* or *theirselves*.

Compound personal pronouns are used *intensively* for emphasis or *reflexively* to refer to a preceding noun or pronoun.

The principal *herself* played in our softball game. (intensive)

John blamed *himself* for the team's defeat. (reflexive)

Exercise A: In the following sentences find the personal pronouns. Find the antecedent of each pronoun.

1. Joe, why are you painting your room that hideous purple?
2. When the children lost their kitten, they were inconsolable.
3. After Sally and her dad had sanded the table, they refinished it.
4. The Campbells have two snowmobiles, but they haven't used them this season.
5. Dad, did Linda tell you about her winning her tennis match?
6. At first the referee signaled a touchdown. Then he nullified it.
7. Ed, the man you listed as a reference, says he doesn't know you.
8. If Cindy calls, tell her I went shopping.
9. Her election came as a complete surprise to Harriet.
10. Nan has a license, but she doesn't have it with her.

Exercise B: Supply the correct compound personal pronoun needed in each of these sentences. Find the antecedent for each compound personal pronoun.

1. We _____ elect representatives to the Student Council.
2. Rodney blamed _____ for his team's defeat.
3. The ceremony _____ was impressive.
4. The referee settled the dispute _____ .
5. Kathleen cut _____ with the sharp knife.
6. You boys will have to raise the money _____ .
7. I hear that you are an experienced electrician _____ .
8. We judged Pam _____ to be the best speaker.

Demonstrative Pronouns

The words *this, that, these,* and *those* are used to point out, or demonstrate, which one or which ones are meant. Since they point to what is meant, they are called **demonstrative pronouns.** They always refer to a definite person or thing, but the words they refer to may come later.

> *This* is the *picture* Eric painted. (*picture* is the word referred to.)
>
> The agents were issued *vials* of poison. *These* were to be used in case of capture. (*vials* is the word referred to by *These*.)

Note: The demonstrative pronouns *this, that, these,* and *those* may also be used as adjectives: *this hat, those curtains.*

Interrogative Pronouns

The pronouns *who, whose, whom, which,* and *what* are used to ask questions. When used in this way, they are **interrogative pronouns.**

> *Who* found the book?   *What* is the number?
> *Whom* did he want?   *Which* route is better?
> *Whose* car is that?

Relative Pronouns

The words *who, whose, whom, which,* and *that* are sometimes used to introduce an adjective clause. They relate the clause to some other word in the sentence. When used in this way, they are called **relative pronouns.**

A relative pronoun is used to introduce a relative clause. It also has a use within the relative clause. See Section 3.6.

Indefinite Pronouns

Some pronouns, such as *anyone* and *anything,* do not refer to a definite person or thing. They are called **indefinite pronouns.** Normally, indefinite pronouns do not have antecedents.

SINGULAR INDEFINITE PRONOUNS

another	anything	either	everything	no one
anybody	one	everyone	neither	someone
anyone	each	everybody	nobody	somebody

PLURAL INDEFINITE PRONOUNS

both   many   few   several

The pronouns *all, some, any,* and *none* may be singular or plural, depending upon their meaning in the sentence.

> *All* of the ice cream *has* melted. (singular)
> *All* the performances *have* been canceled. (plural)
>
> *Some* of the fruit *was* frozen. (singular)
> *Some* of the flights *have* been grounded. (plural)
>
> *None* of the student center *has* been completed. (singular)
> *None* of the hikers *were* found yet. (plural)
>
> *Has any* of the *money* been recovered? (singular)
> *Were any* of the programs good? (plural)

Exercise: List the pronouns in these sentences. Tell what kind each pronoun is.

1. Are these your glasses? They aren't mine.
2. This is my raincoat. Is that yours?
3. They simply ran roughshod over our protests.
4. Has all of the mail been sorted?
5. I asked Molly and her to plan the refreshments.

6. There is no sense in our planning a trip unless you approve of it.
7. Having seen the film myself, I can tell you about it.
8. These are the best samples. Has everyone seen them?
9. From whom did you hear this?
10. Not one of my friends has called me.

1.3 The Verb

Every sentence must contain a word that tells what is happening. This word is the verb.

A verb is a word that tells of an action or state of being.

Grammatically, the verb is the most important word in the sentence. If you can find the verb and manage it properly, many of your grammar and usage problems will be easily solved.

Most verbs change their form (their sound or spelling) to show past time and present time. They are the only words to do so. This fact can help you decide which word in the sentence is the verb.

When repairs *were needed*, the landlord *was* never
in town. (past)
When repairs *are needed*, the landlord *is* never
in town. (present)

The mayor *reacted* strongly to criticism. (past)
The mayor *reacts* strongly to criticism. (present)

Most verbs also change their form to show the difference between singular and plural in the third person.

Mary *finds* calculus interesting. (third person singular)
Tony and Joe *find* reading enjoyable. (third person plural)

Action Verbs

The action asserted by an action verb may be visible, physical action, or it may be invisible action.

Kevin *broke* the window. (visible)
The child *fell* down. (visible)
John *swam* in the school meet. (visible)
Luanne and Russ *enjoyed* the musical. (not visible)
Dad *hoped* for a raise. (not visible)
Maria *disliked* the subzero temperatures. (not visible)

Linking Verbs

A few verbs, such as *be*, link the subject to a noun or adjective. Hence they are called **linking verbs.**

Pat *became* the editor.   Helen *seemed* confused.

The most common linking verb is *be* and with its forms *am, are, is, was, were, been, being.*
Other linking verbs are *appear, become, seem, look, sound, grow, feel, smell, taste, remain, stay.*

The audience *appeared* pleased.   The old tale *sounds* weird.
The silence *became* ominous.   The director *felt* uneasy.
The office *seems* empty.   The bread *smelled* delicious.
Colleen *looks* exhausted.   The milk *tasted* sour.
The crew *grew* anxious as they approached the target.
The room *remained* noisy all afternoon.
George *stayed* longer on the bronco than Fred did.

Many linking verbs may also be used as action verbs.

Jan *grew* ivy in window boxes.   The guard *sounded* the alarm.
José *felt* the bee sting.   We *smelled* the hot tar.
The dog *looked* at the washing machine and barked.
Greg *tasted* the medicine and grimaced.

Main Verbs and Auxiliaries

Many verbs consist of more than one word. They consist of a **main verb** and one or more **auxiliaries,** or helping verbs. The last word in the phrase is the main verb.

There are three verbs that can be used either as main verbs or as auxiliaries. Here are their forms.

DO	HAVE	BE		
do	has	is	was	be
does	have	am	were	been
did	had	are		being

AS MAIN VERB	AS AUXILIARY
I will *do* the dishes.	We *do* like this boat.
Have you the money?	You *have* been remiss.
The stores *were* closed.	The members *were* arguing.

The most frequently used auxiliaries are the forms of *be* and *have*. The most common of the other auxiliaries are the following:

must	may	shall	could	would
might	can	will	should	

AUXILIARY	MAIN VERB	VERB
has	had	has had
had	been	had been
was	doing	was doing
had	done	had done
could have	gone	could have gone
might have been	seen	might have been seen
is being	improved	is being improved

Often the parts of a verb are separated by a modifier or modifiers that are not part of the verb.

He *had* just *bunted.*   The concert *had* not quite *ended.*

Exercise A: Find the verb in each of these sentences. Include all the words that make up the verb. Do not include any word that separates an auxiliary from a main verb.

1. The world's sources of coal and oil are rapidly diminishing.
2. We shall some day turn to the endless resources of atomic power.
3. By 1990 atomic energy may be heating and lighting our homes.
4. Some day the sea will be mined by atomic energy.
5. Gold and silver and platinum will then be plentiful.
6. These metals can be used for nonrusting pipes and tanks.
7. Deserts will be reclaimed with pure, unsalted water.
8. Atomic energy will free streets and airfields of snow and fog.
9. Weather itself will have been guaranteed days in advance.
10. Fruits and vegetables will grow and ripen by atomic light.
11. We are already using radioisotopes in the treatment of certain diseases.
12. Rays from irradiated cobalt or gold have successfully attacked some cancerous tissue.
13. Plant growth has been speeded by radioisotopes.
14. We are firmly and inescapably embarked on the atomic age.

Exercise B: Find each verb and tell whether it is an action verb or a linking verb.

1. That English setter looks particularly intelligent.
2. The collie pup looked inquisitively about him.
3. The dog with the largest number of points was a cocker spaniel.
4. Cautiously Jim smelled the contents of the bottle.
5. The pie in the oven smelled tantalizing.
6. The painter seemed unhappy with his portrait.
7. The younger children grew weary toward the end of the party.
8. They remained quiet all the way home.
9. The governor appeared nervous at his press conference.

10. Radio signals from the rocket were loud and clear.
11. The flowers smelled sweet in the evening air.
12. In 1976 the Cincinnati Reds won their second World Series in a row.
13. Some people have doubts about the value of summit conferences.
14. The man on the other end of the wire sounded angry.
15. Both candidates for mayor were optimistic about their chances.

The Principal Parts

The principal parts of a verb are those from which all forms of the verb are made. They are (1) the *present infinitive* (usually called simply the *present*); (2) the *past*; and (3) the *past participle*.

A **regular verb** is one that forms its past and past participle by adding *-ed* or *-d* to the present.

PRESENT	PAST	PAST PARTICIPLE
paint	painted	painted
close	closed	closed
dance	danced	danced

An **irregular verb** is one that does not form its past and past participle by adding *-ed* or *-d* to the present. See Section 8.1 for usage of irregular verbs.

PRESENT	PAST	PAST PARTICIPLE
hit	hit	hit
bring	brought	brought
ring	rang	rung

The **present participle** of a verb is formed by adding *-ing* to the present form: *close—closing; hit—hitting; talk—talking.*

The Progressive Forms

The **progressive forms** of the verb are used to show on-going action. They are formed by using the forms of *be* with the present participle.

Laura *is studying*.

Cheryl and Alan *are going*.

The passengers *were waiting*.

Ozawa *will be conducting*.

Pam *has been playing* handball.

Protests *had been mounting*.

The costs *must be climbing*.

They *might have been playing*.

The Emphatic Forms

Special emphasis is given to a statement by using *do, does,* or *did* with the present form of the verb. These are examples of **emphatic forms.**

I *did hear* you hammering.

We *do enjoy* apple pies.

Willie *does look* tired.

Transitive and Intransitive Verbs

A **transitive verb** carries over the action from the subject to the object of the verb. An **intransitive verb** expresses an action that is complete in itself; it does not carry action over to an object.

TRANSITIVE	INTRANSITIVE
Matt *vacuumed* the **floor.**	The movie *began.*
Hal *rang* the **buzzer.**	Finally he *left.*
Amy *enjoyed* the **play.**	The plumber finally *came.*
I *considered* my **future.**	They could hardly *wait.*

Many verbs may be transitive in one sentence and intransitive in another.

INTRANSITIVE	TRANSITIVE
Mark *sang.*	Mark *sang* the **first hymn.**
Did Laura *call?*	*Did* Laura *call* the **police?**
I *could* not *hear.*	I *could* not *hear* the **speaker.**

The Active and the Passive Voice

When the subject performs the action expressed in the verb, the verb is in the **active voice.** When the subject receives the action of the verb, the verb is in the **passive voice.** The passive voice is formed by using some form of *be* with the past participle of the verb.

ACTIVE: Roz *polished* the *silver.*
PASSIVE: The silver *was polished* by Roz.

ACTIVE: Our class *is reading Jane* Austen.
PASSIVE: *Jane Austen is being read* by our class.

A transitive verb can be put into the passive voice because it has an object that receives the action of the verb. The object of the active verb becomes the subject in the passive form.

In a sentence containing an intransitive verb, there is no word that receives the action of the verb. For this reason no intransitive verb can be put into the passive voice.

Anton Chekhov *wrote* "The Lost Brooch." (active)
"The Lost Brooch" *was written* by Anton Chekhov. (passive)

The mayor *appointed* the city manager to office. (active)
The city manager *was appointed* to office by the
   mayor. (passive)

Exercise A: Find the verb and tell whether it is active or passive.

1. Astronomers did not discover the planet Pluto until 1930.
2. Many articles about Plains, Georgia, have been published in the newspapers.

3. Mrs. Hill was called to the stand six times.
4. A panel of judges found the defendant guilty.
5. The president of the bank was questioned by reporters.
6. Public indignation forced the mayor to resign.
7. One of our foremost architects designed the terminal.
8. Ornithologists have timed the duck hawk at three miles a minute.
9. The *Titanic* was considered unsinkable by naval architects.
10. Several students misunderstood the instructions.

Exercise B: Change the active verbs to passive and the passive verbs to active.

1. The fuse was ignited by someone.
2. Many responsible citizens signed the petition.
3. The triumphant climbers raised the flag and placed it in a crevice of the rock.
4. A student's outlook is molded by many influences in his or her environment.
5. The President was swept into office by a landslide vote.
6. Many of the tourists bought Evangeline dolls dressed in the Acadian costume of the eighteenth century.
7. The grass was cut, the weeds were pulled, and the flower beds were trimmed by Frank this morning.
8. Fanciful and exaggerated stories are frequently told by children with no intent of deceiving.

Tense

Most verbs change their forms to tell present, past and future time. **Tense** means "time." There are three simple tenses and three perfect tenses for each verb. They are formed as follows:

1. **Present tense.** The present tense is formed from the present or simple form of the verb.

The present forms of verbs usually tell of something that exists at the present moment.

The car *is* in the parking lot. (right now)
The bread *smells* fresh. (at the moment)

The simple or present forms of action verbs, however, are not always used to tell of actions that are going on at the moment. We do not say, "I walk." We are more likely to use the **progressive form** "I am walking" or the **emphatic form** "I do walk." An exception is the use of the present to describe ongoing sports events:

They'*re* in the last lap and Jenner *takes* the lead.

The present forms of action verbs are used to tell of repeated or regular and habitual action.

They *go* to Puerto Rico every winter.
Our team *bowls* with theirs on Tuesdays.
The curtain *rises* at 8:30 sharp.

The present forms of verbs are also used to tell of something that is generally true at all times.

"Power *tends* to corrupt. Absolute power *corrupts* absolutely."

The **historical present tense** is used to tell of some action or condition in the past as though it were occurring in the present:

The assembled *wait,* expectations mixed; then through the wire *crackle* Bell's words, "Mr. Watson, come here, I want you."

2. **Past tense.** Past time is usually told by the past tense, which is the second principal part of the verb: *We waited, they stopped, nobody volunteered.* Continuing past action is shown by the **past progressive:** We *were having* a good time.

3. **Future tense.** Future time is shown by using *shall* or *will* with the present form of the verb: *I shall attend, you will see, we will try.* (For usage of *shall* and *will*, see Section 8.7.)

Future time may be shown by the present tense together with an adverb or phrase that tells time. Future time may also be shown by the use of a form of *be* with *going to* or *about to.*

They are *going to* fly to Hawaii in the fall.
The fleet of helicopters *is about to* take off.
We *get* our grades *tomorrow*. (*tomorrow* is an adverb
    telling time.)
He will try to meet the deadline *from now on*. (*from now on*
    is an adverb phrase telling time.)

4. **Present perfect tense.** The present perfect tense is formed by using *has* or *have* with the past participle (third principal part) of the verb. This tense is used to refer to some indefinite time in the past.

The owner *has begun* the repairs.
I *have* already *fallen* twice on the stairs.

The present perfect is also used to show action that began in the past and continues into the present.

She *has played* the guitar for years. (She still plays.)
You *have been bickering* too much. (present perfect progressive)

5. **Past perfect tense.** The past perfect tense is formed by using *had* with the past participle (third principal part) of the verb. The past perfect tense tells of an action completed in the past before some other action.

EARLIER	LATER
All the roads *had been blocked*	before the President *arrived*.
Maria *had been waiting* an hour	before the bus finally *came*.

6. **Future perfect tense.** The future perfect tense is formed by using *will have* or *shall have* with the past participle of the verb (third principal part). This tense is used to tell of one time completed in the future *before* some other time in the future.

Before the program *is* over, we *will have seen* six commercials.
By the time Jake *reads* his book, I *will have read* three.

Note: The first verb in the present tense indicates far future action. The second verb indicates future action *before* the action of the first verb.

Conjugation of *Work*

Conjugation is a presentation of the various forms of a verb. Usually, verbs are conjugated in the order shown here.

Principal Parts: work, worked, worked **Present Participle:** working
Present Infinitive: to work **Perfect Infinitive:** to have worked

Present Tense

FIRST PERSON:	I work	we work
SECOND PERSON:	you work	you work
THIRD PERSON:	he, she, it works	they work

PRESENT PROGRESSIVE: I am working, you are working, etc.
PRESENT EMPHATIC: I do work, you do work, he does work etc.

Past Tense

FIRST PERSON:	I worked	we worked
SECOND PERSON:	you worked	you worked
THIRD PERSON:	he, she, it worked	they worked

PAST PROGRESSIVE: I was working, you were working, etc.
PAST EMPHATIC: I did work, you did work, etc.

Future Tense

FIRST PERSON:	I shall (will) work	we shall (will) work
SECOND PERSON:	you will work	you will work
THIRD PERSON:	he, she, it will work	they will work

FUTURE PROGRESSIVE: I shall be working, you will be working, etc.

Present Perfect Tense

FIRST PERSON:	I have worked	we have worked
SECOND PERSON:	you have worked	you have worked
THIRD PERSON:	he, she, it has worked	they have worked

PRESENT PERFECT PROGRESSIVE: I have been working, you have been working, he has been working, etc.

Past Perfect Tense

FIRST PERSON:	I had worked	we had worked
SECOND PERSON:	you had worked	you had worked
THIRD PERSON:	he, she, it had worked	they had worked

PAST PERFECT PROGRESSIVE: I had been working, you had been working, he has been working, etc.

Future Perfect Tense

FIRST PERSON:	I shall have worked	we shall have worked
SECOND PERSON:	you will have worked	you will have worked
THIRD PERSON:	he, she, it will have worked	they will have worked

FUTURE PERFECT PROGRESSIVE: I shall have been working, etc.

Exercise: Find each verb and tell its tense.

1. Hurricane Connie has headed out to sea.
2. That croquet set had lain there for years.
3. Will Louise wear her new dress?
4. The man in the seat ahead of us was snoring loudly.
5. After forty moves, Fischer won the chess match with a King's Indian defense.
6. Read the poem carefully.
7. Will you have finished your dinner by seven o'clock?
8. The swimming pool was completed before summer vacation.
9. Janet is playing a Beethoven sonata.
10. Space stations will become springboards for future exploration.
11. The former President is writing his memoirs.

12. The Fosters have been having trouble with termites.
13. The crowd gasps: the diver somersaults into the tiny pool.
14. When I have finished my homework, I usually watch television.
15. When I had finished my homework, I watched television.

Mood

The mood of a verb shows the writer's attitude about the actuality of a happening. The **indicative mood,** which we use most of the time, indicates that we are talking or writing about a fact. That is, we are speaking of something that has happened, is happening, or definitely will happen.

The **subjunctive mood** is used to express only wishes, commands, and conditions that are doubtful or contrary to fact. The forms of the subjunctive mood are like those of the indicative mood except in the third person singular of the present tense where the s ending is omitted.

INDICATIVE: He *obeys* every command.
SUBJUNCTIVE: They insist that he *obey* every command.

The subjunctive form of the verb *be* is a special case. With this verb, the form in the present tense for all persons and numbers is *be*. It is used for clauses contrary to fact, or for statements expressing doubt.

PRESENT TENSE: Jack insisted that he *be* present.
She suggested that the gift *be* returned.

The past subjunctive form of the verb *to be* is *were*.

PAST TENSE: I wish he *were* more trustworthy.
If I *were* President, I wouldn't negotiate at this time.

The **imperative mood** is used to express a command, a directive, or a request. The imperative mood has only one tense—

the present—and is in either the second person or first person plural.

> *Come* to the Community Center on Saturday.
> Please *explain* the problem.
> Let us *leave* immediately.

1.4 The Adjective

To express our point of view fully or to make our meaning clear and definite, we do not rely on nouns and verbs alone. We use other kinds of words to describe or limit or qualify the meaning. We call these words modifiers.

An adjective is a word that modifies a noun or pronoun.

Adjectives are used to tell *which one, what kind, how many,* or *how much* about nouns and pronouns.

WHICH ONE:	this, that, these, those
WHAT KIND:	small, sour, sharp, beautiful
HOW MANY:	some, all, several, four, eight
HOW MUCH:	little, much, plentiful

The Articles

The word *the* is called a **definite article** because it is usually, though not always, used to refer to a definite or specific thing or person.

The words *a* and *an* are called **indefinite articles** because they refer to no particular thing or person. *A* is used before words beginning with consonant sounds. *An* is used before words beginning with vowel sounds. The sound, not the spelling, makes the difference.

> There was *an* exit near the office.
> There is *a* hotel at the foot of the volcano.
> The game was delayed *an* hour.
> It was *a* terrible mistake.

Proper Adjectives

A **proper adjective** is one formed from a proper noun. The proper adjective is always capitalized.

NOUN	ADJECTIVE	NOUN	ADJECTIVE
Denmark	Danish	France	French
Turkey	Turkish	West	Western
Washington	Washingtonian	Napoleon	Napoleonic
Switzerland	Swiss	Asia	Asian

Predicate Adjectives

An adjective is frequently separated from the noun or pronoun it modifies by a linking verb.

Paul seemed *lonely*. (separated)   I was *terrified*. (separated)

An adjective in the predicate that modifies the subject is a predicate adjective.

Exercise: Find each adjective and tell which word it modifies. Ignore the articles.

1. The small green pots contain different types of cacti.
2. The distraught mayor was uncommunicative with reporters.
3. The final edition carried the news in big headlines.
4. The expensive candy that we bought was delicious.
5. Caroline seems optimistic about the new job.
6. Many European students can speak several languages.
7. In the center of the huge quadrangle stood an ornate fountain.
8. Samuel Johnson lived for many years without adequate food.
9. The revolutionary scheme was given scant attention.
10. Texas was an independent republic for nine years.
11. Everyone thought the decision was just.
12. Those brown suede boots are wet and muddy.

13. Historic Plymouth Rock is preserved within a stately monument.
14. Next year I shall be a lowly freshman again.
15. The rough seas and strong winds made sailing treacherous.

Adjectives in Comparisons

Persons and things are compared as to various qualities. The comparison is made by use of two different forms of adjectives.

The **comparative** form of the adjective is formed in two ways:

1. All adjectives of one syllable and a few adjectives with two syllables add -er.

bright—brighter	high—higher
heavy—heavier	tight—tighter

2. Most adjectives with two sylables and all adjectives with more than two syllables use *more* to form the comparative.

studious—more studious	extravagant—more extravagant
helpful—more helpful	willing—more willing

The **superlative** form of the adjective is formed by adding -est or by using *most*. Adjectives that form the comparative with -er form the superlative with -est. Those that form the comparative with *more* form the superlative with *most*.

COMPARATIVE	SUPERLATIVE
neater	neatest
bolder	boldest
more competent	most competent
more satisfying	most satisfying

Irregular Comparisons

We form the comparative and superlative of some adjectives by changing the words themselves.

	COMPARATIVE	SUPERLATIVE
good	better	best
well	better	best
bad	worse	worst
ill	worse	worst
little	less *or* lesser	least
much	more	most
many	more	most
far	farther *or* further	farthest *or* furthest

Exercise: Find the adjectives and tell whether they are in comparative form or superlative form.

1. Jean seems the most likely candidate for the office.
2. The suitcase was heavier than I expected.
3. These berries taste sweeter than those we bought last week.
4. He appears to be more insecure as he grows older.
5. The letter that Ellen wrote was the longest of all.
6. Bill was more cautious after he had made a few errors.
7. Who is the greater poet, Shakespeare or Milton?
8. Tokyo is now the largest city in the world.
9. The most widely used substance for making toys is polyethylene.
10. Few substances are cheaper or more durable.

1.5 The Adverb

Nouns and pronouns are modified by adjectives. Other parts of speech are modified by adverbs.

An adverb modifies a verb, an adjective, or another adverb.

MODIFYING A VERB:	Corky declined the nomination *immediately*.
MODIFYING AN ADJECTIVE:	Sheila is *rather* tired.
MODIFYING AN ADVERB:	Leslie dances *very* gracefully.

Adverbs tell *where, when, how,* or *to what extent:*

WHERE:	We saw soldiers *nearby.*
WHEN:	Letitia saw the President *recently.*
HOW:	The elephant approached *slowly.*
TO WHAT EXTENT:	The symphony is *almost* finished.

Many adverbs are formed by adding *-ly* to an adjective: *wise—wisely, final—finally, rapid—rapidly.* However, not all modifiers ending in *-ly* are adverbs. The following, for example, are adjectives: *lively, homely, friendly, lovely, kindly.*

Some words may be either adjectives or adverbs.

ADJECTIVE	ADVERB
a *still* night	Stand *still.*
She feels *well.*	She sings *well.*
the *right* method	Turn *right* at the corner.

Many adverbs do not end in *-ly.* The negatives *no, not,* and *never* are almost always adverbs. Many time-words, such as *now, ever, almost, soon,* are always adverbs.

Directive Adverbs

Adverbs that tell *where* (place or direction) about the verb are called **directive adverbs.** They normally follow the verb they modify.

Henry came *forward.*	Ms. Roberts brought her bike *inside.*
The instructor looked *up.*	The parade came *near.*
The tree fell *backwards.*	The captain went *outside.*

Many of these directive adverbs are combined with verbs to make idioms: *clear out, clear up, clear away, clear off.* An idiom is a group of words with a meaning different from the literal meanings of the words taken one by one.

Position of Adverbs

A directive adverb normally follows the verb it modifies. An adverb modifying an adjective or another adverb comes immediately before the word it modifies. Other adverbs may be shifted from one place in the sentence to another.

DIRECTIVE: The balloon soared *up*.

ADVERB MODIFYING MODIFIER: It was a *very* silly idea.

He drove *too* fast.

OTHER ADVERBS: *Quickly* he ran for bandages.

He *quickly* ran for bandages.

He ran for bandages *quickly*.

Adverbs in Comparisons

Like adjectives, adverbs are used in comparisons. The comparative and the superlative are formed as follows:

1. Adverbs of one syllable add *-er*.

> The guests stayed *later* than we had expected.
> The team practiced *harder* than ever.

2. Most adverbs ending in *-ly* form the comparative with *more*.

> The first debater spoke *more passionately*.
> I retraced my steps *more carefully*.

3. The superlative form of the adverb is formed with *-est* or *most*. Adverbs that form the comparative with *-er* form the superlative with *-est*. Those that use *more* for the comparative use *most* for the superlative.

COMPARATIVE	SUPERLATIVE
farther	farthest
shorter	shortest
more agreeably	most agreeably
more elegantly	most elegantly

Note: See Section 1.4 for irregular comparisons of adjectives. Some of the words listed there as adjectives may also be used as adverbs and are compared in the same way.

Exercise A: Find each adverb and tell which word or words it modifies.

1. You can still see land if you look hard.
2. The council usually runs this town fairly efficiently.
3. The stranger was dressed neatly but unobtrusively.
4. Unfortunately, all of eastern Europe is still under Communist rule.
5. How can you lie around in this slovenly fashion?
6. Bacteria eventually build up resistance to antibiotics.
7. The skipper started the engine up and cast off the lines.
8. The woman, completely exhausted, was quickly pulled aboard.
9. The thief quietly gave himself up.
10. The labor leaders then voted unanimously to strike.
11. Tab is almost completely noncaloric.
12. Later we heard that our team had won easily.
13. I am still bothered by this slightly queasy feeling.
14. Our garage doors open automatically.

Exercise B: Find the adverbs and show what they tell about the word or words they modify.

1. Andrés Segovia plays classical guitar magnificently.
2. Signals from the Viking I were coming back clearly from Mars.
3. The driver was not badly injured in the accident.
4. Have you ever heard Mr. Kane play the sousaphone?

5. Bill has just returned to school after a rather long absence.
6. Almost all television films are now made in Hollywood.
7. Our neighbors, the Kirks, will be moving away shortly.
8. If you work hard, you will soon see results.
9. The fullback has already fumbled twice.
10. Mt. Hood has not erupted recently.

1.6 The Preposition

The words in an English sentence do not occur in haphazard order. They are arranged in precise patterns in order to convey meaning. The words that go together are joined or linked in a variety of ways. One means of linking words is the **preposition.**

There are seventeen one-syllable prepositions in English.* They are used to show the following relationships.

LOCATION:	at, by, in, on, near
DIRECTION:	to, from, down, off, through, out, past, up
ASSOCIATION:	of, for, with, like

There are also certain two-syllable words that act as prepositions.

about	along	below	during
above	among	beneath	except
across	around	beside	inside
after	before	between	outside
against	behind	beyond	over
			under

A number of prepositions have been formed by combining some of the one-syllable prepositions:

into	upon	without
onto	within	throughout

---

* The word *but* may be used as a preposition with the meaning of *except*.

Objects of Prepositions. A preposition never appears alone. It is always used with a word or group of words that are called its **object.**

A preposition relates its object to some other word in the sentence.

The object of a preposition usually follows the preposition. The only exception occurs in a sentence or clause introduced by an interrogative pronoun or a relative pronoun.

> The driver maneuvered her car *into* the *parking space.*
> The senator marched briskly *down* the *street.*
> *Whom* did you ask *for?*
> The spy did not know *whom* the message was *for.*
> *In* what *quarter* did you kick the field goal?

The object of a preposition may be a single word or a group of words.

WORD:	Angela put the trunk in the *attic.*
WORD:	Herb pointed at *me.*
WORD:	Before voting, we considered the *issues.*

WORD GROUP:	After *boarding the bus,* I read the newspaper.
WORD GROUP:	Before *leaving for work,* have some breakfast.
WORD GROUP:	Dad was ready for *whatever I would say.*

Compound prepositions have been formed by combining a modifier with a preposition or by grouping prepositions, as follows:

according to	out of	on account of	aside from
prior to	owing to	instead of	by means of
in front of	subsequent to	because of	as to

Exercise: Find the prepositions. Tell the object of each one.

1. The powerful rocket rose from its launching pad.
2. With unerring accuracy it sped toward the moon.

3.   The rocket hurtled through space at fantastic speed.

4.   Its progress was followed by scientists throughout the world.

5.   Upon entering the moon's gravitational field, it gained additional speed.

6.   After 36 hours of travel, it crashed into the lunar surface.

7.   On impact, it raised a great cloud of volcanic dust.

8.   They flew directly to London without stopping in New York.

9.   Whom did you go with?

10.   The guidance counselor will give assistance to whoever wants it.

11.   Since 1951, television has broadcast in color.

12.   Most seashore animals make their own shells out of lime from the water.

1.7   The Conjunction

Another kind of word used to tie the parts of a sentence together is the conjunction.

A conjunction is a word which connects words, phrases, or clauses.

There are three kinds of conjunctions: coordinating conjunctions, correlative conjunctions, and subordinating conjunctions.

Coordinating Conjunctions

There are three conjunctions used only to connect like sentence parts. They are called **coordinating conjunctions** because they tie together things of the same kind or order. These coordinating conjunctions are *and,* *but,* and *or.*

>   I am taking physics *and* calculus. (connects nouns)
>   The refugee was frightened *and* ill. (connects adjectives)

Willie acted hastily *but* wisely. (connects adverbs)
I went into the store *and* up the escalator. (connects
 prepositional phrase)
You may practice now *or* wait for Sue. (connects predicates)
Turn on the light *but* leave the door closed.
 (connects clauses)

For is used as a coordinating conjunction only between clauses. *Nor* is used as a coordinating conjunction only when it is preceded by another negative word.

I called him immediately, *for* I was sure that he needed help.
Michael did *not* come by car, *nor* did any of the other boys.
We went on to church, *for* it was certain that Dan was too
 sick to go.

Correlative Conjunctions

A few conjunctions are used in pairs: *not only . . . but (also); either . . . or; neither . . . nor; both . . . and; whether . . . or.* Such conjunctions are called **correlative conjunctions.**

Her temperature was *not only* high *but* alarming.
Either Ms. White *or* Mr. Cole will announce the winner.
Neither Ben *nor* Gussie answered the call.
Both the house *and* the garage were flooded.
Manny must decide now *whether* to keep the car *or* sell it.

Subordinating Conjunctions

Words used to introduce adverb clauses are called **subordinating conjunctions.** These words not only introduce the subordinate clause but link it to the main clause. Their chief function is to make clear exactly what is the relation between the two clauses. The chief relations they show are *time, place,* *cause, result, exception, condition,* and *alternative.* The most common subordinating conjunctions are these:

after	as though	provided	till	whenever
although	because	since	unless	where
as	before	so that	until	wherever
as if	if	than	whatever	while
as long as	in order that	though	when	

Conjunctive Adverbs

Certain adverbs are used to join main clauses. When so used, they are called **conjunctive adverbs.** A conjunctive adverb is preceded by a semicolon and followed by a comma. The most common conjunctive adverbs are these:

accordingly	hence	nevertheless	therefore
consequently	however	otherwise	yet
furthermore	moreover	then	also

Exercise A: Find the conjunctions and conjunctive adverbs. Tell what kind each joining word is.

1. Kathy bought some boots, but she did not like them.
2. Phil looked as if he had been frightened by a ghost.
3. I drove onto the shoulder so that the truck could pass.
4. I have neither the money nor the desire to go.
5. When you see lightning, it has already missed you.
6. We tossed the ball till it was pitch dark.
7. We waxed our skis as we waited.
8. The President visited the town where he had been born.
9. I do not know either how to skate or how to ski.
10. We signaled to the bus driver; however, he didn't stop.
11. She will talk as long as there is someone to listen.
12. You must have your receipt, or no refund will be given.
13. I shall go provided you promise to drive carefully.

14. The road was almost impassable; nevertheless, we kept driving.

15. You must do whatever you think best.

Exercise B: Find the conjunctions. Show what words or word groups they join.

1. Write a report on Harriet Tubman or Sojourner Truth.
2. He failed to read the directions and omitted a question.
3. Neither the book nor the movie was worthwhile.
4. We played tennis as long as the light lasted.
5. If you go, you may use my camera.
6. Kim will go to college provided she wins a scholarship.
7. The question was whether to go to camp or to get a job.
8. Tomatoes, squashes, green beans, and eggplants have seeds and are, therefore, technically not vegetables.

1.8 The Interjection

An interjection is a word or group of words interjected, or thrown, into the sentence. It is usually followed by an exclamation point.

An interjection is a word or word group used to express surprise or other emotion. It has no grammatical relation to other words in the sentence.

Ouch! Oh! Ah! For heaven's sake! Hurrah!
Great! Congratulations!

1.9 Words Used in Different Ways

Some words, such as *are, think, eat,* are always verbs. The personal pronouns *I, me,* etc., are always personal pronouns.

Many words, however, may be used in a sentence in different ways.

> The costume is finished, *but* I may not go. (conjunction)
> No one *but* you can make the final decision. (preposition)
> The *storm* polluted the water for weeks. (noun)
> It is time to buy new *storm* doors. (adjective)
> The enemy *stormed* the garrison. (verb)

Noun or Adjective?

A word used to name a person, place, or thing is a noun. The same word may be used before another noun to tell "what kind." When so used, it is an adjective.

> *Sulpha* is used for many purposes. (noun)
> *Sulpha* drugs are very effective. (adjective)
> *Wednesday* is career day in school. (noun)
> *Wednesday* concerts are very popular. (adjective)

Adjective or Pronoun?

A demonstrative pronoun—*this, that, these,* and *those*—may also be used as an adjective. If the word is used alone in place of a noun, it is a pronoun. If it is used before a noun to tell *which one,* it is an adjective.

> *This* is my Volkswagen. (pronoun)
> *That* is a newer model. (pronoun)
> *These* skates are Anne's. (adjective modifying *skates*)
> *Those* men are surveyors. (adjective modifying *men*)

In a similar way the words *what, which,* and *whose* may be used alone as pronouns or before nouns as adjectives.

> *What* is your name? (pronoun)

W*hat* building is this? (adjective modifying *building*)
W*hich* is your sister? (pronoun)
W*hich* person is the judge? (adjective modifying *person*)
W*hose* is this? (pronoun)
W*hose* story do you believe? (adjective modifying *story*)

The words *your, my, our, his, her, their* are forms of the personal pronouns used to show possession. Used in this way, they perform the job of adjectives. The words *mine, yours, hers, ours,* and *theirs* are always pronouns. The word *his* may be used either as a pronoun or an adjective. See Section 1.2.

That hat of *his* is unique. (pronoun)
The tan luggage is *hers*. (pronoun)
Here is *her* pattern. (adjective use)

Adjective or Adverb?

Several words have the same form whether used as adjectives or adverbs. To tell whether a word is used as an adjective or as an adverb, determine what other word in the sentence it goes with, or modifies. This is a matter of sense, which you can get from the meaning. If it modifies a verb, it is used as an adverb. If it modifies a noun or pronoun, it is used as an adjective. If it tells *how, when, where,* or *how much,* it is an adverb. If it tells *what kind,* it is an adjective.

He shouted as *loud* as he could. (adverb telling *how*
about *shouted*)
A *loud* noise frightened us. (adjective telling *what
kind* about *noise*)

Adverb or Preposition?

A number of words may be used either as prepositions or as adverbs. If the word is followed by a noun or pronoun, it is probably a preposition. The noun or pronoun is its object. If the word in question is not followed by a noun or pronoun, it is probably an adverb. If the word can be moved to another position, it is an adverb.

> The lawyer turned *down* our case.
> The lawyer turned our case *down*.
>> (In both sentences *down* is an adverb. It can be moved without changing the meaning.)
> I turned the press release *in* just before the
>> deadline. (adverb)
> I turned *in* the press release just before the deadline. (adverb)
> Our new representative dropped *in*. (adverb)
> The skiers raced *down* the hill.
>> (*down* cannot be moved; it is a preposition.)

Exercise A: Determine how the italicized word is used in each sentence.

1. The *master* switch is in the basement.
2. Mr. Bowles is not a *well* man.
3. *What* plays can we get tickets to?
4. *What* is the best play to see?
5. The woman on the corner sells *cut* flowers.
6. Where is the *head* usher?
7. Sarah is a stickler for *absolute* accuracy.
8. That candidate received two *write-in* votes.
9. The audience had heard the story *before*.
10. Write a short essay *before* you come to class tomorrow.
11. The expedition set out *before* dawn.
12. Jane, will you put *out* the dog's supper?
13. *This* machine rivets the fenders to the car.
14. Is *this* the machine?
15. The Folger Library in Washington *houses* much valuable Shakespeare material.

Exercise B: Determine how each italicized word is used.

1. The *transatlantic* liner has no funnels whatever.

2. The senator deftly *outmaneuvered* opponents of the bill.
3. Can a Monarch butterfly really migrate so *far?*
4. This plane flies to Los Angeles *nonstop.*
5. *Automobile* manufacturers introduce their new models every autumn.
6. Bones of sabertooth tigers have been found in the *tar* pits of California.
7. Stars are great glowing balls of gas *like* our sun.
8. Our washing machine is not functioning *as* it should.
9. Grasshoppers hatch in the spring and die *before* winter.
10. The *paramedic* team responded to the emergency call.
11. Animals *without* backbones are called invertebrates.
12. The ostrich and the penguin are birds *that* cannot fly.
13. *That* Volkswagen belongs to the Thomases.
14. "*These* are the times that try men's souls."
15. "*Many* are called but *few* are chosen."

1.10   Verbals

There are a number of highly useful words in English that are difficult to classify as parts of speech. These are **infinitives, participles,** and **gerunds.** They are called verbals because all of them are formed from verbs. Like verbs they may all be completed by objects or predicate words. Like verbs they may all be modified by adverbs.

However, each of the verbals has other characteristics. The infinitive may be used as a noun, an adjective, or an adverb. The gerund is used as a noun. The participle is used as an adjective.

1.11   The Infinitive

Usually, but not always, the infinitive is preceded by *to,* which is called the "sign of the infinitive." The kinds of infinitives are as follows:

ACTIVE PRESENT:	to watch
ACTIVE PERFECT:	to have watched
PASSIVE PRESENT:	to be watched
PASSIVE PERFECT:	to have been watched.

The infinitive may appear without its "sign," the word *to*:

He did not dare *trust* him.
One of the passengers saw the boy *fall*.
Mother heard you *come* in.

The infinitive may be used as a noun. It may be subject or object of the verb, or it may be a predicate noun, or an appositive.

To conquer was their only objective. (subject of *was*)
The boss always wants *to quarrel*. (object of *wants*)
Dan's chief objective is *to win* votes. (predicate noun)
Our orders, *to paint* the rec room, were carried
    out. (appositive)

The infinitive may also be used as a modifier. Used as an adjective, it may modify nouns and pronouns.

Ms. Morgan is the banker *to ask*.
Harry is the one *to challenge*.

As an adverb, the infinitive may modify adjectives or verbs.

The fire was dreadful *to watch*. (modifies the
    adjective *dreadful*)

They came *to paint* the posters. (modifies verb *came*)

The Infinitive Phrase. An infinitive itself may have modifiers. It may also have a subject, an object, or a predicate word. An **infinitive phrase** consists of the infinitive together with its modifiers, its subject, object, or predicate word.

The infinitive may be modified by adverbs, phrases, or clauses. These modifiers are part of the infinitive phrase.

> *To work* well requires concentration.
> (*well* modifies *To work*)
>
> *To play* a good game by Saturday, we must practice now.
> (The phrase *by Saturday* modifies *To play*.)
>
> The supervisor said *to stop* when I got the cards addressed.
> (The clause *when I got the cards addressed* modifies *to stop*.)

The infinitive may have a direct object, an indirect object, or a predicate word. These words, completing the meaning of the infinitive, are part of the infinitive phrase.

> *To sign the application*, use this pencil.
> (*application* is the direct object of *To sign*.)
> Marie wanted *to give Pam a gift*.
> (*Pam* is the indirect object and *gift* is the direct object of *to give*.)
> Joe wants *to be a machinist*. (*machinist* is a predicate noun after *to be*.)
> The teller always tries *to be courteous*.
> (*courteous* is a predicate adjective after *to be*.)

The infinitive may have a subject. This subject always follows the main verb and comes directly before the infinitive. Since it follows the main verb and is in the objective case, it is sometimes mistaken for an object of the main verb. The subject of the infinitive is part of the infinitive phrase. In the following examples, the entire phrase is direct object of the verb.

> Willie asked *José to play* basketball.
> The librarian told *me to return the book*.
> The President wanted *the nation to prepare*.

Note: If the main verb is a linking verb (a form of *be, appear, seem,* etc.), the noun following it is a predicate noun. If a predicate noun is followed by an infinitive, the infinitive modifies the noun.

Spaghetti is the dish *to serve.*   She is the person *to ask.*

Exercise A: Find the complete infinitive phrase in each of the following sentences.

1. We tried to find the site of the old narrow-gauge railroad.
2. The team to beat this year is Milwaukee.
3. Lilly works hard to earn money for college expenses.
4. To have accepted the job would have been disastrous.
5. The golfer's dream is to make a hole-in-one.
6. The team is anxious to win this last game.
7. Many a successful businessperson wants to be known as a philanthropist.
8. The desire to succeed is in all of us.
9. The manager's decision to change pitchers was long overdue.
10. To lose in the final seconds of the game was disappointing.
11. Lee's ambition, to be accepted at West Point, has been realized.
12. The next job is to spray the apple orchard.
13. With ten seconds left, USC has decided to try a field goal.
14. Helen's greatest desire is to have her poems published.
15. In the short story "A Christmas Memory," Truman Capote seems to be telling the story of his own life.

Exercise B: Decide how the infinitive phrase is used in each sentence.

1. To make money is not always easy; to keep it is never easy.
2. The Forty-Niners went to California to find gold.
3. My greatest desire is to travel in Europe.
4. When I got home, I decided to call Janet.
5. This is the book to read if you like adventure.
6. Frankly, we would like to go with you.

7. This is the first game to be played in the new gym.
8. After her internship, she can begin to practice medicine.
9. "To err is human; to forgive, divine."
10. "I regret that I have but one life to lose for my country."

1.12   The Gerund

The gerund always ends in *-ing*. It is used in the sentence as a noun and in almost every way that a noun can be used.

> *Typing* can be tiresome. (subject of the verb)
> I enjoy *weaving*. (object of the verb)
> By *signing*, I became a member. (object of the preposition)

The Gerund Phrase. A gerund may be modified by adjectives or adverbs. It may be completed by objects or predicate words. A **gerund phrase** consists of the gerund together with its modifiers, objects, or predicate words.

The gerund may be modified by single adjectives and adverbs or by phrases and by clauses.

> *Good timing* is necessary in skiing.
>   (*Good* is an adjective modifying *timing*.)
> Keith enjoys *bicycling hard*.
>   (*hard* is an adverb modifying *bicycling*.)
> *Skiing down a mountainside* is exhilarating.
>   (*down a mountainside* is a phrase modifying *Skiing*.)
> *Dancing when you are tired* is not fun.
>   (*when you are tired* is a clause modifying *Dancing*.)

Gerunds may be completed by objects or predicate words. These words are part of the gerund phrase.

> *Being provider* for a family is my responsibility.
>   (*provider* is a predicate noun completing *Being*.)
> *Giving Donna a silver chest* is not a good idea.
>   (*Donna* is the indirect object and *silver chest* is the direct object of *Giving*.)

Exercise: Find the complete gerund phrases in these sentences.

1. Cooking gourmet meals is Dad's hobby.
2. Reviewing books can be rewarding work for a person who likes to read.
3. Eli Whitney's cotton gin was a hand-operated contrivance for separating cotton from its seeds.
4. Lynn enjoys covering sports events for the *Register*.
5. Painting and papering can be done by an inexperienced person if he is careful in following instructions.
6. We are all familiar with your thinking on this question.
7. Studying about the past will help you understand the present.
8. Mr. Cobb's occupation is raising pedigreed French poodles.
9. Turning left at the traffic light was our mistake.
10. The mayor reacted by issuing a denial of the story.
11. Painting and writing are arts that require talent and persistence.
12. A busy person can often find relaxation in gardening.
13. Just thinking about space travel intrigues many people.
14. Try seeing it my way.

1.13   The Participle

There are several forms of the participle, all widely used.

PRESENT PARTICIPLE:	painting
PAST PARTICIPLE:	painted
PERFECT PARTICIPLE:	having painted
PASSIVE PERFECT PARTICIPLE:	having been painted

The present participle always ends in *-ing*. The past participle is the third principal part of the verb, and its endings are various. (See Section 1.3.)

The participle is always used as an adjective to modify a noun or a pronoun. In the examples below, the arrow indicates the word modified by the participle.

Running, she managed to reach the station on time.

Frightened, the watchman could not explain the accident.

Having been warned, Jerry avoided the detour.

The Participial Phrase. A participle may be modified by single adverbs or by phrases and clauses. The participle may also be completed by objects or predicate words. A **participial phrase** consists of the participle together with its modifiers, objects, or predicate words.

When a participle is modified by an adverb, a phrase, or a clause, these modifiers are part of the participial phrase.

> *Arriving early,* the critic sat in the wings.
> (*early* is an adverb modifying *Arriving.*)

> *Participating in the tournaments,* Cheryl became a skilled chess player.
> (*in the tournaments* is a phrase modifying *Participating.*)

> *Working while others rested,* Smith developed a new type of plastic.
> (*while others rested* is a clause modifying *Working.*)

When a participle is completed by objects or predicate words, these words are part of the participial phrase. In the examples below, the arrow indicates the word modified by the participial phrase.

> *Having solved the puzzle,* Mrs. Haggarty won the prize.
> (*puzzle* is the direct object of *Having solved.*)

> Alice walked from the principal's office, *looking relieved.*
> (*relieved* is a predicate adjective completing *looking.*)

> *Passing Tony the ball,* Jack danced back.
> (*Tony* is the indirect object and *ball* is the direct object of *Passing.*)

Exercise: Find the complete participial phrase and show which word it modifies.

1. Having written a best seller, the novelist tried to write a play.

2. Built only three years ago, the house already looks shabby.

3. Rising to face his audience, Jack forgot every word of his speech.

4. The Farmers' Bank, established in 1877, has just celebrated its centennial.

5. London, Paris, and Rome are cities often visited by tourists.

6. Seen through the water, a straight stick looks crooked.

7. The play, scheduled for an October opening, had to be postponed until early November.

8. The understudy, appearing in the leading role, gave a splendid performance.

9. Shaking with laughter, the comedian could hardly speak.

10. The papers, scattered by the wind, were collected with difficulty.

11. She stood there for an hour, patiently answering stockholders' questions.

12. Jill is the player now running across the court.

13. Having been rejected by the voters, he returned to the business world.

14. The President, continuing his speech, voiced the will of the nation to defend itself.

15. On April 18, 1906, an earthquake never before equaled in violence in the United States struck the city of San Francisco.

2.0 The Parts of the Sentence

Single words in English are used widely to convey meaning. The words *stop, danger, poison,* for example, express full meaning to the reader. In general, however, meaning is expressed in English by groups of words acting together: *in the morning, playing wide receiver, Sally laughed.*

These groups of words are neither spoken nor written in haphazard order. In the English sentence there are fixed patterns into which words are placed to express meaning. These patterns are learned in childhood. They are learned because they are the chief means by which the child can express his feelings and get what he wants.

A knowledge of what these sentence patterns are and of how they work is essential for effective use of language in adult life.

2.1 The Sentence

For more than 200 years scholars have labored to define the sentence. More than 200 definitions have resulted. The definition favored by many scholars today is this: "Each sentence is an independent linguistic form, not included by virtue of any grammatical construction in any larger linguistic form."*

* Leonard Bloomfield, *Language.*

We shall make use of a simpler definition. Essentially, we shall say that a sentence is an utterance that is grammatically independent of any other. To make use of this definition, we must be clear about the phrase "grammatically independent." We shall see that single words, phrases, and clauses are not grammatically independent. They are tied by various devices to other words, phrases, or clauses within the sentence.

Sentences are used to make statements and to ask questions. To be understood, they must express a complete thought, a complete idea, or a complete question. Now, a complete thought can be expressed by a word or a phrase:

Stop!   Not in school

On the other hand, words and phrases may *not* express a complete idea:

Knowing well   With the curly hair

You know that these expressions are incomplete because they leave you asking *what? what about it? what happened?*

A group of words must express a complete thought or it is not a sentence. We can begin the study of the sentence with this partial definition:

A sentence is a group of words that expresses a complete thought.

INCOMPLETE	The man in the front row (What about him?)
COMPLETE	The man in the front row answered my question.
INCOMPLETE	Mr. James, the banker at Mellon (Did what?)
COMPLETE	Mr. James, the banker at Mellon, is my uncle.
INCOMPLETE	Walking to the subway (Who did what?)
COMPLETE	Walking to the subway, Mike saw the holdup.

Exercise: Which of the following groups of words are sentences?

1. The muskellunge, America's fiercest freshwater gamefish

2. Commonly known as the "musky"
3. The new, officially-approved method of artificial respiration
4. The photographs of Margaret Bourke-White
5. Emily and Charlotte Brontë, seventeenth-century British authors
6. Walking narrow beams hundreds of feet above ground
7. Ruby Dee in *A Raisin in the Sun*
8. The mere thought of using tea bags is abhorrent to Englishmen
9. During the summer, Lili Tomlin and Barbra Streisand, the show's headliners
10. Persian cats often called Angoras
11. A profitable discussion but no decision
12. One faucet for both hot and cold water
13. American Indians the first inhabitants of North and South America
14. Probably came to Alaska from Siberia
15. One of my favorite actresses is Cicely Tyson

2.2 Kinds of Sentences

Sentences may be classified as to structure* or as to the purpose of the speaker or writer. There are four principal purposes served by sentences, as described below.

1. The **declarative sentence** is used to make a statement. The statement may be one of fact, wish, intent, or feeling.

> Babe Didrikson was one of the greatest athletes of all time.
> Thousands of people visit Rome each year.

2. The **imperative sentence** is used to state a command, request, or direction. The subject is always *You.* When the subject

---

* For classification of sentences by form or structure, see Section 3.0.

is not expressed, as is usually the case, it is "understood" to be *You.*

> (You) Please report to the senator at once.
> (You) Close the door before leaving.
> (You) Do not put your hands out the car window.

3. The **interrogative sentence** is used to ask a question. It is always followed by a question mark.

> What program is that?
> Are you interested in that book?
> Are you going to work tomorrow?

4. An **exclamatory sentence** is used to express strong feeling. It is always followed by an exclamation point.

> Look at the fire!   How I wish I could go!

Exercise: What kind of sentence is each of the following?

1. You will never be able to guess the surprise ending.
2. Then you don't think we can afford to take the trip?
3. I wish there were a tourist flight to Los Angeles.
4. Watch the signs as you approach the cut-off.
5. How important is the message?
6. What a bruising sport professional hockey is!
7. Dan Freeburg is the person to see.
8. Before you assemble the folding chair, read these instructions.
9. The directions on the quick-mix package must be followed exactly.
10. Hurricane Belle is headed straight for Long Island.

2.3 Subject and Predicate

There are two parts in every complete sentence (1) The **subject** is the person, thing, or idea about which something is said. (2) The **predicate** is the idea expressed about the subject.

Every sentence must have a subject and a predicate.
The subject of the sentence is the person or thing about which something is said.
The predicate tells something or asks something about the subject of the sentence.

The word *predicate* means "to proclaim, declare, preach, or affirm." The predicate of a sentence therefore "proclaims, declares, preaches, or affirms" something about the subject.

We may say that a sentence is a group of words that tells something (*predicate*) about a person or thing (*subject*). Our definition of a sentence may now be expanded:

A sentence is a group of words expressing a complete thought by means of a subject and a predicate.

SUBJECT	PREDICATE
Tar	sticks.
Fresh tar in the road	sticks to the shoes.
Adversity	strengthens.
Some adversity	strengthens one's character.

2.4 The Simple Predicate

In every predicate, however long, the most important word —the key word—is the **verb.*** In fact, the verb is the key word in the sentence. Sentences may be constructed without nouns, pronouns, or other parts of speech; but, without a verb, there can be no sentence.

The simple predicate of the sentence is the verb.

The verb may be a phrase consisting of more than one word: *have gone, might have gone, is running, had been running.*

---

* The **complete predicate** consists of the verb, its modifiers, and complements. The **complete subject** consists of the simple subject and its modifiers.

The words making up the verb may be interrupted by a modifier. Such a modifier is not part of the verb.

> *has* just *been received*   *had* just *determined*
> *was* never *explained*   *had* almost *reorganized*

The simple predicate, which we shall hereafter call the *verb*, may be compound. The word *compound* means "having more than one part of the same kind." The parts of a compound verb are joined together by a conjunction (*and, or, neither-nor*, etc.).

> She **opened** with Brahms and **closed** with Wagner.
> We **talked, reminisced,** and **sang** at the reunion.
> We **can** either **write** or **call.**

2.5 The Simple Subject

Every verb has a subject. It is the word or the words that answer *who?* or *what?* before the verb.

> The large barn burned.   Liz scored the basket
>   VERB: burned   VERB: scored
>   WHAT BURNED: barn   WHO SCORED: Liz
>   SUBJECT: barn   SUBJECT: Liz

The **simple subject** is the subject of the verb. The subject of the verb may be a word, a phrase, or a clause.

> *To be elegant* is very hard work. (phrase as subject)
> *What they demanded* is still vague. (clause as subject)

The subject of a verb may be an entire phrase, but it is never one word within a phrase.

> **One** *of the crops* was damaged. (Only one was damaged.

One is the subject. The word *crops* lies within the prepositional phrase and is object of the preposition *of*.)

Drying dishes is my bête noire. (The gerund phrase *Drying dishes* is the subject of *is*.)

Algebra, *together with chemistry*, was a frightening prospect. (*Algebra* is the subject of *was*; *chemistry* is the subject of the prepositional phrase *together with*.)

The subject of the verb may be compound. The parts of a compound subject are normally joined by a conjunction.

Kate Jackson and **Valerie Harper** are my favorite TV stars.
Courtesy and **diligence** are required of all diplomats and aides.
Either a **truck** or a **station wagon** will do.

Exercise: Find the verb and its subject.

1. The alarm had been set for five o'clock.
2. Neither the plumber nor his assistant had the right tools.
3. The man with the armful of boxes stumbled and fell.
4. The driver could hardly see the edge of the road.
5. Some of our military secrets have obviously been stolen.
6. No foreigner enters the Forbidden City and returns.
7. A chest of gold coins and jewels was recently found in this cave.
8. Near the airport, the ozone count is always high.
9. Don Wherry tuned in his ham radio and heard a distress signal.
10. He called "Cookie Monster," a friend on Lincoln Street, and warned him.
11. Soon rescue ships and helicopters found a ship in distress.
12. Both Don and his friend were later given medals.
13. To win five out of seven games is the coach's aim.
14. In 1760, a soft-spoken, red-haired storm of energy exploded on the campus of William and Mary.
15. Alexander Hamilton could never have been elected President.

2.6 Subjects In Unusual Positions

In most sentences the subject appears before the verb. This subject-verb order is the normal pattern of English sentences. In many sentences, however, this order is reversed.

Questions. In most questions the subject appears between the words making up the verb phrase.

VERB	SUBJECT	VERB
Did	she	arrive?
Had	you	gone?
May	I	go?
Would	they	have danced?

In most questions beginning with interrogative words such as *where, when, why, how, how much,* the subject falls between the parts of the verb. In questions beginning with *who* or *what,* the verb may follow the subject in normal order:

Who won?   What happened?

Sentences Beginning with *There* and *Here*. Many sentences begin with *There* or *Here* immediately followed by some form of *be: There is, There was, There will be, Here is, Here were,* and so on. In these sentences Here and There are introductory words used to get the sentence started. They are never the subject of the verb. In this kind of sentence, the subject follows the verb.

Here is the decision of the jury. (*decision* is the subject.)
There were three students absent. (*students* is the subject.)
There will be a concert this evening. (*concert* is the subject.)

Note: Not all sentences beginning with *Here* and *There* follow the above pattern: *Here we can pitch our tent. Here he comes. There he goes.* In these sentences, *Here* and *There* are adverbs modifying the verb.

Sentences in Inverted Order. For emphasis or for variety of style, the subject is sometimes placed after the verb.

Into the courtroom walked the *defendant*.
Down into the water plunged the *diver*.
Up into the clouds soared the *rocket*.

Finding the Subject of the Verb. To find the subject of the verb in any sentence, find the verb first. Then ask *who?* or *what?* before it. If the sentence is not in normal word order, change it to normal order, and the subject will become clear.

INVERTED   Onto the stage ran the firemen.

NORMAL   The firemen ran onto the stage.

Exercise A: Find the verb and its subject.

1. There have been many rumors about the governor's future plans.
2. From nowhere there came the deafening boom of a jet plane.
3. Have you or your brother ever ridden in a cable car?
4. There were at least a dozen moths around the light.
5. On the first of every month came the same old bills.
6. Here on this hill were fired the first shots of the Revolution.
7. On the surface of the moon are thousands of huge craters.
8. How fast did the Wright Brothers' plane fly?
9. Directly in front of us stood a bear with her cub.
10. Every day at noon comes the shrill sound of the factory whistle.

Exercise B: Find the verb and its subject.

1. On the table was a copper bowl filled with flowers.
2. In every theatrical production there are many workers behind the scenes.
3. Attached to the letter was a newspaper clipping.
4. Straight toward the hunter the wounded leopard charged.
5. Where is everyone going after the play?
6. On the cliff were the ruins of a medieval fortress.
7. Why has the site of the convention been shifted?
8. Far down at the bottom of the canyon flows the Colorado River.

9. Below the soil are several layers of sedimentary rock.
10. Here are the books on scuba diving.

2.7 The Direct Object

In many sentences the action verb carries action over from the subject to some other word. It serves to tie these words together. The word to which the action is carried from the subject is the **direct object.**

Sometimes the direct object tells what receives the action of the verb. Sometimes it tells the result of the action.

RESULT OF THE ACTION   Sam piloted the PT boat.
(piloted what?)

RESULT OF THE ACTION   Sam secured the PT boat.
(secured what?)

RECEIVER OF THE ACTION   Carol wrote the essay.
(wrote what?)

RESULT OF ACTION   Carol wrote essays. (wrote what?)

Action verbs that carry over the action from subject to object are called **transitive verbs.** Action verbs that are not followed by direct objects are called **intransitive.** Some verbs may be transitive in one sentence and intransitive in another.

The man *was welding.* (intransitive)
The man *was welding* the *joint.* (transitive)

In some so-called action verbs, the action is not visible, nor otherwise evident. However, the verb does carry the thought from subject to object, tying them together.

Sue *has* a large dog. (has what?)
Carol *knows* the lyrics. (knows what?)
She *will need* money. (will need what?)

The direct object is a word or group of words to which the verb carries over the action from the subject.

The direct object may be a word, a phrase, or a clause.

>They intend *to discourage you.* (phrase)
>Hilda enjoyed *digging oysters Saturday.* (phrase)
>I'll paint *whatever you say.* (clause)

The direct object may be compound.

>The hotel caters *parties* and *weddings.* (caters what?)
>We decided *to write* and *to phone.* (decided what?)

A word that completes the meaning of the verb is called a **complement.** The direct object is one kind of complement.

Direct Object or Adverb? To find the direct object, ask *what?* after the verb. An adverb following an action verb tells *how, when, where,* or *how much* about the verb. A direct object tells *what* after the verb.

>The jeep shot *forward.* (where)
>The snake disappeared *suddenly.* (how)
>President Carter presented the *award.* (what)

2.8 The Indirect Object

The indirect object of the verb tells to or for whom, or to or for what, something is done.

>We told the *reporter* what happened. (*to* the reporter)
>Dad bought *Todd* a boat. (*for* Todd)

A verb has an indirect object only if it also has a direct object. Find the direct objects in the examples above.

The indirect object may be compound: I gave *Jay* and *Bob* lunch.

The words *to* and *for* are never placed before the indirect object. When followed by a noun or pronoun, *to* and *for* are prepositions. The noun or pronoun following the preposition is its object.

Jim gave *Mary* the stapler. (*Mary* is the indirect object.)
Jim gave the stapler *to Mary*. (*Mary* is the object of
the preposition)

Sue made *me* a blue sweater. (*me* is the indirect object)
Sue made a blue sweater *for me*. (*me* is the object of
the preposition)

Exercise: Find both the direct and indirect objects.

1. The dealer gave us a good price for our old car.
2. His mother bought Jim a new sports jacket.
3. My guests brought me a box of candy and a basket of fruit.
4. This experience taught the child an important lesson.
5. Mrs. Jenkins, a broker, sold Dad some stocks and bonds.
6. The employer offered Ellen an excellent starting salary.
7. Mr. Grey left the hospital a million dollars for medical research.
8. Their friends at the shore sent Jean and Sue some unusual shells.
9. Ms. Clark told us some exciting stories about her African safari.
10. The hostess served her guests a delicious dinner.
11. The artist showed Steve the pictures in his studio.
12. The manager promised Mary an early answer about the job.

2.9 Predicate Words

The linking verb links its subject to a word in the predicate.
The word in the predicate, so linked, is called a **predicate word.**
The subject may be linked to a **predicate noun,** a **predicate pronoun,** or a **predicate adjective.**

The junior girls will be models at the show. (predicate noun)

The thief could be anyone in the room. (predicate pronoun)

The audience seemed uneasy. (predicate adjective)

A word that completes the meaning of a verb is called a **complement**. Predicate words complete the meaning of linking verbs, and since they refer to the subject, they are called **subject complements.**

Diagraming. The simple sentence with an action verb is diagramed as follows:

Authors write.   Authors write books.

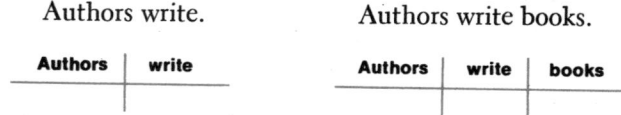

Good authors write carefully.

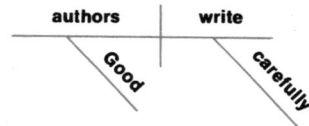

Note: The single-word modifier goes on a slant line below the word it modifies.

The simple sentence with a linking verb is diagramed as follows:

Jo looks happy.   Sanders is governor.

Note: The line following the linking verb slants toward the subject. The action verb with an indirect object is diagramed as follows:

The auditor gave me the total.

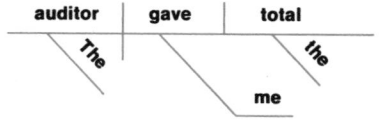

Exercise A: Find the predicate words.

1. For many people, life is a battle.
2. Once every 76 years Halley's comet is visible.
3. The best writer in our group is Joan.
4. The stars look bright in the evening sky.
5. The moon has become a target for rockets.
6. Howard is quite sure of himself.
7. Her remark was a reminder to me of my uncompleted work.
8. Why does this coffee always taste so bitter?
9. The sinking of the *Titanic* was a great maritime disaster.
10. Carol's judgment is unusually good.

Exercise B: Make five columns. Head them *Subject, Verb, Direct Object, Indirect Object,* and *Predicate Word*. Place those parts of the following sentences in the proper columns.

1. In April, 1912, the *Titanic* began her maiden voyage across the Atlantic.
2. Harbor vessels gave the giant ship a gala send-off.
3. Near Newfoundland, in the dead of night, the ship struck an iceberg.
4. The nearby *California* did not hear the vessel's distress signals.
5. The *Titanic* took 1,513 passengers to their doom.
6. Today, radar has eliminated the danger of icebergs.
7. In San Juan, Puerto Rico, we saw an interesting old fort.
8. San Juan is a modern city with a population of one-half million.
9. The many different colors of the Caribbean Sea amazed us.
10. I sent my family many color photographs.

2.10   Compound Parts of Sentences

Subjects, objects, and verbs may all be compound. That is, they may consist of more than one part *of the same kind.* The parts are joined by a conjunction.

COMPOUND SUBJECT	The *intellect* and the *emotions* animate great poetry.
COMPOUND VERB	The flame *sputtered* and *died*.
COMPOUND DIRECT OBJECT	We bought *books* and *records*.
COMPOUND INDIRECT OBJECT	Mom gave *Dan* and *Ed* the tickets.
COMPOUND OBJECT OF PREPOSITION	The Homestead Act provided land for *settlement* and *cultivation*.
COMPOUND PREDICATE WORD	Veterans' Day was *cold* and *damp*.
COMPOUND PREDICATE	The colony *declared itself a republic* and *called for elections*.

Diagraming. Compound sentence parts are diagramed as follows:

Ted and Sue (*compound subject*) met and talked. (*compound verb*).

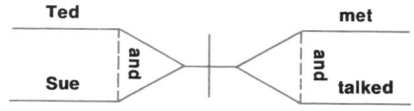

The tailor gave Sylvia and Mary (*compound indirect object*) the wool and linen (*compound direct object*).

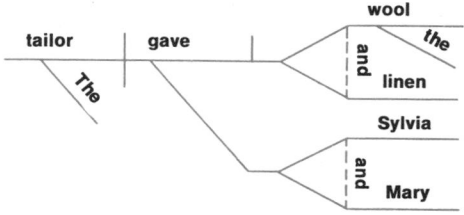

The personalities of the English and Scots (*compound object of the preposition*) are different but complementary (*compound predicate adjective*).

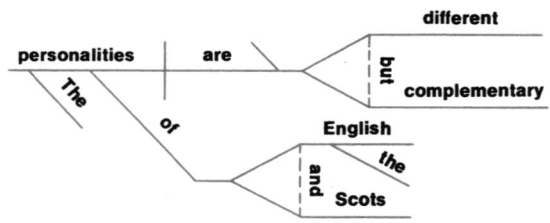

The doctors composed the music and wrote the lyrics (*compound predicate*).

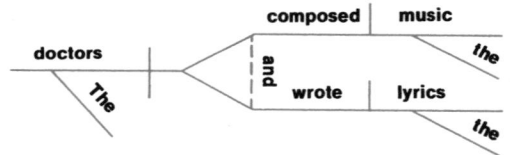

Exercise: Make five columns. Head them *Subject, Verb, Direct Object, Predicate Word,* and *Predicate.* Find the compound parts of the following sentences, and write these parts in the proper columns.

1. Shelley, Keats, and Byron were contemporary poets.
2. The arc lights over the great stadium blinked and went off.
3. The engine sputtered, wheezed, and then stalled.
4. Columbus took with him a compass, an astrolabe, and his own courage.
5. The audience seemed restless and altogether bored.
6. A huge trailer truck had overturned and blocked the road.
7. The Battle of Lexington was short and involved only a few hundred men.
8. Human exploration of other planets seems both possible and probable.

9. Boots barks but never bites.
10. Fir, spruce, and balsam were intermingled with the birches.
11. On the next two holes I hit two trees and one sand trap.
12. I gave Jane a Mexican belt and a pair of hand-made earrings.
13. The hikers found Indian pipes and other wild plants.
14. Mr. Bernstein conducted, played, and lectured.
15. On a certain island in the South Pacific there are no taxes, unemployment, crime, beggars, jazz bands, or inhabitants.

2.11 The Phrase

A phrase is a group of words without a subject and a verb, used as one part of speech.

A phrase is used as one part of speech. A **verb phrase** is two or more words used as a verb: *could sing, might have sung.* A **noun phrase** is two or more words used as a noun: *Edens Expressway, Sears Tower.*

2.12 The Prepositional Phrase

The prepositional phrase consists of the preposition, its object, and modifiers of the object.

> *After that very severe hurricane,* the city rebuilt.
> The Monet hung awkwardly *beside an El Greco.*

The object of a preposition is always a noun, a pronoun, or a group of words used as a noun.

> The lot was full *of* poison ivy. (*poison ivy* is the object of *of.*)
> He insisted that *we* look for her. (*her* is the object of *for.*)
> This is the person *for* whom I auditioned. (*whom* is the object of *for.*)
> *Before* sanding the shelf, I covered the floor. (*sanding the shelf* is a gerund phrase, used as a noun. It is object of *Before.*)

> Terry and I saw a policeman pounding *on* the door. (*door* is object of *on.*)

The prepositional phrase is a modifier. It is used either as an adjective or as an adverb. A prepositional phrase that modifies a noun or pronoun is an **adjective phrase;** that is, it is a phrase used as an adjective.

> Our house is the one *with brown trim.*
> (*with brown trim* modifies the pronoun *one.*)

> I chopped a pound *of onions.* (*of onions* modifies *pound.*)

> The hostility *between the two nominees* grew deeper.
> (*between the two nominees* modifies *hostility.*)

An adjective phrase always comes immediately after the noun or pronoun it modifies.

A prepositional phrase that modifies a verb, an adjective, or an adverb is an **adverb phrase.** That is, it is a phrase used as an adverb to tell *how, how much, when,* or *where* about the word it modifies.

> Jack had been waiting *across the street.* (*across the street* tells *where* about the verb *had been waiting.*)

> It was successful *beyond my fondest expectations.* (*beyond my fondest expectations* tells *how much* about the adjective *successful.*)

> Late *at night* the noise changed somehow. (*at night* tells *when* about the adverb *Late.*)

When two or more prepositional phrases follow each other in succession, they may modify the same word, or one phrase may modify the object in the preceding phrase.

> I drove *to the rally* on *Friday.* (Both phrases modify *drove*; *to the rally* tells *where* and *on Friday* tells *when* about the verb.)

Aunt May hid the phone *on the top shelf of the cupboard.*
(*on the top shelf* modifies *hid*; *of the cupboard* modifies
shelf. It tells *which* shelf.)

We found the culprit *in the middle of a clump of briars.*
(*in the middle* modifies the verb *found*; *of a clump*
modifies *middle*; *of briars* modifies *clump*.)

Diagraming. Prepositional phrases are diagramed as follows:

Julie took the names *of the applicants.* (adjective phrase)

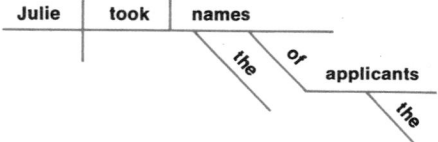

The tide receded late *in the afternoon.* (adverb phrase)

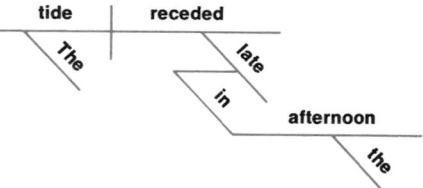

The boat was sunk *near the island.* (adverb phrase)

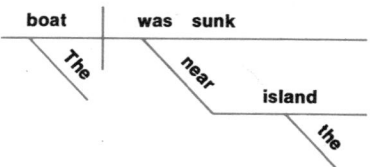

The pile of clothes *in the cellar* got burnt. (adverb phrase)

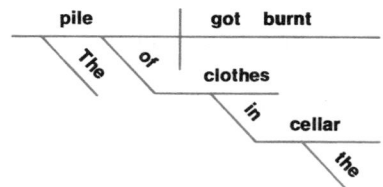

Exercise A: Write each prepositional phrase and the word it modifies.

1. In the 1840's the flood of pioneers over the Oregon Trail began.
2. A company in California sells couples videotapes of their wedding.
3. Will someone in the world please find a cure for asthma?
4. The meaning of *freedom* differs widely between nations and within nations.
5. Some of the scientists were puzzled by the military terminology.
6. Amid a welter of miscues, the play stumbled to an end.
7. The bony structure around the eye protects it against injury.
8. He charmed us with his quick, keen, and altogether delightful humor.
9. Cotton has suffered from competition by the man-made fibers.
10. The deadline for submitting contributions to the contest is May 1.

Exercise B: Write each prepositional phrase and the word it modifies.

1. The hippopotamus usually lies with only its face above water.
2. Does anyone object to our hunting in these woods?
3. Supersonic jets fly from New York to Paris between lunch and dinner.
4. Does the groundhog really emerge from his winter quarters on February 2?
5. Manhattan was purchased for twenty-five dollars' worth of wampum.
6. Peter Stuyvesant was famous for his temper and for his wooden leg.
7. Feeding peanuts to the elephants is part of the fun of going to the zoo.
8. The main secret of survival among animals is being able to eat without being eaten.

2.13   The Infinitive Phrase

Usually, but not always, the **infinitive phrase** begins with *to*. The phrase consists of *to*, the infinitive, its complements and its modifiers. If the infinitive has a subject, that is also part of the phrase.

> I tried *to understand*. (The infinitive phrase is object of the verb *tried*.)
>
> The owner is unwilling *to pay the fine*. (The infinitive phrase modifies the adjective *unwilling*.)
>
> Sherry saw Don *leave*. (The infinitive phrase is object of *saw*. The infinitive is *leave* without the usual *to*. *Don* is subject of the infinitive.)
>
> Ford wanted *to introduce* mass production in his plants. (The infinitive phrase is object of the verb *wanted*.)

Diagraming. The infinitive phrase is diagramed as follows:

He planned to veto the new bill promptly.

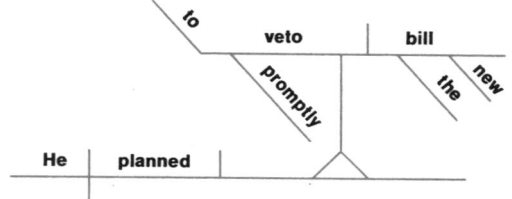

To consider an easy solution is not fair.

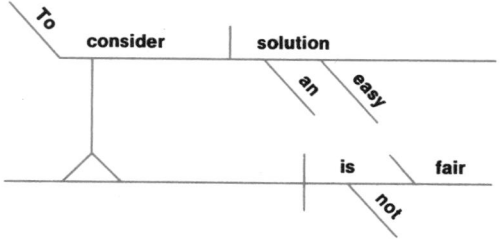

Exercise: Find the infinitive phrases in the sentences below.

1. The Juilliard School is planning to produce an opera.
2. The students have decided to present *The Magic Flute.*
3. Jane Brier has gone to Juilliard to study harmony.
4. The nurse is ready to call the doctor.
5. The speaker was simply impossible to hear.
6. Halle's has advertised a sale to begin in January.
7. To override a Presidential veto requires a two-thirds vote of both Houses.
8. We have decided that this is the house to buy.
9. Nancy is working hard to earn money for college expenses.
10. *The Grapes of Wrath* is about a family's struggle to survive the Depression.
11. The best way to revive a person is to blow your breath into his lungs.
12. To redecorate this room will require time and money.
13. The moon's apparent functions are to provide moonlight for the romanticists and a target for the rocketeers.
14. It is lightning's tendency to seek out the best path offered that makes the lightning rod work.

2.14 The Participial Phrase*

The **participial phrase** usually begins with the participle. The phrase consists of the participle, its modifiers, and its complements. The modifiers and complements may themselves be phrases and clauses.

> I worked until twelve o'clock, *hoping to finish.* (The participial phrase modifies the pronoun *I.* The infinitive phrase *to finish* modifies the participle *hoping.*)

> *Knowing the exact route,* Joe didn't get lost. (The participial phrase modifies *Joe.*)

* See also Section 1.13.

Disturbed by the noise, the editor accomplished nothing. (The participial phrase modifies *editor.*)

Knowing what the university needed, the dean decided wisely. (The participial phrase modifies *dean.* The noun clause *what the university needed* is the object of the participle *knowing.*)

Diagraming. The participle and the participial phrase are diagramed as follows:

Laughing slyly, the comedian sauntered off.

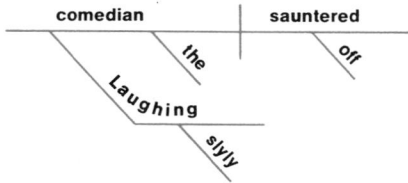

Whistling the aria softly, Sanders left the auditorium.

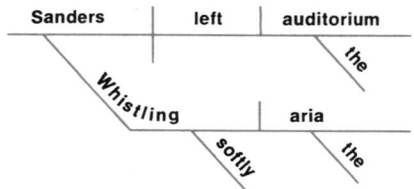

Exercise: Find the participial phrases. Tell the word each phrase modifies. Do not overlook phrases made from past participles and present participles.

1. The magazines lying on the table were back numbers.

2. Utterly bewildered, the new employee sought aid from her supervisor.

3. Stung by his critics, the mayor called a press conference.

4. Having broken her ankle, Eleanor missed the dance.

5. A large crowd heard the evidence presented by the prosecution.

6. Running and leaping, the fawn disappeared into the woods.

7. These houses, built before 1900, are still sturdy.

8. Flowers grown in a greenhouse wilt sooner than those grown in a garden.

9. Mary Hays, better known as Molly Pitcher, was a heroine of the Revolutionary War.

10. We saw the Alps, looming above us and covered with snow.

11. Approaching the city, we saw the skyscrapers etched against the sky.

12. The snow, having lain on the ground for months, melted swiftly in the warm sunshine.

13. Having forgotten his lines, Howie rushed offstage.

14. Repulsed in New York, General Washington led his dwindling forces across New Jersey.

2.15   The Gerund Phrase

The **gerund phrase** consists of the gerund, which always ends in *-ing,* and the modifiers and complements of the gerund. The modifiers themselves may be phrases or clauses. The gerund phrase is always used as a noun.

> *Loud talking in the bus* distracts the driver. (The gerund phrase is the subject of the verb *distracts.*)
>
> She dreaded *hearing the news.* (The gerund phrase is the object of *dreaded.*)
>
> By *smuggling contraband goods,* the colonists evaded English taxes. (The gerund phrase is the object of the preposition *By.*)
>
> *Asking directions as you travel* makes very good sense. (The gerund phrase is the subject of the verb *makes.* The adverb clause *as you travel* modifies the gerund.)

Diagraming. The gerund and the gerund phrase are diagramed as follows:

Thinking is hard work.

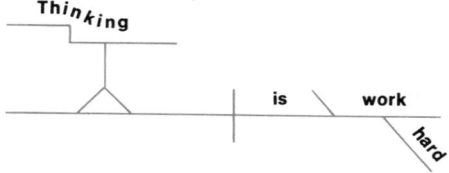

Careful planning made the difference.

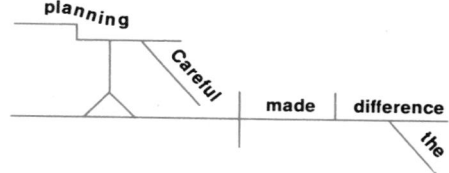

I considered appealing the decision.

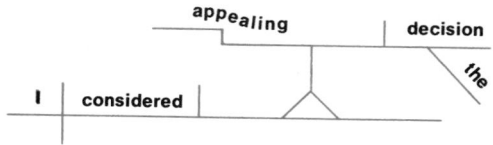

After crawling through the tunnel, they escaped.

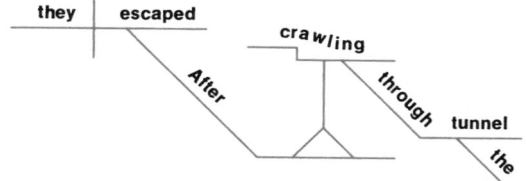

Exercise A: Find the gerund phrases. Tell how each is used.

1. Postponing a dreaded job only makes it more difficult.
2. The secretary's duties are recording the minutes and sending notices to club members.
3. No one could have accused my father of sparing the rod.
4. The tourists were reprimanded for taking pictures of the garden.
5. Mr. King enjoys his hobby, collecting and repairing old clocks.
6. Listening to their complaints drives me mad.
7. A rereading of the book will surely convince you.
8. The law forbids parking a car near a fire hydrant.
9. You start the dishwasher by simply pushing this button.
10. His method of investing every dollar made him wealthy.
11. Taking sonar soundings enables scientists to determine the depth of the ocean.
12. His occupation, testing jet planes, is quite hazardous.
13. A favorite sport of Indians was playing the game of lacrosse.
14. By adding a fourth speaker, you can get a quadraphonic effect.

Exercise B: Find the verbals.

1. Having won seven races, Mark Spitz took home seven Olympic gold medals.
2. Learning to identify birds is not really difficult.
3. The chapter on writing gave the students many helpful suggestions to follow.
4. The tanker exploded in the harbor, injuring many men.
5. The refugees came to this country to find freedom.
6. Singing and whistling are antidotes to worrying.
7. Nancy has her work to do, and she does it without complaining.
8. By mowing the neighbors' lawns, Jack earns money.
9. Surrounded by mountains, the village becomes inaccessible in winter.
10. The picture hanging on the wall is a Gauguin reproduction.

2.16   The Appositive Phrase

An appositive is a word placed after another word to explain or identify it.

> The mayor, *Donald Gabo*, demonstrated how to vote.
> Sir Georg Solti, *the conductor*, arrived first.

The appositive always appears after the word it explains or identifies. It is always a noun or pronoun, and the word that it explains is also always a noun or pronoun.

An **appositive phrase** consists of the appositive and its modifiers, which themselves may be phrases or clauses.

> The painting, *an old portrait that we cherished*, was never found. (The appositive phrase identifies *painting*. The adjective *old* and the adjective clause *that we cherished* modify the appositive *portrait*.)
>
> Napoleon III selected Maximilian, *a tall, thin man with a beard*. (The italicized words are the appositive phrase, identifying *Maximilian*. The adjectives *tall* and *thin* modify the appositive *man*, as does the adjective phrase *with a beard*.)

Note: The compound personal pronoun used intensively is not regarded as an appositive. It is used for emphasis and does not explain or identify the word to which it refers: The speaker *himself* was not sure of the answer.

Diagraming. The appositive is diagramed as follows:

> Howard Lock, the new trainee, worked in Schenectady.

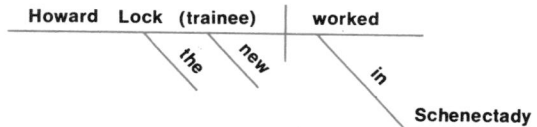

2.17 Diagraming the Simple Sentence

Meaning is conveyed in English by word-groups arranged in definite order in the sentence. Diagraming will help you see which words go together and how they are arranged.

The base of the simple sentence is composed of subject-verb-complement. These words are placed on the base line of the diagram. The indirect object is placed below the verb.

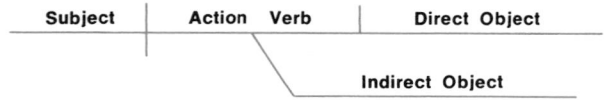

The introductory word *There* or *Here* is placed above the base line. The subject of an imperative sentence, *you* (understood), is placed in parentheses. Note the slant line after the linking verb.

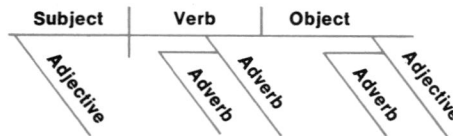

A single-word modifier is placed on a slant line below the word it modifies. An adverb modifying an adjective or adverb is placed as shown below.

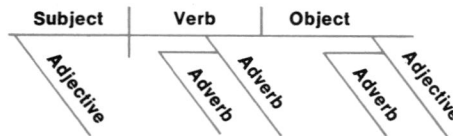

The prepositional phrase is attached to the word it modifies, as follows:

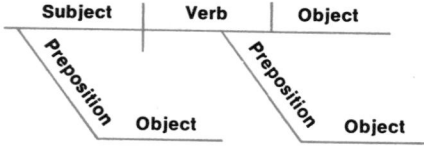

The participial phrase is shown as follows:

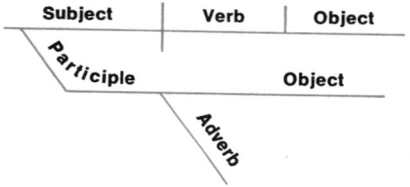

The gerund phrase is placed above the base line unless it is the object of a preposition.

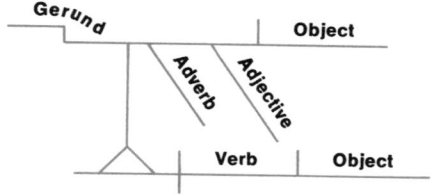

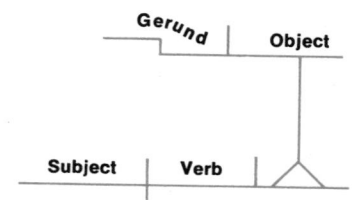

The infinitive phrase is shown in this way:

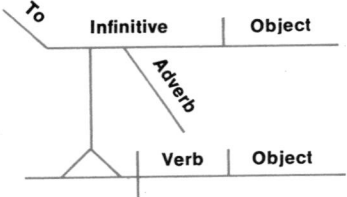

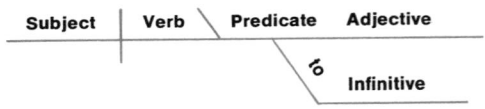

3.0 Sentence and Clause

We have seen (Section 2.2) that sentences can be classified according to the purpose of the speaker: *declarative, imperative, interrogative,* and *exclamatory*. This classification is helpful in problems of punctuation.

For help in writing better sentences, there is another, more useful classification. This is the classification by form. There are three basic forms of sentences: the *simple sentence,* the *compound sentence,* and the *complex sentence.* A fourth kind, the *compound-complex sentence* is a combination of other forms.

3.1 The Simple Sentence

A simple sentence contains only one subject and predicate. Both the subject and the predicate may be compound.

You will recall that *compound* means having two or more similar parts.

> COMPOUND SUBJECT   The *author* of the book and the *publisher* went to the convention. (The author went; the publisher went.)

COMPOUND VERB   The audience *cheered* and *applauded*. (The audience cheered; the audience applauded.)

COMPOUND PREDICATE   The rains *fell to the earth* and *flooded the fields*. (The rains fell; the rains flooded.)

COMPOUND SUBJECT AND COMPOUND PREDICATE   The *elevator operator* and the *superintendent started the elevator* and *called the police*. (The elevator operator and the superintendent started; the elevator operator and the superintendent called.)

All of the preceding sentences are simple sentences. In these sentences both parts of a compound subject go with the same verb. Or both parts of a compound verb have the same subject. In all of these sentences there is only one subject-verb connection.

For contrast, note that in the following sentence the first subject goes with the first verb while the second subject goes with the second verb. There are two subject-verb connections. This is not a simple sentence:

Nero fiddled; Rome burned.

The Compound Predicate. The compound predicate is worth special attention because it is most useful in writing clear, smooth sentences.

The compound predicate consists of two verbs having the same subject. At least one of the verbs has a complement.

Heavy rains *flooded streets* and *damaged* many *homes*.
Van Gogh *died impoverished* but *painted pictures* worth millions.

Exercise: Identify the compound parts in the following sentences. Look for compound subjects, compound verbs, and compound predicates.

1. Seminole Indians live and raise cattle in the Everglades.

2. Blackfeet Chief Weasel Feather shook our hands and welcomed us to Glacier Park.

3. Botany and zoology are both branches of biology.

4. The advertising department apologized and refunded my money.

5. The wisteria tree in our back yard slowly withered and died.

6. Viking 2 tipped over a rock and scooped up some of the soil that had been under it.

7. He designed the scenery and built it himself.

8. Snowy dogwoods and showy azaleas make Georgia a showplace in the spring.

9. William Faulkner invented Yoknapatawpha County in the deep South and used it as the setting for his novels.

10. Eugene O'Neill's romantic and poetic nature and his psychological insight into character gave his tragedies their greatness.

3.2 The Compound Sentence

The compound sentence consists of two or more simple sentences put together.

The parts of a compound sentence are put together: (1) with a comma and a coordinating conjunction (*and, but, or, for, nor*); (2) with a semicolon.

> The trial ended, *and* the jurors were dismissed.
> The diamond was beautiful, *but* he did not buy it.
> Willie has a pleasing personality, *and* he is well-liked by everyone.
> You must know the rules of the game and follow them, *or* you can ignore them and be disqualified.
> She knew U.C.L.A. well, *for* she had once taught there.
> The governor would not call a press conference, *nor* would she release the information to her secretary.
> She knew U.C.L.A. well; she had once taught there.
> The filibuster ended; a vote was taken.

Conjunctive adverbs (*then, however, moreover, hence, consequently,* etc.) are also used to join the parts of a compound sentence. The conjunctive adverb is preceded by a semicolon.

His advice was not taken; *consequently,* he was angry.
I want to go shopping; *however,* I have no money.
The prime minister paused for a moment; *then* applause broke out.

Diagraming. The compound sentence is diagramed on two parallel base lines as follows:

The house was nearly destroyed, but she ran in.

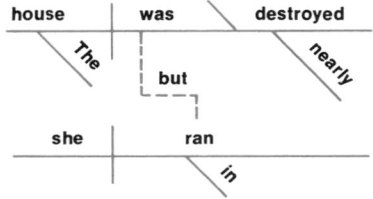

My father built the wall; my mother put up the wallpaper.

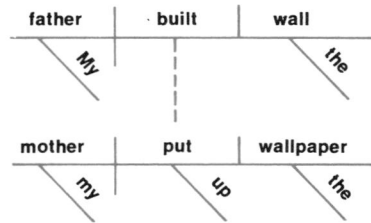

Compound Sentences and Compound Predicates. In the compound predicate every verb has the same subject. In the compound sentence, each verb has a different subject. This difference can be seen readily in diagrams.

SIMPLE SENTENCE WITH COMPOUND PREDICATE:

Nelson waged many battles and won them.

COMPOUND SENTENCE:

Nelson waged many battles, and his sailors won them.

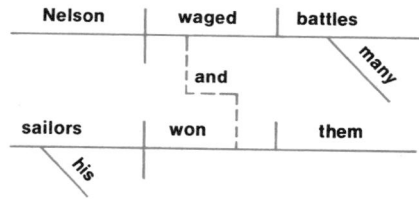

Exercise: Decide which of these sentences are compound and which are simple. In the simple sentences identify all compound predicates.

1. Russ and Janet performed well and were warmly applauded.
2. We tried to hurry but the crowd delayed us.
3. His data were accurate; he simply interpreted them incorrectly.
4. Willie joined the navy as a boy and came out a man.
5. Darla has held important positions in Iran and Turkey and is now working in Beirut.
6. You can buy this western-type hat for four dollars or you can buy the same hat with bullet holes for five dollars.
7. The horn of a rhinoceros is not a real horn; it is a closely packed bundle of hair.
8. Beatrice and Benedick, two witty characters in Shakespeare's *Much Ado About Nothing*, seem very modern to audiences today.

9. Jacques-Yves Cousteau is a widely known ocean explorer and is co-inventor of the aqualung.

10. Public awareness was indicated by the interest in the campaign and by the huge turnout of voters on election day.

11. Captain Queeg lost his head in the middle of a typhoon and almost wrecked the *Caine*.

12. The original ancestor of many Western languages is called Indo-European, but no written documents exist in this language.

13. In 1860, the Pony Express carried the mail from St. Joseph, Missouri, to Sacramento, California, in eight days and captured the imagination of the people.

14. California has already surpassed New York in population; it may eventually emerge as America's number-one center of political, economic, and social power.

15. Angelenos joke about the smog, but they recognize it as a serious problem.

3.3 The Clause

A clause is a group of words containing a verb and its subject.

According to this definition, a simple sentence is a clause. Indeed, the simple sentence is sometimes defined as consisting of one main clause. However, we shall find it simpler to use the word *clause* to name a *part* of a sentence.

Each part of a compound sentence has its own verb and subject. These parts of the compound sentence are therefore clauses.

Each clause in a compound sentence can be lifted out and written separately as a simple sentence.

A clause that can stand by itself as a sentence is a main clause.

We have defined a compound sentence as consisting of two or more simple sentences put together. We can now also define it as consisting of two main clauses.

A clause that cannot stand by itself as a sentence is a subordinate clause.

> _{s.} _{v.}
> After she had screamed . . . (What happened?)

> _{s.} _{v.}
> Until you act properly . . . (What?)

> _{s.} _{v.}
> If you have the courage . . . (Then what?)

Phrase or Clause? A clause has a subject and a verb. A phrase does not.

> We watched the Pittsburgh Pirates *gradually fading.* (phrase)

> _{s.} _{v.}
> We watched the Pittsburgh Pirates *as they gradually faded.* (clause)

> It was in the book of *quotations.* (phrase)

> _{s.} _{v.}
> It was in the book *that lists quotations.* (clause)

Exercise: Are the italicized words in each sentence a phrase or a clause?

1. Most of the people *who frequent this restaurant* are actors.
2. *Although she started her career as an actress,* Marlo Thomas is now a producer.
3. The list of things *to be packed* is on the hall table.
4. *Built in 1810,* the building is now a National Landmark.
5. Three of Shakespeare's plays are tragedies *which suddenly turn into comedies.*
6. *To pursue new opportunities,* Mary Tyler Moore ended her successful television series.
7. The members recessed *to eat their lunch.*
8. *On my first attempt at flycasting,* I snared a trout.
9. Turtles are the only reptiles *that have shells.*
10. *With the help of several drama students,* Rita Moreno performed at the assembly.

3.4 The Complex Sentence

The complex sentence consists of one main clause and one or more subordinate clauses.

In a complex sentence, the subordinate clause is always used as a noun or a modifier. If it is used as a modifier, the subordinate clause modifies a word in the main clause.

> I can wait *until the cows come home.* (clause modifies *can wait.*)
>
> *If the emergency continues,* water will be rationed. (clause modifies *will be rationed.*)
>
> This is the magazine *that you ordered.* (clause modifies *magazine.*)

In each example above, the main clause can stand as a sentence by itself: *I can wait, water will be rationed, This is the magazine*

The subordinate clauses, however, cannot stand alone because their meaning is incomplete.

> until the cows come home . . . (What then?)
> If the emergency continues . . . (What will happen?)
> that you need . . . (What is it?)

Complex sentences containing noun clauses are somewhat different. The noun clause may be used as a noun *within the main clause.* The noun clause, in other words, is part of the main clause.

> *What he thinks* means nothing under the circumstances.
>   (Noun clause is subject of *means.*)
> *What Jan said* is true but irrelevant. (Noun clause is subject of *is.*)
> We are working toward *what is possible and just.*
>   (Noun clause is object of preposition *toward.*)
> Mother said *that he was found.* (Noun clause is object of *said.*)

In these sentences, neither the main clause nor the noun clause can stand by itself. Nonetheless, a sentence containing one main clause and a noun clause is regarded as a complex sentence.

Exercise A: Indicate whether each sentence below is simple, compound, or complex.

1. We enjoyed Katherine Hepburn and John Wayne, but some of the students preferred Hepburn.
2. Both are fine performers, and I had no preference.
3. The modern woman makes up her mind without assistance.
4. The tourists who attended the auction were looking for bargains.
5. Having made a study of bookplates, Frank was able to design one for the library.
6. Texas became an independent nation in 1836.
7. When "Old Faithful" erupts, it sends water as high as a twelve-story building.
8. Bumblebees carry clover pollen from flower to flower and help make clover seed develop.
9. How migrating animals find their way on their long journeys is a great mystery.
10. The light that reaches our eyes from some stars started on its way before Columbus discovered America.

Exercise B: Find the subordinate clause in each sentence below.

1. Superstitions, which are beliefs in magic and chance, proceed from ignorance or fear.
2. That a black cat crossing your path will bring you bad luck is a common superstition.
3. A number that is supposed to bring bad luck is thirteen.
4. When Friday comes on the thirteenth of the month, superstitious people regard the day as unlucky.
5. If one breaks a mirror, he is likely to have bad luck for seven years, according to the superstition.
6. Some people who are otherwise rational are superstitious.

7. Superstitions, which are learned in childhood, can become a part of one's emotional background.

8. Because they are not based on facts, superstitions and prejudices are similar.

9. Since some people are governed by emotion instead of reason, they continue to have superstitions and prejudices.

10. People who are superstitious or prejudiced are fearful.

11. If you were to list your superstitions, what would you include?

12. You may decide that you are not superstitious.

3.5 The Compound-Complex Sentence

A compound-complex sentence consists of two or more main clauses and one or more subordinate clauses.

The main clauses are joined by a coordinating conjunction (preceded by a comma), a conjunctive adverb (preceded by a semicolon), or by a semicolon alone. The subordinate clause modifies a word in one of the main clauses or acts as a noun within one of them.

MAIN CLAUSE   MAIN CLAUSE   SUBORDINATE CLAUSE
I ran back to school, and there I found the notes that I had lost.

MAIN CLAUSE   MAIN CLAUSE   SUBORDINATE CLAUSE
I'll go to England; however, don't be surprised if I get to France, too.

3.6 The Adjective Clause

The single-word adjective, the adjective phrase, and the adjective clause are used in the same way. They modify a noun or pronoun.

An adjective clause is a subordinate clause used to modify a noun or pronoun in the main clause.

Introductory Words. A majority of the adjective clauses in modern writing begin with an introductory word. There is a growing tendency, however, to use adjective clauses with no introductory word.

> This is the rink *where I skate.* (*where* is an introductory word.)
>
> May 7 is the date *when I leave.* (*when* is an introductory word.)
>
> This is the coat *I made.* (no introductory word.)
>
> This is the coat *that I made.* (*that* is an introductory word.)
>
> The doctor *you want* is on vacation. (no introductory word.)
>
> The doctor *that you want* is on vacation. (*that* is an introductory word.)

In the first two examples above, the introductory words *where* and *when* are both used within the subordinate clause as modifiers of the verb: *skate* **where;** *leave* **when.**

Relative Pronouns. The pronouns *who, whose, whom, which,* and *that* are used to introduce adjective clauses. Used in this way they refer to a word in the main clause and are used in place of that word. That word is the antecedent of the pronoun. It is also the word modified by the adjective clause.

> Carol is the girl *who belongs to the dance troupe.*
> (*girl* is the antecedent of *who* and is modified by the adjective clause.)
>
> That is the man *whose judgment I question.*
> (*man* is the antecedent of *whose* and is modified by the adjective clause.)
>
> The trees *which line our driveway* are red maples.
> (*trees* is the antecedent of *which* and is modified by the adjective clause.)

An adjective clause introduced by a relative pronoun is sometimes called a relative clause.

The relative pronoun has two functions. It introduces the clause, and it is used as a sentence-part within the clause.

Is this the tie *that you borrowed?*
> (*that* is the direct object of *borrowed.*)

Eleanor Roosevelt was the delegate *whom everybody
admired.* (*whom* is the direct object of *admired.*)

The company *for which I work* is well known.
> (*which* is the object of the preposition *for.*)

Our neighbors are people *who enjoy giving parties.*
> (*who* is the subject of *enjoy.*)

Diagraming. The adjective clause is joined to the word it modifies in the main clause. A dotted line leads from this word to the introductory word. Note that the relative pronoun is placed to show its use in the sentence.

The necklace that she borrowed belonged to Mme. Forestier.

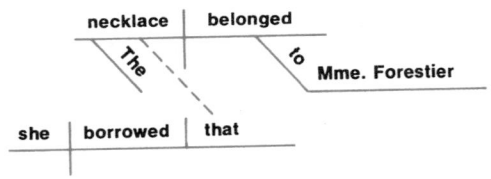

This is the spot where the avalanche started.

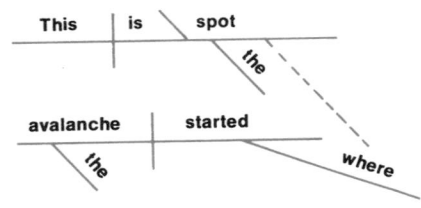

Exercise: Find each adjective clause and the word it modifies.

1. The three-legged stool which stands near the fireplace is an antique.

2. I met Tom and Bill, who were waiting for me at the airport.

3. In 1609 Henry Hudson discovered the great river that bears his name.

4. The camel has long eyelashes which keep sand out of its eyes.

5. The blue jeans I bought at The Century are pre-washed.

6. Appomattox, where Lee surrendered, is visited by many tourists.

7. Each year many books are written about the Revolutionary War, which was fought almost two hundred years ago.

8. Many of the exhibits we saw at the museum were science-oriented.

9. The ashes that come from wood fires can be sprinkled around rose bushes.

10. Frogs have long, sticky tongues that are excellent for catching insects.

11. Most of the seniors who will graduate this June are going to college.

12. The flowers we gathered last week have withered.

13. We have come to the day when we must go back to work.

14. We visited Mount Vernon, where Washington lived and is buried.

15. Is this the novel you were telling me about?

3.7 The Adverb Clause

The single-word adverb, the adverb phrase, and the adverb clause are all used in the same way. They are used to modify verbs, adjectives, and adverbs.

An adverb clause is a subordinate clause used to modify a verb, adjective, or adverb in the main clause.*

Adverb clauses tell *when, where, why, how, to what extent,* and *how much* about the word they modify.

---

* Some authorities suggest that an introductory adverb clause may modify an entire main clause rather than a single word in it.

ADVERB CLAUSES MODIFYING VERBS

I **put** the oil *where the hinges squeaked.* (where)
When the pain starts, **take** two aspirin. (when)
The project **looked** *as if it would fail.* (how)
I **came** *simply because you asked.* (why)

ADVERB CLAUSES MODIFYING ADJECTIVES

Tony is as **capable** *as his sister is.* (to what extent)

The Federal debt is **higher** *than it ever was.* (how much)

ADVERB CLAUSE MODIFYING AN ADVERB

Paul works **harder** *than his partner does.* (how much)

Subordinating Conjunctions. Every adverb clause is introduced by a subordinating conjunction. The function of this word is to show how two clauses are related. By use of the subordinating conjunction, one clause is made to tell *how, why, when, where, to what extent,* or *how much* about another.

When a subordinating conjunction is placed before a clause, the clause can no longer stand alone.

Your account is already overdrawn. (*complete*)
If your account is already overdrawn . . . (*incomplete*)
Since your account is already overdrawn . . . (*incomplete*)

The Presidential election is over. (*complete*)
When the Presidential election is over . . . (*incomplete*)
Until the Presidential election is over . . . (*incomplete*)

A subordinating conjunction may be placed before either of two main clauses to tie it to the other. Which clause is subordinated depends upon the meaning the writer wants to express.

The porch looked fine, *although* Bill painted it himself.
Although the porch looked fine, Bill painted it himself.
The audience left *because* he did not finish.
Because the audience left, he did not finish.

Subordinating conjunctions can be used to show a great variety of relationships between main ideas. The careful choice of conjunctions will enable you to express your ideas clearly and exactly.

TIME:	as, after, before, since, until, when, whenever, while
CAUSE OR REASON:	because, since
COMPARISON:	as, as much as, than
CONDITION:	if, although, though, unless, provided
PURPOSE:	so that, in order that

Note how the meaning changes with the change in conjunctions in these sentences.

Until the principal arrived, I was unconcerned.
Because the principal arrived, I was unconcerned.
Although the principal arrived, I was unconcerned.

Elliptical Clauses. The word *elliptical* comes from *ellipsis,* which means "omission of a word." An **elliptical clause** is one from which words have been omitted.

While he was a small child, Mozart showed great musicianship.
While a small child, Mozart showed great musicianship.

When you are addressing the chairperson, speak courteously.
When addressing the chairperson, speak courteously.

Diagraming. The adverb clause is diagramed on a separate line:

When the buggy started, we ran alongside.

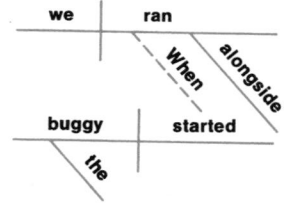

Exercise: Find each adverb clause and the word it modifies.

1. When the plane landed, people cheered.
2. She overslept again because nobody could get her up.
3. If we win this game, the trophy will be ours.
4. I drove slowly so that we could enjoy the view.
5. I can't play tennis until I get my racket restrung.
6. Pitch your tent wherever you can find a dry place.
7. Although we pleaded with him, he refused to wear the kilts.
8. Dad will be here before dinner if his train arrives on time.
9. Quickly she hid the letter where no one could find it.
10. Laura makes friends easily wherever she goes.

3.8 The Noun Clause

A noun clause is a subordinate clause used as a noun.

The noun clause may be used as subject or direct object of the verb, as a predicate noun, as object of a preposition, or as an appositive.

> A good teacher knows *whether or not you study.*
>   (direct object)
> There is no report on *what the mayor plans.* (object
>   of preposition)
> The theory *that life exists on Mars* is being tested.
>   (appositive)
> *Who you know* may be important. (subject)
> The foolish part to me is *why she bothered.*
>   (predicate noun)

Introductory Words. As the examples above clearly show, noun clauses may be introduced by some of the same words that introduce adverb clauses: *when, where.* Used with noun clauses, these words are not regarded as subordinating conjunctions. They are merely introductory words, used as adverbs within the noun clause.

Similarly, noun clauses may be introduced by the same words used to introduce relative clauses: *who, whose, whom, which, that, when, where.* Used in noun clauses, these words are not regarded as relative pronouns, but they may serve as subjects or objects within the noun clause.

> I know **where** *the fuses are.* (noun clause as the object of *know*.)
>
> We waited **where** *we were told.* (adverb clause modifying *waited*.)
>
> Is that the one **that** *fell?* (adjective clause modifying *one*.)
>
> **Who** *wins the prize* is important. (noun clause as the subject of *is*.)

Many noun clauses are written without any introductory word. Every direct quotation preceded by words such as *she said, I replied, Bob asked* is a noun clause without the introductory word. Every indirect quotation is a noun clause preceded by the introductory word.

> She said *that there is no electricity.* (noun clause as the object of *said*.)
>
> She said, *"There is no electricity."* (noun clause as the object of *said*.)

Diagraming. The noun clause is diagramed as shown below. Note that the use of the noun clause determines its position in the diagram.

I hope that she is successful.

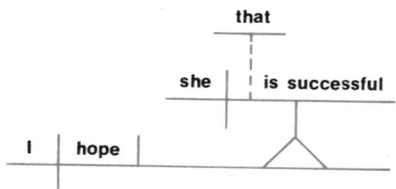

He found problems in whatever seemed simple.

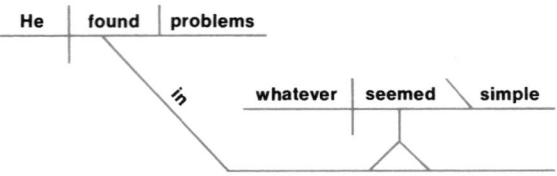

Exercise: Identify each noun clause. Tell how it is used in the sentence.

1. Scientists believe that the planet Venus has an atmosphere.
2. What I want and what you want are two different things.
3. The children knew why they were being called.
4. His attitude is what I am referring to.
5. The coach said that he was counting on an upset victory.
6. Why you have come here is a mystery to me.
7. She always approves of what her children say and do.
8. The question was where we would go for our vacation.
9. My idea that we should go early met with approval.
10. We found, however, that the road was under construction.
11. They took whatever they could lay their hands on.
12. I don't understand why he made such a speech.
13. The jury's belief was that the man was not guilty.
14. The freight agent can tell you when your trunk will arrive.

3.9 The Sentence Redefined

We are now ready to complete the definition of a sentence that we started in Sections 2.1 and 2.3. We may begin by noting once again the differences between phrases, clauses, and sentences.

A **phrase** is a group of words used within a sentence as a single part of speech. A phrase may be used as a noun, a verb, an adjective, or an adverb. It does *not* contain a subject and verb.

A **clause** is a group of words which contains a subject and its verb. It may be used within the sentence as a noun, an adjective, or an adverb.

> PHRASE: Running for the train . . .
>
>   s.   v.
> CLAUSE: While *I was running* for the train . . .

A main clause can stand by itself as a sentence. A subordinate clause cannot stand by itself.

> MAIN CLAUSE   MAIN CLAUSE
>
> The air seemed smoky, but the fire had been put out.
> The air seemed smoky. (*complete*)
> The fire had been put out. (*complete*)

> SUBORDINATE CLAUSE   MAIN CLAUSE
>
> Although the air seemed smoky, the fire had been put out.
>
> The fire had been put out. (*complete*)
> Although the air seemed smoky . . . (*incomplete*)

Clauses and phrases are sentence parts. The sentence itself is not part of any other grammatical construction. (The paragraph is not a grammatical construction.) Our complete definition of a sentence then is in three parts:

A sentence is a group of words that

1. expresses a complete thought,

2. contains a subject and verb,

3. is not part of any other grammatical construction.

4.0 Complete Sentences

Uncompleted sentences are more often a problem in writing than in speaking. If you use an uncompleted sentence in speaking with someone face-to-face, he or she can interrupt and ask you what you mean. In writing, you usually do not have a second chance.

The sentence is the best means you have for getting your meaning across to someone else in writing. Through study and practice, you can learn to write effective and forceful sentences. To write effectively, however, you must learn to avoid two kinds of sentence error: (1) the sentence fragment, and (2) the run-on sentence. Both of these errors cause confusion for the reader.

4.1 Fragments Resulting from Incomplete Thought

An uncompleted sentence is called a **sentence fragment.** It is only a part, or fragment, of a sentence.

You can think much faster than you can write. Many of your sentence errors, if you make them, happen because your mind has raced on ahead of your hand. You have started to write a second thought before you have finished writing the first. Or, perhaps in haste, you have left out a key word necessary for a complete sentence. Suppose you intended to say something like this:

> Bob and Helen had a bitter quarrel. After the quarrel, they went home in separate cars. They did not speak to each other for a week.

In the hurry to get on with your writing, however, what you put down was something like this:

> Bob and Helen had a bitter quarrel. After they went home in separate cars. They did not speak to each other for a week.

The second group of words is not a sentence. It causes confusion. The reader may suppose that you meant to say, "Bob and Helen had a bitter quarrel after they went home in separate cars."

Exercise A: Find the sentence fragments. Add the words needed to make each fragment a sentence.

1. Then we saw Pete. Running down the road as fast as he could go.
2. The plan to give everyone two choices in the election.
3. After we had climbed up a long succession of hills.
4. We had trouble from the outset. To begin with, something wrong with the motor.
5. The judge, an old friend of Bob's mother.
6. The taxi turning around in the middle of the block.
7. No one saw us. Into the back of the auditorium, closing the door quietly.
8. There is a prize. The student entering the best experiment in the Science Fair.
9. The truck halfway up the mountain road.
10. When rain comes to the desert, a carpet of little flowers.

Exercise B: Three of the following groups of words are sentences. The rest are fragments. Find the fragments and add words needed to make them sentences.

1. The firemen were overcome by the heat and the smoke
2. After the fire had subsided
3. The house which had burned, a beautiful colonial mansion
4. No one was fatally injured
5. Because the firemen had worked heroically to rescue the occupants
6. A small child who had to be dropped from a second-story window.
7. The child frightened but not injured by the fall
8. Everyone praised the firemen who had fought the blaze
9. The owner grateful to the firemen for rescuing his child
10. A financial loss of thirty thousand dollars

4.2 Fragments Resulting from Incorrect Punctuation

The first word of a sentence begins with a capital letter. The sentence is closed by a punctuation mark: *period, question mark,* or *exclamation mark.* A great many sentence fragments are written simply because the writer inserts a period and a capital letter too soon. This error is sometimes called a **period fault.**

FRAGMENT	*At the beginning of the third act.* The audience walked out.
SENTENCE	At the beginning of the third act, the audience walked out.
FRAGMENT	Beethoven composed the *Ninth Symphony.* *While he was deaf.*
SENTENCE	Beethoven composed the *Ninth Symphony,* while he was deaf.

FRAGMENT   *Although Jane had her license.* She was afraid
to drive.

SENTENCE   Although Jane had her license, she was afraid
to drive.

Exercise: Find the fragments. Correct them by changing the punctuation or by adding the words needed to make a sentence.

1. Larry likes to dance. In spite of the fact that he is usually shy.
2. Sixty million Americans are overweight. According to a survey.
3. Address the envelopes. As you have been instructed.
4. I'd try to remain neutral. If I were you, Jim.
5. I haven't seen Jeff once. Since I left Peoria in 1975.
6. Ships, large and small, came into the harbor. From many countries.
7. I must resign my position. Since I have no other choice.
8. Although the pianist played with fervor. He made many mistakes.
9. Hearing the five-o'clock siren. We knew it was time to leave.
10. I'd mow the lawn this afternoon. If I weren't so lazy.

4.3 Phrases as Fragments

You know that a phrase is a group of words that does not contain a verb and its subject. A phrase, therefore, cannot be a sentence by itself. It is a *part* of a sentence.

You are not likely to mistake a prepositional phrase for a complete sentence. If you write a long prepositional phrase or a series of phrases as a sentence, it is probably because you have punctuated incorrectly.

FRAGMENT   He planned to transfer. *At the end of the
school year.*

SENTENCE   He planned to transfer at the end of the
school year.

You are more likely to mistake a verbal phrase for a complete sentence. This error occurs because verbals look like verbs and function somewhat like verbs. Like verbs, they may be modified by adverbs. They may be followed by objects or predicate words. They are not complete verbs, however, and they cannot be used as the main verb of a sentence.

The most troublesome verbals are those that end in *-ing*. All gerunds and present participles end in *-ing*. You will avoid many sentence errors if you will remember this fact:

No word ending in *-ing* can be a verb unless it is a one-syllable word like *sing, ring,* or *bring.*

If an *-ing* word is preceded by *is, are, was,* or some other form of *be,* the two words together are a verb.

PARTICIPLE	COMPLETE VERB
baking	is baking
writing	had been writing
traveling	were traveling

A long infinitive phrase may sometimes be mistaken for a complete sentence. Such a phrase sounds like a sentence since it often has everything that a sentence requires except a subject.

INCOMPLETE	Sue has an idea. *To go to the box office at lunch hour.*
COMPLETE	Sue has an idea. She plans to go to the box office at lunch hour.
INCOMPLETE	Jacqueline was thrilled. *To be chosen as a delegation officer.*
COMPLETE	Jacqueline was thrilled to be chosen as a delegation officer.

An appositive phrase is sometimes written incorrectly as a complete sentence. Although it may seem like a sentence, it always lacks a verb.

FRAGMENT	Jonathan Swift, *an important English author*
SENTENCE	Jonathan Swift was an important English author.
SENTENCE	Jonathan Swift, an important English author, wrote *Gulliver's Travels*.
FRAGMENT	The confusion, *a result of inadequate instructions.*
SENTENCE	The confusion was a result of inadequate instructions.

Exercise: Rewrite the groups of words beside each number below to make a complete sentence. You may need to add words in some instances.

1. I sometimes get up at six. The best time to do homework.
2. Playing chess and watching TV instead of studying.
3. Jack spends weekends on his hobby. Eating cheeseburgers.
4. The interest rate is too high. My only objection.
5. I enjoyed the prom. The high point of the weekend.
6. Unexpected frosts costing fruit growers millions of dollars.
7. The President is calling a special session of Congress. A serious emergency.
8. "The Stars and Bars," another name for the Confederate flag.
9. The films having proved that the runner stepped out of bounds.
10. Nina had left. To drive Mother to the station and then pick up Don.
11. I read that the liver is the warmest part of the body. About 101 degrees.
12. Eight percent of the earth's crust is composed of aluminum. One of the lightest of the metals.
13. Detroit anxious to get rid of its oversupply of last year's models.
14. The two village churches, simple white buildings with tall spires.
15. Snowshoe rabbits are perfectly adapted to winter climates. Often blending right into the snow.

4.4 Clauses as Fragments

A subordinate clause cannot stand alone as a sentence. See Section 3.3. A sentence may be changed into a subordinate clause by having a subordinating conjunction placed before it.

SENTENCE	I was watching the preliminary diving
SUBORDINATE CLAUSE	*As* I was watching the preliminary diving . . .

Writers sometimes mistakenly place a period before or after a subordinate clause as though it were a sentence.

FRAGMENT	*When I knew him.* He was extraordinarily lazy.
SENTENCE	When I knew him, he was extraordinarily lazy.
FRAGMENT	Jean considered Michigan. *Because it was near home.*
SENTENCE	Jean considered Michigan because it was near home.

Exercise: Rewrite the word groups below to eliminate the fragments.

1. We never could find out. Who sent us the tickets for the concert.
2. He heard the news. When he reached his office.
3. The defeat was hard for Paul to accept. Since he had worked so hard for so long.
4. The final victory came as a surprise. Although it had never been in doubt.
5. Dr. Bell decided to return to Hawaii. Where he had spent so many years.
6. Jack swam out to the boat. Which had obviously been abandoned.
7. Don't fail us now. No matter what the newspapers say.
8. Come again. Whenever you can.
9. Do not remove the cap. Until you are ready to use the ink.
10. If it says "Wet Paint." Don't touch it.

Review Exercise: In this exercise you will find examples of many kinds of fragments. Change them into sentences.

1. A famous vacation spot is Cape Cod. Situated near Boston.
2. Shakespeare's plays fall into three categories. Comedies, histories, and tragedies.
3. The volunteer firemen scramble. Whenever the whistle blows.
4. Washington's first inaugural address was short. And not well delivered.
5. We decided not to get a foreign car. The difficulty of getting parts.
6. The snowstorm suddenly stopped. As if it had been switched off.
7. Harvard is the most famous university in America. Although by no means the largest.
8. Little is known about Shakespeare's life. Except for a few facts.
9. I figured out the trouble. Dirt in the carburetor.
10. The early American painters studied in Europe. Then returned to America to paint.

4.5 Run-on Sentences

A **run-on sentence** is two or more sentences written as though they were one sentence. That is, the writer fails to use a period or other end mark at the end of the first sentence.

RUN-ON   I had my hair cut Saturday it looked awful.
SENTENCE   I had my hair cut Saturday. It looked awful.

RUN-ON   She left willingly then she was sorry.
SENTENCE   She left willingly. Then she was sorry.

The most common run-on sentence error is the joining of two sentences by a comma. This error is called the **comma fault**.

COMMA FAULT	Joan came to see *Hamlet,* she had read it in English.
SENTENCE	Joan came to see *Hamlet.* She had read it in English.
COMMA FAULT	Dr. Kay X-rayed the foot, he found a fractured toe.
SENTENCE	Dr. Kay X-rayed the foot. He found a fractured toe.

In all of the foregoing examples, notice that the two sentences are closely related and that the second sentence begins with a personal pronoun: *it, he, she.* Watch for situations like these in your own writing and avoid the comma fault.

4.6 Avoiding the Run-on Sentence

There is no objection to joining two or more closely related statements into one sentence. In fact, it is often better to join them than to write them separately. There are three ways in which closely related sentences can be joined to make a compound sentence: (1) with a comma and a coordinating conjunction; (2) with a semicolon; (3) with a semicolon and a conjunctive adverb.

RUN-ON	Jose has two choices. He can work part-time and finish school, he can take a full-time job.
SENTENCE	Jose has two choices. He can work part-time and finish school, or he can take a full-time job.
RUN-ON	I considered the situation carefully and conscientiously, then I made my decision foolishly.
SENTENCE	I considered the situation carefully and conscientiously; then I made my decision foolishly.

RUN-ON   Many people believe that Shakespeare did not write his plays, consequently they try to prove that others did.

SENTENCE   Many people believe that Shakespeare did not write his plays; consequently, they try to prove that others did.

Note: When a conjunctive adverb such as *consequently, however, moreover, therefore,* and *nevertheless* introduces a second main clause, it is preceded by a semicolon. Usually, it is followed by a comma.

Exercise A: Correct each of the following run-on sentences in one of these ways: (1) by using a period and a capital letter; (2) by using a semicolon; or (3) by using a comma and *and, but,* or *or.*

1. Antique automobiles are popular, pictures of them appear on match covers.
2. The room was cleared for dancing, no one seemed to want to dance.
3. He ordered a deluxe hot dog, I ordered a hamburger.
4. Lee reads many historical novels, his main interest is science fiction.
5. The Battle of Lexington was short, it involved only a few hundred men.
6. Carol bought a new sweater, it was the wrong color.
7. We signaled to the bus driver, he didn't see us.
8. The bass flogged the water, then it pulled on the line.
9. I'll bring the sandwiches, Jack, you bring the Coke.
10. The lady sounded very British, I was surprised to hear a British accent in San Diego.
11. The road was almost impassable, nevertheless, we kept driving.
12. I read "A Scandal in Bohemia," in this story Sherlock Holmes is actually defeated.

Exercise B: The first part of a sentence is given on each line that follows. Add a second main clause, beginning it with the word in parentheses at the end of the line. If the word is a conjunctive adverb, place a semicolon before it and a comma after it. If the word is a personal pronoun, use a semicolon or use a comma with a coordinating conjunction.

1. Not only did the winners get a free trip to Hawaii (they)
2. That beam is full of termites (it)
3. Most of the peaches were bruised (nevertheless)
4. That plane is a crop-duster (it)
5. There have been many requests for tickets (in fact)
6. Our team's prospects look gloomy (however)
7. Kerry had never played soccer before (nevertheless)
8. I heard the screech of brakes (then)
9. Frank made no reply (he)
10. In speaking, Helen uses no notes (however)
11. Many fine books are published in paperback form (they)
12. The engine sputtered briefly and stopped (consequently)
13. Tad and Kris have completed paramedic training (they)
14. In the confusion, three prisoners escaped (however)
15. The pitcher fanned the first two batters (then)

5.0 The New Grammar of English

People have been interested in the study of language for many centuries. Many of the grammatical terms and categories that we use today were first developed over two thousand years ago —long before there was an English language—by the Greeks. This Greek grammar was later applied to Latin and became Latin grammar. In the eighteenth century, when scholars first worked out a description of the English language, they borrowed from Latin grammar. Thus, although Greek and Latin and English are quite different languages, they are described in much the same way.

In recent years linguists have attempted to describe English in its own terms, rather than in terms suitable for another language. One of the most important of the new developments in English grammar is called **transformational grammar.** In this section we will discuss some of the features of this new approach. You will gain some new insights by looking at English from this point of view.

5.1 Basic Sentences

In order to explain the different ways that English words can be combined to form English sentences, we must distinguish between two different kinds of English sentences—*basic sentences* and *transformed sentences*. These two kinds of sentences are formed in different ways and must therefore be described in different ways. In this section we will discuss basic sentences. Later we will explain some of the ways in which these basic sentences can be turned into transformed sentences.

The Basic Sentence Patterns

Every basic sentence consists of a subject followed by a predicate. The **subject** is always a noun or pronoun. Noun subjects are often accompanied by words like *the, a, my, those, some,* or *several.* Words like these are often called **determiners.**

The **predicate** of a basic sentence always begins with a verb. The rest of the sentence—that is, the part of the predicate that follows the verb—is called the **complement.** Notice the following tables. The first table shows sentences divided into subjects and predicates. The second table shows how these predicates can be divided into verbs and complements.

SENTENCE = SUBJECT	+ PREDICATE
Several people	were on the boat.
We	congratulated everyone.
The dogs	barked.
Mrs. Jones	gave the neighbors some rabbits.

PREDICATE = VERB	+ COMPLEMENT
were	on the boat
congratulated	everyone
barked	—
gave	the neighbors some rabbits

All basic sentences begin with a noun followed by a verb, but many different kinds of complement are possible. Basic sentences are therefore usually classified according to the kind of complement they have. In this chapter we will list only the most common basic sentence patterns.

Pattern One

NOUN	VERB	(ADVERBIAL)
Everybody	laughed.	
The policeman	laughed	uproariously.
Nothing	happens	here.
The dogs	barked.	
Those birds	tweet	constantly.
My father	works	at night.
We	went	to a movie.
Several guests	arrived	late.

Pattern One sentences may consist of only a noun and a verb, or they may have an adverbial element, such as an adverb or a prepositional phrase, as a complement. Verbs that occur in Pattern One sentences are called **intransitive verbs.**

Pattern Two

NOUN	VERB	ADVERBIAL
Cheryl	is	at the party.
My parents	are	in Seattle.
Everyone	is	here.
Jason	was	in a quandary.
Your hat	is	on the table.
Several people	were	on the dock.
The Lindstroms	were	not there.

In Pattern Two sentences the verb is always some form of *be*, such as *is*, *am*, *are*, *was*, or *were*, and there is always an adverbial element as a complement. The adverbials in Pattern Two sentences always express time or place rather than manner.

Pattern Three

NOUN	VERB	ADJECTIVE
The clerk	was	quite rude.
The crowd	seemed	friendly.
Everyone	became	rich.
Their lawn	looks	very neat.
Her story	is	incredible.
His trip	sounded	exciting.

Verbs that occur in Pattern Three sentences are called **linking verbs.** There are thousands of intransitive verbs, but only about a dozen verbs are used frequently as linking verbs. The most common linking verbs are *seem, become,* and the various forms of *be.* The complement in Pattern Three sentences is always an adjective. The adjective is sometimes accompanied by words like *very, quite, rather,* and *too,* which are often called **intensifiers.**

Pattern Four

NOUN	VERB	NOUN
His parents	are	acrobats.
Our driveway	became	a mudhole.
Colin	remained	captain.
My grandfather	was	a doctor.
We	remained	friends.
Her aunt	is	a systems analyst.

The only verbs that regularly occur in Pattern Four sentences are *be, because,* and *remain.* These verbs are also called linking verbs.

Pattern Five

NOUN	VERB	NOUN
Maria	wove	wall hangings.
The driver	skipped	our stop.
Ray	wrote	that editorial.

My parents	visited	Seattle.
The shortstop	bobbled	several grounders.
The store	guarantees	this radio.

Pattern Four and Pattern Five sentences have the same sequence: noun-verb-noun. We can always tell them apart, however, because they contain different kinds of verbs. The verbs used in Pattern Four produce sentences in which the subject noun and the complement noun refer to the same person or thing. The verbs that occur in Pattern Five, on the other hand, produce sentences in which the two nouns refer to different persons or things. These verbs are usually called **transitive verbs.**

The noun following the verb in Pattern Four is called a **predicate noun;** in Pattern Five, it is called a **direct object.**

Pattern Six

NOUN	VERB	NOUN	NOUN
We	told	our mother	the news.
Several colleges	offered	Joy	scholarships.
Mrs. Moore	gives	the children	fudge.
The mayor	gave	the press	an interview.
My aunt	sent	me	a telegram.
Mrs. Conway	taught	Eric	French
Richard	built	Elizabeth	a castle.

Pattern Seven

NOUN	VERB	NOUN	NOUN
Her classmates	elected	Maria	president.
They	consider	him	a bore.
The principal	appointed	Frank	leader.
Perseverance	made	him	a success.
Delia	called	Henry	a flirt.

Pattern Six and Pattern Seven sentences contain transitive verbs which are followed by two nouns. The verbs that occur in Pattern Six produce sentences in which the two nouns following the verb refer to different persons or things. The first noun is called an **indirect object;** the second noun is a direct object. In Pattern Seven sentences, the two nouns in the complement refer to the same person or thing. The first noun is a direct object; the second is called an **object complement.** Some of the verbs that occur in Pattern Seven can also produce sentences in which an adjective replaces the second noun:

> Perseverance made him successful.
> They consider Frank quite intelligent.
> The court declared the law unconstitutional.

Exercise A: The sentences below are all basic sentences. Read each sentence carefully and tell which of the seven patterns it follows.

1. Her relatives are quarrelsome.
2. The guests are outside.
3. This material feels luxurious.
4. My brother gave our dog a shampoo.
5. The neighbors became very sarcastic.
6. Frank leaves tomorrow.
7. Our guests waited outside.
8. My father remained in the house.
9. The audience remained quiet.
10. No one invited them.
11. Many people envy them their success.
12. Our parrot calls the neighbors names.
13. It rained very hard.
14. We find this medicine effective.
15. Several guests braved the elements.
16. Eric brought Mrs. Conway an apple.

Exercise B: Write five sentences that conform to each of the following sentence patterns. Nouns that are marked with an asterisk (*) should refer to the same person or thing.

1. Noun   Verb   (Adverb)
2. Noun*   Verb   Noun*
3. Noun   Verb   Adjective
4. Noun   Verb   Noun*   Noun*
5. Noun   Verb   Noun
6. Noun   Be   Adverb
7. Noun   Verb   Noun   Noun

5.2 Adding Auxiliaries to Verbs

Look again at the verbs used in the examples of basic sentences in Section 5.1. Notice that each verb consists of a single word which can take one of three forms: the simple form is used with plural subjects (*they want*), a form ending in -*s* with singular subjects (*John wants*), and a form usually ending in -*ed* for the past tense (*they wanted; John wanted*). Before considering some of the ways that basic sentences can be turned into transformed sentences, we will describe the various ways that verbs can be made more complex through the addition of auxiliaries.

Three Kinds of Auxiliaries

There are three groups of auxiliaries: the modals, forms of *have*, and forms of *be*.

MODALS:	can, could, shall, should, will, would, may, might, must
FORMS OF HAVE:	has, have, having, had
FORMS OF BE:	is, am, are, was, were, be, being, been

Each of these groups of auxiliaries combines with verbs in a different way.

Adding a Modal. The modal auxiliaries can precede any of the verbs in the basic sentences. When a modal is used, the verb that follows takes the simple form.

PATTERN ONE: John leaves tomorrow.
John may leave tomorrow.

PATTERN THREE: The graduates are lined up.
The graduates should be lined up.

PATTERN FIVE: Everyone likes that movie.
Everyone will like that movie.

These auxiliaries are called "modals" because they often express the "mood," or attitude, of the speaker toward what he is saying. *John leaves tomorrow,* for example, is stated as a fact, but *John may leave tomorrow* is stated as a possibility. In a similar way, *John should go tomorrow* is a statement of obligation, and *John must go tomorrow* is a statement of necessity. A complete description of the different shades of meaning that the modals can express would be quite extensive.

Adding *Have* + pp. Any verb in the basic sentences can also be preceded by *have* + pp. The "pp" means that any verb which follows a form of *have*—that is, *has, have,* or *had*—must be in the past participle form. With regular verbs, the past participle form ends in *-ed* just as the past tense does (*rent, rented; receive, received*), but some past participle forms are irregular (*drive, driven; ring, rung; hit, hit; be, been*). (For a list of irregular past participle forms, see Section 9.)

PATTERN TWO: His parents are in Seattle.
His parents have been in Seattle.

PATTERN FOUR: Our village became a city.
Our village has become a city.

PATTERN SIX: Mr. Wilson lends us his sprinkler.
Mr. Wilson has lent us his sprinkler.

Adding *Be* + *-ing*. Still another way to expand verbs is to add *be* + *-ing*. The appropriate form of *be* (*is, am, are, was,* or *were*) precedes the verb, and the *-ing* is added to the end to form the present participle.

PATTERN ONE: My father works at night.
                My father is working at night.

PATTERN THREE: They are very foolish.
                They are being very foolish.

PATTERN FIVE: My brother mows the lawn.
                My brother is mowing the lawn.

Combining Auxiliaries

As we have seen, a verb may be expanded by adding a modal, adding *have* + pp, or adding *be* + *-ing*. A verb may also be expanded by adding any two of these or even all three, as long as the auxiliaries are added in the right order. We can best show how this system works by stating a formula.

Subject   Tense   (Modal)   (Have + pp)   (Be + -ing)   Verb

"Tense" represents the choice between endings for a singular subject (the *-s* form), a plural subject (the simple form), or the past tense (the *-ed* form). It is placed first because the tense indication is added to the auxiliary or verb that immediately follows. Parentheses indicate that the item may or may not occur.

Leaving out the items in parentheses for the moment, let us see how the formula works:

SUBJECT	TENSE	VERB	
Paul	present	wait	Paul waits.
The men	present	wait	The men wait.
Paul	past	wait	Paul waited.
The men	past	wait	The men waited.

If we add one of the modals, we get:

SUBJECT	TENSE	MODAL	VERB	
Paul	present	can	wait	Paul can wait.
The men	present	can	wait	The men can wait.
Paul	past	can	wait	Paul could wait.
The men	past	can	wait	The men could wait.

When a modal is used, it, rather than the verb, shows the tense. When the tense is present, the modals have only one form, regardless of whether the subject is singular or plural. When the tense is past, *can* becomes *could, will* becomes *would, shall* becomes *should,* and *may* becomes *might. Must* has no past form. In addition to their uses in past time context, these modals have developed many special meanings which are not related to the idea of past time.

Suppose that we add *have* + pp instead of a modal:

SUBJECT	TENSE	HAVE + PP	VERB	
Paul	present	have + pp	wait	Paul has waited.
The men	present	have + pp	wait	The men have waited.
The men	past	have + pp	wait	The men had waited.

Again, the word that follows, in this case a form of *have,* shows the tense. The word that follows the form of *have* takes the past participle form: *wait* + pp becomes *waited.* If we add *be* + *-ing* instead of *have* + pp, it is the form of *be* that shows the tense, and the *-ing* is added to the following verb:

SUBJECT	TENSE	BE + -ING	VERB	
Paul	past	be + -ing	wait	Paul was waiting.
Paul	present	be + -ing	wait	Paul is waiting.
The men	present	be + -ing	wait	The men are waiting.
The men	past	be + -ing	wait	The men were waiting.

Now let us see how the formula works when more than one auxiliary is added. No matter what combination is used, the tense ending and any -ing or pp affects the auxiliary or verb that follows.

SUBJECT	TENSE	MODAL	HAVE + PP	BE + -ING	VERB
Paul	present	will		be + -ing	wait
Paul will be waiting.					
Paul	past	can	have + pp		wait
Paul could have waited.					
Paul	past		have + pp	be + -ing	wait
Paul has been waiting.					
Paul	present	may	have + pp	be + -ing	wait
Paul may have been waiting.					

Using the formula, we can put together verb phrases with the words in the right order and with each verb and auxiliary taking the right form. This formula is an excellent example of the kind of system upon which the English language is based. It demonstrates that verb phrases are really simple—even mechanical—although they appear to be complex.

It is this underlying simplicity that makes it possible to learn a language. Someone learning English would find it simpler to learn the formula for building verb phrases, however long it might take, than to memorize different verb phrases one at a time. For, once he has mastered the system, the learner can juggle verbs and auxiliaries without effort or error.

Exercise: Write sentences that match the formulas given below. Use a variety of subjects and verbs. (X) stands for material, if any, that follows the verb.

1. Subject present have + pp Verb (X)
2. Subject present can have + pp Verb (X)
3. Subject past may be + -ing Verb (X)
4. Subject present have + pp be + -ing Verb (X)
5. Subject present be + -ing Verb (X)
6. Subject past can be + -ing Verb (X)

7. Subject present will have + pp Verb (X)
8. Subject past may have + pp be + -ing Verb (X)
9. Subject past have + pp be + -ing Verb (X)
10. Subject present must have + pp Verb (X)
11. Subject past will have + pp be + -ing Verb (X)
12. Subject present may have + pp be + -ing Verb (X)
13. Subject past be + -ing Verb (X)
14. Subject present have + pp be + -ing Verb (X)
15. Subject past can Verb (X)
16. Subject present have + pp Verb (X)
17. Subject present shall Verb (X)
18. Subject present must be + -ing Verb (X)
19. Subject present may have + pp Verb (X)
20. Subject past shall be + -ing Verb (X)
21. Subject past can have + pp be + -ing Verb (X)
22. Subject past have + pp be + -ing Verb (X)
23. Subject present be + ing Verb (X)
24. Subject present have + pp be + -ing Verb (X)
25. Subject past shall have + pp Verb (X)

5.3 Transforming Basic Sentences

Compare the sentences in each of the following groups:

Jane will go tomorrow.
Jane will not go tomorrow.
Will Jane go tomorrow?

Frank brought the refreshments.
Who brought the refreshments?
What did Frank bring?

Mary has misplaced that book.
That book has been misplaced by Mary.
That book has been misplaced.

The first sentence in each of these groups is a basic sentence; the other sentences in each group are not basic sentences, but they are obviously related to the first sentence of their respective groups. Sentences that have this kind of relationship with a basic sentence are called **transformed sentences.** The various ways in which transformed sentences can be derived from basic sentences are called **transformations.** In other words, transformations are rules which state how sentences of one type can be changed, or transformed, into sentences of another type. English is organized in such a way that once we are given the basic sentences, we can produce all other sentences by applying one or more transformations.

The Negative Transformation

The **negative transformation** is one of several that operate on the auxiliaries. We can make any affirmative sentence negative by adding *not* or *-n't* after the first auxiliary, which may be a modal, a form of *have,* or a form of *be.* Here is an example of each case:

> Jane can go tomorrow.
> ⟶ Jane cannot go tomorrow.
> ⟶ Jane can't go tomorrow.
>
> Mr. Jones has left.
> ⟶ Mr. Jones has not left.
> ⟶ Mr. Jones hasn't left.
>
> He was driving very fast.
> ⟶ He was not driving very fast.
> ⟶ He wasn't driving very fast.

The *not* or *-n't* is added in the same way even when a form of *be* functions as a verb rather than as an auxiliary:

> John was there.
> ⟶ John was not there.
> ⟶ John wasn't there.

The neighbors are very friendly.
⟶ The neighbors are not very friendly.
⟶ The neighbors aren't very friendly.

But how is the negative transformation applied to sentences such as the following that do not contain an auxiliary?

She looks very healthy.
Jack won first prize.
My parents enjoy television.

In cases like these, a form of *do* is inserted in the sentence in order to make the transformation possible. When this is done, it is the form of *do*, rather than the verb, that expresses the tense and agreement with the subject:

She looks very healthy.
⟶ She does not look very healthy.
⟶ She doesn't look very healthy.

Jack won first prize.
⟶ Jack did not win first prize.
⟶ Jack didn't win first prize.

My parents enjoy television.
⟶ My parents do not enjoy television.
⟶ My parents don't enjoy television.

This use of do as a "dummy" auxiliary occurs throughout English wherever a transformation that requires an auxiliary is applied to a sentence that does not contain one.

The Emphatic Transformation

Whenever we wish to emphasize the truth of a particular sentence, we apply the **emphatic transformation.** In speech, this is done by saying the first auxiliary in the sentence with extra stress. In writing, the emphasis given the first auxiliary is usually indicated by underlining or the use of italics. The emphatic transformation works much like the negative transformation. Here are examples with a modal, a form of *have,* a form of *be* as an auxiliary, and a form of *be* used as a verb:

>   We must be on time.
>   ⟶ We *must* be on time.

>   Both boys have paid their dues.
>   ⟶ Both boys *have* paid their dues.

>   Jane is going tomorrow.
>   ⟶ Jane *is* going tomorrow.

>   I was there on time.
>   ⟶ I *was* there on time.

Whenever the emphatic transformation is applied to a sentence that does not contain an auxiliary, a form of *do* is inserted to carry the extra stress:

>   Mr. Jenks drives too fast.
>   ⟶ Mr. Jenks *does* drive too fast.

>   The neighbors seem very friendly.
>   ⟶ The neighbors *do* seem very friendly.

>   We invited everyone.
>   ⟶ We *did* invite everyone.

The Question Transformation

The **question transformation** also operates on the auxiliaries. It works in much the same way as the negative and emphatic transformations except that it is applied by changing the word order rather than by an addition to the sentence. Any statement can be turned into a question by moving the first auxiliary in the sentence to a position before the subject:

>   Susie will bring some cookies.
>   ⟶ Will Susie bring some cookies?

The Bentleys have been on vacation.
⟶ Have the Bentleys been on vacation?

John is going to the game.
⟶ Is John going to the game?

Their fathers were very angry.
⟶ Were their fathers very angry?

When the question transformation is applied to a sentence that does not have an auxiliary, a form of *do* with the appropriate tense ending is placed at the beginning of the sentence:

Frank broke that window.
⟶ Did Frank break that window?

Those books belong on this shelf.
⟶ Do those books belong on this shelf?

Mrs. Bauer owns this building.
⟶ Does Mrs. Bauer own this building?

There is another way of turning statements into questions. Can you explain the mechanism by which the following have been formed?

Susie will bring some cookies, won't she?
The Bentleys have been on vacation, haven't they?
John is going to the game, isn't he?
Their fathers were very angry, weren't they?

This kind of question is often called a **tag question,** because it is formed by adding material at the end of the sentence. With sentences that do not contain an auxiliary, different forms of *do* are used in the tag:

Frank broke that window, didn't he?
Those books belong on this shelf, don't they?
Mrs. Bauer owns this building, doesn't she?

When negative statements are turned into tag questions, the tag is made positive:

> John isn't going to the game, is he?
> Frank didn't break that window, did he?

The two types of questions that we have considered are both called **yes/no questions.** That is, they are the kind of question that can be answered by "yes" or "no," or sometimes with words like "probably," "maybe," or "perhaps." If we wish to produce the kind of question that asks for specific information, we must use a question word such as *who, what, where,* or *when.* Before we can apply the **question-word transformation,** we must first apply the regular question transformation. We can then substitute an appropriate question word for some element and move the question word to the beginning. Here is how this double transformation works:

> Frank broke that window.
> ⟶ Did Frank break that window?
> ⟶ Did (who) break that window?
> ⟶ Who broke that window?

> Frank broke that window.
> ⟶ Did Frank break that window?
> ⟶ Did Frank break (what)?
> ⟶ What did Frank break?

Thus, *who* is substituted for nouns referring to people and *what* for nouns referring to things. Notice in the first example how *did* drops out in the final operation because it is no longer needed to show the tense. Here are three more examples of this transformation:

> Jack is going to the game tomorrow.
> ⟶ Is Jack going to the game tomorrow?
> ⟶ Is (who) going to the game tomorrow?
> ⟶ Who is going to the game tomorrow?

Jack is going to the game tomorrow.
⟶ Is Jack going to the game tomorrow?
⟶ Is Jack going to the game (when)?
⟶ When is Jack going to the game?

Jack is going to the game tomorrow.
⟶ Is Jack going to the game tomorrow?
⟶ Is Jack going (where) tomorrow?
⟶ Where is Jack going tomorrow?

In these examples *who* has been substituted for a noun referring to a person, *when* for an adverbial expressing time, and *where* for an adverbial expressing place.

Notice the difference in word order in these examples. When the question word replaces the subject and is moved to the beginning, it reverses the question transformation, and the final question has normal word order: subject-auxiliary-verb. When the question word replaces something besides the subject, however, the resulting question still has transposed word order: auxiliary-subject-verb.

This difference in word order is an example of how the concept of transformation helps us to explain English briefly and simply. If we tried to explain every English sentence in terms of word order as we did the basic sentences, we would have an endless list of possible patterns. Once we look at English from the standpoint of transformation, however, we can explain a great many sentence types as variations of a limited number of basic patterns.

The Passive Transformation

The **passive transformation** is applied only to sentences that contain a transitive verb—that is, to sentences that follow Pattern Five, Pattern Six, or Pattern Seven. Since it is a good deal more complicated than the transformations we have discussed so far, it is most simply expressed as a formula:

Noun 1   (Aux)   Verb   Noun 2

⟶ **Noun 2   (Aux)   *be* + pp   Verb   (*by* Noun 1)**

Thus, the passive is produced by making the object of the original sentence the subject and adding *be* + pp just before the verb. The subject of the original sentence may or may not appear as the object of the preposition *by*. If the sentence being made passive does not contain any auxiliaries, *be* takes a form that agrees with the subject and shows the tense of the sentence:

> Students prepare the meals.
> ⟶ The meals are prepared by students.

> John mowed the lawn.
> ⟶ The lawn was mowed by John.

> The double play pleased the fans.
> ⟶ The fans were pleased by the double play.

However, if the sentence being made passive contains auxiliaries, *be* takes the form dictated by the auxiliary that precedes it. The following examples demonstrate the various possibilities:

> My father will sell the car.
> ⟶ The car will be sold.

> Frank has painted the house.
> ⟶ The house has been painted by Frank.

> Jane is writing the dialogue.
> ⟶ The dialogue is being written by Jane.

Thus, you can see that when *be* + pp is added to the verb phrase, it follows the same pattern as the auxiliaries which we described in Section 5.2. Since *be* + pp is always the last auxiliary, the verb in a passive sentence always has the past participle form.

The indirect object in a Pattern Six sentence can also serve as the subject of a passive sentence:

The neighbors told Mother the news.
⟶ Mother was told the news by the neighbors.

They will give us some candy.
⟶ We will be given some candy.

The transformations that we have considered—negative, emphatic, question, tag question, question word, and passive—have all, in one way or another, been concerned with the auxiliaries, which were discussed in Section 5.2. By looking at English from the point of view of transformation, we have been able to see a simple and consistent system underlying sentences that on the surface are quite different.

Exercise A: Apply the negative transformation to each of the odd numbered sentences below. Then apply the emphatic transformation to the even-numbered sentences. Be sure to underline the word that receives extra stress.

1. Frank mows lawns to earn extra money.
2. Jane crossed the street against the light.
3. The heavy rains delayed the guests.
4. Mary is living in Seattle.
5. He was expecting a surprise party.
6. The Bentleys go on vacation next month.
7. Mrs. Conway was the leader of the group.
8. Frank had brought some refreshments.
9. She has asked for some new clothes.
10. Fran will borrow his brother's car.
11. He should improve his telephone manners.
12. John goes to Chicago every weekend.
13. His mother is president of that company.
14. They like their new neighbors very much.
15. Jack was president of the hiking club last year.
16. The blomps are klooking on the splock.

17. Their galumphs might fleeken the smops smoomiously.
18. Those bleefs are fleeky galumphs.
19. The gloobs have splickled.
20. Each smibble was a schnickly martip.

Exercise B: Apply the question transformation to the sentences in Exercise A.

Exercise C: Transform each of the yes/no questions you produced for Exercise B into question-word questions by substituting an appropriate question word for the part of the sentence listed below:

1. to earn extra money	11. his telephone manners
2. Jane	12. to Chicago
3. the heavy rains	13. that
4. in Seattle	14. very
5. a surprise party	15. last year
6. next month	16. on the splock
7. Mrs. Conway	17. smoomiously
8. some refreshments	18. fleeky galumphs
9. some new clothes	19. the gloobs
10. his brother's	20. a schnickly martip

Exercise D: Apply the passive transformation to each of the following sentences. Omit the *by*-phrase whenever the passive sounds better without it.

1. The farmer chased the boys out of the orchard.
2. Barbara has asked several questions.
3. We could give that passage several interpretations. (Transform in two ways.)
4. Everyone is reading that book.
5. Some man lifted the child onto the scales.

6.0 Agreement of Subject and Verb

In grammar the word *agreement* means "likeness." To make two words agree is to make them alike in some respect. Words may agree in number, gender, and case.

A common error in American speech is the failure to make subject and verb agree in number (*you was, we was, he don't*). Errors of agreement in speaking are sometimes difficult to avoid. In writing, however, these errors should be easier to avoid because the writer always has the time and the opportunity to revise his work before presenting it to a reader.

6.1 Subject-Verb Agreement in Number

There are two numbers in grammar: **singular** and **plural.** A word is singular in number if it refers to one person or thing. A word is plural if it refers to more than one person or thing.

Except for *be*, English verbs show a difference between singular and plural only in the third person and only in the present tense. The third person singular present form ends in *s*.

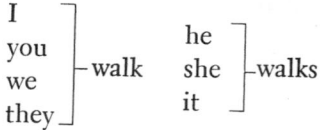

The verb *be* presents several special problems in agreement. First, the second person pronoun *you* is always used with the plural form of the verb: *you are, you were.* Second, the difference between singular and plural is shown in the past tense as well as in the present tense.

SINGULAR	PLURAL	PRESENT TENSE	PAST TENSE
I *was*	we *were*	I *am*	we *were*
you *were*	you *were*	you *are*	you *were*
he, she, it *was*	they *were*	he, she, it *is*	they *were*

The most common errors with *be* are *you was, we was, they was.*

A singular verb is used with a singular subject.

A plural verb is used with a plural subject.

The subject determines whether the verb is singular or plural. The verb does not agree with any other part of the sentence.

> The machine (singular) *is* useful.
> The machines (plural) *are* useful.
>
> He (singular) *swims* gracefully.
> They (plural) *swim* gracefully.

Note: A verb also agrees with its subject in *person.* When there are two or more subjects that differ in person, the verb agrees with the subject nearest to it.

> Neither she nor I am planning to try out.
> Either Kip or you are going to get the part.

6.2 Plural Words Between Subject and Verb

The verb agrees only with its subject. Occasionally a word with a different number from that of the subject occurs between the subject and the verb. This word usually has no effect upon the number of the verb even though it is closer to the verb than the subject is.

> The *bus,* loaded with people, *is* stalled in the parking lot.
> (*bus* is the subject.)
> *One* of the books *is* overdue at the library.
> (*One* is the subject.)
> The *maps* in that encyclopedia *distort* the South Pole.
> (*maps* is the subject.)
> The weak *arguments* of the prosecution *infuriate* the judge.
> (*arguments* is the subject.)

The words *with, together with, along with, as well as* are prepositions. The objects of these prepositions have no effect upon the number of the verb.

> *Caesar,* together with his followers, *enters* the Forum.
> (*Caesar* is the subject.)
> Her *intelligence,* as well as her charm, *impresses* them.
> (*intelligence* is the subject.)
> The *captain,* with his crew, *walks* to the hangar.
> (*captain* is the subject.)

Exercise: Choose the right verb from those given in parentheses.

1. Beth, with some friends, (is, are) taking a tour of Europe.
2. The most damaging testimony against the two defendants (was, were) given by the neighbors.
3. Discovery of atomic particles called quarks (were, was) not made until recently.
4. One of the most dangerous kinds of mushrooms (are, is) the death angel.

5. The glass in these doors (have, has) been treated to prevent sweating.

6. The number of robberies in summer homes (has, have) decreased.

7. Nobody except children and their parents (are, is) allowed to attend the matinee.

8. The campers with their equipment (is, are) being lowered to safety.

9. Films of our team in action (is, are) shown after every game.

10. A schedule of arrivals and departures (are, is) posted on the wall.

11. The gestures accompanying the speech (was, were) too dramatic.

12. His arrogance, as well as his ignorance, (annoy, annoys) them.

13. The sound of the drums and the trumpets (was, were) deafening.

14. The director of the project, together with several prominent scientists, (is, are) studying the data.

6.3 Indefinite Pronouns

Some indefinite pronouns are always singular. Others are always plural. Some may be either singular or plural.

SINGULAR			PLURAL
each	everyone	anyone	several
either	everybody	someone	few
neither	no one	somebody	both
one	nobody		many

No one is going to get in without paying admission.
Does either of you plan to see the Cornell-Yale game?
Both of us *do.*
Neither is under consideration for membership.
In the script, *somebody notifies* the Treasury Department.

Many come; few remain.
Several of the manuscripts *were* found to be authentic.

SINGULAR OR PLURAL

some	all	most
none	any	

Some, all, most, none, and *any* are singular when they refer to a quantity. They are plural when they refer to a number of individual items.

Some of the milk *was* sour. (quantity)
Some of the styles *were* unfashionable. (number)

Most of the money *was* frittered away. (quantity)
Most of the advantages *are* enumerated. (number)

All the light *was* refracted. (quantity)
All of the avocados *were* mottled. (number)

None and *any* may be either singular or plural depending on whether the writer is referring to one thing or to several.

None of the programs *is* worth an Emmy. (not one)
None of the programs *are* worth Emmys. (no programs)

Any of these stocks *is* valuable. (any one)
Any of these stocks *are* valuable. (any stocks)

Exercise: Choose the right word from the two given.

1. Many of the ship's passengers (was, were) Sunday sailors.
2. One of Grant Wood's best-known paintings (are, is) "American Gothic."
3. Anyone who wants to help collect funds (are, is) welcome.
4. Not one of the guests (was, were) aware of the mishap.
5. Neither of these books (interest, interests) me.
6. One of the least beautiful of mammals (are, is) the hippopotamus.
7. (Do, Does) either of you have change for a dollar?

8. Neither of the programs (has, have) been successful.
9. Several of the trees (has, have) been replaced by pin oaks.
10. Nobody in the House or Senate (dare, dares) oppose the bill.
11. Not one of our basketball players (are, is) over six feet tall.
12. One of the best disc jockeys (are, is) Wolfman Jack.
13. Either of the cars (is, are) available.
14. Not one of my friends (is, are) able to go.
15. Several of the fuses (have, has) blown.
16. Everyone in the Bahamas (seem, seems) friendly to tourists.
17. Neither Betsy or Carl (was, were) invited to the barbecue.
18. Each of you (has, have) a funny look on his face.

6.4 Compound Subjects

Compound subjects joined by <u>and</u> are plural.*

> A new department store and new office buildings
> *are* planned.

Singular words joined by <u>or</u>, <u>nor</u>, <u>either-or</u>, <u>neither-nor</u> to form a compound subject are singular.

> Neither her short story nor her novel *has* been published.
> Either a bulldozer or a wrecker *is* feasible.
> Curry powder or charcoal seasoning *flavors* chicken nicely.

When a singular word and a plural word are joined by <u>or</u> or <u>nor</u> to form a compound subject, the verb agrees with the subject that is nearer to it.

> Neither the President nor his aides *approve* the decision.
> (*aides* is closer to the verb than *President*.)
> Atomic energy or huge amounts of fuel *are* essential.
> Neither the new taxes nor the fiscal crisis *is* pleasant.

---

* If the words making up the compound subject are habitually used together to refer to a single thing, the subject may be used with a singular verb: *bread and butter, macaroni and cheese,* etc.

Exercise: Find the errors in subject-verb agreement in these sentences. Write the sentences correctly. Two of the sentences are correct.

1. Neither Rick nor his classmates was prepared for the test.

2. Working and going to college at the same time takes all of Bill's energy.

3. To kick a field goal or to complete a long pass seem impossible.

4. Neither the mayor nor his assistant have released any information.

5. The doctor or her assistant are always on duty.

6. Neither the students nor the teacher is immune to criticism.

7. Both the orchestra and the conductor was aware of the disturbance.

8. To go to the city and to stay there is all that I ask.

9. Either my brothers or my sister are going with me.

10. Neither the quarterback nor the two tackles were eligible.

11. Have either the doctor or the dentist made an appointment for you?

12. Which is more beautiful, spring flowers or autumn flowers?

13. In the basement is a power saw and an electric drill.

14. Either Mary or her brothers has bought a new car.

15. Are your father or your mother going to the meeting tonight?

6.5   Subject Following Verb

The most difficult agreement problem in speech arises when the subject follows the verb. The speaker must think ahead to the subject in order to decide whether the verb is to be singular or plural.

This problem arises in sentences beginning with *There* and *Here*. It also arises in questions beginning with *who, why, where, what, how.*

NONSTANDARD Here's the books for Salvatore.
STANDARD Here *are* the books for Salvatore.

NONSTANDARD There's four players waiting to use the tennis courts.
STANDARD There *are* four players waiting to use the tennis courts.

NONSTANDARD Who's the three people in that photograph?
STANDARD Who *are* the three people in that photograph?

NONSTANDARD What's the arrangements for the meeting?
STANDARD What *are* the arrangements for the meeting?

NONSTANDARD Onto the stage *comes* the players and the musicians.
STANDARD Onto the stage *come* the players and the musicians.

6.6 Predicate Words

The linking verb agrees with its subject, *not* with the predicate word.

NONSTANDARD More powerful weapons *is* not the solution.
STANDARD More powerful weapons *are* not the solution.

NONSTANDARD John's penchant *are* Russian novels.
STANDARD John's penchant *is* Russian novels.

NONSTANDARD Honesty and perseverance *is* the answer.
STANDARD Honesty and perseverance *are* the answer.

6.7 Don't and Doesn't

The word *does* and the contraction *doesn't* are used with singular nouns and with the pronouns *he, she,* and *it.* The word *do* and the contraction *don't* are used with plural nouns and with the pronouns *I, we, you,* and *they.*

DOES, DOSEN'T	DO, DON'T
the boat does	the boats do
he doesn't	we don't
she doesn't	you don't
it doesn't	they don't

Exercise: Choose the right word from the two given in parentheses.

1. There (goes, go) the governor and her husband.
2. Why (don't, doesn't) she pick up the tickets after work?
3. There (hasn't, haven't) been any fresh strawberries for a week.
4. Bifocals (are, is) probably what Dad needs.
5. An advertisement and a bill (are, is) today's exciting mail.
6. Attending the Constitutional Convention at Philadelphia in 1789 (was, were) many able people.
7. The main unfinished business (is, are) the disarmament negotiations.
8. Heading toward Japan (is, are) torrential rains driven by a 100-mile-an-hour wind.
9. There (happen, happens) to be ready four boxes of equipment.
10. (Here's, Here are) some economic forecasts that point to a bright future.
11. Posted on every bulletin board (are, is) a copy of the rules.
12. The fruit I like most (is, are) bananas.
13. (There's, There are) no restaurants on the turnpike for thirty miles.
14. Why (don't, doesn't) the list of contributors include my name?
15. Frankly, there (were, was) times when I regretted my decision.

6.8 Collective Nouns

A collective noun names a group of people or things: *committee, team, jury, council, crowd.*

When the writer refers to a group acting together as one unit, the collective noun is used with a singular verb. When the writer refers to the individuals in the group acting separately, one by one, the collective noun is used with a plural verb.

> The crowd *is* complacent. (united action)
> The crowd *were* milling excitedly. (separate actions)
>
> The crew *works* harmoniously together. (united action)
> The crew *were* studying their navigation plans.
>   (separate action)

Once the writer decides whether the collective noun is a unit or a group of individuals, he must abide by his choice. Later in the same sentence he may not use a verb or pronoun of different number.

> NONSTANDARD   The council *has* (singular) withdrawn *their*
>   (plural) support.
> STANDARD   The council *has* withdrawn *its* support.

6.9 Nouns Plural in Form

Some nouns are plural in form but are regarded as singular in meaning. That is, they end in *s* as most plural nouns do, but they do not stand for more than one thing: *news, mumps, measles.* Therefore, they are used with a singular verb.

There are many words ending in *-ics* that may be either singular or plural: *economics, athletics, civics, politics.* These words are singular when they are used to refer to a school subject, a science, or a general practice. When singular in meaning, they are not usually preceded by *the, his, some, all* and singular modifiers.

> Politics *is* an art in which they excel. (singular)
> His politics *are* subject to question. (plural)
> Ethics *is* the study of moral values and responsibilities.
>   (singular)
> Her professional ethics *are* sound. (plural)
> The new mathematics *is* puzzling to many parents.
>   (singular)
> Lee's hysterics *indicate* a more significant disturbance.
>   (plural)
> News *is* censored in totalitarian countries. (singular)

6.10   Titles and Groups of Words

The title of a book, play, story, film, musical composition, or other work of art is used with a singular verb. The name of a country is used with a singular verb. Such words, even though they may be plural in form, refer to a single thing.

> The United States *is* engaged in long-range space operations.
> The Netherlands *has* a land area of 12,504 square miles.
> Cheviot Hills *is* a mountain range along the English-
>   Scottish border.
> *To Kill a Mockingbird was* written by Harper Lee.
> *I Know Why the Caged Bird Sings is* a novel by Maya Angelou.

Any group of words referring to a single thing or thought is used with a singular verb.

> What we need *is* friends.
> "The thing of which I have most fear is fear," was said
>   by Montaigne.

6.11   Words of Amount and Time

Words or phrases that express periods of time, fractions, weights, measurements, and amounts of money are usually regarded as singular.

> Two tons *is* the capacity weight for that bridge.
> Two-thirds of the community fund *has* been distributed.
> Sixty minutes *is* to be spent preparing each lesson.
> Twelve dollars *is* too much to charge for a ticket.

If a prepositional phrase with a plural object falls between the subject and the verb, the verb is singular if its subject is considered as a single thing or thought. The verb is plural if its subject is felt to be plural.

> Two boxes of candy *was* what Carl ordered.
>   (singular meaning)
> Boxes of candy *were* displayed in the shop window.
>   (plural meaning)

Exercise: Choose the right words from those given in the parentheses.

1. What this project needs (is, are) sponsors.
2. Molasses (are, is) the secret ingredient in these cookies.
3. Ten weeks (is, are) the time required for the course.
4. Two-thirds of our farm (was, were) flooded.
5. Measles (are, is) a potentially dangerous disease.
6. The jury (has, have) been unsuccessful in their efforts to agree.
7. Two pounds of ground beef (is, are) enough.
8. There (was, were) six feet of water in the hold.
9. The class (is, are) planning its annual picnic.
10. The jury (is, are) about to give its verdict.
11. The class (are, is) having their pictures taken for the yearbook.

12. The National Aeronautics and Space Administration (sponsor, sponsors) the project.

13. Politics (are, is) not for those who cannot stand ridicule.

14. Lasker's *Chess Secrets* (have, has) improved my game considerably.

15. Four-fifths of the words in common use (are, is) of Anglo-Saxon origin.

16. One-tenth of the people in rural areas (is, are) illiterate.

17. Forty dollars (is, are) too high a price for your car.

18. Medicine (offers, offer) many people interesting careers.

19. The United Nations (are, is) sending observers to the Indian border.

20. Over one-fourth of the people on earth (is, are) Chinese.

6.12   Relative Pronouns

A relative pronoun stands in place of its antecedent (the word to which it refers). If that antecedent is plural, the relative pronoun is plural. If the antecedent is singular, the relative pronoun is singular.

A relative pronoun agrees with its antecedent in number.

When a relative pronoun is used as subject of the verb in the relative clause, the number of the verb depends upon the number of the pronoun's antecedent.

These are the *delegates* (plural) who (plural) *are* going to Atlanta.

Bridget is the *girl* (singular) who (singular) *reads* the announcements in the auditorium.

Tom is one of those *people* who *are* always late. (*People* are always late.)

Mrs. Berry is the only *one* of the reporters who *has* a direct line to Washington. (Only *one* has a direct line.)

The problem of agreement arises in the sentences above because there are two words, either of which *might* be the antecedent of the relative pronoun. Usually the meaning of the sentence shows which word *is* the antecedent.

Exercise: Choose the right word from those given in parentheses.

1. You are the only one of the members who (has, have) failed to vote.

2. This is the longest of the selections that (is, are) to be played.

3. This is one of the European cars that (has, have) automatic transmission.

4. The rose is one of the flowers which (requires, require) great care.

5. The bluejay is one species which (visits, visit) the feeder frequently.

6. The spruce is one of the evergreens which (grow, grows) abundantly in New England.

7. Of all the sports that (develops, develop) strong bodies, swimming is best.

8. Track is the sport which (help, helps) most to develop stamina.

9. The sea anemone is one of the animals that (has, have) to wait for their food to come to them.

10. Janice is one of those girls who (gets, get) everywhere on time.

7.0 Pronoun Usage

In grammar, the term *inflection* has a special meaning. It means "a change in form to show how a word is used in a sentence." Prepositions, conjunctions, and interjections do not change their form. All other parts of speech do. Usually, the change in form is just a change in spelling:

ADVERB: big — bigger — biggest
ADJECTIVE: hard — harder — hardest
NOUN: person — person's — persons — persons'
VERB: walk — walks — walked — walking

Often, however, the change involves the use of a completely new word:

VERB: go — went — gone
PRONOUN: I — me — mine

Pronouns change their form in both ways. The changes in pronouns correspond to their use in sentences. These changes are called the **cases** of pronouns. The cases are the **nominative, possessive,** and **objective.**

You will recall that pronouns can be used in sentences in the following ways:

subject of the verb	object of a preposition
object of the verb	appositive
predicate pronoun	modifier

Nearly all pronouns change their form for different uses in the sentence. The indefinite pronouns have the least change. They change only when used as modifiers. As modifiers, they are in the possessive case:

POSSESSIVE

everyone	—	everyone's
nobody	—	nobody's
anyone	—	anyone's

The pronouns *this, that, these, those, which,* and *what* do not change their forms to indicate case. None of these has a possessive form.

The pronoun inflections are as follows:

NOMINATIVE	POSSESSIVE	OBJECTIVE
I	my, mine	me
we	our, ours	us
you	your, yours	you
he	his	him
she	her, hers	her
it	its	it
they	their, theirs	them
who	whose	whom
whoever	whosever	whomever

7.1 The Pronoun as Subject of a Verb

The nominative form of the pronoun is used as subject of a verb.

The problem of which pronoun form to use as subject arises chiefly when the subject is compound. The compound subject may be made up of pronouns or of both nouns and pronouns.

To decide which pronoun form to use in a compound subject, *try each part of the subject by itself with the verb.*

> Sherry and (I, me) went shopping for antiques.
> (Sherry went; I went, *not* me went.)

> The Wendels and (they, them) are Californians.
> (The Wendels are; they are, *not* them are.)

> George and (they, them) met at the subway.
> (George met; they met, *not* them met.)

> Jack and (I, me) work at the hardware store.
> (Jack works; I work, *not* me works.)

The plural forms *we* and *they* sound awkward in many compounds. They can be avoided by recasting the sentence.

> AWKWARD The girls and we are leaving.
> BETTER We and the girls are leaving.

> AWKWARD We and they planned the reception.
> BETTER We planned the reception with them.

7.2 The Predicate Pronoun

The verb *be* is a linking verb. It links the noun, pronoun, or adjective following it to the subject. A pronoun so linked is called a **predicate pronoun.**

The nominative pronoun form is used as a predicate pronoun.*

The problem of which form to use in a predicate pronoun occurs primarily after the verb *be*. The rule applies to all verb phrases built around forms of *be: could have been, can be, should be,* etc.

---

* Standard usage permits the exception in both speech and writing of *It is me.*

It was **I** whom they called.
Could it have been **she** who left?
It *must have been* **they** who rang the alarm.

Sometimes the nominative form sounds awkward. The awkwardness can be avoided by recasting the sentence.

AWKWARD The instigators are she and Bill.
BETTER She and Bill are the instigators.

AWKWARD It was we who planned the symposium.
BETTER We are the people who planned the symposium.

7.3 The Pronoun as Object of a Verb

The objective pronoun form is used as direct or indirect object.

The problem of which pronoun form to use as object of the verb arises chiefly when the object is compound. The compound object may consist of pronouns or of both nouns and pronouns.

To decide which pronoun form to use in a compound object, *try each part of the object by itself with the verb.*

The police officer gave Tina and (I, me) the directions.
(gave Tina; gave me, *not* gave I)
The denial angered Paul and (he, him).
(angered Paul; angered him, *not* angered he)
Dr. Marshall told both (they, them) and (we, us) about Van Gogh's life. (told them, *not* told they; told us, *not* told we)
Do you want (she, her) and (I, me) to stay longer?
(want her, *not* want she; want me, *not* want I)

Exercise A: Choose the right form from those given in parentheses.

1. Mother sent Karen and (I, me) to the bank.
2. Are you implying that it was (she, her)?

3. The co-captains of the volleyball team are Betty and (she, her).

4. (She, Her) and Ben will give the commencement speeches.

5. We met Tim and (he, him) at the Winter Carnival.

6. If I were (he, him), I'd accept the invitation.

7. How many goals did (he, him) and Al make?

8. The song sent the parents and (we, us) into gales of laughter.

9. Give Howard or (I, me) the directions for getting there.

10. The Rotary Club gave Jan and (I, me) $500 scholarships.

11. The guests of honor were the mayor and (I, me).

12. The police found (he, him) and his little sister asleep in the woods.

13. (Him, He) and his parents have just returned from a camping trip.

14. Joyce and (he, him) have been accepted at Oberlin College.

15. Was it (them, they) who were doing all that shouting?

Exercise B: Choose the right form from those given in parentheses.

1. I am sure it was (him, he) who called last night.

2. I saw (him, he) and his sister at the Aquarium.

3. Did you or (he, him) sing in the concert?

4. It must have been (they, them) who waved at us.

5. The woman kept poking Betty and (I, me) with her umbrella.

6. If I were (she, her) I would apply for the job.

7. It was (he, him) who first spotted the rocket.

8. How many tickets did (she, her) and Ruth sell?

9. Neither the Clarks nor (we, us) have been invited to the barbecue.

10. The judge sentenced (him, he) and his accomplice to a year in jail.

11. Did you know that Peggy and (he, him) are engaged?

12. I have no doubt that it was (them, they).

13. Will you help Larry and (I, me) put up the storm windows?

14. Wasn't it (she, her) who discovered radium?

15. The conductor told Hal and (I, me) about the derailment.

7.4 The Pronoun as Object of a Preposition

The objective pronoun form is used as object of a preposition.

The problem of which pronoun form to use as object of a preposition arises only when the object is compound. The compound object may consist of pronouns or of both nouns and pronouns.

To decide which pronoun to use in a compound object of a preposition, *try each part of the object by itself with the preposition.*

> The Internal Revenue Service sent a refund check to Mike
>   and (I, me). (to Mike; to me, *not* to I)
> Christina received lovely gifts from (they, them) and
>   David. (from them; *not* from they)
> The telephone operator had messages for Irene and (we, us).
>   (for Irene; for us, *not* for we)

The preposition *between* causes especially noticeable errors in pronoun usage. Use only the objective pronoun forms after *between*.

> between you and him, *not* between you and he
> between him and me, *not* between he and I

7.5 The Pronoun Used with a Noun

In a construction such as *we girls* or *us boys*, the use of the noun determines the case form of the pronoun.

> We girls cannot dispute his premise.
>   (*girls* is the subject of *cannot dispute*; the nominative
>   pronoun is therefore required.)

> The record shop offers us students a ten percent discount.
>   (*students* is indirect object of *offers*; the objective pronoun
>   is therefore required.)

To decide which pronoun form to use in a construction such as *we boys,* try the pronoun by itself with the verb or preposition.

> The insurance agent asked (we, us) witnesses to describe the accident.
> (asked us, *not* asked we)
> (We, Us) skeptics must learn to accept the inevitable without question.
> (We must learn, *not* Us must learn)

Exercise A: Choose the right form from those given in parentheses.

1. There is no real disagreement between you and (I, me).
2. The counselor gave special attention to Alice and (he, him).
3. The company agent asked (us, we) seniors to consider the jobs.
4. Everyone went to the senior dance except Ray and (I, me).
5. For (us, we) seniors, the commencement exercises should be impressive.
6. I have ordered tickets for you and (me, I).
7. (We, Us) students discussed our plans for the summer.
8. The principal's remarks were meant for Jim and (me, I).
9. The auditorium was decorated by Melinda, George, and (I, me).
10. Everyone will receive a diploma except Charlie and (she, her).
11. Several of (us, we) girls play in the band.
12. The speaker directed his remarks at all of (we, us) seniors.
13. The automobiles were driven by Kelly and (I, me).
14. Why don't you wait for Hal and (I, me) in the lobby?
15. Just between you and (I, me), the speech was too long.

Exercise B: Choose the right form from those given in parentheses.

1. The band sat below Ted and (I, me) at the stadium.
2. Ann and Mike are going to the dance with Bill and (me, I).
3. The only passengers on the bus were (us, we) two girls.

4. The director says she will need (we, us) stagehands for tomorrow's rehearsal.

5. The money is being held in trust for Walt and (he, him).

6. There was not a single failure among all of (us, we) seniors.

7. Did you hear the news about (her, she) and her sister?

8. The bus waited while (we, us) boys looked for the missing book.

9. To (we, us) three, the fire seemed to be coming in our direction.

10. Shouldn't (we, us) older girls make the major decisions?

11. The secret must remain between you and (I, me).

12. The class play was written by Kate and (he, him).

13. Who sat between you and (he, him) on the platform?

14. The coach spoke to my parents and (I, me) after the game.

15. For (her, she) and Bob everything looks positive.

7.6 Who and Whom in Questions

The pronouns *who* and *whom* are used as interrogative pronouns in questions. Within the question, the pronoun may be the subject of the verb, object of the verb, or object of the preposition.

In standard usage, the nominative form *who* is used as the subject of the verb. The objective form *whom* is used as the object of the verb or of a preposition. (In informal usage there is a growing tendency to use *who* at the beginning of a sentence, whether subject or object.)

The pronouns *whoever* and *whomever* follow the same rules as *who* and *whom*.

To decide which form to use, determine how the pronoun is used within the question.

> To (who, whom) did the President give praise?
> > (*whom* is correct as the object of the preposition *to*.)
> (Who, Whom) were the Iconoclasts?
> > (*Who* is correct as the subject of the verb *were*.)

(Who, Whom) are you waiting for?
    (*Whom* is correct as the object of the preposition *for*.)
(Who, Whom) was he calling?
    (*Whom* is correct as the object of the verb *was calling*.)
(Whoever, Whomever) did Sir Richard Steele satirize?
    (*Whomever* is correct as the object of the verb *did satirize*.)

Do not be misled by parenthetical expressions like *do you think, can you imagine, do you suppose, do you believe*. They do not determine the case of the interrogative pronoun.

Who do you suppose will be chosen?
    (*Who* is the subject of *will be chosen*.)
Whom do you think she called?
    (*Whom* is the object of *called*.)
Who do you believe is deceiving them?
    (*Who* is the subject of *is deceiving*.)

7.7 <u>Who</u> and <u>Whom</u> in Clauses

The pronouns *who* and *whom* may be used as relative pronouns to introduce adjective clauses or as introductory words in noun clauses. These pronouns also perform a job within the clause they introduce.

Whoever and *whomever* follow the same rules as *who* and *whom* when used as introductory words.

The use of the pronoun within the clause determines whether the nominative or objective form is used.

The superintendent did not know *whom the repairman wanted*. (Noun clause; *whom* is the object of the verb *wanted* within the clause.)

Joan of Arc was a courageous woman *whom we must admire*. (*whom* is the object of *must admire* within the clause.)

Horace Wells was the man *who* first *used* nitrous oxide as an anesthetic. (*who* is the subject of the verb *used* within the clause.)

No one knows *who inspired* Shakespeare's sonnets to a "dark lady." (Noun clause; *who* is the subject of the verb *inspired* within the clause.)

Anna Pavlova is the ballerina *about whom she was asking.* (*whom* is the object of the preposition *about* within the clause.)

Whoever volunteers must realize fully the dangers involved. (*Whoever* is the subject of the verb *volunteers* within the noun clause.)

The troops are ready for *whoever might attack.* (The noun clause is the object of the preposition *for*; *whoever* is the subject of the verb *might attack* within the clause.)

Mr. Bossard can award the contract to *whomever he wants.* (The noun clause is the object of the preposition *to*; *whomever* is the object of the verb *wants* within the clause.)

Exercise: Choose the right form from those given in parentheses.

1. (Whom, Who) do you think will be nominated?
2. She is the one (whom, who) the committee has endorsed.
3. The speaker urged the members to support (whomever, whoever) is elected.
4. These are the men (who, whom) drew up the platform.
5. Party unity depends on those (who, whom) are willing to compromise.
6. Should we praise someone (who, whom) merely does his duty?
7. A person (who, whom) faces obstacles can often overcome them.
8. Mr. Briggs speaks to (whomever, whoever) he sees.
9. It concerns various characters (who, whom) are involved in the Spanish Civil War.
10. If there is anyone (whom, who) disagrees, let him say so now.

11. Give the note to (whoever, whomever) opens the door.

12. (Who, Whom) does the director want to see?

13. The wallet goes to (whoever, whomever) can describe it accurately.

14. I gave the package to the postman, (who, whom) was making his rounds.

15. (Whom, Who) did you say was driving the car?

16. Faulkner is an author (who, whom) I'm sure you know.

7.8 Pronouns in Comparisons

Sometimes a comparison is made by using a clause that begins with *than* or *as.*

> Holly is better at discerning symbolism than Tina is.
> Stephen admires Maxine Kumin's poetry as much as he admires Sylvia Plath's poetry.

Sometimes the final clause in the comparison is left incomplete.

> Holly is better at discerning symbolism than Tina (is).
> Mr. Berry is a better reporter than Mr. Hodget (is).

To decide which pronoun form to use in an incomplete comparison, complete the comparison.

> Bernie had a higher batting average than (I, me).
> (Bernie had a higher batting average than I had.)
> The senator has a better voting record than (I, me).
> (The senator has a better voting record than I have.)

7.9 Possessive Case with Gerunds

The possessive form of the pronoun is used when the pronoun immediately precedes a gerund.

All gerunds end in *-ing,* and they are all formed from verbs. The present participle also ends in *-ing,* and it, too, is formed from a verb. If the *-ing* word is used as a modifier, it is a participle. If it is used as a noun, it is a gerund.

The possessive form of the pronoun is used before a gerund. The nominative and objective forms are used before a participle.

> The other skiers saw *him careening* down the slopes.
> (*careening* is a participle modifying *him.*)

> The professor discouraged *her talking* during the lecture.
> (*talking* is a gerund, the object of the verb *discouraged.*)

> Mr. Lacey's *writing* provides much insight into world affairs.
> (*writing* is a gerund, the subject of the verb *provides.*)

> The foreman heard *them complaining* about their salaries.
> (*complaining* is a participle modifying *them.*)

7.10   The Pronoun with Infinitives

The objective form of the pronoun is used as the subject, object, or predicate pronoun of an infinitive.

> The official ordered *him to leave* the game. (*him* is the subject of *to leave.*)
> Mrs. Salas asked *him to modify* the original design. (*him* is the subject of *to modify.*)
> The teachers thought *him* to be *me.*
>   (*him* is the subject of *to be,* and *me* is the predicate pronoun following *to be.*)
> Ellen left in time *to meet them.*
>   (*them* is the object of *to meet.*)
> The announcer believed the victor *to be him.*
>   (*him* is the predicate pronoun following *to be.*)

7.11 The Pronoun as an Appositive

The form of a pronoun used as an appositive is determined by the use of the noun to which it is in apposition.

> The candidates, *Mr. Hierlihy* and *I,* urged all members to vote. (*Mr. Hierlihy* and *I* are in apposition to *candidates,* which is the subject of *urged.* Therefore, the nominative form of the pronoun is required.)

> For the brothers, *Paul* and *him,* the judge's decision was heartbreaking. (*Paul* and *him* are in apposition to *brothers,* which is the object of the preposition *For.* Therefore, the objective form of the pronoun is required.)

> We gave the winners, *Ross* and *her,* a warm welcome. (*Ross* and *her* are in apposition to *winners,* which is the indirect object of *gave.* Therefore, the objective form of the pronoun is required.)

To determine which form of the pronoun to use in apposition, try the appositive by itself with the verb or preposition.

> Those interns, Chet and (him, he), have bright futures. (Chet and he have, *not* Chet and him have.)

> Those wires are from two of your clients, Mrs. Coe and (him, he). (Those telegrams are from him, *not* from he.)

7.12 Compound Personal Pronouns

Compound personal pronouns are used only when their antecedents appear in the same sentence.

> STANDARD   The impresario appeared pleased with himself.
> STANDARD   He ruined himself in business.

NONSTANDARD	She made the adjustment for Ms. Burke and myself.
STANDARD	She made the adjustment for Ms. Burke. and me.

NONSTANDARD	I bought me a new pair of hockey skates.
STANDARD	I bought myself a new pair of hockey skates.

Exercise: Choose the standard form from those given in parentheses.

1. Pat and (myself, I) are directors of the music festival.
2. The twins are both taller than (she, her).
3. Few people are better educated than (him, he).
4. The prize was awarded jointly to Bill and (me, myself).
5. Mr. Briggs didn't like (us, our) playing touch football on his lawn.
6. Did you hear about (him, his) winning the first prize?
7. I hope no one heard (my, me) talking to myself.
8. I'd like to be (him, he) for just one week.
9. The Rotary Club gave two students, Meg and (I, me), scholarships.
10. Helen and (I, myself) will be glad to help you.
11. The teacher must have thought Ginny to be (I, me).
12. Janet worked harder for the bazaar than (me, I).
13. Please return the unsold envelopes to Jo Anne or (me, myself).
14. The investigators suspected the embezzler to be (him, he).
15. Is anyone in favor of (me, my) showing some slides?
16. No one can make the decision but (yourself, you).
17. Trisha went to the party with Jim and (myself, me).
18. Sally and (I, me, myself) bought the material for the new drapes.
19. Nobody in the audience laughed except (ourselves, us).
20. I did not like (him, his) crashing the party.

7.13 Pronouns and Antecedents

A pronoun agrees with its antecedent in number, gender, and person.

Agreement in Number. If the antecedent of a pronoun is singular, a singular pronoun is required. If the antecedent is plural, a plural pronoun is required.

The indefinite pronouns that are singular in meaning cause the greatest difficulty. The following are referred to by singular pronouns:

anybody	either	neither	somebody
anyone	everybody	nobody	someone
each	everyone	one	

Each of the men had *his* own preconceived ideas.
One must determine *his* personal plan of action.
Someone has forgotten *his* overcoat.

Note: The general rule does not always apply to *everyone* and *everybody*. In certain sentences these words must be referred to by plural pronouns to make good sense.

POOR   *Everyone* left when *he* learned of the cancellation.
BETTER *Everyone* left when *they* learned of the cancellation.

POOR   Everyone read *his* favorite books.
BETTER *Everyone* read *their* favorite books.

In the sentences above, the verbs are all in the past tense. Verbs in the past tense do not change form to show singular and plural. If the verbs were in the present tense, the singular verb would be required and the singular personal pronouns (he, his) would also be required.

Everyone *leaves* when *he* hears of the cancellation.
Everybody *reads* his part with animation.

Two or more singular antecedents joined by <u>or</u> or <u>nor</u> are referred to by a singular pronoun.

Either Sally or Terri will bring *her* dictionary.
Neither Alex nor Bob has left *his* room all day.

Collective nouns may be referred to by either a singular or plural pronoun, depending upon the emphasis desired.

The night staff *has its* new parking area.
The night staff *have* signed *their* new contracts.

The indefinite pronouns <u>all</u>, <u>some</u>, <u>any</u>, and <u>none</u> may be referred to by either a singular or plural pronoun, depending upon the meaning intended.

All of the crew *has* lost *its* camaraderie.

Some of the meat *has* lost *its* flavor.

None of the women *have* left *their* gloves.

Some of the committee *have* given *their* decision.

Note: In all of the foregoing examples, the collective nouns and indefinite pronouns are used as subjects. The number of the verb and the number of the pronoun referring to them must be the same.

NONSTANDARD	All of the advisory council *are* casting *its* vote.
STANDARD	All of the advisory council *are* casting *their* vote.
NONSTANDARD	None of the congressmen *was* forgetting *their* duty.
STANDARD	None of the congressmen *were* forgetting *their* duty.
STANDARD	None of the congressmen *was* forgetting *his* duty.

Agreement in Gender. Masculine gender is indicated by *he, his, him.* Feminine gender is indicated by *she, her, hers.* Neuter gender is indicated by *it* and *its*. These pronouns must be the same in gender as the word to which they refer.

> The woman searched for change in *her* handbag. (feminine)
> The President read *his* State-of-the-Union address. (masculine)
> The dog ran to *its* master. (neuter)

When a singular pronoun must refer to both feminine and masculine antecedents, the phrase "his or her" is acceptable. It is, in fact, preferred by some people who wish to avoid what they consider to be sexist language.

> STANDARD   Every participant will bring *his* or *her* sketch pad.
> STANDARD   Every participant will bring *his* sketch pad.

Agreement in Person. A personal pronoun must be in the same person as its antecedent. The words *one, everyone,* and *everybody* are in the third person. They are referred to by *he, his, him, she, her, hers.*

> NONSTANDARD   *Everyone* should present *your* thoughts on automation.
> STANDARD   *Everyone* should present *his* thoughts on automation.

> NONSTANDARD   *I* find that a long, quiet walk is good for *your* soul.
> STANDARD   *I* find that a long, quiet walk is good for *my* soul.

Exercise: Find and correct the errors in agreement of these sentences. Make sure that both verb and pronoun are correct.

1. Neither the director nor the producer received their salary on time.

2. Everyone offered their criticism of the rehearsal.

3. Each of the out-of-town tryouts were full of flaws.

4. Either the set designer or the costume designer will have to change their color scheme.

5. Each playwright has their own agent.

6. The dancing troupe is rehearsing their routine.

7. Each of them aspire to be *première danseuse*.

8. Neither Wayne nor Diana have been to a dance recital before.

9. If one goes to dramatic school, you can learn a lot about acting.

10. Everyone chosen was rehearsing their role.

11. Neither the actress nor her understudy were using the proper make-up.

12. Does the leading man or leading woman know their parts yet?

13. Everybody off-stage stood waiting for their cue.

14. Did you notice anyone ad-libbing their lines?

15. Everyone is assigned to their own dressing room.

7.14　Indefinite Reference

To avoid any confusion for the reader, every personal pronoun should refer clearly to a definite antecedent.

INDEFINITE The battle was won, and *they* set out for Concord.

BETTER The battle was won, and the British troops set out for Concord.

INDEFINITE *It* says in the newspaper that Sartre declined the Nobel Prize.

BETTER The newspaper says that Sartre declined the Nobel Prize.

INDEFINITE You should see the exhibit if *it* is open.

BETTER You should see the exhibit if the museum is open.

The pronoun *you* is sometimes used when it is not meant to refer to the person spoken to. The effect is usually confusing.

INDEFINITE	In civics class, *you* have an opportunity to learn how *your* government functions.
BETTER	In civics class, *students* have an opportunity to learn how *their* government functions.
INDEFINITE	In the new atlas *you* have many maps to consult.
BETTER	In the new atlas *there* are many maps to consult.

Exercise: Revise the sentences below to remove all indefinite reference of pronouns.

1. It says in the paper than an American pilot is being held prisoner.
2. Before we could get to our seats, they began to play.
3. In our assignment it says to read Conrad's *Lord Jim*.
4. In ancient Greece you could see plays given in outdoor theaters.
5. At my summer camp, they don't have competitive sports.
6. In the days of the Romans you had to use honey instead of sugar.
7. Bill wants to be a diplomat because it will give him a chance to travel.
8. It said in a book that Christopher Marlowe wrote Shakespeare's plays.
9. In the new Ford automobiles, it takes much less maintenance.
10. In the advertisement they tell you about a new type of shampoo.

7.15   Ambiguous Reference

The word *ambiguous* means "having two or more possible meanings." The reference of a pronoun is ambiguous if the pronoun may refer to more than one word. This situation arises whenever a noun or pronoun falls between the pronoun and its true antecedent.

AMBIGUOUS	Remove the dishes from the trays and wash *them*.
BETTER	Wash the dishes after you remove them from the trays.
AMBIGUOUS	They gave us directions but *they* got lost.
BETTER	The directions they gave us got lost.
AMBIGUOUS	Take the silver from the cabinet and polish *it*.
BETTER	Polish the silver after you take it from the cabinet.
AMBIGUOUS	Please stitch the hems of both dresses and press *them*.
BETTER	Please stitch and press the hems of both dresses.

Exercise: Revise the sentences below to remove all ambiguous pronoun references.

1. The firemen fought the flames until they disappeared.
2. The reporters told the listeners that they were confused about the issue under discussion.
3. Repair the locks on both doors and oil them.
4. Betty assured her mother that her headache was of no importance.
5. Sam convinced Al that his solution to the puzzle was correct.
6. Fred told his father than his Volvo had been stolen.
7. Matt told Jerry that the book belonged to him.
8. Remove the curtains from both windows and wash them.
9. Sue bet Barb that her team would win.
10. Jack told the doctor that he thought he looked tired.

7.16   Vague Reference

The words *this, which, that,* and *it* are sometimes used to refer to a preceding idea or chain of ideas. The reader is confused by this vague reference.

VAGUE   Jason was an unsuccessful poet and writer, *which* is
the reason he was so desperately unhappy.

BETTER   Jason was desperately unhappy because he was an
unsuccessful poet and writer.

VAGUE   Sonia had overslept and she had missed the bus. *It*
made it impossible for her to get to work on time.

BETTER   It was impossible for Sonia to get to work on time
because she had overslept and had missed the bus.

VAGUE   The snow had not been cleared from the streets by
the sanitation department, and the parking ban
was being put into effect. *That* made people
quite angry.

BETTER   People were quite angry because the snow had not
been cleared from the streets by the sanitation
department and the parking ban was being put
into effect.

VAGUE   Stan received his driver's license, and he passed
his final examination in algebra. *This* made
him happy.

BETTER   Stan was happy because he received his driver's
license and he passed his final examination
in algebra.

Exercise: Revise the sentences below to remove all vague references of pronouns.

1. Our timetable was outdated, which made us miss our train.

2. Paperbacks are inexpensive, which means we can all afford them.

3. Lincoln spoke briefly at Gettysburg. It was destined to become famous.

4. Physics is frequently called a difficult subject. This frightens many students.

5. Some of us missed two rehearsals, which infuriated the conductor.

6. The contractor built many different kinds of houses in the new development. This gives a pleasing variety.

7. Someone's car broke down in the tunnel, which delayed us.

8. The new novels present realistically the tragic problems of man in the modern world. That makes them depressing to read.

9. Bill practiced with his seven iron for weeks. This helped make him a better golfer.

10. Laura made a very high score on the test and it won her a scholarship.

Review Exercise: Revise the sentences below to remove vague, indefinite, or ambiguous reference of pronouns.

1. Tom told his father that his automobile needed new tires.

2. At college they expect you to take care of yourself.

3. They say that inflation is dangerous to our economy.

4. Pour the mixture into a mold when it is cold.

5. The survivors' faces showed no emotion, which amazed us.

6. I ate my lunch early, which meant that I was hungry before dinner time.

7. Betty and Jane were talking about her sister.

8. Forest fires destroy trees, which leads to erosion of the land.

9. Jean told her mother that she needed a new pair of boots.

10. The summer resort I like best is in Maine, and it is a good place to live.

11. The news from the Far East is bad, and this is disturbing.

12. Ed goes jogging each day. That keeps him healthy.

13. They say that you should eat some fruit each day.

14. Shakespeare was born in 1564 and died in 1616, which was not a very long life.

15. The American people must conserve their natural resources, for this may mean the difference between wealth and poverty in the future.

8.0 Adjective and Adverb Usage

Certain adverbs are formed by adding -ly to adjectives, as *sweet—sweetly*. The problem then is whether to use the modifier with or without the -ly ending after a verb.

8.1 Adverbs with Action Verbs

When a modifier comes just before an action verb, it is always an adverb, and no problem arises. When the modifier follows the action verb, there is a temptation to use an adjective rather than an adverb.

The problem is made more difficult by the fact that many adverbs have two forms, one with and the other without the -ly ending.

Shut the door *tight*.   Drive *slow*.   Don't play so *loud*.

All of the words used above as adverbs are also used as adjectives: a *loud* noise, a *slow* stream, a *tight* fit, and so on.

Most of the words that may be either adjectives or adverbs are words of one syllable. Adjectives of two or more syllables almost never have the same form for the adverb.

The *cautious* man crossed the street. (adjective)
The man crossed the street *cautiously*. (adverb)

The *thoughtful* writer prepared his letter. (adjective)
The writer *thoughtfully* prepared his letter. (adverb)

After an action verb use the _-ly_ form of the modifier if the modifier has two or more syllables.

8.2 Adjectives with Linking Verbs

Linking verbs are usually followed by adjectives rather than adverbs. The adjective is a predicate adjective and modifies the subject.

There is no problem with modifiers following the form of *be*, the most common linking verb. Most of the other linking verbs, however, may also be used as action verbs. As action verbs, they may be followed by adverbs.

The messenger *appeared swiftly*.
   (*appeared* is an action verb modified by an adverb.)

The messenger *appeared swift*.
   (*appeared* is a linking verb followed by a predicate adjective.)

The nurse *looked hurriedly* at her watch.
   (*looked* is an action verb modified by an adverb.)

The nurse *looked hurried*.
   (*looked* is a linking verb followed by a predicate adjective.)

The following verbs are linking verbs. Most of them may also be used as action verbs.

| look | appear | smell | stay | grow | seem |
| sound | feel | taste | remain | become | |

To decide whether a verb is used to link or to show action,

try substituting a form of *be*. If the sentence still makes sense, the verb is a linking verb.

The ambassador *grew* (apprehensive, apprehensively).
(*The ambassador was apprehensively* does not make sense. *The ambassador was apprehensive* makes sense; *grew* is a linking verb here.)

The ambassador *looked* (apprehensive, apprehensively) around the conference table. (*was* does not make sense with either modifier; *looked* is an action verb here.)

Exercise A: Choose the standard form from those given in parentheses.

1. Our team looks (envious, enviously) every time the other team is mentioned.
2. The students were looking (envious, enviously) at Bill's new Skyhawk.
3. The music sounded (soft, softly) as it came across the lake.
4. Emily looked (unhappy, unhappily) at the broken window.
5. Teresa played the accompaniment (perfect, perfectly).
6. Joe sprained his ankle (bad, badly) as he rounded second base.
7. Elaine is (real, really) happy about winning the scholarship.
8. It snowed (steady, steadily) for six hours.
9. The bride looks (beautiful, beautifully) in her wedding dress.
10. The novelist writes (beautiful, beautifully) about his native country.

Exercise B: Decide whether the italicized modifier is standard or nonstandard. If it is nonstandard, substitute the standard form.

1. The fish defrosted and began to smell *badly*.
2. Sally's voice sounds *strange* over the intercom.
3. When the boss is away, Bob acts *different*.
4. Jack handled the ball *clumsily* during the first quarter.
5. Take the bandage off as *gentle* as you can.

6. The music of Schoenberg sounds *harshly* to me.
7. See how *easy* the drawers slide in and out.
8. The coach feels quite *confidently* about Saturday's game.
9. The bread in the oven smells *tantalizingly*.
10. The directions for making frozen eggnog are not written *clear*.

8.3 This—These; That—Those

This and *that* modify singular words. *These* and *those* modify plural words. The words *kind, sort,* and *type* require a singular modifier.

NONSTANDARD	These kind of materials are not good quality.
STANDARD	This kind of material is not good quality.
NONSTANDARD	These sort of hats flatter her.
STANDARD	This sort of hat flatters her.

8.4 Them—Those

Those may be either a pronoun or an adjective. *Them* is always a pronoun and never an adjective.

NONSTANDARD	Did Joan use *them* remnants?
STANDARD	Did Joan use *those* remnants? (adjective)

8.5 Bad—Badly

In standard usage, *bad* is always used after linking verbs.

Linda felt bad. (*not* Linda felt badly)
Linda looked bad.
The meat smells bad.
The weather became bad.

8.6   Good—Well

Good is used only as an adjective to modify nouns and pronouns.

Well is an adjective when it means "in good health, of good appearance, or satisfactory." *Well* is used as an adverb to modify an action verb when it means that the action was performed properly or expertly.

> The dishwasher runs *well* now. (adverb)
> Mr. Gage seems *well* in spite of his difficulties. (adjective)
> Jill played *well* during tennis practice. (adverb)

8.7   Fewer—Less

Fewer is used to describe things that can be counted. *Less* refers to quantity or degree.

> Sheila is less friendly than her sister.
> He has had fewer disturbances today than yesterday.
> Mr. Maxwell is less ambitious than his partner.

Exercise: Decide whether the italicized words are standard or nonstandard usage. Substitute a standard form for each nonstandard one.

1. Scientists are paid *good* these days.
2. The team played *well* until Simmons was hurt.
3. I set out *them* tomato plants last week end.
4. Marion feels *badly* about losing the nomination.
5. Where can you get a better car for *less* money?
6. Since his operation, Mr. Bieler has been looking *well*.
7. Dennis, that suit looks especially *well* on you.
8. Dealers are reporting *less* demand for big cars.
9. *Them* andirons are over two hundred years old.
10. The sponge cake requires *less* sugar and *less* eggs.

11. Pumpkin doesn't taste very *well* unless you put it in a pie.
12. *Those* kind of rumors should be traced to their source.
13. This pen never writes very *good.*
14. How *well* do you play chess?
15. Each year *fewer* people attend the lectures.
16. Roy needs help and he needs it *bad.*
17. The room doesn't look *bad* with chartreuse walls.
18. Since we introduced the new machines in our accounting department, we have had far *less* errors.
19. *Fewer* people turned up at this meeting than at the last one.
20. I have never used *these* kind of paint sprayer before.

8.8 Comparative and Superlative

The comparative form is used to compare two things; the superlative is used in comparing more than two.

STANDARD   He may read the poems of T. S. Eliot or Robert Frost, but he will find Frost easier. (*not* easiest)

STANDARD   They lived both in Hartford and in Yonkers, but they liked Hartford better. (*not* best)

STANDARD   Of the five countries, the United States has the greatest nuclear force. (*not* greater)

8.9 The Double Comparison

The comparative form of a modifier is made either by adding -*er* or by using *more.* It is nonstandard to use both.

The superlative form of a modifier is made either by adding -*est* or by using *most.* It is nonstandard to use both.

NONSTANDARD   Bridget's home is much more larger than we thought.

STANDARD   Bridget's home is much larger than we thought.

NONSTANDARD	Sarah is more smarter than Mike.
STANDARD	Sarah is smarter than Mike.

NONSTANDARD	Rhode Island is the most smallest state in the union.
STANDARD	Rhode Island is the smallest state in the union.

8.10 Illogical Comparisons

The word _other_ is required in comparisons of an individual member with the rest of the group.

ILLOGICAL	The Times' James Reston is read by more congressmen than any columnist in the country. (Reston is also a columnist.)
CLEAR	The Times' James Reston is read by more congressmen than any _other_ columnist in the country.

ILLOGICAL	Shakespeare towered over every playwright in England.
CLEAR	Shakespeare towered over every _other_ playwright in England.

The words _than_ or _as_ are required in a compound comparison.

ILLOGICAL	Gas is as clean if not cleaner than oil.
CLEAR BUT AWKWARD	Gas is as clean _as_ if not cleaner than oil.
BETTER	Gas is as clean _as_ oil, if not cleaner.

ILLOGICAL	John had as many front-page stories if not more than the other reporters.
CLEAR	John had as many front-page stories _as_ the other reporters, if not more.

ILLOGICAL   Penn's chances of winning the Ivy League title
are as good if not better than Columbia's.

CLEAR   Penn's chances of winning the Ivy League title
are as good *as* Columbia's, if not better.

**Both parts of a comparison must be stated completely if there
is any chance of its being misunderstood.**

CONFUSING   The Soviets trust the Americans more than
the Chinese.

CLEAR   The Soviets trust the Americans more than the
Chinese *do.*

CLEAR   The Soviets trust the Americans more than
they trust the Chinese.

ILLOGICAL   The post of ambassador is more important
than a diplomat.

CLEAR   The post of ambassador is more important
than *that of* a diplomat.

BETTER   An ambassador's post is more important than
a diplomat's *is.*

Exercise: Revise the following sentences to make the comparisons
clear.

1. Sylvia is more interested in golf than Joe.

2. Which of the two plans do you think will be the
most workable?

3. Of all the students, Carol answered the questions
more thoughtfully.

4. The voters thought more highly of Mrs. Williams than
her opponent.

5. Of the two boys, John works fastest and most accurately.

6. When his integrity was questioned, he became more angrier
than ever.

7. Elliott is as charming if not more charming than his brother.

8. This suit is probably as expensive if not more expensive than that one.

9. The traffic on Interstate 57 is heavier than any highway in the country.

10. Vegetables are much more cheaper this month than last.

11. Of the two Irish dramatists, the best one, in my opinion, is Yeats.

12. The work of a file clerk is less interesting than a private secretary.

13. Herbert draws better than any student in his art class.

14. Your explanation is just as clear if not clearer than Joan's.

15. Bill likes his science teacher more than Gus.

16. We enjoyed *Macbeth* more than any of Shakespeare's plays.

17. Peggy insisted that she liked Ann as well as Charlotte.

18. Of the co-captains, Claire is really the best player.

8.11 The Double Negative

A double negative occurs when a negative word is added to a statement that is already negative The double negative is nonstandard usage.

NONSTANDARD	I wasn't doing nothing.
STANDARD	I wasn't doing anything.

NONSTANDARD	We don't have no bananas.
STANDARD	We don't have any bananas.

Hardly or *barely,* used with a negative word, is nonstandard.

NONSTANDARD	There wasn't hardly any fudge left.
STANDARD	There was hardly any fudge left.

NONSTANDARD	She couldn't scarcely believe it.
STANDARD	She could scarcely believe it.

Exercise: These sentences cover all of the problems of adjective and adverb usage in this section. Choose the standard form from those in parentheses.

1. There (is, isn't) hardly any bread left for sandwiches.
2. The chairperson doesn't speak (clear, clearly) enough.
3. Who is the (oldest, older), you or Sandy?
4. Of the two cities, Cleveland is the (most, more) densely populated.
5. I had a (real, really) good time at the party.
6. We had (less, fewer) interruptions in physics class than usual.
7. The workers grew (angry, angrily) when their foreman was dismissed.
8. This money (won't, will) be hardly enough to meet my financial obligations.
9. The blue vase looks (well, good) on the marble-topped table.
10. Mrs. Hadley (can, can't) get hardly any trained managers.
11. I slept (good, well) after that stiff basketball workout.
12. Judd is (easy, easily) the best player on the team.
13. He is good at playing guard, and he does (good, well) at center, too.
14. The oil painting looks particularly (good, well) over the fireplace.
15. Please take your places as (quiet, quietly) as possible.
16. You are sure to get results if you study (regular, regularly).
17. I haven't tightened (those, them) bolts on the fenders yet.
18. I (can, can't) hardly see with these old glasses.

9.0   Verb Usage

Most of the several thousand English verbs cause no problems of usage at all. They are **regular verbs.** That is, the past tense is formed by adding *-ed* or *-d* to the present, and the past participle is the same as the past tense form:

PRESENT	PAST	PAST PARTICIPLE
talk	talk*ed*	talk*ed*
print	print*ed*	print*ed*
crawl	crawl*ed*	crawl*ed*

There are about sixty commonly used verbs, however, whose past forms do not follow this pattern. They are **irregular verbs.** The most commonly used verbs, *be* and *have,* not only form the past tenses irregularly but change from person to person in the present tense: *I am, you are, he is, I have, he has.*

9.1   The Past Forms

The main problem with irregular verbs is the choice between the past form and the past participle form. These are two of the **principal parts** of every verb. (See Section 1.3.) All forms of any verb are made from the principal parts. Since they are always given in the same order in dictionaries and reference books, learning them in that order will make usage choices easier.

The past tense form is used alone. The past participle form is used with forms of *be* or *have*.

> Ben Franklin first *went* to work as a soap boiler. (past)
> The free gifts were *gone* quickly. (past participle with form of *be*)
> The troops *had* already *gone*. (past participle with form of *have*)

There are five groups of irregular verbs.

Group 1. The easiest of the irregular verbs are those that have the same form in all principal parts.

PRESENT	PAST	PAST PARTICIPLE
burst	burst	burst
cost	cost	cost
hit	hit	hit
hurt	hurt	hurt
put	put	put
set	set	set

Group 2. A second group that causes little difficulty is composed of verbs that have the same form for the past and the past participle.

PRESENT	PAST	PAST PARTICIPLE
bring	brought	brought
catch	caught	caught
dive	dived *or* dove*	dived
fight	fought	fought
flee	fled	fled

* Where two forms are given, both are standard usage, but the first is more common.

PRESENT	PAST	PAST PARTICIPLE
fling	flung	flung
get	got	got *or* gotten
lead	led	led
lend	lent	lent
lose	lost	lost
say	said	said
shine	shone	shone
sit	sat	sat
sting	stung	stung
swing	swung	swung

Exercise A: In the sentences below, the present form of the verb is given in parentheses. Substitute either past or past participle, whichever the sentence requires.

1. Marie (bring) me a French newspaper.
2. Rob has already (catch) two rainbow trout.
3. The fall from the tree had (hurt) the tiny sparrow.
4. Marcia has been (sting) by a hornet.
5. Jake has (lose) his status as an amateur by playing professional ball.
6. The bank has (lend) Mr. Fielding some money for home repairs.
7. When the river began to rise, the campers (flee).
8. Banners had been (swing) from wires across the street.
9. The dispute may be (bring) before the United Nations.
10. The wind had (fling) the Christmas decorations to the pavement.
11. The election of 1976 (bring) Jimmy Carter to the White House.
12. The prisoner had (lose) count of the days.
13. The danger of an infected leg was (bring) to my attention.
14. The shortstop (catch) the ball with a spectacular backhand stab.
15. The eye ointment (sting) at first.

Exercise B: Choose the correct form from those in parentheses.

1. A water main (burst, bust, busted) and flooded the street.
2. The pilot's parachute was (catched, caught) in a tree.
3. The aurora borealis (shined, shone) brightly in the sky.
4. The shaving lotion (stang, stung) too much to suit Bill.
5. The colonel (swang, swung) reinforcements into the battle.
6. Roberta (lended, lent) me her umbrella.
7. Nancy had already (losed, lost) one of her new earrings.
8. Uncle Ed had a picture of the tuna he had (catched, caught).
9. The cheerleaders (flang, flinged, flung) their arms into the air.
10. The animals (fleed, fled) as the hunters approached.
11. The officer (leaded, led) the dazed residents to safety.
12. The cat's eyes (shined, shone) brightly in the glare of the headlights.

Group 3. Another group of irregular verbs adds **n** or **en** to the past form to make the past participle.

PRESENT	PAST	PAST PARTICIPLE
bear	bore	borne*
beat	beat	beaten
bite	bit	bitten
break	broke	broken
choose	chose	chosen
freeze	froze	frozen
speak	spoke	spoken
steal	stole	stolen
swear	swore	sworn
tear	tore	torn
wear	wore	worn

Exercise A: Choose the standard form from those in parentheses.

1. The Steuben glass vase was (broke, broken) beyond repair.

* Note that *borne* retains the final *e*.

2. The candidate (beared, bore) all of the campaign expenses himself.

3. Marcia has been (chose, chosen) queen of the winter festival.

4. The letter had been (tore, torn) into bits and thrown on the floor.

5. The sherbet (froze, frozen) quickly in the new refrigerator.

6. Nan and Abbey (weared, wore) their band uniforms to the game.

7. The defendant (sweared, swore) under oath that he was innocent.

8. Two valuable paintings have been (stole, stolen) from the museum.

9. The Senate minority leader (spoke, spoken) persuasively.

10. Leslie (teared, tore) the advertisement from the paper and took it to the store.

11. While fishing, Mr. Sloan was (bit, bitten) by black flies.

12. The fender was dented and the taillight was (broke, broken).

13. The coach has (bore, borne) this heavy schedule for years.

14. My compass was (broke, broken), so I drew the circles with a jar lid.

15. Wilmington has (beat, beaten) us three years in a row.

16. Mike has already (broke, broken) three test tubes in chemistry class.

17. Lynn has hardly (spoken, spoke) to me since my arrival.

18. Have you (beat, beaten) the cream yet, Chris?

19. I have no desire to be (bit, bitten) by a black widow spider.

20. Have you (chosen, chose) a college yet, Paula?

Exercise B: The present form of the verb is given. Substitute past or past participle, whichever the sentence requires.

1. Somehow the robber (break) through the police barricade.

2. The lake froze over in October and remained (freeze) until May.

3. The students had (wear) a path across the grass.

4. The new President was (swear) in by the Chief Justice.

5. Pat cannot read because she has (break) her glasses.

6. All employees' salaries have been temporarily (freeze).
7. The Governor (speak) about the proposed bond issue.
8. Has the Dramatic Club (choose) its next play?
9. Our outboard motor was (steal) from our summer cottage.
10. I haven't (speak) a word of French since I left Quebec.
11. Fran was (beat) badly in the semifinals.
12. The gale had (tear) the election posters down.
13. The X-rays showed that Gary's leg had been (break).
14. Has the Most Valuable Player been (choose)?
15. The insurance company (bear) all of Phil's medical expenses.
16. Joe (tear) his jacket on the edge of his locker.
17. Sam has (choose) *The Bermuda Triangle Mystery—Solved* for his report.
18. Our TV set has been (break) for two weeks.
19. The rain had (freeze) on the windshield.
20. The defendant (swear) that he had never met the witness.

Group 4. Another group of irregular verbs is alike in changing the middle vowel from **i** in the present, to **a** in the past, and to **u** in the past participle. Memorize these seven verbs as a unit. They are the only verbs to follow this pattern. Let no other verbs into this group.

PRESENT	PAST	PAST PARTICIPLE
begin	began	begun
drink	drank	drunk
ring	rang	rung
sing	sang	sung
sink	sank *or* sunk	sunk
spring	sprang *or* sprung	sprung
swim	swam	swum

Exercise: The present form is given in parentheses. Substitute the past or past participle, whichever the sentence requires.

1. Cheers (ring) out when the first baseman dropped the ball.
2. A pipe in the basement has (spring) a leak.

3. The ship had already (sink) when the Coast Guard cutter arrived.

4. Larry (swim) the length of the pool in twenty seconds.

5. The choir (sing) portions of Handel's *Messiah*.

6. Just as I was leaving the house, the telephone (ring).

7. The men (spring) to their feet when the colonel entered.

8. Ed, have you (begin) writing your research paper?

9. The skin divers (swim) down to 100 feet.

10. The director stopped us after we had (sing) a few bars.

11. A tree had (spring) up through a crack in the basement.

12. The defeated governor (sink) into obscurity.

13. They (drink) a toast to their winning team.

14. The patient had faithfully (drink) the prescribed liquors.

15. The audience rose and (sing) "The Star-Spangled Banner."

16. Our relay team (swim) in the state finals.

17. Jerry has already (sink) eight long shots.

18. I was so thirsty I (drink) two bottles of ginger ale.

19. The geologists (sink) a deep hole in the mountain.

20. We (drink) a whole case of Coke at the party.

21. The excavation for the new high school was (begin) last month.

22. You ought to have (ring) for the nurse.

23. By five o'clock the crowd had (begin) to thin out.

24. The ore freighter *Edmund Fitzgerald* (sink) in Lake Superior.

25. By spring the economic outlook had (begin) to improve.

Group 5. Another group of irregular verbs is alike in making the past participle from the present form rather than from the past form.

PRESENT	PAST	PAST PARTICIPLE
blow	blew	blown
come	came	come
do	did	done

PRESENT	PAST	PAST PARTICIPLE
draw	drew	drawn
drive	drove	driven
eat	ate	eaten
fall	fell	fallen
give	gave	given
go	went	gone
grow	grew	grown
know	knew	known
ride	rode	ridden
rise	rose	risen
run	ran	run
see	saw	seen
shake	shook	shaken
slay	slew	slain
take	took	taken
throw	threw	thrown
write	wrote	written

Exercise A: Choose the standard form from those in parentheses.

1. Has Phil (wrote, written) to you since he was transferred overseas?

2. The students have (gone, went) for registration and placement tests.

3. We (blew, blowed) on our soup before tasting it.

4. Sid has (gone, went) to the cellar for the cider.

5. Fran must have (knowed, known) where we were going.

6. The governor had (shaken, shook) hands with a thousand people.

7. Have you ever (driven, drove) across the continent?

8. Wild roses have (grown, grew, growed) here for many years.

9. Mr. Jenner was badly (shaken, shook) by his near accident.

10. Our drive for funds (fallen, fell) short of our goal.

11. This parsley was (growed, grew, grown) in our own back yard.

12. Just as we sat down, the fuse (blew, blowed) again.

13. Tom had never (rid, rode, ridden) on an elephant before.

14. The catcher (throwed, threw) the ball over the second baseman's head.

15. He (ran, run) the pump all night to keep his cellar dry.

16. I (saw, seen) a good play last night.

17. I had never (seen, saw) a Broadway play before.

18. Maureen would have (gone, went) if she had not made other plans.

19. The Declaration of Independence was (wrote, written) by Thomas Jefferson.

20. The basket that won the game was (thrown, threw) by my sister.

Exercise B: The present form is given in parentheses. Substitute the past or past participle, whichever the sentence requires.

1. I (see) a fawn in the woods this morning.

2. A wealthy alumnus has (give) a million dollars to the college library.

3. Laura is lonely because her friends have (go) to camp.

4. Angrily, he (throw) his racket down on the court.

5. Paul has (write) letters to half a dozen agencies.

6. Mr. Voss (do) his best to convince us we were wrong.

7. We (drive) slowly because we were looking for the exit to Scarsdale.

8. The senior class (go) to New York by chartered plane.

9. The daffodils (grow) rapidly in the warm sunshine.

10. The ship's whistle (blow) a final warning to the visitors.

11. The buses were (draw) up in a neat row.

12. Have you ever (eat) a mango?

13. Mr. Cross (give) the school his collection of rare books.

14. The storm had (shake) most of the apples off the trees.

15. The room clerk insisted that he had (do) the best he could.

16. I should have (know) it was too far to walk.

17. Someone had (take) my suitcase by mistake.

18. Custer and most of his men were (slay) by Chief Sitting Bull.

19. Stocks have (fall) sharply in the last week.

20. Ms. Knowles has (rise) from teller to vice-president in ten years.

Exercise C: The present form is given. Substitute the past or past participle as the sentence may require.

1. The Secretary of State has (know) their intentions for a long time.

2. The material in this book was (draw) from many sources.

3. The minister (do) all he could for the unfortunate man.

4. Some American economists have (go) to advise the Iranians.

5. The mechanic had (take) an hour to recharge the battery.

6. Mr. Sloane's small business has (grow) into a large corporation.

7. The witness said that he had (know) the defendant for many years.

8. Tom (draw) an amusing cartoon for the school paper.

9. Janice (see) an interesting editorial in yesterday's paper.

10. We (do) what we could to repair the damage.

11. Mrs. Quinn brought us a cake just after we had (eat) our dessert.

12. The burglar (run) when the dogs began to bark.

13. The wind had (blow) great drifts of snow against the garage door.

14. By March 7, Cologne had (fall) to the Allies.

15. Hurricane winds have (blow) ships from their moorings.

16. Have you (ride) in Joe's new Chevette?

17. The manager has (give) Bill a substantial raise.

18. Maureen would have (go) if she had been invited.

19. Has Phil (write) to you since he was transferred to Lakehurst?

20. Dee has already (give) two pints of blood to the Red Cross.

9.2 Problem Pairs of Verbs

Three pairs of verbs are often confused because the meanings of each pair are closely related. They are related, but they are not identical. To use these verbs correctly, it is important to keep their meanings distinct.

Lie and lay. The verb *lay* means "to put or place something." The verb *lie* has eight or nine meanings, all having in common the idea of "being in a horizontal position, or to remain, or to be situated."*

Lie is always an intransitive verb. It never has an object. *Lay* is a transitive verb. It almost always has an object. The principal parts of these verbs are as follows:

PRESENT	PAST	PAST PARTICIPLE
lay	laid	laid
lie	lay	lain

Sit and set. The verb *sit* usually means "to rest with the legs bent and the back upright," but there are many other related meanings. The verb *set* means "to put or place something."

Sit is an intransitive verb; it never has an object. *Set* is a transitive verb; it almost always has an object. The principal parts of the verbs are as follows:

PRESENT	PAST	PAST PARTICIPLE
sit	sat	sat
set	set	set

Rise and raise. The verb *rise* means "to go to a higher position." The verb *raise* means "to lift to a higher position."

Rise is intransitive; it never has an object. *Raise* is transitive; it almost always has an object. Things *rise* by themselves; they are *raised* by something else. The principal parts of these verbs are as follows:

* There is a homonym meaning "to tell an untruth." The principal parts of this verb are *lie, lied, lied*.

PRESENT	PAST	PAST PARTICIPLE
rise	rose	risen
raise	raised	raised

Note: It is very difficult to make any general statements about English usage that will hold without exception. There are exceptions to the statements given above about the three pairs of verbs:

> The sun *sets*. (intransitive)
> The mixture will *set* in an hour. (intransitive)
> *Sit* her up. (transitive)
> The hens are *laying* well. (intransitive)

Exercise A: Choose the standard form from those in parentheses.

1. Donna told the dog to (lay, lie) down.
2. I was (lying, laying) down when the telephone rang.
3. The taxi drivers (laid, lay) the blame on the mayor.
4. My books (lay, laid) where I had left them.
5. The salesperson (lay, laid) some samples on the table.
6. A large tree was (laying, lying) across the road.
7. The Secretary-General (laid, lay) his plan before the Security Council.
8. Joe's wallet had (laid, lain) in the driveway all night.
9. At the foot of Hallet Peak (lies, lays) Dream Lake.
10. The Atlantic cable was (laid, lain) in 1858.
11. The box of colored slides is (laying, lying) on the sofa.
12. Grandfather (lays, lies) down every afternoon for an hour.
13. Have you (laid, lain) aside enough money for the trip?
14. Beyond that ridge (lies, lays) Asheville.
15. The document was (lying, laying) unheeded on the floor.
16. The capital is to (lie, lay) untouched until the children become of age.
17. They have already (laid, lain) the foundations for the new school.
18. Andy (lay, laid) the birch logs in the fireplace.

Exercise B: Choose the standard form from those in parentheses.

1. Lightning does not strike the ground but (raises, rises) from it.
2. The sun (rose, raised) at six-fifteen this morning.
3. This new hybrid corn was (raised, risen) in Iowa.
4. The stockholders (raised, rose) a storm of protest.
5. Prices of consumer goods have continued to (rise, raise).
6. The money for an orchestra was (raised, risen) by private subscription.
7. Everyone (raised, rose) when the President entered the stadium.
8. The American colonies (raised, rose) in revolt against the unjust taxation.
9. His testimony (raises, rises) some interesting questions.
10. The curtain was just (raising, rising) as we got to our seats.
11. Murmurs of astonishment (raised, rose) from the audience.
12. My cake didn't (raise, rise) because I forgot the baking powder.
13. The ICC gave the bus line permission to (raise, rise) its fares.
14. Dave (raised, rose) quickly and picked up the receiver.
15. Will everyone in favor please (rise, raise) his hand?
16. The price of steel has (raised, risen) four dollars per ton.
17. Our spirits (raised, rose) when we heard the half-time score.
18. The ranger saw smoke (raising, rising) from the woods.
19. New buildings have (risen, raised) on every street.
20. A flag pole was (risen, raised) in front of the school.

Exercise C: Choose the standard form from those given in parentheses.

1. You will either have to stand or (sit, set) on the floor.
2. Several students were (sitting, setting) at the soda fountain.
3. (Set, sit) the tomatoes on the window sill.
4. We had to (sit, set) in the waiting room for an hour.
5. You can (sit, set) the box on the floor.
6. Every long run (sat, set) the stadium in an uproar.

7. We were (setting, sitting) on the fifty-yard line.
8. I was so nervous I couldn't (set, sit) still.
9. Please (sit, set) the music racks and chairs on the stage.
10. We (set, sat) the flats for the scenery against the wall and painted them.
11. Shall we (set, sit) in the balcony or in the orchestra?
12. Have you ever (sat, set) for your portrait?
13. Luanne wanted me to (sit, set) with her at the concert.
14. The Pates (set, sat) up a trust fund for their children.
15. That old house has been (sitting, setting) there for a century.

9.3 Distinguishing Two Actions in the Past

In telling of things that have happened in the past, it is sometimes necessary to tell of one thing that happened before another.

The past perfect tense is used to tell about the earlier of two past happenings.

	EARLIER	LATER
STANDARD	I *had come* here	before the war began.

	LATER	EARLIER
STANDARD	I just learned that	you *had* not *eaten* lunch.

NONSTANDARD	I told that editor that I *have* sold the manuscript.
STANDARD	I told that editor that I *had* sold the manuscript.

NONSTANDARD	The guide mentioned places we already *saw*.
STANDARD	The guide mentioned places we *had* already *seen*.

NONSTANDARD	Anita began to realize what she *has* done.
STANDARD	Anita began to realize what she *had* done.

9.4 The Tense of Infinitives

The perfect infinitive (see Section 1.11) is used to show an action earlier than that of the main verb. The present infinitive is used to show action at the same time as that of the main verb, or later.

Sid is happy *to have had* the opportunity. (earlier time)
Sid was happy *to have had* the opportunity. (The perfect infinitive shows the earlier of the two past times.)

Ms. Allen is pleased *to review* it. (same time)
Ms. Allen was pleased *to review* it. (same time)

Alicia plans *to volunteer* Monday. (later time)

The present infinitive is used if the main verb contains some form of the verb *have*.

NONSTANDARD	Lisa would have liked *to have seen* it.
STANDARD	Lisa would have liked *to see* it. (same time)
STANDARD	Lisa would like (now) *to have seen* it. (earlier)

NONSTANDARD	Jeff planned *to have given* you the key. (The intention preceded the giving.)
STANDARD	Jeff had planned *to give* you the key.
STANDARD	Jeff planned *to give* you the key.

9.5 The Split Infinitive

When a modifier appears between *to* and the verb in an infinitive phrase, the infinitive is said to be split. It is wise to avoid splitting the infinitive. Usually, the modifier can be placed before or after. There are some sentences, however, in which a split infinitive is the only means of avoiding clumsy expression.

NEEDLESSLY SPLIT	The spy planned to quickly destroy the code.
IMPROVED	The spy planned to destroy the code quickly.
NEEDLESSLY SPLIT	The Phoenix appeared to swiftly rise from the ashes.
IMPROVED	The Phoenix appeared to rise swiftly from the ashes.
AWKWARD	The plan was substantially to reduce costs.
PERMISSIBLE	The plan was to substantially reduce costs.

9.6 The Tense of Participles

The present participle and the past participle show an action or state of being at the same time as that of the main verb.

Being confident, Lisa enjoys a challenge.
(Present participle; same time as main verb.)
Aggravated by her refusal, Jim left the premises.
(Past participle; same time as main verb.)
Being basically clumsy, the waiter spilled the soup.
(Present participle; same time as main verb.)

The perfect participle shows an action or state of being earlier than that of the main verb.

STANDARD	*Having won* the match, Bjorn Borg *left* the court. (The winning occurred before the leaving.)
STANDARD	*Having signed* the treaty, the President *announced* the nuclear weapons ban. (The signing took place before the announcement.)

NONSTANDARD	*Appearing* in two hits, the actor *became* famous.
STANDARD	*Having appeared* in two hits, the actor *became* famous.
NONSTANDARD	*Being* famous, the actor *adopted* a superior air.
STANDARD	*Having become* famous, the actor *adopted* a superior air.
NONSTANDARD	*Being* a "prima donna," he soon *became* unemployed.
STANDARD	*Having become* a "prima donna," he soon *became* unemployed.

Exercise: Change the nonstandard usage to standard usage in the following sentences.

1. I knew I met you somewhere before.
2. Aren't you going to ever join our club, Jerry?
3. Notre Dame scored a touchdown before we reached our seats.
4. Gaining an upset victory, the team left the field in high spirits.
5. Betty would have preferred to have visited the Guggenheim Museum.
6. I planned to have called you last week about the picnic.
7. Dave is determined to somehow raise a hundred dollars.
8. Marie would have liked to have gone to the exhibit.
9. We planted the trees that we have brought from Maine.
10. Sinking eight long shots, Mark was easily the hero of the game.
11. We are hoping to eventually buy a cottage at the lake.
12. We hoped to have finished the job before now.
13. Receiving an invitation to testify, Ms. Marks prepared to leave for Washington, D.C.
14. Helen's family was delighted to hear that she won a National Merit Scholarship.
15. The new mayor put into effect all the reforms he promised during the campaign.

16. Reading the instructions more carefully this time, Dad revised his income-tax report.

17. The local fans expected their heroes to easily win the World Series.

18. Never eating pizza before in her life, Aunt Beth hesitated to order it.

9.7 Shall and Will

Earlier practice, which some people still insist upon, is as follows:

Future time is shown in the first person by *shall* with the verb. Future time is shown in the second and third persons by *will* with the verb.

Emphasis or determination about future action is shown in the first person by *will* and by *shall* in the second and third persons.

	FUTURE TIME	EMPHASIS
FIRST PERSON:	We shall leave later.	We will vote.
SECOND PERSON:	You will dine there.	You shall vote.
THIRD PERSON:	They will answer soon.	They shall answer now.

Today, however, the usage of *shall* and *will* is undergoing rapid change. In speech, the general custom is to use the contractions *I'll, he'll, you'll* which suit either *shall* or *will*. In good writing today, the tendency is to use *will* for all three persons.

9.8 The Subjunctive

The subjunctive form of the verb is used to express (1) a statement contrary to fact; (2) a request or command; (3) a wish, hope, or prayer.

> *If he were here,* he would have the solution. (contrary
>   to fact)
> The general demanded *that they surrender.* (command)
> The Lord *be* with you and with your spirit. (prayer)

The subjunctive forms of the verb *be* are as follows: *be* with all persons in the present tense except for clauses contrary to fact, which take *were.*

> If this *be* the reason, I am pleased.
> If I *were* you, I would learn it.

For all other verbs, the only difference between regular forms and the subjunctive is that the *s* is dropped in the third person singular.

> Charles urged that she *grant* the audience.
> The queen insisted that he *leave* at once.

The words <u>would have</u> are not used in a clause beginning with if or <u>even though</u>.

NONSTANDARD	If she would have asked, she could have been helped.
STANDARD	If she *had* asked, she could have been helped.
NONSTANDARD	If the Harts would have testified, it would be over now.
STANDARD	If the Harts *had* testified, it would be over now.

Exercise: Find the nonstandard usage in each of the following sentences. Supply the standard form.

1. If Pete would have kept his boat in the garage, it would not have been damaged.

2. If I was you, Pat, I would take a foreign language.

3. We would be there by now if the car would not have stalled.

4. If the children would have waited, I would have given them the money.

5. If Marion was here, we could leave now.

6. If I would have studied for the test, I would have made a higher grade.

7. I move that the meeting is adjourned.

8. If the air-conditioning was on, we would be more comfortable.

9. The Fire Chief has ordered that the school holds more fire drills.

10. If your instructions would have been more detailed, I would not have made these mistakes.

11. I know what I would do if I was in charge.

12. Even if you would have sent the letter yesterday, it would not have arrived in time.

13. The parents request that a nurse is in attendance daily.

14. If he would have given us a ride, we would be there now.

15. Even though we would have worked hard, we could not have finished in time.

10.0 The Right Word

The preceding pages of this Handbook have been concerned with problems of usage. They have presented choices of words and constructions that are accepted as **standard usage**—the kind of usage that is appropriate at all times and in all places.

Some forms and constructions have been marked **nonstandard usage.** While these may go unchallenged or unnoticed on the playing field or in the locker room, they are nonstandard because they are not acceptable everywhere. In many situations they mark the user as careless or untrained in the English language.

American English is not composed of just *standard* and *nonstandard* usages. Every good dictionary makes other distinctions such as *colloquial, slang, dialectal, archaic, poetic.* These labels limit the areas in which a word or construction is accepted. Thus, some words are acceptable in poetry but nowhere else. Slang expressions are acceptable only in everyday speech, not in writing.

A special note should be made of the term **colloquial.** Colloquial language is the homely, informal language of everyday speech and writing. You would not expect to find it in a government document or in a religious service, but there is no objection to colloquial usage in school, in business, or in ordinary everyday situations.

The glossary that follows lists alphabetically (a) usage items not covered in the preceding pages, and (b) words commonly confused as to meaning. Many of the usage items deal with idiom, the normal way of combining words to convey meaning in English.

This glossary is too short to cover all the problems and questions that may arise. It is intended only as a first resort; if it fails, consult a good dictionary.

Distinctions of Meaning and Items of Usage

accept, except To *accept* is to agree to something or to receive something willingly. *To except* is to exclude or omit. As a preposition, *except* means "but" or "excluding."

> Jane *accepted* the invitation hesitantly. (verb)
> The union will *except* all unskilled workers. (verb)
> No one *except* Rob remained to finish the job. (preposition)

advice, advise You *advise* someone. What you give him is *advice*.

affect, effect *Affect* is a verb meaning either to influence or to pretend. *Effect* as a verb means to accomplish or to produce as a result. As a noun, *effect* means result.

agree to, with, on You agree *to* something such as a plan of action. You agree *with* someone else. Or, something such as spinach does not agree *with* you. You agree with others *on* a course of action.

allusion, illusion, delusion An *allusion* is a reference to something. An *illusion* is a false idea or a faulty interpretation of the facts. A *delusion* is a belief in something that is contrary to fact.

> The professor made an *allusion* to her excellent essay.
> Jean had the *illusion* that promptness was unimportant.
> Carol suffers from the *delusion* that wealth is happiness.

anywheres, nowheres, somewheres   The final *s* is in error. The words are *anywhere, nowhere, somewhere.*

alumna, alumnus   An *alumna* is a female graduate; the plural is *alumnae.* An *alumnus* is a male graduate; the plural is *alumni.* Male and female graduates of a coeducational college or high school are referred to *alumni.*

all right   The misspelling *alright* is nonstandard usage. The two words are separate.

all the   Clumsy and nonstandard in such expressions as "all the longer," "all the farther," and so on.

> NONSTANDARD   Is that all the longer he made it?
> STANDARD   Didn't he make it any longer than that?

altogether, all together   *Altogether* means entirely or on the whole. *All together* means that all parts of a group are considered at once.

> His account of the facts is *altogether* incorrect. (entirely)
> The family went to church *all together.*

among, between   *Between* expresses the joining or separation of *two* people or things. *Among* refers to a group of three or more. There are some group situations in which *between* is clearly wrong. There are others when it is clear, accurate usage, but only when pairs of people or things within a larger group are being considered.

> NONSTANDARD   *Between* the six of them, they planned
>   the escapade.
> STANDARD   *Among* the six of them, they planned
>   the escapade.
> STANDARD   There were a number of clashes *between*
>   the fans at the championship game.

amount, number   *Amount* is used to indicate a total sum of things. It is usually used to refer to items that cannot be counted. *Number* is used to refer to items that can be counted.

The *amount* of effort is staggering. (*effort* cannot
be counted)
The *number* of complaints increased. (*complaints* can
be counted.)

angry at, with You are angry *with* a person and angry *at* a
thing.

apt, likely, liable These three words have in common the
meaning of *probable*. However, they cannot be substituted for
each other at random. With respect to probability, *apt* means
"naturally inclined to." *Likely* means "something that can reasonably be expected." *Liable* means "subject to something,
usually something unpleasant."

Children are *apt* to be cranky when they are tired.
The southern senators are *likely* to filibuster.
Norris is *liable* to fail if he doesn't study.

bad, badly See Section 8.5

because Do not use *because* to introduce a noun clause.
This is a common fault in student compositions.

AWKWARD   Because he sprained his ankle is the reason
he is out.

BETTER   He is out *because* he sprained his ankle.

AWKWARD   The reason they spoke is *because* they
were angry.

BETTER   They spoke *because* they were angry.

being This completely acceptable present participle is most
safely used as part of a main verb. Used as a modifier it creates
extremely awkward sentences. *Being as* and *being that* are not
satisfactory substitutes for *since* or *because*.

AWKWARD   Being a partner in the corporation, she had to
address the stockholders.

BETTER   Because she is a partner in the corporation, she
had to address the stockholders.

beside, besides   *Beside* means at the side of. *Besides* means in addition to.

Sitting *beside* the mayor was the chief of police.
There were icy roads *besides* poor visibility to worry about.

between each   *Between* cannot be followed by a singular noun.

NONSTANDARD	Between each class, Jane went to the library.
STANDARD	Between *classes,* Jane went to the library.
NONSTANDARD	Between every quarter, he bought a hot dog.
STANDARD	Between *quarters,* he bought hot dogs.

borrow, lend   *Borrow* and *lend* are verbs. You *borrow from* someone. You *lend to* someone.

NONSTANDARD	Will she *borrow* me her curling iron?
STANDARD	Will she *lend* me her curling iron?
STANDARD	May I *borrow* your curling iron?

bring, take   *Bring* means motion toward someone or some place; *take* means motion away from someone or some place.

I will *take* her to the railroad station. (*away* from here)
They will *bring* us the newspaper clippings. (*toward* us)

but that, but what   The word *but* has a negative meaning. If it is preceded by another negative, it creates a double negative situation.

NONSTANDARD	I have *no* doubt *but that* she will take the job.
STANDARD	I have *no* doubt that she will take the job.
NONSTANDARD	There is not a chance *but what* Peter won't go.
STANDARD	There is not a chance that Peter won't go.

continual, continuous   *Continual* means occurring repeatedly or at intervals over a long period. *Continuous* means extending without interruption in space or time.

The meeting was delayed by his *continual* interruptions.
The *continuous* absence of rain increases the danger of
forest fires.

compliment, complement A *compliment* is a remark spoken
in praise. A *complement* is something needed to complete a
whole.

can, may *Can* means able or having the power to do something. *May* is used to ask or to grant permission. It also expresses the probability of something happening.

Can you complete the assignment? (ability)
May I take the car tonight? (permission)
They *may* arrive too late. (probability)

Could is the past tense of *can;* might is the past tense of *may.*

differ from, with One thing or person differs *from* another in
characteristics. You differ *with* someone when you disagree with
him.

different from In most situations *different from* is better
usage than *different than.* However, there are some situations
in which *than* must be used to avoid awkward expression.

Jane's experiment is different *from* mine.
Susan's attitude is much different *than* his.

emigrate, immigrate To *emigrate* is to leave one's homeland.
To *immigrate* is to enter a country for the purpose of settling
there. An *emigrant* is one who is on his way from a former
home. An *immigrant* is one who has arrived in a new country.

etc. The abbreviation for *et cetera,* meaning "and so forth,"
or "and others." The abbreviation is avoided in most writing.
If it is used, it must not be preceded by *and,* because the *et*
means "and."

fewer, less See Section 8.7.

formally, formerly *Formally* means in a formal manner. *Formerly* means previously.

> He was *formerly* associated with that insurance company.
> It was presented *formally* to the Board of Directors.

good, well See Section 8.6.

had of, off of The *of* is both unnecessary and undesirable.

NONSTANDARD	We wish you *had of* called first.
STANDARD	We wish you *had* called first.

NONSTANDARD	Please take the scarves *off of* the bureau.
STANDARD	Please take the scarves *off* the bureau.

hanged, hung Criminals are *hanged*. Things are *hung* on walls, hooks, or elsewhere.

> In some countries, criminals are still *hanged*.
> The bunting was *hung* from the rafters.

in, into *In* means inside something. *Into* tells of motion from the outside to the inside of something.

NONSTANDARD	The milk was put *in* the refrigerator.
STANDARD	The milk was put *into* the refrigerator.

NONSTANDARD	The crowd poured *in* the stadium.
STANDARD	The crowd poured *into* the stadium.

imply, infer A speaker or writer suggests or *implies* something. The reader, listener, or observer comes to a conclusion or *infers* something on the basis of what he sees and hears.

> The delegate *implied* that he was anti-American.
> His colleagues *inferred* that he would vote against it.

ingenious, ingenuous *Ingenious* means clever and resourceful. *Ingenuous* means frank and honest.

kind, sort, type See Section 8.3.

kind of a, sort of a The *a* is unnecessary and ungrammatical.

NONSTANDARD	What *kind of a* job did Juan look for?
STANDARD	What *kind of* job did Juan look for?

lay, lie See Section 9.2.

leave, let *Leave* means to go away from. *Let* means permit. The principal parts are *leave, left, left,* and *let, let, let.*

NONSTANDARD	Please *leave* Henry stay longer.
STANDARD	Please *let* Henry stay longer.
NONSTANDARD	He should have *left* the child go.
STANDARD	He should not have *let* the child go.
STANDARD	*Leave* her alone or she will be angry. (Depart.)
STANDARD	*Let* her alone. (Do not interfere.)

like, as, as if There is a tendency to accept *like* as a conjunction introducing a clause, but this usage is not yet fully established. *Like* is better used as a preposition.

NOT ACCEPTED	She feels *like* we do about that magazine.
BETTER	She feels *as* we do about that magazine.
NOT ACCEPTED	Kathy acts *like* she is certain of the promotion.
BETTER	Kathy acts *as if* she is certain of the promotion.

majority This word can be used only with items that can be counted. It is incorrectly used in speaking of time or distance.

NONSTANDARD	The *majority* of the grass was mowed.
STANDARD	*Most* of the grass was mowed.
NONSTANDARD	The *majority* of the air is polluted.
STANDARD	*Most* of the air is polluted.
NONSTANDARD	The *majority* of the population knows the danger of narcotics.
STANDARD	*Most* of the population knows the danger of narcotics.

of When *could have, might have, must have,* and similar phrases are spoken, they usually come out as contractions: *could've, might've, must've,* and so on. Because the contracted form *'ve* sounds like *of,* some persons write mistakenly *would of, might of, must of.*

> NONSTANDARD   Kim *must of* gone home.
> STANDARD   Kim *must have* gone home.

percent, percentage *Percent* is correctly used only when preceded by a number. When there is no preceding number, *percentage* is correct.

> Nearly 10 *percent* of the proceeds was taken.
> A large *percentage* of our taxes are used for defense.

raise, rise See Section 9.2.

reason is because The less awkward expression is *The reason is that.*

> AWKWARD   The reason for his sorrow is *because* he was
> turned down.
> BETTER   The reason for his sorrow is *that* he was
> turned down.

> AWKWARD   The reason his car wouldn't stop is *on account
> of* the brakes didn't work.
> BETTER   The reason his car wouldn't stop is *that* the
> brakes did not work.

seldom ever The *ever* is unnecessary. You can say instead *seldom, very seldom,* or *hardly ever.*

> AWKWARD   They seldom ever went to the sports events.
> BETTER   They very seldom went to the sports events.

so There is a good deal of objection to this completely acceptable conjunction on the grounds that it is overused. If you overuse it, try some other connective. *So* as a conjunction usually indicates result. The clause it introduces states the result; the main clause states the cause. You can eliminate the *so* entirely by changing the main clause to a subordinate clause introduced by *since* or *because*.

        CAUSE   RESULT

    The play was a hit *so* the cast rejoiced.

        CAUSE   RESULT

    Since the play was a hit, the cast rejoiced.

So is correctly used in place of *so that* to indicate result.

    Peg left Jill's house immediately *so that* she would get to work on time.

    Peg left Jill's house immediately *so* she would get to work on time.

So should never be used for emphasis unless it is followed by a clause beginning with *that*.

    NONSTANDARD   They were *so* impatient.

       STANDARD   They were *so* impatient *that* they annoyed everyone.

way, ways   *Ways* is misused when it refers to distance.

11.0 Capitalization

11.1 A.D., B.C., I, O

Capitalize the abbreviations *A.D.* and *B.C.*, the pronoun *I*, and the interjection *O*.

The abbreviations B.C. and A.D. occur only with the number of a year: 1001 B.C., A.D. 1492. The interjection O occurs in poetry, in the Bible, or in prayers or petitions: O Lord, O King, O Master.

O is quite different from the explosive interjection *oh*, which is capitalized only at the beginning of a sentence.

11.2 First Words

Capitalize the first word of a sentence, a direct quotation, and a line of poetry.

1. What brought the man to our hideout?

2. "I have come," he said, "to repay a debt."

3. Whenever Richard Cory went down town,
   We people on the pavement looked at him:
   He was a gentleman from sole to crown,
   Clean favored, and imperially slim.*

Note: The second example above is a divided quotation.
The second part of a divided quotation does not begin with
a capital letter unless it starts a new sentence. See Section 15.2.

11.3 Proper Nouns and Adjectives

A **common noun** is the name of a whole group of persons,
places, or things. A **proper noun** is the name of an individual
person, place, or thing. A **proper adjective** is an adjective formed
from a proper noun.

COMMON NOUN	PROPER NOUN	PROPER ADJECTIVE
country	England	English
state	Texas	Texan
city	Paris	Parisian

Proper nouns and adjectives occur in many compound words.
Capitalize only the parts of these words that are capitalized
when they stand alone. Do not capitalize prefixes such as
pro-, un-, anti- attached to proper nouns and adjectives.

un-American   pro-French   Spanish-speaking people

Proper nouns occur in great variety. The following rules with
their illustrations will help you solve the capitalization problems that proper nouns present.

---

* From *Richard Cory* by E. A. Robinson, quoted by permission of the Macmillan Company.

11.4 Geographical Names

In a geographical name capitalize the first letter of each word except articles and prepositions.

The article *the* appearing before a geographical name is not part of the geographical name and is therefore not capitalized.

CONTINENTS: Australia, Africa, Europe

BODIES OF WATER: the Atlantic Ocean, San Francisco Bay, the Mississippi River, the Great Lakes, the Strait of Magellan, the Firth of Forth, Cape Cod, New Hampton Roads

LAND FORMS: the Gobi Desert, the Rocky Mountains, the High Plains, Crystal Cave, Mount Hood, Shenandoah Valley

POLITICAL UNITS: the United States of America, the Republic of Texas, the Commonwealth of Massachusetts, the Province of Quebec, St. Louis County, Newcastle Township, the City of Detroit, Stratford-on-Avon, the Fields of Dan, the Department of Health, Education, and Welfare

PUBLIC AREAS: Glacier National Park, Mammoth Cave, Big Hole Battlefield, Fort Laramie, Joshua Tree Monument

ROADS AND HIGHWAYS: Fifth Avenue, New Jersey Turnpike, U.S. Highway 1, Twelfth Street, London Road, Thirty-fourth Street, Michigan Boulevard

11.5 Common Nouns in Names

A common noun that is part of a name is capitalized. A common noun used to define or refer to a proper noun is not capitalized.

PART OF THE NAME	REFERENCE OR DEFINITION
New York State	the state of Minnesota*
New York City	the city of Buffalo
the Western Plains	plains in the West
Hudson Valley	the valley of the Hudson

11.6 Words Modified by Proper Adjectives

The word modified by a proper adjective is not capitalized unless adjective and noun together are a geographical name.

the Indian Ocean	the Indian nation
the Swiss Alps	a Swiss watch
the English Channel	the English language
the Irish Sea	Irish songs

Exercise: Copy the following sentences, supplying necessary capitals.

1. The romans ruled britain from a.d. 43 until a.d. 410.

2. At the mouth of the nile lies the great city of cairo.

3. Judy's european tour includes a trip down the rhine.

4. On the plains of abraham, wolfe and montcalm were fatally wounded.

5. The puerto ricans are a spanish-speaking people.

6. The st. lawrence seaway was officially opened in 1959.

7. The students went to stratford, connecticut, to see a shakespearean play.

8. Shakespeare was born and is buried in stratford-on-avon.

9. The most famous road in italy, the appian way, was built in 312 b.c. by appius claudius, a roman ruler.

10. How would you define "anti-american practices"?

---

* In official documents, words like city, state, and county are capitalized when they are a part of the name of a political unit: *the City of Chicago, the State of Illinois, the County of Westchester.*

11. The ottoman empire, a former turkish sultanate, was powerful for six centuries.

12. The british ship *lusitania* was sunk by a german submarine.

13. We live in the valley of the connecticut river.

14. The japanese date the beginning of their nation with the reign of the mythical emperor jimmu 660 years before the birth of christ.

15. Formosa, a large island off the coast of china, is also called taiwan.

16. The chief island in the state of hawaii is oahu.

17. The greek playwright sophocles wrote his tragedies between 495 b.c. and 406 b.c.

18. Thousands of people of polish descent marched down fifth avenue in the pulaski day parade.

11.7 Directions and Sections

Capitalize names of sections of the country but not of directions of the compass.

The South is now heavily industrialized.
The climate attracts settlers to the West.
To the north lies Kalamazoo.
We are going south this winter.
Los Angeles is east of Reno, Nevada.
You will find mountains to the west of here.
The wind is from the southwest.

Capitalize proper adjectives derived from names of sections of the country. Do not capitalize adjectives derived from words indicating direction.

a westerly breeze   a Midwestern university
a northbound flight   a Southern state

Exercise: Copy the following sentences, supplying the necessary capitals.

1. We travel south from Concord to get to our cottage in Maine.

2. We sailed to the Canary Islands, which lie to the west of Morocco.

3. North Carolina is perhaps the most industrialized of the southern states.

4. "Go west, young man" was Horace Greeley's advice.

5. The Andes Mountains run down the west side of south America.

6. The wind from the northeast brought snow and lower temperatures.

7. The tall mountains to the west of the village look purple in the twilight.

8. From Paris, we traveled to the middle east.

9. Cotton and tobacco are important crops in the south.

10. Many eastern Congressmen were in the midwest for political rallies.

11. The speech of southerners is easily distinguishable from that of northerners.

12. The hero of the play is a cowboy of the old west.

13. The Brandenburg Gate divides the eastern part of Berlin from the western part.

14. The path of the gale changed from a northwesterly to a northeasterly route.

15. The scene of the novel is the Pacific northwest.

16. Bolivia, Peru, Colombia, and Venezuela border the south American country of brazil.

11.8 Languages, Races, Nationalities, and Religions

Capitalize the names of languages, races, nationalities, and religions and the adjectives formed from them.

the Caucasian race	Buddhism	Jew
the Spanish language	Catholic	Brazilian
Mexican history	Protestant	Dutch

11.9   Organizations and Institutions

Capitalize important words in the names of organizations, buildings, firms, schools, churches, and other institutions. Do not capitalize *and* or prepositions. Capitalize an article (*a, an,* or *the*) only if it appears as the first word in a name.

Chicago Symphony Orchestra	Evanston Township High School
	Standard Gas, Incorporated
University of Alabama	Library of Congress
St. Luke's Hospital	Chicago and Northwestern
Book-of-the-Month Club	Railroad

Note: In brand names, the common noun is not capitalized: *a Volkswagen bus; Indian River grapefruit; Crest toothpaste.*

Exercise: Copy the following sentences, supplying necessary capitals.

1. The professor made a study of brahmanism when he was in india.

2. A graduate of the university of iowa, jim stanton is now attending dental school.

3. In 1869 the cincinnati red stockings became the first professional baseball team.

4. The philadelphia museum of art contains the paintings of old masters as well as contemporary french, american, and mexican art.

5. The indian government has protested chinese communist violations of its borders.

6. The seniors arranged their class trip to disneyland in california through the foster travel agency.

7. About thirty-nine percent of the population of hawaii is caucasian.

8. The league of women voters is having a membership drive.

9. The university of michigan is playing the university of southern california in the rose bowl.

10. Pennsylvania state teachers college is located in different parts of the state.

11. My birthday gift was a subscription to *sports illustrated.*

12. The campaign is sponsored by the chamber of commerce and the better business bureau.
13. Have you tried dandix tooth powder?
14. Jack's father bought stock in the western motors corporation.
15. Our french teacher has studied at the sorbonne in paris.

11.10 Titles of Persons

Capitalize words that show rank, office, or profession, when they are used with a person's name.

Doctor Walsh	Aunt Mary	Father Flynn
Lieutenant Flagg	Rabbi Jacobs	Judge Wright
Chief Joseph	Controller Bucklin	Dean Smith

The titles of high officials are capitalized even when they are used without the official's name.

the President of the United States	the Governor
the Secretary of State	the Pope
the Prime Minister	the Bishop

The prefix *ex-* and the suffix *-elect* are not capitalized when attached to titles: *ex-President Ford,* the *Senator-elect.*

11.11 Family Relationships

Capitalize the name of a family relationship when it is used with a person's name.

Aunt Ruth   Uncle Bill   Grandma Moses

When words like *mother, father, dad,* and *mom* are used alone in place of a particular person's name, they are capitalized. When modified by a possessive pronoun, as in *your mother,* they are not capitalized. When these and other words of family relationship do not stand for a particular person, they are not capitalized.

My Uncle Phil will be here tomorrow.
We have a letter from Grandpa Swanson.
Bob asked Dad for the car yesterday.
I saw your father at the airport.
Does Alice have a sister?

11.12 Titles of Books and Works of Art

Capitalize the first word and every important word in the titles of books, stories, articles, poems, films, works of art, and musical compositions.

The only words considered as not important are conjunctions, articles (*a, an,* and *the*) and prepositions containing fewer than five letters. These are capitalized when used as the first word in a title.

The Old Man and the Sea	*Danger under the Moon*
The Last Supper	*The Uses of Enchantment*
A Midsummer Night's Dream	"The Stars and Stripes Forever"

Exercise: Copy each word that requires a capital in these sentences.

1. Robert asked aunt mary to lend him *all the president's men.*

2. Harding appointed ex-president taft chief justice of the supreme court.

3. The first nonstop transatlantic jet flight was made by colonel schilling.

4. The prime minister invited the senator-elect to lunch.

5. Alice saw the secretary of state at o'hare airport in chicago.

6. Leonardo's *mona lisa* was once stolen from the louvre.

7. Michelangelo created great works of art for the pope.

8. Our mothers and dads met us at the station.

9. The band always plays "hail to the chief" when the president appears.

10. At the metropolitan opera house we heard *il trovatore.*

11. The class read and discussed thomas gray's "elegy written in a country church-yard."

12. My father announced that the family was invited to uncle bill's cottage.

13. In 1876, general custer and his men were massacred by the indians led by chief sitting bull.

14. *Murder in the cathedral* is about the murder of the archbishop of canterbury in 1170.

15. In 1755, doctor johnson's *dictionary of the english language,* one of the first dictionaries, was published in England.

11.13 The Deity

Capitalize all words referring to the Deity, the Holy Family, and to religious scriptures.

God	Jehovah
the Father	Allah
the Son	the Bible
the Holy Ghost	the Gospel
the Virgin Mary	the Torah
the Lord	the Talmud
the Almighty	the Koran

Capitalize personal pronouns but not relative pronouns that refer to the Deity.

May God make His light to shine down upon you.
Praise God from whom all blessings flow.

11.14 Days, Months, Holidays

Capitalize the names of days of the week, of months, and of holidays. Do not capitalize the names of the seasons.

Monday	the Fourth of July	autumn
January	Washington's Birthday	Veterans Day

11.15 Historical Names

Capitalize the names of historical events, documents, and periods.

Declaration of Independence   the Middle Ages
Battle of the Bulge   the Jacksonian Period

Exercise A: Copy the words that require capitals in these sentences.

1. In maine and massachusetts, the nineteenth of april, patriots' day, is a holiday.
2. The magna carta, a famous document in english history, marks the beginning of english liberties.
3. Of historic importance in the united states is the emancipation proclamation; its author, abraham lincoln, issued it on january 1, 1863.
4. The fourteenth of february, st. valentine's day, is not a legal holiday.
5. The first five books of the old testament are known collectively as the pentateuch.
6. The period following the civil war is known as the reconstruction era.
7. The sacred book of the mohammedans is the koran.
8. The almighty is another name for god.
9. The united states senate rejected the treaty of versailles after world war I.
10. The marshall plan brought economic aid to europe after world war II.

Exercise B: The following exercise reviews all the uses of capitals in this chapter. Copy the words that need capital letters.

1. My mother and father will attend graduation exercises at northside high school.
2. The secretary of state will arrive in buenos aires, argentina, on wednesday, april 12.

3. My sister is visiting our aunt callie, who lives in the west.

4. The people of laos are buddhists.

5. The president of the united states visited the british prime minister.

6. I listened to a program of french and english folk songs.

7. Have you read *leaves of grass* by walt whitman?

8. The norman conquest occurred in a.d. 1066.

9. The walter reed army medical center is in washington, d. c.

10. After the war of independence, john paul jones became an admiral in the russian navy.

12.0 End Marks and Commas

12.1 Periods at the Close of Sentences

Place a period at the close of every declarative sentence and of most imperative sentences.

A period is also used at the close of groups of words that are used as sentences even though they are not complete sentences.

> Please hand me the broom.
> Oh, no. We were not near the fire.

12.2 Periods in Abbreviations

Place a period after every part of an abbreviation.

E. A. Robinson	Edwin Arlington Robinson
A.D.	Anno Domini
U. S. A.	United States of America
Washington, D. C.	Washington, District of Columbia

Since the 1930's it has become the custom not to use periods in abbreviations of certain government agencies and of international organizations.

ICC	Interstate Commerce Commission
FHA	Federal Housing Authority
FBI	Federal Bureau of Investigation
UN	United Nations
HEW	Department of Health, Education, and Welfare

12.3 Exclamation Points

Place an exclamation point after an exclamatory sentence and after an exclamation set off from a sentence.

Great! We can't lose now. Wow! I don't believe it!
What a pass! We want Jackson!
Hold that line! Wilson for Senator!

12.4 Question Marks

Place a question mark after an interrogative sentence or after a question that is not a complete sentence.

The word order in questions is sometimes the same as in declarative sentences. In speech, the speaker raises his voice at the end of the sentence to show that it is a question. In writing, the question mark performs the same function.

Is it worth seeing? It is worth seeing?
Do you call that wisdom? That is wisdom?
Is it snowing? The weather? It is snowing.

Exercise: Copy these sentences, using end marks and punctuation as required for sentences and abbreviations. Use question marks only for sentences in normal interrogative form.

1. You can stay, can't you
2. Look There goes a 747 jet
3. Just set the parcel on the stool, please

4. Helen received her M A degree from the University
of Michigan
5. Send these articles C O D to St Louis, Mo
6. The winner was J B Prescott, a student at U C L A
7. "Where did you find your wallet" she asked
8. Send the parcel to this address: 60 Fifth Ave, New York,
N Y 10021
9. Write to your senator, The Honorable E D Smith,
Washington, D C
10. What an interesting person your mother is

Uses of the Comma

12.5 Introductory Words

**Introductory words such as _yes, no, well, why_, and _oh_ are fol-
lowed by a comma.**

> Oh, no, I didn't intend to buy it.
> Yes, I realize that it is a direct quote.
> Well, there are several French "anti-novelists."

Adverbs such as *besides, however, anyhow, nonetheless* at the
beginning of a sentence are set off by commas.

12.6 Introductory Phrases and Clauses

**A participial phrase at the beginning of a sentence is followed by
a comma.**
**A long adverbial clause at the beginning of a sentence is fol-
lowed by a comma.**
**A succession of prepositional phrases at the beginning of a sen-
tence is set off by commas.**

> *Hoping to win,* he played with determination.
>   (participial phrase)

When we heard the first siren, we evacuated the building.
(adverbial clause)
In the vase on top of the mantelpiece, we found the missing
earring. (succession of prepositional phrases)

12.7 Transposed Words and Phrases

Words and phrases moved to the beginning of a sentence from their normal position are usually set off by a comma.

Yeats was quite naturally interested in Irish mythology.
(normal order)
Quite naturally, Yeats was interested in Irish mythology.
(transposed order)
He had little success, unfortunately. (normal order)
Unfortunately, he had little success. (transposed order)

Exercise: Copy the following sentences, inserting commas where necessary. Three of the sentences are correct.

1. Anyhow that is what I thought the announcer said.
2. Before starting to cook the boys carefully planned their menus.
3. Why this is the movie I saw on TV.
4. From the beginning of the trip to the end Ed wanted to see everything.
5. Well I see that you are as good as your word.
6. Constantly bemoaning your fate will not improve your situation.
7. If you will tune in to Channel 9 tonight you will see some of your classmates.
8. In preparation for the panel discussion I made a detailed outline.
9. Why there are many amateurs who do excellent repair work.
10. When you are ready to invest this broker will help you.
11. Although Robert Frost is often called a New England poet his poetry has universality.

12. Even if you don't like poetry you might enjoy "The Death of the Hired Man."
13. To have accepted the job of waterfront director would have been unwise.
14. Learning to play squash is easier than it looks.

12.8 Appositives

An appositive is set off from the rest of the sentence by commas.

Mr. Rivera, *an anthropologist,* discussed man's origin.
The English writer, *Joseph Conrad,* was actually Polish.

12.9 Words of Direct Address

Words of direct address are set off by commas.

David, will you please move your car?
Don't forget to leave a tip, *Debbie.*
People doubt, *Mary,* that your views are correct.

12.10 Parenthetical Expressions

Words and phrases used to explain or qualify a statement are called **parenthetical expressions.** These same words and phrases may also be used as basic parts of the sentence. It is only when they are parenthetical that they are set off by commas.

As a matter of fact Keats did study medicine.
Keats, *as a matter of fact,* did study medicine. (parenthetical)
I understand that Keats died at twenty-five.
Keats, I understand, died at twenty-five. (parenthetical)

Parenthetical expressions are set off by commas.

Some expressions often used parenthetically are:

of course	as a matter of fact	for example	indeed
in fact	I believe (think)	on the other hand	

Conjunctive adverbs (see Section 1.7) used parenthetically within the sentence are set off by commas: *therefore, moreover, nevertheless, however, consequently,* and so on.

Yeats, *nevertheless,* continued to write plays.
The President, *therefore,* prepared a White Paper.
The bill, *however,* was passed despite the filibuster.

Occasionally, words like *however, therefore, and consequently* are used to modify a word in the sentence. As modifiers they are an essential part of the meaning of a sentence. Since they are essential, they are not set off by commas.

The heroic soldier was consequently honored by France.
Ambassador Stevenson could not convince the Russians
however hard he tried.
Mr. Jones was therefore justified in closing his shop.

12.11 Dates, Addresses, Geographical Names

In dates and addresses of more than one part, set off every part after the first from the rest of the sentence.

We visited the baseball museum in Cooperstown. (one part)
In Cooperstown, New York, we visited the museum.
(two parts, the second set off by commas)
The package arrived on June 6. (one part)
Wisconsin entered the Union on May 29, 1848.
(two parts with a comma after the first)
The letter was addressed to 280 East End Avenue,
Pleasantville, Ohio 43148, as you requested.
(three parts, the second and third set off by commas)

Note: The day of the .month and the month are one item. The name of the street and the house number are one item. The name of the state and the zip code number are one item.

June 6   240 East Thirty-first Street   Illinois 60610

Exercise: Copy these sentences, inserting the necessary commas.

1. The Governor's Horse Guard a troop of mounted cavalry rode in the parade.
2. May I say a few words Mrs. Berman?
3. Bees for example are industrious insects.
4. Colorado the Centennial State entered the Union on August 1 1876.
5. *Hamlet* probably the most famous of Shakespeare's plays is a drama of revenge.
6. The address of the White House is 1600 Pennsylvania Avenue Washington D.C. 20006
7. We moved to our new home at 500 Cook Boulevard Bradley Illinois 60915 on December 10 1976.
8. Warren you can be sure can be trusted to do his best.
9. This is to say the least a disconcerting discovery.
10. You must remember of course that all modern music is not jazz.
11. The ideas of a reformer as you may know frequently meet with opposition.
12. The use of anesthesia in surgery for example was once severely criticized.
13. I saw Lynn's father a retired army colonel.
14. See me if you can before you leave town for the summer.
15. Rudolf Nureyev the famous dancer is appearing at the Kennedy Center in Washington.
16. The promotion was I believe the first she had received in years.
17. He contends on the contrary that slow driving causes as many accidents as fast driving.
18. My grades are on the whole above those required for recommendation for college.

12.12 Nonrestrictive Modifiers

A clause that identifies or points out the person or thing it modifies is a **restrictive clause.** It is essential to the meaning of the sentence. It cannot be dropped out without confusing the meaning or making the meaning incomplete.

> Mrs. Amato hired a person *who could audit the books.* (The clause tells an essential characteristic of the person hired.)
> The house *that burned down* belonged to them. (The clause tells *which* house.)
> A man *who is conscientious* will succeed. (Without the clause, the sentence has no specific meaning.)

Restrictive clauses are not set off from the rest of the sentence by commas.

A **nonrestrictive clause** does not contain information essential to the meaning of the sentence. It presents merely added information. It can be dropped without confusing the meaning of the sentence.

> Linemen, *who are just as important to football success as the backs,* seldom get any of the glory.
> These shoes, *which are certainly better looking,* cost more than I can pay.

Nonrestrictive clauses are set off by commas from the rest of the sentence.

Participial phrases that identify or point out the thing or person they modify are restrictive.

> The boy *standing on the chair* is the director. (Without the phrase, the sentence loses its meaning.)
> The paper *attached to the handle* gives the directions for using the sharpener. (The phrase identifies the paper.)

Nonrestrictive participial phrases merely add meaning. They are not essential and can be dropped without making the sentence meaning incomplete.

Climbing fast, we arrived at the top out of breath.
José Sandoval, *carrying the flag,* advanced to the stage.

Nonrestrictive participial phrases are set off from the rest of the sentence by commas. Restrictive phrases are not set off by commas.

Exercise: Number your paper 1–18. Decide whether the adjective clause or the participial phrase is restrictive or nonrestrictive. After each number write *restrictive* or *nonrestrictive.* Copy and insert commas in the sentences in which commas are needed.

1. A car having defective brakes is a hazard to highway safety.
2. The book which brought fame to James Hilton was *Lost Horizon.*
3. His music which was essentially romantic offended some critics.
4. People who live in glass houses shouldn't throw stones.
5. The bills passed by the legislature await the Governor's signature.
6. A clock which loses time is better than no clock at all.
7. This boat which was repaired last month should hold water.
8. Her sister Joan who lived near us in Tulsa is now eighteen years old.
9. Ralph Smith is the man who owns the TV repair shop.
10. The girl boarding the bus is Janet Slocum.
11. Mexico is a place that you would like to visit in winter.
12. The city's transit system which had long been criticized was now under investigation.
13. The additional taxes for which the Governor asked were to be used for state roads.
14. The construction of highway shopping centers is a trend which helps to alleviate traffic jams.
15. The training which college gives tends to develop one's problem-solving abilities.

16. Muscular coordination which every dancer needs is acquired and maintained through daily practice.
17. The person who filled their gas tank did not notice their license number.
18. This lyric which was written early in Tennyson's life expresses his youthful sorrow and skepticism.

12.13 Compound Sentences

Place a comma before the conjunction that joins two main clauses in a compound sentence.

We must win this game, *or* we will be out of the running.
The elevator has stopped running, *and* everyone is late to work.
I could not remember the title of the book, *nor* could I remember the author.

When the clauses are quite short, the comma may be omitted.

John arrived early but Paul was late.
The train arrived and we got on.

12.14 Series

A **series** is a group of three or more items of the same kind.

SERIES OF NOUNS: *Dogs, children,* and *clowns* were suddenly mixed in a tangled mass.

SERIES OF VERBS: The old car *coughed, lurched* forward, then *shuddered* to an obstinate standstill.

SERIES OF ADJECTIVES:	The food was *greasy, tasteless,* and *insufficient* for our hunger.
SERIES OF PHRASES:	We searched *under the rug, behind the pictures,* and *in the desk drawers.*

Commas are used to separate the parts of a series.

No comma is required after the last item in a series. When the last two items of a series are joined by *and* or *or,* the comma is sometimes omitted. To avoid all possibility of misunderstanding, it is wise to use a comma before the conjunction.

Do not use a comma if all parts of the series are joined by *and, or,* or *nor.*

We swam and ate and slept for five days.
Milk or water or even ink would have tasted good to us.

12.15 Coordinate Adjectives

Commas are placed between coordinate adjectives that modify the same noun.

The hot, humid day drew to a close.
The blinding, blistering, interminable heat bore down on us day after day.

To determine whether adjectives are coordinate, try placing an *and* between them. If it sounds natural, they are coordinate, and a comma is needed.

PROBLEM	The loud irritating noise persisted all day.
NATURAL	The loud *and* irritating noise persisted all day.
SOLUTION	The loud, irritating noise persisted all day.
PROBLEM	It was a light, warm pleasant room.
NATURAL	It was a light, warm, *and* pleasant room.
SOLUTION	It was a light, warm, pleasant room.

PROBLEM   Turn left at the big red barn.
NOT NATURAL   Turn left at the big *and* red barn.
SOLUTION   Turn left at the big red barn.

In general, it is safe to omit the comma before numbers and adjectives of size, shape, and age.

CORRECT   the little old man
CORRECT   a huge round dome
CORRECT   five square pieces of paper

Exercise: Copy these sentences, placing commas where they are needed.

1. Bring skis snowshoes and plenty of warm clothes.
2. Did you know that the apple the plum the peach and the quince are members of the rose family?
3. The wind roared around the house shook the doors and windows and then stopped abruptly.
4. The room was large cheerful and tastefully decorated.
5. Mary wrote that she needed a new dress a new pair of shoes and a new raincoat.
6. The book holds one's interest but it is of little permanent value.
7. The squirrel ran across the lawn up a tree and out onto a telephone wire.
8. The line of weary hungry students moved slowly into the cafeteria.
9. I am going to college to acquire knowledge to make new friends and to equip myself for a career.
10. The work is not dangerous nor is it remunerative.
11. A long low wail interrupted our conversation.
12. The great wide old door swung slowly shut.
13. Different metals are added to alloys to make them stronger more workable more heat-resistant or more rust-resistant.
14. The noise was loud and annoying but we paid no attention to it.

15. Oil is discovered by sounding by magnetic testing or by studying the rocks.

16. We did not see the landslide nor did we hear the warning cries.

17. The botanist studies the world's plants—where they grow how they are related and what their fruits and flowers are like.

18. The bus stopped and we got off.

12.16 Clarity

Use a comma to separate words or phrases that might be mistakenly joined in reading.

There are three common situations in which words may be mistakenly read together. The first occurs when the conjunctions *but* and *for* are mistaken for prepositions.

CONFUSING   They were all skilled in carpentry but one
                          was superior.
CLEAR   They were all skilled in carpentry, but one
                          was superior.

CONFUSING   Joan spoke for Dana was still eating.
CLEAR   Joan spoke, for Dana was still eating.

A second source of confusion is a noun following a verbal phrase.

CONFUSING   After kicking the boy ran down the field.
CLEAR   After kicking, the boy ran down the field.

CONFUSING   Before leaving Barbara closed the windows.
CLEAR   Before leaving, Barbara closed the windows.

CONFUSING   To learn to sew a person should take lessons.
CLEAR   To learn to sew, a person should take lessons.

A third source of confusion is the word that may be either adverb, preposition, or conjunction at the beginning of the sentence.

CONFUSING	Beneath the car was rusted.
CLEAR	Beneath, the car was rusted.
CONFUSING	Outside the air was crisp.
CLEAR	Outside, the air was crisp.

12.17 Words Omitted

Use a comma when words are omitted from parallel word groups.

John Berry wrote the editorial; Jim Kelly, the captions.
Lee won the English prize; Joel, the History prize.
The more, the merrier.

Exercise: Copy these sentences, placing commas where necessary to avoid confusion.

1. Inside the gaiety continued for many hours.
2. If you can write to me tomorrow.
3. While they were eating the fire started.
4. To George Henry is an opportunist.
5. Arlene is going to law school; Henry to West Point.
6. In summer we buy peaches and berries; in autumn apples and pears.
7. Sheila told a romantic story; Lee a hair-raising mystery.
8. To study a person should have a good light and a quiet place.
9. On top the mountain is covered with small shrubs.
10. Ann matriculated at Oberlin College; Bill at the University of California at Los Angeles.

13.0 The Semicolon, the Colon, the Dash, and Parentheses

13.1 Semicolons Between Main Clauses

A semicolon is placed between the main clauses of a compound sentence when they are not joined by a conjunction.

The clauses of a compound sentence are closely related in thought. That is the reason for joining them into one sentence rather than writing them as separate sentences.

In some sentences the semicolon is more effective in joining main clauses than one of the conjunctions. This is especially true when *and* or *but* add little meaning to the joined clauses.

Ben Jonson was a poet, and he was also a bricklayer.
Ben Jonson was a poet; he was also a bricklayer.

The fire was caused by an electrical short circuit, and it
spread throughout the block.
The fire was caused by an electrical short circuit; it spread
throughout the block.

13.2 Semicolons and Conjunctive Adverbs

A semicolon is used between main clauses joined by conjunctive adverbs or by phrases like _for example_, _in fact_, _for instance_.

> Every human cell records stimuli and responses; in fact, such "tape recordings" persist during an entire life span.
> Many fabrics today are wrinkle-proof and stain-resistant; nevertheless, they do require laundering or cleaning.
> Man is a slave to his conveniences; for example, he works to pay for water, gasoline, electricity, and conditioned air.
> Thoreau is known as a dreamer and a philosopher; however, he designed a practical graphite pencil.

Note that the conjunctive adverb or phrase is followed by a comma in the examples above.

13.3 Semicolons Between Word Groups Containing Commas

A sentence containing a great many commas is difficult to read. If commas precede the conjunction between man clauses, another comma at this point would lose its value as a guide to the reader.

A semicolon is used between main clauses joined by a conjunction if the clause before the conjunction contains commas.

> Darius Milhaud, George Gershwin, and Aaron Copland used jazz themes; but George Antheil created an electronic synthesis.
> Many modern architects adapt Greek, Roman, and Georgian concepts; but Wright and Le Corbusier attempted original designs.

A semicolon is used between a series of phrases if they contain commas.

Gertrude Stein was one American expatriot; Ernest
Hemingway, another; and F. Scott Fitzgerald, a third.
During the class, Lois reported on Sisyphus; Henry, on
Daedalus; and Margaret, on Prometheus.
Cello is a short form for *violoncello;* piano, for *pianoforte;*
and *oboe,* for *hautboy.*

Exercise: Two of the following sentences need no semicolons.
For the other sentences, indicate the point at which a semicolon
should replace a comma.

1. He had waited for years before attempting to get his novel
published, moreover, he was prepared to wait longer if necessary.

2. Everyone signed up for the outing, however, only
twenty came.

3. Hamilton believed more factories would help the nation
grow, Jefferson argued for better farms.

4. The Senate confirmed Mrs. Perry's nomination, Mrs. Perry,
however, did not accept the post.

5. The movers packed the china, glassware, and silver carefully,
nothing was broken in the process of moving.

6. The daffodils come up first, then the tulips, and finally, the
iris and day lilies.

7. Brad waited anxiously for the reply to his application, in fact,
he met the postman at the corner each day.

8. Some octopi are small, but others are so large they can
overturn a small boat.

9. The chairperson called for questions, no one responded.

10. The singer was trembling violently, nevertheless, she
continued to sing.

11. A dense fog enveloped the city and the surrounding area, as
a result, all airports were closed down.

12. *Caves of Steel,* by Isaac Asimov, combines both science
fiction and detective story techniques, hence, it has wide appeal.

13. The lobster's right claw is usually the crusher, the left claw,
the cutter.

14. History reveals the past, illuminates the present, and
sometimes can foretell the future.

13.4 Colons To Introduce Lists

The colon is used to throw the reader's attention forward to what follows. It is in some respects like an equal sign, saying that what follows is the explanation or equivalent of what has gone before.

A colon is used to introduce a list of items.

Usually, a colon is required when a list is preceded by the words *the following* or *as follows*. A colon is not used before a series of modifiers or complements immediately following the verb.

Pulitzer prizes are awarded in the following areas:
fiction, drama, history, biography, and poetry. (list)
His itinerary included the following: Italy, a week; France,
eight days; and England, a fortnight. (list)
Good writing requires organization, a precise vocabulary,
and revision. (series of complements)
The virus is found in wastes, in milk, and in water. (series
of modifiers)

13.5 Colons with Formal Quotations

A colon is used to introduce a formal quotation.

The president opened the meeting with these words:
"We are beginning a period of expansion in which all of
you will play a key role. Many of you will have added
responsibilities; others will have entirely new responsibilities."

13.6 Colons Before Explanatory Statements

A colon is used between two sentences when the second explains the first. The second sentence begins with a capital letter.

The alternatives are obvious: You either do the work and
learn or you do nothing and fail the course.
Sir Francis Bacon made valuable contributions to science:
He stimulated inquiry and pointed out logical fallacies.

13.7 Other Uses of the Colon

A colon is used (1) after the formal salutation of a letter,
(2) between hour and minute figures of clock time, (3) in
Biblical references, (4) between the title and subtitle of a
book, (5) between numbers referring to volume and pages of
books and magazine.

Dear Sir or Madam:	Genesis 2:4-7
Dear Ms. Sims:	*The Wide World: A High School*
6:15 A.M.	*Geography*
	Volume II: pages 65–72

13.8 The Dash To Show Break in Thought

A dash is used to show an abrupt break in thought.

In dialogue, the break in thought is often caused by uncer-
tainty or hesitancy as in the first example below.

"I was on my way to the—that is, I was asked—the principal
wanted to see me."
Connecticut is a beautiful—look at that car go!
We should invite some of the people—whom did you say
to ask?

13.9 The Dash with Interrupters

A dash is used in the same way that commas and parentheses are used: to set off a long explanatory statement that
interrupts the thought.

Thomas Hardy—he wrote *The Mayor of Casterbridge*—
spans the jump from Victorian to modern novels.
He came slithering down that rope—and he didn't burn his
hands at all—as though he were a monkey.

13.10 The Dash Before a Summary

The dash is used after a series to indicate a summarizing statement.

John F. Sullivan, Charles J. Correll, Freeman F. Gosden,
Benjamin Kubelsky, Edward I. Iskowitz, James E. Jordan,
Isaiah Leopold—these were famous comedians during the
golden age of radio.
Rustling programs, discreet coughs, murmurs of conversation
—all are part of the cacophony preceding a concert.

Exercise: Copy the following sentences, inserting semicolons, colons, and dashes where necessary.

1. We have read the following books in English class *The
Return of the Native, The Scarlet Letter,* and *Wuthering Heights.*

2. These were her assets a good mind, good health, and a
determination to succeed.

3. The title of the book is *From Past to Present A
World History.*

4. The toastmaster introduced the guests of honor Senator
Gordon Williams, Congressman Joseph O'Brien, and Judge
Henry Houghton.

5. Dogwood trees in bloom, students sauntering along the walks,
grass that looks like green velvet these I see from my window.

6. The class president made one request that all dues be
paid promptly.

7. We might have some hamburgers and oh, I'm afraid I forgot
to buy groceries today.

8. They have a summer home, a sailboat, and well everything
a person could want.

9. The detective listed the clues that had led to the solution of the murder first, the fingerprints on the revolver were not those of the dead man second, the fingerprints matched those of his friend third, the landlord had heard the murdered man and his friend quarreling violently before the shot rang out.

10. The singer had only one desire she wanted to sing in the Metropolitan Opera House in New York.

11. The vaccine 75,000 shots in all was stolen by masked gunmen.

12. We saw those huge rays of bluish-green light the aurora borealis in the northern sky.

13. What Dan said was but probably I should not repeat it.

14. The letter from the admissions office listed the requirements for a degree one hundred twenty-four credits, an average grade of C, and the successful completion of the required courses in a major and a minor.

15. This quotation comes from *The Raven The Life of Sam Houston* Volume I, pages 98–100.

16. The conference dates are as follows October 8–11, December 20–22, and March 7–10.

17. The meeting of the Student Council will be held at 3 30 P.M.

18. In the early days of the United States there were only four members in the President's cabinet the Secretary of State, the Secretary of War, the Secretary of the Treasury, and the Attorney-General.

13.11 Parentheses To Enclose Supplementary or Explanatory Words

Commas, dashes, or parentheses are used to set off words that are supplementary or explanatory. Commas are used when the material set off is fairly close to the main thought of the sentence. Dashes are used to set off material more loosely connected, and parentheses are used to set off material so loosely related to the main thought that it might be made a separate sentence.

There are few occasions in high school writing when parentheses are needed. The safest course for the student is to use commas, or even dashes, to set off parenthetical matter. If the material is so distantly related as to require parentheses, the passage might better be rewritten to place the parenthetical material in a separate sentence.

COMMAS ADEQUATE: Mark's best point, *which he saved for the end*, was that every group needs leadership.

DASHES REQUIRED: Modern science no longer deals directly with the visible world—that is, it deals directly only with ions, atoms, electrons, and other particles that are too small to be seen.

PARENTHESES APPROPRIATE: She speaks French and Arabic (her family has lived in France and the Middle East) but English is her first language.

PARENTHESES AVOIDED: She speaks French and Arabic, since her family has lived in France and the Middle East, but English is her first language.

13.12 Punctuation Within Parentheses

Commas, semicolons, and periods are placed outside the closing parenthesis. The question mark and exclamation point are placed inside if the parenthetical material is itself a question or exclamation; otherwise, outside.

Open the package carefully (do not puncture the carton).
We were astonished (as anyone should have been!) at the precision of the marching routines during half-time.
No one was prepared (why should they have been?) for the attack.
Lauri played guitar; Harry, drums; Joe, bass (he doubles on mandolin); and Pete, piano.

13.13 Brackets

Brackets are used to enclose corrections or material inserted by a writer who is quoting someone else's material.

> "On the 4th [5th] of March, Hayes took office." (correction)
> The letter read: "We have him [Jordahl] at our mercy."
> (explanatory word inserted by the writer)

13.14 Ellipses

Indicate the omission of unused parts of a quotation by ellipses: three dots (. . .) to indicate an omission within a sentence and four dots (. . . .) to indicate an omission at the end of a sentence.

> When the old monks had tired themselves out in fighting the devil, did they not have places to which they retired for rest . . . called retreats? I think of making this office one of my retreats. It is so quiet and restful here. . . . —ABRAHAM LINCOLN

14.0 The Apostrophe

The apostrophe is used with nouns to show possession or ownership: *Mr. Carr's station wagon, Bob's boat, the doctor's coat.* The apostrophe is also used to show the following:

CLOSE RELATIONSHIP:	Jane's friend, someone's mother
SOURCE OR ORIGIN:	Ed's speech, Betty's idea
IDENTIFYING CHARACTERISTICS:	the lady's expression, Bob's tone of voice, Terry's temper

14.1 The Possessive of Singular Nouns

The possessive form of a singular noun is usually made by adding an apostrophe and s ('s) to the noun.

boy + 's = boy's   city + 's = city's
Charles + 's = Charles's   Ross + 's = Ross's

When a singular noun of more than one syllable ends in *s,* the possessive may be formed by adding only the apostrophe.

waitress + ' = waitress'   witness + ' = witness'
Phyllis + ' = Phyllis'   Jesus + ' = Jesus'

14.2 The Possessive of Plural Nouns

If a plural noun does not end in s, add both apostrophe and s ('s) to form the possessive.

men + 's = men's   children + 's = children's

alumni + 's = alumni's   women + 's = women's

If a plural noun ends in s, add only the apostrophe to form the possessive.

horses + ' = horses'   waiters + ' = waiters'

actors + ' = actors'   editors + ' = editors'

Exercise: Number 1–20 on your paper. Write *correct* for each sentence in which the possessive form is correct. If the form is incorrect, write it correctly.

1. "Pauls Wife," Robert Frosts poem, tells of Paul Bunyans wife.
2. Bill Jones sweater was left in the Thomases car.
3. It was Mr. Warners daughters coat.
4. Mr. and Mrs. Browns childrens birthdays all come in May.
5. The captains' dinner is held on the ship's last night at sea.
6. The housekeeper's first job is to pack the hunter's lunches.
7. The wild ducks' cries alerted the dogs.
8. The muskrat's skins had to be dried and stretched.
9. The weasels' foot was caught in the trap.
10. Sportsmens' apparel is now on sale.
11. The waitress' uniform has not arrived.
12. The men's clothing department is on the third floor.
13. That bicycle is Charles'.
14. Jack Brooks' talk was much too long.
15. Bess' answer was the only correct one.
16. All of the critic's reviews praised the pianist's performance.
17. The princesses' tour had been carefully planned.
18. The speaker's voices were difficult to hear.
19. The childrens' playground is well equipped.
20. That butterflys' wings have beautiful markings.

14.3 The Possessive of Compound Nouns

A **compound noun** is a noun composed of more than one word. Some compound nouns are written with hyphens between the parts.

Only the last part of a hyphenated noun shows possession.

editor-in-chief + 's = editor-in-chief's
brother-in-law + 's = brother-in-law's

Nouns such as *the Queen of England, the President of the United States, the Secretary of State* form the possessive by adding an apostrophe and *s* to the last word only: the *Secretary of State's name.* However, this awkward construction can be avoided by using an *of* phrase.

the jewels of the Queen of England
the address of the President of the United States
the name of the Secretary of State

14.4 Joint Ownership

When the names of two or more persons are used to show joint ownership, only the name of the last person mentioned is given the possessive form. Add an apostrophe or an apostrophe and *s* in accord with the spelling of that name.

Beth and Tom's family
fathers and sons' banquet
author and critic's correspondence

The rule applies also to firm names and to names of organizations.

Clarke and Taylor's sale
Brown, Jackson and Company's building
The League of Women Voters' pamphlet
Johnson and Andrews' advertisement

14.5 Separate Ownership or Possession

If the names of two or more persons are used to show separate ownership, each name is given the possessive form.

Adams' and Jefferson's careers
Webster's and Clay's orations

This construction may become awkward. It can be avoided by using an *of* phrase.

the careers of Adams and Jefferson
the orations of Webster and Clay

14.6 Possessive of Indefinite Pronouns

Use an apostrophe and *s* to form the possessive of indefinite pronouns.

someone + 's = someone's   nobody + 's = nobody's
another + 's = another's   anyone + 's = anyone's

The apostrophe and *s* are added to the last word in forms like *someone else, anybody else, no one else:*

no one else's   anybody else's

The apostrophe is not used to form the possessive of personal pronouns.

NONSTANDARD   their's, your's, her's, our's, it's
STANDARD   theirs, yours, hers, ours, its

14.7 Expressions of Time and Amount

When used as adjectives, words expressing time and amount are given the possessive form.

a day's wages   ten minutes' walk
an hour's time   three days' wages

> a month's delay   two hours' time
> a week's vacation   four months' delay
> a dollar's worth   two decades' history

Exercise: Copy the italicized words, changing them to show ownership or possession correctly.

1. The *Representative from Iowa* vote was in the negative.
2. What is the *Chief Justice* name?
3. It is *Grace and Marion* turn to provide refreshments.
4. The strike caused a *month* delay in deliveries.
5. "I don't think *their's* is as good as *our's*," said Martha.
6. *Someone* umbrella was left in the hall.
7. Many diplomats attended the *Governor General* reception.
8. Cindy borrowed her *brother-in-law* tennis racket.
9. The *editor-in-chief* comment was terse.
10. The *owner* and *agent* signatures were on the document.
11. A *moment* delay may make a great difference.
12. We are planning to take three *week* vacation.
13. Mutual defense is *America* and *England* problem.
14. *Brown and Allen* store has been robbed.
15. The PTSA gave the *new students and parents day* lunch.
16. *Everybody* business is said to be *nobody* business.
17. *Smith, Craig, and Beane* School of Drama might fill your need.
18. She bought *two dollar* worth of gasoline.
19. The *Secretary of Agriculture* proposal displeased the farmers.
20. *G. Fox and Company* expansion program is under way.

14.8   Apostrophes To Show Omissions

An apostrophe is used to show the omission of letters or figures.

> the gold rush of '49   *1849*
> the class of '79   *1979*
> o'clock   *of the clock*
> doesn't   *does not*

14.9 Plurals of Letters, Words, Numbers, and Signs

An apostrophe is used to show the plurals of letters, words, numbers, and signs used as words.

How many *s's* are there in Mississippi?
Beware of using too many *and's* in your themes.
His *7's* look like *9's*.
Make sure that your +*'s* look different from your —*'s*.

Note: The plurals of letters, numbers, signs, and words used as words are always italicized in print. In manuscript and typescript they may be underlined or placed in quotation marks. (See Section 15.7.)

Exercise A: Copy the following sentences, inserting an apostrophe (and *s*) where needed. This exercise reviews all the uses of apostrophes.

1. Havent you received a single days wages yet?
2. No, I haven't, but I expect to receive a check in a weeks time.
3. This students theme contains too many *thens*.
4. Womens clubs are popular in the United States.
5. Johnson and Brothers store has been completely modernized.
6. Barbaras *os* and *as* look exactly alike.
7. Shes a friend of my sisters.
8. Is this book yours, or is it your brothers?
9. Havent you read any of Dickens novels?
10. Lewis and Clarks expedition was Thomas Jeffersons idea.
11. The master of ceremonies mannerisms were tiresome.
12. Please buy me a dimes worth of candy.
13. The Attorney-Generals office is on the second floor.
14. Will you return in five minutes time?
15. The man in the streets word is often taken too seriously.
16. Washingtons and Jeffersons homes are national shrines.

17. We saw Jeffersons home, Monticello, during the summer of 76.
18. James pony ran away but Dales returned to its stall.
19. Janet calls her dentists assistant "the torturers apprentice."
20. Mt. Rushmore, in South Dakotas Black Hills, bears Gutzon Borglums sculptures of famous American patriots.

Exercise B: Write the possessive singular and the possessive plural of each of the following words:

1. day	6. salesperson	11. mouse
2. city	7. sister	12. woman
3. class	8. son-in-law	13. country
4. children	9. country	14. Jones
5. baby	10. lady	15. deer

Exercise C: The following sentences contain errors in the use of apostrophes. Copy the sentences, correcting all errors.

1. The teachers answered the parents's questions.
2. Bess' painting received honorable mention.
3. You can get those items at Smith's and Strevig's store.
4. Mabel, Joan, and Sallys' biology project is almost finished.
5. Sheila's and Stella's project is already completed.
6. Heres the book; Ive mended it's cover.
7. We couldnt keep from laughing at my sister-in-laws story.
8. Students themes often contain too many *sos*.
9. John Adams terms of office preceded Jeffersons'.
10. Lori and Jess's applications were sent on to Morgan's and Company vice-president.
11. In the 1800s the three *Rs* made up the schools curricula.
12. The *os* and *es* in Jeffs' old typewriter looked alike.
13. Someone elses books were lying on the teachers' desk.
14. Molly's and Don's father, after an evenings' work, hadnt finished Ms. Holmes bookcase.
15. "Its still anybodys game," croaked the hoarse announcer.

15.0 Quotations

15.1 Quotation Marks Are Used To Enclose a Direct Quotation

In a direct quotation, the words of the speaker are directly quoted exactly as he spoke them.

> "Sign it. This is your last chance," shouted the enemy general.
> "Sign it," shouted the enemy general. "This is your last chance."

An indirect quotation reports the meaning expressed by the speaker but does not give his exact words.

> INDIRECT   The spy cried for justice.
> DIRECT   "I want justice," the spy cried.

Quotation marks are not used with an indirect quotation.

15.2 Punctuation of Direct Quotations

Punctuation and capitals are used as follows in direct quotations:

1. **In dialogue the first word of the quotation is capitalized.** The material quoted from another writer may begin in the middle of a sentence. If so, the first word is not capitalized.

May we, then, "make haste slowly."

2. **The speaker's words are set off from the rest of the sentence.** Note the placement of commas in these examples:

"That flight is scheduled for Monday," said the pilot.
The pilot said, "That flight is scheduled for Monday."

3. **When the end of the quotation is also the end of the sentence, the period falls inside the quotation marks.**

4. **If the quoted words are a question or an exclamation, the question mark or the exclamation point falls inside the quotation marks.** In this situation no comma is needed.

"May we attend the opening?" the artist's children asked him.
"That is untrue!" shouted the defendant.

5. **If the entire sentence is a question or an exclamation, the exclamation point or question mark falls outside the quotation marks.**

What is the meaning of "laissez faire"?
He saw the burglar and he shouted "Stop"!

6. **The colon and the semicolon at the close of a quotation fall outside the quotation marks.**

Read Hemingway's "The Killers"; then write a short story of your own using no dialogue.
These items are "top priority": a tax cut, medicare, housing, and the war on poverty.

7. **Both parts of a divided quotation are enclosed in quotation marks. The first word of the second part is not capitalized unless it begins a new sentence.**

"We can't promise," said Lieutenant Martinez, "that your jewels will be found."
"We've found them," the lieutenant said. "They're here."

8. In dialogue, a new paragraph and a new set of quotation marks show a change in speaker.

"But I gave your aide," said the ghost writer to the senator, "the only copy of the speech."

"You did not!" shouted the aide, Healy, excitedly. "I don't have it in my briefcase, and I never lose anything."

"Gentlemen," remarked the senator, "get out your typewriters and start writing another. I am scheduled to speak in two hours."

15.3 Quotations Within Quotations

Single quotation marks are used to enclose a quotation within a quotation.

"I believe it was Aesop who said 'United we stand, divided we fall,' " said Susan.

"But Mrs. Eaton said, 'Do not report to French class,' " cried the bewildered student.

"She said, 'Do not be late for French class,' " I replied.

15.4 Long Quotations

A quotation may be several paragraphs in length.

In long quotations, begin each paragraph with quotation marks. Place quotation marks at the end of the last paragraph only.

Exercise: Copy the following sentences, adding the necessary punctuation marks and capital letters.

1. Where is this morning's paper Father roared I can't find it
2. Mother insisted that she had not seen the paper at all
3. The title of my theme was Political Parties Jane said what did you write about Marjorie

4. Sally will you please look up the meaning of the word *recondite* Miss Forrest requested and report to the class tomorrow

5. We missed the train Debbie said and we had to spend the night in Boston

6. I'd like to go to the dance Jean admitted but we may go away that weekend

7. Put not your trust in money goes an old American saying put your money in trust.

8. Will you drive me to the airport asked Frank the plane leaves in an hour

9. In a town in Nevada said Jack we saw a sign that said yes we have no bonanzas

10. Sir said the policeman don't you see that sign that says don't walk

11. Was it Jefferson asked Bob who said we mutually pledge to each other our lives our fortunes and our sacred honor

12. Of all noises said Samuel Johnson I think music the least disagreeable

15.5   Setting Off Titles

The title of a book, magazine, newspaper, long pamphlet, or bulletin is usually italicized in print. In your own writing, you indicate the italics by underlining.

To distinguish the title of a *part* of a book, magazine, or newspaper, quotation marks are used.

Use quotation marks to enclose the titles of chapters and other parts of books and to enclose the titles of stories, poems, essays, articles, and short musical compositions.

I enjoyed A. L. Weeks' "Struggle at the Top" which was published in *The New Leader*.

In *The Collected Poems of W. B. Yeats* I read "The Cap and Bells."

15.6 Words Used in Special Ways

Words used in special ways or special senses are enclosed in quotation marks.

A writer may want to show that he is using a word as someone else has used it. The writer can make clear that he himself does not accept this use of the word by enclosing it in quotation marks.

Slang words and phrases are also enclosed in quotation marks to indicate that the writer does not accept them as standard usage.

Is that dance called "The Bus Stop"?
These countries are the "non-aligned nations" we read about in the newspaper this morning.
Jean Paul Sartre, who is an "existentialist," refused the Nobel Prize for Literature.
The congressman's speech was labeled "derisive"; his book was called a "tribute."

Note: When a comma or period immediately follows the quoted word, it falls *inside* the quotation marks. The semicolon falls *outside* the quotation marks. See the last example above. If the quoted word appears at the end of a question or exclamation, the question mark or exclamation point falls *outside* the quotation marks. See the first example above.

15.7 Words Used as Words

A word referred to as a word is italicized in print. In writing, the word is underlined.

Do not confuse the words *quiet* and *quite.*
What does the word "serendipity" mean?

When a word and its definition appear in the same sentence, the word is italicized or underscored in writing, and the definition is placed in quotation marks.

The word *perspicuity* means "clearness of expression."

Exercise: Copy the following sentences. Insert quotation marks where necessary. Indicate italics by underlining.

1. I am reading a chapter called Father and Daughter in Dombey and Son by Dickens.
2. Reckon is a word that is sometimes used to mean think or suppose.
3. Who writes The Talk of the Town in The New Yorker?
4. In the dictionary, the abbreviation Colloq. stands for colloquial and means acceptable in conversation.
5. The verb to be is used alone and with other verbs.
6. My pet peeves in words are factor, contact, and the suffix wise in such words as weather-wise and health-wise.
7. Some writing today is described by the word gobbledygook.
8. From *Hamlet* we have the phrases flaming youth, mind's eye, and primrose path.
9. How do you spell iguana, and what kind of animal is it?
10. Intellectuals are sometimes referred to as eggheads.
11. Iron pyrites is often called fool's gold because it looks so much like the true metal.
12. The word protozoa comes from proto, meaning first, and zoa meaning animals.

16.0 Spelling

If you have trouble with spelling, you may be consoled by the fact that other students for generations back have also had trouble. If you are interested in improving your spelling, you may be encouraged to know that many generations of poor spellers before you have learned to spell.

There is no simple way to teach you to spell. There is no easy way to learn. If you are concerned about the problem, however, there are several helpful suggestions:

1. **Proofread all your writing.** Even the ablest scholar may write "their" for "there" or "here" for "hear" in a first draft. Many apparent errors are not spelling errors at all They are mistakes caused by carelessness and too much haste.

2. **Learn to look at the letters in a word.** Most of us have learned to read by recognizing whole words or parts of words. Spelling errors are errors in the letters that compose a word. You will find it helpful to break a word into its parts to see and to memorize the spelling of each part.

3. Keep a list of your spelling errors. The point is that you can spell correctly most of the words you use. Your errors fall within a narrow range. If you will concentrate on this range—provided by your list—you may show quick improvement.

4. Practice on your own spelling problem. There is no reason why you cannot totally eliminate spelling errors *if you want to.* One recommended procedure is to use a card pack. Print your problem words on cards in large letters. Take a card from the pack. Look at every letter and let the order of the letters sink into your mind. Pronounce each part of the word separately. Turn the card over. Write the word on a piece of paper. Turn the card over and compare what you have written with the correct spelling.

5. Memorize and apply the few rules of spelling given below. Be sure you understand the rules, or your memory work will be wasted. Practice using the rules so that their use becomes automatic and you can write *bragging, reference, occurrence,* and so on, quickly.

Exercise: Divide these words into syllables. Do not be concerned as to whether they conform to the dictionary division. Just make sure that every word part has a vowel sound.

1. occurrence	7. humorous	13. italicize
2. accidentally	8. specifically	14. miniature
3. accommodate	9. necessary	15. extraordinary
4. incredible	10. disappearance	16. secretarial
5. miscellaneous	11. mimeograph	17. athletic
6. maintenance	12. immediately	18. privilege

16.1   The Final Silent e

When a suffix beginning with a vowel is added to a word ending in a silent e, the e is usually dropped.

believe + ing = believing   architecture + al =
invite + ation = invitation   architectural
ice + y = icy   admire + able = admirable
create + ive = creative   fame + ous = famous
imagine + ary = imaginary

When the final silent e̲ is preceded by c̲ or g̲, the e̲ is usually retained before a suffix beginning with a̲ or o̲.

courage + ous = courageous   peace + able = peaceable
notice + able = noticeable

When a suffix beginning with a consonant is added to a word ending in a silent e̲, the e̲ is usually retained.

state + ment = statement   safe + ty = safety
same + ness = sameness

The following words are exceptions: *truly, argument, judgment, wholly, awful.*

16.2   Words Ending in y̲

When a suffix is added to a word ending in y preceded by a consonant, the y is usually changed to i.

There are two exceptions: (1) When -ing is added, the y does not change. (2) Some one-syllable words do not change the y: *dryness; shyness.*

merry + ment = merriment   sixty + eth = sixtieth
city + es = cities   hazy + ness = haziness
hurry + ed = hurried   carry + ing = carrying

When a suffix is added to a word ending in y̲ preceded by a vowel, the y̲ usually does not change.

delay + ing = delaying   employ + er = employer
enjoy + ed = enjoyed

Exceptions: day + ly = daily, gay + ly = gaily.

Exercise A: Find the misspelled words in these sentences and spell them correctly.

1. The arriveal of the fameous actress caused quite a stir.
2. Bill's arguement was truely ridiculous.
3. The administrateion may soon be forced to take disciplineary action.
4. The icey air was exhilarateing.
5. Their efforts toward a peacable settlement were both creative and courageous.
6. The sofa bed, the heavyest item, was immoveable.
7. The guideance counselor is in his office dayly.
8. Dan's lazyness is outragous.
9. Her motives are not wholely admireable.
10. Believeing that the inviteation was meant for him, Joe accepted.
11. Some of Frank Lloyd Wright's architectureal achievements are truely exciteing.
12. The Americans easly overran the Spanish fortifycations.
13. The merryment lasted until an incrediblely late hour.
14. We are planning a surprise celebrateion for my grandparents' fiftyeth anniversary.
15. We enjoyed drifting lazyly down the stream.
16. Mark staggered clumsyly with the two heavyest suitcases.
17. The defendant's hazyness in recalling certain details was noticable.
18. Tolkien's characters, though imagineary, are thoroughly believeable.

Exercise B: Add the suffixes as shown and write the new word.

1. mystery + ous	7. amaze + ing	13. enjoy + able
2. relay + ing	8. insure + ance	14. create + ive
3. body + ly	9. grease + y	15. copy + ing
4. frenzy + ed	10. situate + ion	16. educate + ion
5. appraise + ed	11. worry + ing	17. assemble + age
6. waste + ful	12. carry + ed	18. wide + ly

19. constitute + ion   23. charge + ing   27. merry + ly
20. like + able   24. hurry + ing   28. ease + ly
21. move + ment   25. debate + able   29. day + ly
22. change + able   26. hasty + ly   30. argue + ment

16.3 The Suffixes -ness and -ly

When the suffix -ly is added to a word ending in l, both l's are retained. When -ness is added to a word ending in n, both n's are retained.

gradual + ly = gradually   even + ness = evenness
actual + ly = actually   thin + ness = thinness

16.4 The Addition of Prefixes

When a prefix is added to a word, the spelling of the word remains the same.

dis + appear = disappear   dis + similar = dissimilar
mis + spell = misspell   re + commend = recommend
im + mobilize = immobilize   trans + ship = transship
il + legal = illegal   re + enter = re-enter

Note: When a prefix ending in a vowel is joined to a word beginning with the same vowel, a hyphen is sometimes used: re-enter, pre-empt.

16.5 Words with the "Seed" Sound

Only one English word ends in sede: supersede.
Three words end in ceed: exceed, proceed, succeed.
All other words ending in the sound of seed are spelled cede: secede, accede, recede, concede, precede.

Exercise A: Correct the spelling errors in these sentences.

1. This faded old map is virtually ilegible.
2. Kansas is being penalized fifteen yards for ilegal proceedure.
3. The eveness of the two teams made the game unusualy exciting.
4. A re-examination of our foreign policy was considered unecessary.
5. The meeting is usualy preceeded by a pot luck supper.
6. Breaking a leg normaly imobilizes a person for months.
7. The captain's sterness caused disatisfaction among his crew.
8. Rays from iradiated cobalt or gold have successfully attacked cancerous tissue.
9. The SEC investigates iregularities in the stock market.
10. Scientists dissagree as to whether the nose cone actually re-entered the atmosphere.
11. This exceptionaly brilliant youngster should be unusualy successful.
12. The officer answered civily that driving without a license was ilegal.
13. Atomic-powered ships will eventualy supercede conventionaly powered types.
14. The prosecuting attorney dissagreed that the evidence was irelevant.

Exercise B: Add the suffixes and prefixes as indicated. Write the new word.

1. thin + ness
2. mis + stake
3. ir + relevant
4. im + moderate
5. dis + satisfied
6. co + operate
7. incidental + ly
8. im + mobilize
9. uneven + ness
10. im + moral
11. confidential + ly
12. re + examine
13. ir + radiate
14. cordial + ly
15. dis + solution

16.6   Words with ie and ei

When the sound is long e (ē), the word is spelled _ie_ except after _c_.

i before e

relieve	priest	chief
believe	shield	yield
piece	brief	niece

except after c

receive	ceiling	deceit
perceive	conceive	receipt

Exceptions: either, neither, financier, weird, species, seize, leisure. You can remember these words by combining them into such a sentence as: _Neither financier seized either weird species of leisure._

Exercise A: Correct the spelling errors in these sentences.

1. My neice is here for a breif visit.
2. In her leisure time, she often yeilds to mischeif.
3. I am releived that I have found the reciept.
4. Across the feild raced the Labrador retreiver.
5. I beleive this is a rare speceis of butterfly.
6. The Vikings siezed the initiative on the first play and never yeilded it.
7. Can you peice together these wierd happenings?
8. The releif pitcher did not yeild a single hit.
9. The financeir had decieved his best freind.
10. A wierd shreik peirced the stillness of the night.
11. The cheif of police cornered the theif at the end of a peir.
12. The power that Hitler weilded was almost inconcievable.
13. Niether driver would yeild the right of way.
14. This crossbeam should releive the wieght on the cieling.
15. C. M. Bowra's book _The Greek Experience_ sums up the whole acheivement of Greek civilization.

Exercise B: Copy the words below, filling the blank spaces with *ie* or *ei*.

1. perc__ve	6. f__rce	11. gr__vance
2. n__ther	7. n__ce	12. hyg__ne
3. c__ling	8. sh__ld	13. p__r
4. rec__pt	9. s__ze	14. spec__s
5. repr__ve	10. p__ce	15. l__sure

16.7 Doubling the Final Consonant

Words of one syllable, ending in one consonant preceded by one vowel, double the final consonant before adding a suffix beginning with a vowel.

1. Words of one syllable ending in one consonant:

heat   sleep   near   foot

The rule does not apply to these one-syllable words because two vowels precede the final consonant.

2. Words of one syllable ending in one consonant preceded by one vowel:

big   brag   slug   fat

These words are the kind to which the rule applies.

These words double the final consonant if the suffix begins with a vowel.

fat + er = fatter   slug + er = slugger
big + est = biggest   plan + ing = planning

3. The final consonant is doubled in words of more than one syllable:
When they end in one consonant preceded by one vowel.
When they are accented on the last syllable.

re·fer′   o·mit′   con·cur′

The same syllable is accented in the new word formed by adding the suffix:

o·mit′ + ed = o·mit′ted
re·fer′ + ed = re·fer′red
con·cur′ + ence = con·cur′rence

If the newly formed word is accented on a different syllable, the final consonant is not doubled.

re·fer′ + ence = ref′er·ence
pre·fer′ + ence = pref′er·ence

Exercise A: Copy these words, indicating with an accent mark (′) where each word is accented.

1. control	7. allot	13. defer
2. excel	8. impel	14. benefit
3. limit	9. travel	15. admit
4. resist	10. distill	16. differ
5. omit	11. forget	17. infer
6. regret	12. murmur	18. propel

Exercise B: Add the ending indicated, and write the new word.

1. control + ing	11. put + ing	21. admit + ance
2. bat + ed	12. get + ing	22. let + ing
3. compel + ed	13. plan + ing	23. pad + ed
4. bed + ing	14. prefer + ed	24. murmur + ing
5. differ + ence	15. sit + ing	25. repel + ed
6. limit + ed	16. remit + ance	26. omit + ed
7. commit + ed	17. transfer + ing	27. commit + ed
8. book + ed	18. nod + ing	28. ton + age
9. fur + y	19. begin + ing	29. allot + ed
10. disappear + ed	20. expel + ed	30. defer + ed

17.0 The Plurals of Nouns

17.1 Regular Formation of Plurals

The plural of most nouns is formed by adding s.

employee + s = employees   door + s = doors

sense + s = senses   badge + s = badges

17.2 Plurals Formed with es

The plural of nouns ending in s, sh, ch, x, and z is formed by adding -es.

fox + es = foxes   church + es = churches

sash + es = sashes   class + es = classes

17.3 Plurals of Nouns Ending in y

When a noun ends in y preceded by a consonant, the plural is formed by changing the y to i and adding es.

city   citi + es = cities

beauty   beauti + es = beauties

company   compani + es = companies
worry   worri + es = worries

When a noun ends in _y_ preceded by a vowel, the plural is formed by adding _s._

play + s = plays   holiday + s = holidays
galley + s = galleys   alloy + s = alloys
delay + s = delays   valley + s = valleys

17.4   Plural of Nouns Ending in _o_

The plural of nouns ending in _o_, preceded by a vowel, is formed by adding _s._

studio + s = studios   radio + s = radios
rodeo + s = rodeos   ratio + s = ratios
folio + s = folios   duo + s = duos

The plural of most nouns ending in _o_, preceded by a consonant, is formed by adding _s_, but for some nouns of this class the plural is formed by adding _es._

piano + s = pianos   auto + s = autos
solo + s = solos   alto + s = altos
credo + s = credos

tomato + es = tomatoes   echo + es = echoes
potato + es = potatoes   hero + es = heroes

There are some words ending in -o with a preceding consonant that may form the plural with either _s_ or _es: motto, mango, mosquito._ The safest thing to do is to memorize the few words that add -es and to consult the dictionary when in doubt about others.

17.5 Plural of Nouns Ending in f or ff

The plural of most nouns ending in f or ff is formed regularly by adding s.

waif + s = waifs   proof + s = proofs
chief + s = chiefs   gulf + s = gulfs
staff + s = staffs   sheriff + s = sheriffs

The plural of some nouns ending in f or fe is formed by changing the f or fe to ve and adding s.

leaf—leaves   knife—knives   life—lives
wife—wives   loaf—loaves   elf—elves
wolf—wolves   sheaf—sheaves   thief—thieves

Since most of these words with irregular plurals are in common use, careful listening may help you to spell them correctly. If you are doubtful about spelling, however, look up the singular form of the word in a dictionary. If the plural of a word is irregularly formed, the plural will be given immediately after the singular.

17.6 Nouns with Irregular Plurals

The plural of some nouns is formed by a change of spelling.

foot—feet   goose—geese
man—men   mouse—mice
woman—women   ox—oxen
child—children   basis—bases
datum—data   phenomenon—phenomena
index—indices *or* indexes   hypothesis—hypotheses

The plural and singular forms are the same for a few nouns.

sheep   corps   Chinese
deer   cattle   Portuguese

17.7 The Plural of Names

The plural of a name is formed by adding <u>s</u> or <u>es</u>.

George Wolf—the Wolfs   Joyce Williams—the Williamses
John Perry—the Perrys   Henry Jones—the Joneses

17.8 The Plural of Compound Nouns

When a compound noun is written without a hyphen, the plural is formed at the end of the word.

handful + s = handfuls   teaspoonful + s = teaspoonfuls
cupful + s = cupfuls   doghouse + s = doghouses

When a compound noun is made up of a noun plus a modifier, the plural is added to the noun.

sisters-in-law (the phrase *in law* is a modifier.)
commanders-in-chief (the phrase *in chief* is a modifier.)
attorneys-general (*general* modifies *attorneys*.)
notaries public (*public* modifies *notaries*.)
hangers-on (*on* modifies *hangers*.)
bills of sale (the phrase *of sale* modifies *bills*.)

The following are exceptions: *smash-ups, stand-bys, lean-tos.*

Exercise A: Form the plural of each of the following words.

1. turkey	11. quarry	21, Eskimo
2. phenomenon	12. tomato	22. tablespoonful
3. deer	13. banana	23. hero
4. echo	14. quality	24. parenthesis
5. alloy	15. credo	25. opportunity
6. corps	16. knife	26. ambassador-at-large
7. chief	17. shelf	27. sister-in-law
8. handful	18. memento	28. notary public
9. waif	19. ratio	29. register of deeds
10. mastiff	20. loaf	30. bill of lading

Exercise B: Find the errors in plural forms in the following sentences.

1. The thiefs took two silver trophys.
2. Use two cupsful of flour and three teaspoonsful of sugar.
3. The strike against the steel companys added to the President's worrys.
4. The sopranoes drowned out the altoes.
5. We used two loafs of bread to make the sandwichs.
6. Have you read *Echos of Greece?*
7. Not many monarchys exist today.
8. In Southeast Asia, oxes have not yet been replaced by autoes.
9. The sportsmans hunted for deers and foxs.
10. Cattles and sheeps were grazing in the vallies.
11. On modern highways you encounter many rotarys.
12. We need sharper knifes to cut these loafs.
13. Before the holidays the grocers stock their shelfs with cranberrys.
14. Cattles from many countys were exhibited at the State Fair.
15. Mices ate the bulbs from the tulips.
16. Some of the best marble quarrys are in Vermont.
17. The commander-in-chiefs of the two armys met to discuss armistice terms.
18. We have lily-of-the-valleys in our window boxes.
19. The scientists advanced different hypothesis.
20. The tomatoes were canned and stored on the shelfs.
21. Both of my sister-in-laws are notary publics.
22. There are over a hundred varietys of potatos.
23. Coachs at the large universitys are well paid.
24. The knifes were sharpened to cut the loafs of fresh bread.
25. Both of the studioes had two grand pianoes.

18.0 The Forms of Letters

In general, there are two classes of letters: (1) *friendly letters,* and (2) *business letters.* Any letter written for business purposes is a business letter; all other letters—love letters, apologies, invitations, letters written home, etc.—are called friendly letters.

The terms *friendly* and *business* are simply means of designating different forms. They do not refer to the tone in which the letter is written. A business letter may be extremely cordial and friendly. A friendly letter may be most businesslike. A friendly letter may, actually, be cold and unfriendly in tone.

There are two aspects to the forms of letters. The first pertains to the "letter picture," that is, to the arrangement of the content on the page. The second pertains to punctuation, forms of address, and other aspects of content.

18.1 The Friendly Letter

1. It is generally considered that a handwritten letter is more friendly, thoughtful, and considerate than a typed letter. Nonetheless, friendly letters may be typewritten if the circumstances make typing appropriate.

2. Handwritten letters are written on personal stationary, which comes in assorted sizes and colors. Scented papers and papers of unusual color are not considered to be in good taste.

If a friendly letter is typed, plain white typing paper 8½" by 11" is appropriate.

3. While there is some choice as to the size, shape, and color of correspondence paper, there is no choice as to the writing instrument. Pen and ink are required; pencil is not appropriate.

The Picture of the Friendly Letter

Indented Style

Heading

201 Walton Lane
Toledo, Ohio 43619
May 3, 1977

Dear Joe,   Salutation

Body

Complimentary close   Sincerely yours,

Signature   Jack

Block Style

Heading
201 Walton Lane
Toledo, Ohio 43619
May 3, 1977

Dear Joe, Salutation

_____

_____ Body

_____

_____

Complimentary close Sincerely yours,

Signature Jack

Style of the Friendly Letter

1. **The Heading.** The heading consists of the writer's address and the date. It is better not to use any abbreviations, but if you abbreviate one item such as Street (St.) or Avenue (Ave.), use abbreviations throughout. The date, by the way, is always important.

No commas appear at the ends of lines. Commas appear only between the city and state and between the day and the year. Note that the state and zip code are not separated by a comma.

2. **The Salutation.** The salutation begins with the word _Dear_ which is capitalized. The phrase _My dear—_ is too formal for friendly letters. The word _Dear_ is not used with a person's last name alone. The salutation, for example, is _Dear Mr. Jones,_ not _Dear Jones._

The salutation of a friendly letter is followed by a comma.

3. **The Body.** The first paragraph begins with a paragraph indention. Each later paragraph begins with the same indention. The left margin is even, on a vertical line below the first letter of *Dear—*. The right margin should be kept as even as possible. It is better to let a line run short than to hyphenate a word at the end of a line. Hyphens are not appropriate at the ends of lines in a friendly letter.

4. **The Close.** The close of a friendly letter varies with the situation. The only inappropriate close is *Very truly yours,* which is suitable only in business letters. The close may be *Yours truly, Yours, Love, With Love, Sincerely, Cordially,* etc.

The first letter of the first word in the close is capitalized. No other capitals are used. The close is followed by a comma.

The Envelope

The picture of the envelope follows that of the letter itself. If the letter uses the indented style, for example, the envelope uses it too. The writer's address is placed in the upper left corner as a convenience to postal authorities.

Indented Style

James L. Cawder
1421 Northwood Drive
Pleasantville, New York 10570

Ms. Anne Byers
1401 Seminole Road
Wilmette, Illinois 60091

18.2   The Business Letter

The Picture of the Business Letter

Block Form

Heading

6 Evergreen Terrace
Maplewood, New Jersey 07040
February 6, 1977

Costa Brothers
142 Millburn Avenue   Inside address
Camden, New Jersey 08107

Dear Sir or Madam :   Salutation

_____
_____
_____
_____   Body

_____
_____
_____

Complimentary close   Sincerely yours,

Signature   Kelly O'Shea

Modified-Block Form

Heading *6 Evergreen Terrace*
Maplewood, New Jersey 07040
February 6, 1977

Costa Brothers
142 Millburn Avenue Inside address
Camden, New Jersey 08107

Dear Sir or Madam: Salutation

_____
_____
_____
_____ Body

_____
_____
_____

Complimentary close *Sincerely yours,*
Signature *Kelly O'Shea*

The only difference between the block form and the modified block form is the indention of paragraphs, in modified block form, each paragraph begins three letter spaces in from the margin. In the block form, there is no paragraph indention.

In both typed and handwritten business letters, it is desirable to keep the right margin even. The left margin must be kept even. In both forms of business letters, a full line space is left between paragraphs.

1. **The Heading.** The heading of a business letter follows the form of that in the friendly letter except that it is always in block form without indented lines. The letterheads of business firms always have the address printed on them. The heading, then, consists only of the date.

2. **The Inside Address.** The inside address is the address of the person or organization to whom the letter is written. If the writer wants the letter to go to a particular person in the organization, he may use either of two forms:

Ms. J. B. Bennett, Vice-President
The Powers Company
421 Main Street
Madison, Wisconsin 53703

The Powers Company
421 Main Street
Madison, Wisconsin 53703
Attention: Ms. J. B. Bennett, Vice-President

3. **The Salutation.** The salutation of a letter addressed to a business firm or to an organization is *Dear Sir or Madam*. The salutation of a letter addressed to an individual is *Dear* —. If the writer knows intimately the person to whom he is writing, he may use that person's first name: *Dear Henry*.

The salutation of a business letter is always followed by a colon.

4. **The Close.** The close of a business letter is usually one of the following:

Very truly yours,   Yours truly,
Yours very truly,   Sincerely yours,
Yours sincerely,

Only the first letter of the first word in the close is capitalized. The close is followed by a comma.

5. **The Signature.** In all typed business letters, the writer's name is typed below the close. The writer then signs his name above the typed name. The reason for typing the name is that many signatures are difficult to read.

The Envelope

The writer's name and address appear in the upper left corner. The punctuation is the same as that of the heading. The first line of the address is placed just above the lower half of the envelope.

Ms. Jane Allen
9 Satter Road
Red Oak, Iowa 51566

Payne and Company
1402 Massachusetts Avenue
Boston, Massachusetts 02138

Attention:
Personnel Manager

19.0 Good Manuscript Form

It is well established that readers will grade a paper higher if it is neat and legible than if it is messy in appearance and hard to read. Good manuscript form assures a good hearing for what you have to say. Many high schools and colleges have regular forms that students are expected to follow. Others require manuscripts to follow the form described below.

19.1 Legible Writing

Few schools require that student papers be typewritten. A typed paper, however, is easier to read than one written by hand.

If a paper is written by hand, it should be written with pen and a dark blue or black ink. An ink of any other color is not acceptable. Letters should be formed so that there is no doubt as to what they are: *a*'s and *o*'s should be distinctly different; *u*'s and *i*'s should be distinct; if *i*'s are dotted, there can be no chance of their being mistaken for *e*'s.

19.2   Margins and Spacing

Leave a margin of an inch at the top, the bottom, and the right side of each page. The left margin should be slightly wider. If a paper is typed, the left-hand margin must be carefully maintained. The right-hand margin should be approximately the same, and it should be as even as possible without an excess of hyphens to show the break in a word. It is a good rule not to permit more than two successive lines to end with a hyphen.

All typed copy should be prepared with a double space between lines. Usually five letter spaces are provided for each paragraph indentation. One space separates each word; two spaces follow the end punctuation of a sentence. If material must be deleted, it can be struck out by x's or capital M's.

19.3   Proper Labeling

Your teacher will give you instructions on the heading for your papers. Follow these instructions exactly. Usually, you will be expected to place your name at the upper right-hand corner of the first page. On a line below your name, you will place the name or number of the course, and on a third line, you will place the date.

Number each page beginning with page two. (Do not number the first page.) The number may be placed in the upper right-hand corner. To guard against loss or misplacement, you may place your name under the page number.

19.4   Placement of the Title

The title of a paper appears only on the first page. Place the title two lines below the last line of your heading, and center it. Allow two lines between the title and the first line of your copy.

Capitalize the first word and all important words in the title. See Section 11.12. If you are typing, do not capitalize every letter but only the initial letters. Do not underline the title; do not place it in quotation marks unless it is a quotation from some other source.

If a paper is longer than three or four pages, your teacher may ask you to supply a title page. This is a separate page containing the heading in the upper right-hand corner and the title centered on the page.

19.5   Preparation of Final Copy

No one can write a paper exactly as he or she wants it the first time. After you have written your first draft, read it over carefully. Revise and correct it. After you have completed your revision, make a final copy. Then read over this copy.

You may find that you have left out words, or you may find errors. You can insert words neatly by writing above the line where they should appear and by using a caret (∧) to show their position. You can make corrections neatly by drawing a line through a word and writing the correction above it. If more than two or three corrections per page are necessary, recopy the page.

19.6   Numbers in Writing

Numbers that can be expressed in fewer than four words are usually spelled out; longer numbers are written in figures.

The company spent *two million* dollars on research.
We had traveled *twenty-one hundred* miles.
The cast spent *four* hours at the first rehearsal.
A new car in 1976 cost approximately $5,000.

A number beginning a sentence is spelled out.

Eighty-seven delegates attended the convention.
Eleven art students exhibited paintings.

19.7   Figures in Writing

Figures are used to express dates, street and room numbers, telephone numbers, page numbers, decimals, and percentages.

The bridge was opened February 1, 1977.
The nurse told us that Jim's room number was 207.
The address of the hospital is 2099 Lexington Avenue.
The company's telephone number has been changed
to 620–4500.
On page 12 there is a map showing the sites of the battles.
The policeman said that a .36 caliber revolver was used.
Almost 80 percent of the congress voted for the bill.

Note: Commas are used to separate the figures in sums of money or expressions of large quantities. They are not used in dates, serial numbers, page numbers, addresses, or telephone numbers.

CORRECT   The estimated high school enrollment
was 11,700,000.

CORRECT   Students contributed a total of $3,486.25 to
the fund.

INCORRECT   The Olympics were held in Montreal in 1,976.
CORRECT   The Olympics were held in Montreal in 1976.

Exercise: Copy these sentences, correcting any errors in the writing of figures. Three of the sentences are correct as they stand.

1. She paid two hundred dollars for that coat.
2. The Plush family owns 3 automobiles.
3. In nineteen hundred and five, the poet published his first poem.
4. We live at 1,534 Drake Drive.

5. 15 people have been invited to the party.
6. We would like to buy a house for less than 38,000 dollars.
7. Shakespeare was born on April twenty-third, fifteen sixty-four.
8. Yesterday we had three and two-tenths inches of rain.
9. Now turn to the map on page five.
10. The population of India is almost six hundred million.
11. India's population is eighty-three per cent Hindu.
12. My telephone number is 476–7660.
13. We sent a check to the hospital for 1000 dollars.
14. Last night the temperature fell eighteen and six-tenths degrees.
15. His balance was four thousand three hundred and fifty-two dollars.

19.8   Abbreviations in Writing

Abbreviations may be used for most titles before and after proper names, for names of government agencies, and in dates.

BEFORE PROPER NAMES:	Dr., Mr., Mrs., Ms., Messrs., Rev., Hon., Gov., Capt.
AFTER PROPER NAMES:	Jr., Sr., D.D., Ph.D.
GOVERNMENT AGENCIES:	FBI, FCC, AEC
DATES AND TIME:	A.D., B.C., A.M., P.M.

There are no periods after abbreviations of government agencies.

The abbreviations of titles are acceptable only when used as part of a name. It is not acceptable to write *The secy. of the club is a dr.* The titles *Honorable* and *Reverend* are not abbreviated when preceded by *the: The Honorable John Ross.* They appear with the person's full name, not just the last name. Abbreviations are not appropriate for the President and Vice-President of the United States.

In ordinary writing, abbreviations are not acceptable for names of countries and states, months and days of the week, nor for words that are part of addresses or firm names.

UNACCEPTABLE   My cousin lives in N.D.

BETTER   *My cousin lives in North Dakota.*

UNACCEPTABLE   It was good to be back in the U.S.

BETTER   It was good to be back in the United States.

UNACCEPTABLE   Ellen got a job with the Elgin Mfg. Co.

BETTER   Ellen got a job with the Elgin Manufacturing Company.

UNACCEPTABLE   I went to my first class on Mon., Sept. 28.

BETTER   I went to my first class on Monday, September 28.

In ordinary writing, abbreviations are not acceptable for the following: names of school courses, *page, chapter, Christmas,* and words standing for measurements such as *bu., in., hr., min., sec.*

Exercise: Correct the errors in abbreviation in the following sentences.

1. Helen became ill on Wed., and we had to send for a dr. on Thurs.
2. The capt. of the team was chosen on Fri.
3. We drove across the Miss. River last Aug.
4. The union had a contract with the Gaines Mfg. Co.
5. Look at the diagram on the second p. of Chap. 3.
6. Jeff makes better grades in Eng. than in math and sci.
7. Eugene O'Neill was born on B'way in N.Y.C.
8. Address the letter to the Hon. Jonathan Howard.
9. Chas. Gordon, Jr., is treas. of the 1st Natl. Bank.
10. Thomas Burke of the U.S. won the first Olympic 100 m. run.
11. He ran it in twelve sec. and won a gold medal for the U.S.
12. The Sen. is not interested in running for Vice-Pres.

19.9   Italics for Titles

The word *italics* is a printer's term. It refers to a kind of type. When a writer wants the printer to set a word in italic type, he underlines it in his manuscript.

Titles of complete books and plays, of newspapers, magazines, works of art, and musical compositions are printed in italics. The names of ships, trains, and airplanes are also printed in italics.

PRINTED FORM   *Fidelio* is Beethoven's only completed opera.

MANUSCRIPT FORM   Fidelio is Beethoven's only completed opera.

PRINTED FORM   A replica of Rodin's *The Cathedral* was advertised in *The New York Times.*

MANUSCRIPT FORM   A replica of Rodin's The Cathedral was advertised in The New York Times.

PRINTED FORM   George Orwell's *Animal Farm* is considered one of the best political satires of our time.

MANUSCRIPT FORM   George Orwell's Animal Farm is considered one of the best political satires of our time.

19.10   Italics for Foreign Words and Phrases

Many foreign words have become so widely used that they are now part of the English language: *chauffeur, cul-de-sac, entrepreneur.* These naturalized words are printed in regular type. Foreign words and phrases that have not become naturalized in our language are printed in italics: *cum laude, bon vivant, mirabile dictu.*

The only way to be sure whether a word or phrase of foreign origin should be printed in italics (underlined in manuscript) is to consult the dictionary.

19.11 Italics for Words, Letters, or Figures

Italics are used for words, letters, or figures referred to as such.

In printed works, words, letters, or figures referred to as such are in italics. In writing, they are underlined.

PRINTED FORM	How do Westerners pronounce the *er* in *father?*
MANUSCRIPT FORM	How do Westerners pronounce the <u>er</u> in <u>father?</u>
PRINTED FORM	*Chemist* is the British word for *druggist.*
MANUSCRIPT FORM	<u>Chemist</u> is the British word for <u>druggist.</u>

19.12 Italics for Emphasis

Italics (underlining) are used to give special emphasis to words or phrases.

The tendency in modern writing is to avoid the use of italics for emphasis. One reason for this is that italic type is considered harder to read than regular (roman) type, particularly if there is a great deal of it. Another reason is that modern writers are developing a direct, straightforward style which gives emphasis to important words without use of printing devices.

In high school writing, use italics (or underlining) for emphasis only to make meaning clear.

Although I could not decide what was amiss, *something* was wrong.

You misunderstood. I said that I was *not* going.

19.13 Correction Symbols and Revision

Both in high school and in college your teachers will make marginal notes on your themes and reports before returning them to you. These notes will indicate errors or awkward passages that require rewriting. The correction of errors will make you alert to their recurrence in your later writing. Practice in rephrasing an awkward sentence will give you greater skill in turning out careful, clear writing that means what you want it to mean.

Many schools and colleges have their own system of indicating writing faults briefly. If your school has such a system of abbreviations, it will be made available to you. Your teachers may prefer to use the symbols listed below. These are symbols used by professional copyreaders who work for publishers. The manuscript bearing the marks is returned to the author, no matter how experienced or professional he may be, for correction and revision before the manuscript is set in type.

ab   *Abbreviation.* Either the abbreviation is not appropriate, or the abbreviation is wrong. Consult a dictionary.

agr   *Agreement.* You have made an error in agreement of subject and verb or of pronoun and antecedent. Consult Sections 6.1 and 7.13 in your Handbook.

awk   *Awkward.* The sentence is clumsy. Rewrite it.

cap   *Capital letters.* You have omitted necessary capitals. Consult Section 11 in your Handbook.

cf   *Comma fault.* You have joined two sentences together with a comma. Change the punctuation.

dang   *Dangling construction.* You have written a verbal phrase in such a way that it does not tie up to another word in the sentence. Rewrite the sentence.

frag   *Sentence fragment.* You have placed a period after a group of words that is not a sentence. Join the fragment to an existing sentence or add words to complete the thought.

ital   *Italics.* You have omitted italics that are needed.

k   *Awkward.* See *awk* above.

lc   *Lower case.* You have mistakenly used a capital letter where a small letter is required.

ms   *Manuscript form.* You have not followed the proper manuscript form. Consult Section 19 in your Handbook.

no ¶   *No paragraph.* You have started a new paragraph too soon. Join these sentences to the preceding paragraph.

¶   *Paragraph.* Begin a new paragraph at this point.

nc   *Not clear.* Your meaning is not clear. Rewrite the passage to say what you mean.

om   *Omission.* You have left out words that are needed for clarity or smoothness of style.

p   *Punctuation.* You have made an error in punctuation. Consult Sections 12–15 in your Handbook for sentences like the one you have improperly punctuated.

par   *Parallelism.* You have committed an error in parallel structure. Consult Chapter 3.

ref   *Reference.* There is an error or a weakness in the reference of pronoun to antecedent. Consult Section 7 in your Handbook.

rep   *Repetition.* You have repeated a word too often, or you have repeated something you wrote in preceding sentences.

shift   *Shift.* You have shifted point of view or tense needlessly.

sp   *Spelling.* You have misspelled a word. Consult a dictionary.

t   *Tense.* You have used the wrong tense form. Consult Section 9 in your Handbook.

tr   *Transpose.* You have misplaced a modifier; consult Chapter 4. Or, your meaning would be clearer if a sentence or passage were placed at another point.

wd   *Wrong word.* You have confused homonyms, or you have used a word that does not fit the meaning, or you have used a slang word inappropriately. Consult Section 10 in your Handbook, or a dictionary.

Sources of Quoted Material

Chapter 1, pages 2, 3, and 4: Grateful acknowledgment is made to Collins + World Publishing Co., Inc. for material from *Webster's New World Dictionary,* Students Edition; copyright © 1976 by William Collins + World Publishing Company, Inc. Chapter 1, page 25–26, paragraph 1 by Martin B. Margolies from *New York State English Council Newsletter.* Paragraph 2 by Leonard Fleischer from *New York State English Council Newsletter.* Paragraph 3 by Legouis and Cazamian from *A History of English Literature.* Paragraph 4 by John Ciardi from *How Does a Poem Mean?* Paragraph 5 by Elizabeth Drew from *Poetry: A Modern Guide to Its Understanding and Enjoyment.* Paragraph 6 by Thomas Merton from *No Man Is an Island.* Paragraph 7 by Igor Stravinsky from *Poetics of Music.* Chapter 6, page 87 by William E. Leuchtenburg from *The Perils of Prosperity.* Page 89, paragraph 1: Grateful acknowledgment is made to American Heritage Publishing Co., Inc. for material from *"The World Trade Center: Does Mega-architecture Work?"* by Thomas Meehan in *Horizon;* copyright 1976 American Heritage Publishing Co., Inc., reprinted by permission from *Horizon* (Fall 1976). Pages 90–91, paragraph 1 by William E. Leuchtenburg from *The Perils of Prosperity.* Page 91, paragraph 2 by J. I. Biegeleisen from *Careers in Commercial Art.* Pages 91–92, paragraph 4 by Barbara W. Tuchman from *The Historian's Opportunity.* Page 92, paragraph 5 by Frederick Lewis Allen from *Horatio Alger, Jr.* Page 94, paragraph 1 by H. A. Overstreet from "Education as Maturity." Page 95, paragraph 2 by Donald E. Carr from "The Lost Art of Conversation." Paragraph 3 by Sonny Kleinfield from "Dwarfs." Pages 95–96, paragraph 4 by William E. Leuchtenburg from *Perils of Prosperity.* Page 96, paragraph 5 by Beaumont Newhall from "Photographing the Reality of the Abstract." Page 98 by Buffalo Bill from *An Autobiography of Buffalo Bill.* Pages 98–99, paragraph 1 by Frederick Lewis Allen from *Horatio Alger, Jr.* Page 99, paragraph 2 by Frank Donovan from *Dickens and Youth.* Paragraph 3 by Edward W. Cronin, Jr. from "The Yeti." Page 100, paragraph 4 by Joseph Wood Krutch from "Is Our Common Man Too Common?" Paragraph 5 by Herbert A. Otto from "New Light on the Human Potential." Page 101, paragraph: Grateful acknowledgment is made to Hawthorn Books, Inc. for material from *Mark Twain* by Stephen Leacock. Pages 101–102 by Eleanor Roosevelt from "Must We Hate To Fight?" Page 102, paragraph 1 by Stephen Spender from "The Age of Overwrite and Underthink." Pages 102–103, paragraph 2 by H.A. Overstreet from "Education as Maturity." Page 103, paragraph 3 by Thomas Griffith from "Yours Sincerely, A Party of One." Pages 104–105 by Samuel Hopkins Adams from "The Man Who Spoke Latin." Page 106, paragraph 2 by Robert Barr from "The Absent-Minded Coterie." Pages 106–107, paragraph 4 by Mary Dewees Fowler from "Man of Distinction." Page 107, paragraph 5 by William Henry Schultz from "The Shirt Off Their Backs." Page 108, paragraph 1: Grateful acknowledgment is made to The Atlantic Monthly Company for material by Warren King Moorehead from Letter to *Atlantic,* "An Archaeologist Speaks." Page 108, paragraph 2 by Agnes De Mille from *Dance to the Piper.* Chapter 7, page 112 by Arnold Toynbee from "Why and How I Work." Page 114, paragraph by Buffalo Bill from *An Autobiography of Buffalo Bill.* Pages 116–117 by Gerard de Vaucouleurs from "Mars." Pages 117–118, paragraph by Elizabeth Enright from "The Operator." Page 118, paragraph by Voltaire from *Candide.* Page 119, paragraph 1 by Shirley Ann Grau from "Joshua." Pages 119–120, paragraph 2 by Thomas Henry Huxley from "The Method of Scientific Investigation." Paragraph 3 by R. V. Cassill from "The Inland Years." Pages 120–121, paragraph 4 by Hugh Garner from "A Trip for Mrs. Taylor." Page 121, paragraph 1 by Orville Wright from "How I Learned To Fly." Pages 121–122, paragraph 2 by Judith Groch from *You and Your Brain.* Page 122, paragraph 3 from "Auto Racing" in *Atlantic,* Oct. 1975. Paragraph 4 by Judith Groch from *You and Your Brain.* Page 123 by Mark Twain from *A Tramp Abroad.* Pages 124–125 by Billie Jean King from *Billie Jean.* Grateful acknowledgment is made to American Heritage Publishing Co., Inc. for material from "The Time of Man" by Loren Eiseley; © 1962 American Heritage Publishing Co., Inc.; reprinted by permission from *Horizon* (March 1962). Page 126 by Frances Koltun from "Edinburgh: A City Awakens." Pages 128–129 by Elizabeth Enright from "The Operator." Page 129, paragraph 1 by Gabrielle Roy from "Wilhelm" in *Street of Riches.* Page 130, paragraph 2 by Avram Davidson from "The Affair at Lahore Cantonment." Paragraph 3 by Robert L. Fish from "The Adventure of the Artist's Mottle." Paragraph 4 by Stuart Cloete from "The Soldiers' Peaches." Pages 130–131, paragraph 5 by Cornell Woolrich from "Hotel Room." Page 131, paragraph 6 by Stephen Vincent Benét from "The Devil and Daniel Webster." Page 132 by Conrad Aiken from "Impulse." Page 133, paragraph by Maurice Leblanc from "The Red Silk Scarf." Pages 133–134, Paragraph 1 by Gilbert K. Chesterton from "The Secret Garden." Page 134, paragraph 2 by Sinclair Lewis from *Cass Timberlane.* Page 134–135, paragraph 3 by Charles Dickens from *A Tale of Two Cities.* Chapter 8, pages 142–143 by Isak Dinesen from *Out of Africa.* Page 144, paragraph by Nathaniel Hawthorne from *The Scarlet Letter.* Page 146–147, paragraph by Goerge Zebrowski from "Science Fiction and the Visual Media." Page 147, paragraph by Weston La Barre from *The Human Animal.* Page 148, paragraph by Jack Allen *et al* from *The Problems and Promises of American Democracy.* Page 148, paragraph by Percival Spear from *India.* Page 149, paragraph by Lin Yutang from *Importance of Living.* Pages 150–151, paragraph by Klaas Toxopeus from *Flying Storm.* Page 151, paragraph by Henry C. King from *The World of the Moon.* Page 153–154, paragraph by Keith Clayton from *The Crust of the Earth.* Page 154, paragraph by Percival Spear from *India.* Page 156, paragraph by William Ebenstein from *American Democracy in World Perspective.* Pages 157–158, paragraph by William E. Leuchtenburg from *The Perils of Prosperity.* Pages 159, 160, 161, paragraphs by Donald H. Riddle from *The Problems and Promise of American Democracy.* Page 162, paragraph by Norman Cousins from "Modern Man is Obsolete." Pages 162–163, paragraph by John H. Troll from "The Thinking of Men and Machines." Page 163, paragraph 1 by Alice Walker from "Her Sweet Jerome" from *In Love & Trouble.* Pages 164 and 165, paragraphs 2 and 4 by Keith Clayton from *The Crust of the Earth.* Page 164, paragraph 3 by Henry Garnett from *Treasures of Yesterday.* Page 165, paragraph 5 by Edward Rowe Snow from *True Tales of Pirates and Their Gold.* Pages 165–166, paragraph 6 by N. Scott Momady from "February 27" in *House Made of Dawn.* Page 166, paragraph 7 by Thomas Henry Huxley from "A Liberal Education." Pages 166–167, paragraph 8 by Keith Clayton from *The Crust of the Earth.* Page 167, Paragraph 10 by Alice Walker from "Her Sweet Jerome" from *In Love & Trouble.* Chapter 10, pages 239–253: Grateful acknowledgment is made to Craig Pirrong for use of his research paper, "The Realism of Henry Fleming in Stephen Crane's *The Red Badge of Courage.*"

Handbook Sections 2 and 3: Diagrams by Ken Izzi. Handbook Section 18: Handwritten letters by Pamela Kimball.

Index

Index

Correction Symbols

ab	abbreviation
agr	agreement
awk	awkward
cap	capital letters
cf	comma fault
dang	dangling construction
frag	sentence fragment
ital	italics
k	awkward
lc	lower case
ms	manuscript form
no ¶	no paragraph
¶	paragraph
nc	not clear
om	omission
p	punctuation
par	parallelism
ref	reference
rep	repetition
shift	shift
sp	spelling
t	tense
tr	transpose
wd	wrong word

For a detailed explanation of these correction symbols, see Handbook **Section 19.13.**

Handbook

The page numbers for the Handbook (the second half of this book) appear in red.

8.0 Adjective and Adverb Usage 166

9.0 Verb Usage 176

10.0 The Right Word 196

11.0 Capitalization 206

12.0 End Marks and Commas 218

13.0 The Semicolon, the Colon, the Dash, and Parentheses 232

14.0 The Apostrophe 241

15.0 Quotations 248